PERSONALITY ASSESSMENT IN AMERICA

A Retrospective on the Occasion of the Fiftieth Anniversary of the Society for Personality Assessment

PERSONALITY ASSESSMENT IN AMERICA

A Retrospective on the Occasion of the Fiftieth Anniversary of the Society for Personality Assessment

Edited by

Edwin I. Megargee
Florida State University

Charles D. Spielberger
University of South Florida

Routledge
Taylor & Francis Group
LONDON AND NEW YORK

First published 1992 by Lawrence Erlbaum Associates, Inc.

Published 2019 by Routledge
2 Park Square, Milton Park, Abingdon, Oxon OX14 4RN
52 Vanderbilt Avenue, New York, NY 10017

Routledge is an imprint of the Taylor & Francis Group, an informa business

Library of Congress Cataloging-in-Publication Data

Personality assessment in America : a retrospective on the occasion of the fiftieth anniversary of the Society for Personality Assessment / edited by Edwin I. Megargee, Charles D. Spielberger.
p. cm.
Includes bibliographical references.
ISBN 0-8058-0928-7
1. Personality assessment—United States. I. Megargee, Edwin Inglee. II. Spielberger, Charles Donald, 1927- . III. Society for Personality Assessment.
BF698.4.P475 1992
155.2'8—dc20 92-362
CIP

ISBN 13: 978-0-8058-0928-2 (hbk)
ISBN 13: 978-1-138-97824-9 (pbk)

Contents

Preface

Contemporary consumers expect to receive product information with every purchase. This book is no exception. In this Preface we provide the information you need to obtain maximum usefulness and service from this volume. We have also provided some technical notes to assist you in using the bibliographic materials.

The contents of this book are unique in several respects. No matter how diligently you search among the psychology volumes on the shelves of your library, you will not find another quite like the one you are holding. What distinguishes it from the others? Whereas most psychology books discuss current or future trends, this one focuses on the past. It consists of a collection of important and historically significant writings by a select group of men and women who, over the past 50 years, were honored by their colleagues for their distinguished contributions to the field of personality assessment.

Chapter 1 is a brief overview of the history of personality assessment and of the Society for Personality Assessment (SPA). Our introductory chapter also includes a general commentary on the 16 selections that appear in the body of the text and an explanation of how these articles were chosen. Published from 1939 through 1989, most of the papers were SPA Presidential addresses or presentations by the recipients of the Society's Distinguished Contributions Award. Taken as a whole, they provide a unique perspective on the evolution of personality assessment in America from the viewpoint of those who made important contributions to that history.

Our initial purpose in assembling this volume was to celebrate the SPA's Fiftieth Anniversary with a commemorative volume, but this goal was soon transcended. As we searched through the 55 volumes of the Society's journals that had accumulated in the archives, we began to feel like museum curators who stumble on a storeroom filled with forgotten masterpieces. The writings we discovered were not merely of historical interest, but intrinsically important scientific contributions, some of which were in danger of being lost or forgotten. We felt that it was important to preserve and pass on this valuable legacy for the education and edification of later generations. Our only regret is that page limitations imposed by fiscal realities forced us to reduce the volume we initially envisioned by 50 percent.

Unlike many others, this book does not promise to put you at the "cutting edge" of some narrow subject by providing a review and analysis of the latest findings and speculations. It is not the edge, but the body of a knife, that determines its quality. With the edge you can scratch the surface, but with a strong, tempered blade encased in a sturdy haft you can penetrate deeper. The writings in this book provide the background and perspective that are needed to cut through to the fundamentals of personality assessment. You can then dissect the meaning and importance of current theory and findings as they are encountered.

It is not only its historical perspective that makes this book unique. There are many fine texts that summarize the problems and progress of personality assessment over the years. But given the choice between reading a clinical report or examining a Rorschach protocol or an MMPI profile for ourselves, we prefer to study the primary source material. This book provides first-hand discussions of crucial issues in personality assessment written by the gifted men and women who were actually grappling with these problems at the time, not knowing what the outcome would be.

If this seems dry, dull, and tedious, rather like wading dutifully through a five-foot shelf of "great books," rest assured it is not. In preparing their Presidential speeches and Award addresses, these men and women were responding to a challenge, a once-in-a-lifetime opportunity to share with their peers their paramount concerns about personality assessment and to pass on the most important lessons they had learned over the course of their distinguished careers. Moreover, as some explicitly noted, the contributors to this volume were acutely aware of the presence of former honorees in the audience, and were eager to match or exceed the standards of excellence established by their predecessors. Thus, the resulting papers are anything but dull.

As a person who is interested in personality assessment, you have a special treat in store. It is axiomatic that we can learn a great deal about people by studying their artistic and imaginative creations. These papers are no exception. Our authors were vigorous individuals with trenchant opinions. Over the years there have been some noteworthy disputes and rivalries within the Society, which has itself gone through some difficult times. Readers will find that these papers provide insights not only into the conflicts and controversies, but also into the ideas, attitudes, and emotions of the men and women who took part in them. We believe you will have almost as much fun reading this book as we did editing it.

During the 50 years covered by this retrospective, citation styles have changed considerably. Before the American Psychological Association established the current convention of citing a reference by author's name and year of publication, some selections used footnotes on each page while others employed consecutive numbers in the text. To eliminate the confusion engendered by this multiplicity of styles, all of the older manuscripts have been retyped so that they conform with modern usage.

The reference lists for each selection posed a related but different problem. The simplest solution would have been to reprint each article with its references as it originally appeared. However, because many of the articles cited the same sources, we discovered we could save a great deal of space by presenting a comprehensive reference list at the end of the book. Therefore, the references from each article were incorporated into a single reference list, according to the guidelines specified in the current APA *Publication Manual.* This procedure was followed insofar as the information provided in the initial reference list allowed, but some older references, for example, did not include page numbers.

When the names of journals were abbreviated, as was the custom through the early 1950s, we retained the abbreviated spelling. Because some of these journals are no longer published and some are in German or French, readers attempting to track down these sources may have some difficulty deciphering the citations. It may help to know that, in those days, custom dictated that adjectives in the titles of journals were in lower case letters while nouns were capitalized.

When articles were cited as being "in press," we attempted to determine the actual date of publication and update the reference. This was not always possible, so some are still listed as being "in press" or "in preparation." Three articles published during the 1970s utilized consecutively numbered Reference Notes to cite sources that were not generally available. The Reference Notes for these articles appear before the comprehensive reference list.

The collaboration that culminated in this volume began in the late 1960s when Charles D. Spielberger, then Director of Clinical Training at Florida State University, recruited Edwin I. Megargee to develop a solid graduate training program in psychological assessment. Almost immediately, Megargee enrolled Spielberger into the Society for Projective Techniques and Personality Assessment. Two decades later, Megargee called Spielberger, who by then was President of the Society, to suggest that "someone" should gather together the Klopfer Award addresses for distribution to the members attending the forthcoming Fiftieth Anniversary Celebration in New York City. Spielberger suggested instead that they work together on a book commemorating the anniversary.

In preparing this volume, Megargee took the main responsibility for searching through the archives, selecting articles for inclusion, preparing the manuscript and reference list for publication, and writing the initial drafts of the introductory and concluding chapters. In addition to reviewing and editing these materials, Spielberger had primary responsibility for corresponding with the authors, arranging for the publication permissions with the Society, and working with the publisher. Throughout the preparation of this book both editors were involved in all aspects of the project and consulted extensively with one another.

We are grateful to all the living authors, to the families and estates of those authors who are now deceased, and to the Society for Personality Assessment for granting us permission to reprint copyrighted material. The paper by Krugman (1939) and Rickers-Ovsiankina (1943) first appeared in the *Rorschach Research Exchange*. Those by Kutash (1955), Beck (1955), B.

Klopfer (1957), Bellak (1958), and Holt (1958) were published in the *Journal of Projective Techniques.* The papers by Henry and Cumming, (1959), Shneidman (1962), W. G. Klopfer (1968), and Hertz (1970) were published in the *Journal of Projective Techniques and Personality Assessment.* The articles by Meehl (1979), Exner (1980), Weiner (1983), Dana (1984), and Blatt (1990) all appeared in the *Journal of Personality Assessment.*

A number of people assisted in the preparation of this book. Karen Lawson and Liana Pena assisted in library research, Debra Bonds entered the references into the comprehensive bibliography, and she and Sharon Wittig retyped the older articles in modern style. Virginia Berch, Tamera Fontenot, Diane Gregg, and Eric Reheiser contributed to the technical details of preparing the introductory and final chapters for publication. We thank them all for their careful and painstaking efforts. Finally, we thank Lawrence Erlbaum, our publisher, for having the vision to appreciate the value of this endeavor and for helping us convert our fantasy into reality, and Art Lizza, LEA Vice-President for Production, for his invaluable assistance in helping us to resolve immeasurable problems in adapting the selected papers for this volume.

Edwin I. Megargee, London, UK
Charles D. Spielberger, Tampa, FL

Personality Assessment in America: An Introduction

EDWIN I. MEGARGEE
CHARLES D. SPIELBERGER

The history of the projective test movement and the evolution of the Society for Personality Assessment both began with the Rorschach Inkblot Technique. Hermann Rorschach published his inkblots and the monograph reporting his research with them in 1921. He was only 38 when he died from appendicular peritonitis a year later. His associate, Emil Oberholzer, became the executor of Rorschach's intellectual legacy, arranging for the posthumous publication of Rorschach's blind analysis of a case (Rorschach & Oberholzer, 1923).

Oberholzer was also active in teaching the Rorschach technique to others, one of whom was David Levy, who introduced the technique in the United States in 1924 (Beck, 1972; Pichot, 1984). That same year, an English translation of Rorschach's posthumous paper (Rorschach & Oberholzer, 1923) appeared in the *Journal of Nervous and Mental Diseases.* In 1928, Levy taught the Rorschach technique to Samuel Beck, who used the instrument in his doctoral dissertation and, in 1930, published the first original work on the Rorschach in English (Beck, 1972).

In the early 1930s, Beck studied the Rorschach technique with Oberholzer in Zurich, and Marguerite Hertz and Zygmunt Piotrowski began their pioneering work with the instrument. In 1935, Bruno Klopfer, who had learned the technique in Switzerland, arrived on the scene. He founded the Rorschach Institute and the *Rorschach Research Exchange* which, respectively, evolved into the Society for Personality Assessment and the *Journal of Personality Assessment.* We shall discuss the history of the Society and its journals below.

Rorschach's master work on his technique, *Psychodiagnostik: Methodik und Ergebnisse eines Wahrnehmungs-diagnostichen Experiments* (Rorschach, 1921), which was available only in German until 1942, merely provided the broad outlines of his technique. Without Rorschach to supervise its development, different followers began to diverge in their conception of the particulars of administration, scoring and interpretation. Over the years, Samuel Beck, Bruno Klopfer, Marguerite Hertz, Zygmunt Piotrowski and, somewhat later, David Rapaport each developed their own distinctive approaches.

By the 1950s, as John Exner (1980) notes in his article "But it's only an inkblot," there were at least five different, competing, "Rorschachs" in America, each with its own partisans. These schools were not above criticizing one another. For example, in the *Journal of Personality Assessment,* which had been founded by Bruno Klopfer and was then being edited by his son, Walter, Samuel Beck criticized the senior Klopfer's system as being, ". . . hazardous because it is subjective (Beck, 1972, p. 107)."

Meanwhile, two other personality assessment instruments were being developed in America, each of which would serve as the prototype for a number of other tests. At Harvard, Henry Murray (1943) was pursuing research that would culminate in the publication of the Thematic Apperception Test (TAT), an instrument closely related to his theory of personality. The development of the TAT would inspire Murray's students to create a number of related apperceptive techniques such as the Children's Apperception Test (Bellak, 1954) and the Make-A-Picture-Story (MAPS) (Shneidman, 1949) test. Like the Rorschach, the apperceptive tests were administered individually, and differing approaches to administration, scoring and interpretation soon emerged.

Further west, Starke Hathaway and J. C. McKinley (1967) were developing the Minnesota Multiphasic Personality Inventory (MMPI), an empirically derived paper-and-pencil self-report inventory. Because it could easily be administered to large groups and scored by various automated devices, its 556 items would serve as a spawning ground for hundreds of other scales, some derived empirically and some rationally. In the years that followed, other researchers would develop a wide array of structured personality inventories.

By the middle of the century, there were a number of competing instruments available for the assessment of personality characteristics. Each had its own set of adherents, and competition could be fierce. Such rivalries are hardly surprising. Before the advent of high-speed electronic computers and substantial government grants, developing a new test was an even more demanding, labor-intensive task than it is today. Test authors did not invest the years of time and effort required to construct and validate a new test unless they had serious reservations about the instruments already available and were convinced of the superiority of their own approach.

Differences among the instruments developed to assess personality were exacerbated by the fact that the proponents of rival tests often differed in their theoretical orientations. Rorschach workers were partial to dynamic and gestalt approaches, whereas Murray's followers preferred his need-press schema. The "dust-bowl empiricists" of the Midwest seemed to the Easterners to be atheoretical, or at least not especially influenced by theoretical concerns.

Proponents of projective and structured techniques also differed in their approaches to research. Neither the Rorschach nor the TAT was easily amenable to conventional statistical analyses, or to the commonly accepted methods for establishing reliability and validity (Krugman, 1939). Their advocates favored "idiographic" research involving the extensive and intensive study of a few individual cases. In contrast, the MMPI and its cousins yielded quantitative scores that appeared more amenable to conventional statistical and psychometric analyses. Because these tests were designed for group administration, it is not surprising that the MMPI's proponents were more partial to "nomothetic" research involving large samples.

With America's entry into the Second World War, many service personnel were trained as military psychologists. After the War, the Veterans Administration began a major program of training clinical psychologists, and, in the late 1940s and early 1950s, personality assessment was a primary focus. The stage was set for a vigorous debate. Which methods were best? What criteria should be used to evaluate them? Is it possible to validate projective techniques? Do structured instruments reflect anything other than response sets? Which is better, clinical or statistical prediction? What techniques and approaches should be taught to graduate students? These were the questions confronting clinicians when many of the papers in this book were being written.

In retrospect, the advocates of structured and projective approaches actually had more in common than they realized, but, as is often the case, it was the polarized theoretical orientations and methodological predilections that produced the polemics. Later, in the 1960s and early 1970s, the whole enterprise of personality assessment came under attack from several quarters. As Marguerite Hertz (1970) and Irving Weiner (1983) note in their contributions to this volume, "Projective techniques in crisis" and "The future of psychodiagnosis revisited," radical behaviorists who felt relearning techniques could correct all disorders regardless of etiology questioned the need for diagnosis, as did those humanists who felt that categorization and classification stripped clients of their humanity.

Behaviorists such as Walter Mischel (1968), who contended that behavior was primarily determined by situational circumstances, also challenged trait-based personality theories and techniques of assessment. Others questioned the morality of a clinical psychology devoted to the diagnosis and treatment of individuals when there were broad social issues affecting the welfare of large groups of people that needed to be addressed. During this period, the questions became more fundamental. Should projective techniques or any other form of individual assessment be taught at all? Are not personality assessment techniques simply another tool used to suppress the disenfranchised? How can a Society for Personality Assessment (SPA) justify its existence? Before we turn to the papers that address these issues, let us first sketch the history of the SPA during this period.

A BRIEF HISTORY OF THE SOCIETY FOR PERSONALITY ASSESSMENT

The Society traces its roots to the Rorschach Institute founded in 1939 by Bruno Klopfer, who served as its Director until 1947. Over the years a gradual process of what we might term "ecumenical evolution" took place. In 1948 the Rorschach Institute was renamed the "Society for Projective Techniques and the Rorschach Institute," and in 1959 it became simply the "Society for Projective Techniques."

By the 1960s, the Society had become the only professional psychological organization exclusively devoted to personality assessment, but many members and potential members were interested in structured as well as projective techniques. In 1965, their interests were formally recognized as the name of the Society was changed to "Society for Projective Techniques and Personality Assessment." In 1970 this cumbersome title was simplified to "The Society for Personality Assessment," which it has remained for over 20 years.

In 1936, even before he established the Rorschach Institute, Bruno Klopfer had begun the *Rorschach Research Exchange.* This mimeographed *Journal,* which was probably one of the earliest "desktop publications," quickly became the primary publication outlet for articles dealing with the Rorschach. Beginning in 1939, the *Exchange* became the official publication of the Rorschach Institute, and of the societies that evolved from it, altering its name to keep pace with the broadening interests of the Society. The name of the Society's journal was first changed to *The Journal of Projective Techniques,* then it became the *Journal of Projective Techniques and Personality Assessment* and finally the *Journal of Personality Assessment.* Throughout this evolution, the volumes have been numbered consecutively to reflect its origin in 1936 as the *Rorschach Research Exchange.* For 35 years, Bruno Klopfer served as the Editor, from 1936 through 1971. After Bruno Klopfer's death, his son Walter edited the *Journal* until shortly before his death. Robert Davis served as interim editor, followed by Irving B. Weiner who became Editor in 1985. Selections from each period of the *Journal's* history are included in the present volume.

In 1970 and 1971, there was a major debate over whether the 32-year-old Society could, or even should, continue as an autonomous professional organization. Relatively few of the Society's 800 members participated in its activities or governance, most seeming content simply to receive the *Journal* regularly. As Marguerite Hertz noted in her 1970 "Great Man" address, "Projective techniques in crisis," many questioned the need for and, especially, the validity of personality assessment. President-Elect Arthur C. Carr wrote, "At present there is a diminished interest in and a general pessimism among psychologists about the future of personality assessment, resulting in a potential threat to the existence of our Society" (1971, p. 203).

By this time, the Society had adopted the custom of meeting in conjunction with the annual convention of the American Psychological Association, but it was becoming increasingly difficult for autonomous organizations such as SPA to obtain time on the APA program. In view of these complications, and in response to the perceived threats to the Society's survival as an autonomous organization, then-current SPA President Norman Farberow and Past-President Kenneth B. Little suggested that the Society affiliate with APA, either as a separate Division or as a Section of the Division of Clinical Psychology (Farberow & Little, 1970). Calling these proposals "defeatist in nature and ill-advised in action," President-Elect Arthur Carr (1971) argued that the Society should remain autonomous:

> Our Society unites all those who believe in the continuity of assessment. We believe assessment will be here long after more current fads often prominently espoused at APA conventions cease to be considered fashionable. Our group believes that the valid criticisms leveled against current techniques of assessment can be met only through continued research and education. . . . (p. 203).
>
> As a Society our membership must continue to work for those objectives in which we believe. It would seem that our present efforts can best be organized, our future goals best realized through an organization maintained specifically and solely for its main purpose,—the perpetuation and enhancement of relevant theories of and techniques for personality assessment (p. 204).

Carr's position prevailed and the SPA retained its independence. As the decade progressed, advances in psychometric theory and methods, coupled with progress in computer technology, paved the way for the development of new assessment techniques, and revisions and improvements in already existing measures. As Irving Weiner points out in his 1983 selection, "The future of psychodiagnosis revisited," the emergence of new specialty areas such as behavioral medicine and geropsychology, advances in understanding the etiology of psychopathology, and the development of a variety of different interventions all served to reinvigorate psychodiagnosis and assessment.

The 1980s witnessed a period of new and more vigorous leadership. Efforts to expand the membership base were quite successful, and the Society now sponsored a popular Midwinter Meeting. Spielberger and Piotrowski (1992) recently reported:

> Over the past three years, membership in SPA has increased dramatically. The Society now has over 2,000 members, more than double the number in 1987. . . . The large increase in membership and the changing orientation and interests of SPA members have contributed to a substantial expansion in the number of published pages in the *Journal of Personality Assessment,* which now covers a significantly broader range of relevant topics.

Some of this growth can be attributed to increased interest in cognitive psychology among clinicians and researchers alike. As Sidney Blatt (1990) notes in his paper that concludes this book, this movement has given new life to assessment techniques, such as the Rorschach and TAT, which provide samples of cognitive behavior that can be related to personality functioning. Blatt's views are borne out by a recent survey of the SPA membership. Although a majority of the members still describe themselves as adhering to a psychodynamic (42.0%) or psychoanalytic (13.1%) orientation, 23.6% now claim a cognitive or cognitive-behavioral orientation (Spielberger & Piotrowski, 1992). Less than 2% indicate a behavioral orientation.

As it enters its second half century, the Society for Personality Assessment is once again active and vigorous. Nev ertheless, there are still challenges to be faced. The declining emphasis on personality assessment in graduate training programs, the advent of largely unvalidated, computerized interpretive programs, controversial revisions in major assessment techniques, and the proliferation of new tests are but a few. These issues are discussed in the concluding chapter of this volume.

HISTORY OF THE DISTINGUISHED CONTRIBUTION AWARD

Because a number of the papers that we have included in this volume were prepared as Award addresses, the history of this honor should be outlined. What is now known as the "Bruno Klopfer Distinguished Contribution Award" was originally known as the "Great Man Award." Samuel J. Beck was the first recipient in 1965, followed by Bruno Klopfer (1966), Henry A. Murray (1967) and Robert R. Holt (1969). (No Award was presented in 1968.)

In 1970, Marguerite Hertz received the "Great Man Award." In presenting it, Past-President Louise Bates Ames dryly noted, "Though as far as I know, neither of us is an active member in the Women's Liberation Movement, I am delighted that [Marguerite Hertz] should be the first woman to receive our Great Man Award." Hertz was the last person to receive the "Great Man" award, which thereafter became the "Distinguished Contribution Award" until Bruno Klopfer's death, when the Society renamed it in his honor. Hertz was also the first honoree who delivered an Award address that was printed in the Society's *Journal,* along with the photograph and lifetime bibliography of the recipient.

In subsequent years, the Award was presented to Zygmunt A. Piotrowski (1971), Molly R. Harrower (1972), William E. Henry (1973), Louise Bates Ames (1974), Sylvan S. Tomkins (1975), Edwin S. Shneidman (1976), Albert I. Rabin (1977), Roy Schafer (1978), Paul E. Meehl (1979), John E. Exner, Jr. (1980), Martin Mayman (1981), Gordon F. Derner (1982), Irving B. Weiner (1983), Richard H. Dana (1984), Stephen A. Appelbaum (1985), Walter G. Klopfer (posthumous, 1985), Harrison G. Gough (1987), Wayne H. Holtzman (1987), Sidney J. Blatt (1989), Charles D. Spielberger (1990) and Leopold Bellak (1991). Most, but not all, delivered addresses that were published in the Society's Journal. The 1992 Award will be presented to Lee J. Cronbach (1992).

SELECTION OF PAPERS

We bring forth this volume with mixed feelings of pride and regret, pride for the valuable contributions being made available to a new generation of readers, and regret for the many other fine papers that could not be included. In assembling this collection, we acted like museum curators with a large collection of valuable paintings and only a limited amount of space in which to hang them. How did we choose?

Because this is a retrospective celebrating the first 50 years of the Society, we limited ourselves to articles published in the Society's Journal during that period. Next we decided to focus on works by men and women who had either served the Society as President or who had received the Great Man/Distinguished Contribution Award. By and large, we found that their Presidential or Klopfer Award addresses fitted best with our desire to select papers that dealt with the theoretical and conceptual issues that concerned the Society, and which commented on historical trends over its first 50 years. However, for several of these individuals whose presentations were not available, we selected other works. Our goal throughout was to choose papers that would be interesting and relevant to modern readers. This generated a list of potential selections that we fine-tuned to eliminate overlap and ensure coverage of the major issues over the entire 50-year period.

Overview and Commentary on the Selected Papers

In this section, we introduce the 16 selected articles spanning the full range of the Society's first half century, and comment on some of the issues and trends they illustrate. The articles are presented in the order of their publication. To observe how the ideas developed and how the issues have changed over the years, we recommend that you read the papers in their chronological order.

1. *Morris Krugman (1939).* Our retrospective begins with the first Presidential Address delivered by Morris Krugman in 1939 to the newly founded Rorschach Institute. Krugman first reviews the use of inkblots prior to Rorschach's experiments and then describes the development of the technique after Rorschach's death. [Readers wishing to explore this history further can consult articles by Beck (1972), Pichot (1984), and Rosenzweig (1944).]

Many of the issues Krugman raises have continued over the years to be of significant concern. One was the need for adequate standardization and norms, especially on special groups such as children and the elderly. Louise Bates Ames (1974) would later make this a major focus of her life's work. However, until John Exner (1974; 1978) developed his comprehensive scoring system, the lack of a single generally accepted scoring system hindered standardization efforts.

Another persistent concern is the need for more convincing evidence of validity. In his paper, Krugman discusses the fact that projective tests such as the Rorschach are not amenable to conventional statistical analyses and paradigms for establishing reliability and validity. In the years to come, the development of more sophisticated multivariate and nonparametric statistical techniques and Cronbach and Meehl's (1955) introduction of the concept of "construct" validity would help researchers address these problems. But to this day no completely satisfactory solutions have been found.

A third important issue that Krugman addresses is the qualifications of clinicians who administer and interpret the Rorschach. Decades later, Edwin Shneidman's 1962 address discusses the fact that validation research in projective techniques cannot separate the test from the skill of the person using it. Krugman's call for "extensive and intensive training in the various branches of psychology for all Rorschach workers" is, no doubt, even more cogent today than it was over 50 years ago.

Finally, Krugman outlines L. K. Frank's (1939) then-recent formulation of the "projective" hypothesis as a model to explain why Rorschach and TAT phenomena relate to personality processes. This marked one of the first attempts to ground projective assessment in psychological theory, an issue which is of central concern to the authors of the next three papers.

2. *Maria Rickers-Ovsiankina (1943).* By the time Maria Rickers-Ovsiankina delivered her Presidential Address at the Fourth Annual Meeting of the Rorschach Institute, the Rorschach technique was over 20 years old and seemed firmly established in psychology and psychiatry. In her talk, Rickers-Ovsiankina notes that clinical and empirical applications of the Rorschach and the concomitant accumulation of clinical data had outstripped the technique's theoretical foundations. She raises the question of how Rorschach data fit into the broader body of psychological research and theory on perceptual processes and personality theory.

After examining basic psychological research on perceptual processes among humans and animals as well as anthropological data, Rickers-Ovsiankina observes that the data are consistent with certain Rorschach color hypotheses. She concludes that: "The Rorschach method presents an empirical demonstration of a fundamental relationship between the perceptual pattern of a person and his personality makeup . . . [and it] . . . has an important contribution to make to the science of personality." In later years she would explore these points in greater depth in her book *Rorschach Psychology* (Rickers-Ovsiankina, 1977).

3. *Samuel B. Kutash (1955).* In this, his 1954 Presidential address to the Society for Projective Techniques, Samuel Kutash recalls Rickers-Ovsiankina's appeal for a closer integration of projective test data with psychological theory. He then discusses seven ways in which projective tests have positively influenced psychological science.

Rejecting the notion that projective assessment procedures are not amenable to scientific investigation, Kutash cites other disciplines such as astronomy and physics that have similar problems, and argues that "science" subsumes more than one narrowly construed methodological approach. Citing Hammond's (1954) call for more representative designs, Kutash maintains that projective techniques have contributed to basic science by emphasizing the interdependence of phenomena on one another and the importance of holistic research methods that preserve the gestalt.

4. *Samuel J. Beck (1955).* Samuel Beck was both a President of the Society for Projective Techniques and the first recipient of what would become known as the Bruno Klopfer Distinguished Achievement Award. In this rather demanding essay, Beck's 1955 Presidential Address to the Society, he continues to pursue the theme of integrating the Rorschach with basic research in personality.

Beck explores the similarities among three different clinical approaches, each having a different language and frame of reference. The first is neuropsychiatry as exemplified by Hughlings Jackson. The second is Freudian psychoanalysis as explicated by Roy R. Grinker. The third, of course, is the Rorschach. Using schizophrenia as an illustrative example, Beck explores the convergencies among the three approaches while commenting on the logic of scientific inquiry. He concludes, ". . . that it is possible to have a scientific approach to the study of personality, one consistent with clinical theory and with scientific logic."

5. *Bruno Klopfer (1957).* Bruno Klopfer was also both President of the Society and an early recipient of what was then known as the "Great Man Award." Although this paper, which was Klopfer's Presidential Address, was prepared in 1957, modern medical psychologists should find it absorbing. Klopfer describes how he was able to differentiate the Rorschach protocols of cancer patients who rapidly expired from those who went into remission, based primarily on his clinical judgment of ego strength. Similar discriminations were obtained with the MMPI.

In attempting to account for the relationship between psychological status and medical prognosis, Klopfer comments on the effects of the patients' psychological will to live and confidence in their treatment, describing a dramatic case of remission due to the placebo effect in a man with terminal cancer. This clinical report is consistent with anecdotal evidence form a surprising source 15 years later.

In a symposium commemorating Bruno Klopfer's death, his son, Walter, revealed that he and his father had given each other Rorschachs from time to time, partly as a form of communication and partly to determine if their increasing sophistication with the instrument would detract from the validity of their interpretations (W. Klopfer, 1974). On the last occasion that Walter administered the test to Bruno, he was disturbed because his father did not respond with his usual precision and animation. In his symposium paper, Walter reported: "I wondered whether this was the precursor of some degenerative disorder that might afflict Bruno Klopfer later on. In fact this is precisely what happened. Not long afterwards he chose to retire rather than continue working at less than his best" (W. Klopfer, 1974, p. 422).

6. *Leopold Bellak (1958).* This is the first of four selections by contributors to personality assessment who are best known for their work with apperceptive techniques. Henry A. Murray, who developed the Thematic Apperception Test (TAT), received the Great Man Award in 1967, the third person to be so honored. Unfortunately there is no record of a talk by Murray, nor were we able to find any other writings by him in the Society's archives.

This brief paper by Leopold Bellak, who was President of the Society in 1958 and the recipient of its Distinguished Contributions Award in 1991, was a tribute to Murray on the occasion of his 65th birthday. In it, Bellak provides a brief glimpse of the man who inspired so many in the Society.

7. *Robert R. Holt (1958).* Whereas the scoring and interpretation of the Rorschach depends more on how the respondent perceives the blot and utilizes the stimulus material than it does on the content of the responses, the opposite has been true of the TAT, in which most scoring systems focus on the content of the stories. In this article, Robert R. Holt, who was the first person after Murray to receive the Great Man Award, observes that Murray's major interest in the motivational aspects of personality led him to focus on the content, the "needs" of the hero and the "press" impinging upon him.

Holt's thesis is that a study of *how* a story is told, that is the formal and structural aspects of the stories such as their length, types of words used, comprehension of the stimulus and so forth, can be as revealing as the study of story content, perhaps even more so. Conceding that thus far studies of the formal aspects of the TAT had not been encouraging, Holt argues that this is because previous studies used *a priori* categories instead of empirically discovering the meaningful relationships between personality characteristics and TAT signs. He then cites data obtained in studies of psychiatric residents and labor mediators to demonstrate the potential value of considering formal aspects of the TAT as well as the content.

8. *William E. Henry and Elaine Cumming (1959).* William E. Henry was President of the Society in 1959 and he received the Distinguished Achievement Award in 1974. This paper, which was his Presidential Address, is one of the selections that focus on an area of application rather than on a particular assessment technique. In it, Henry considers old age, a topic that also interested several other Award recipients (Ames, 1974; W. Klopfer, 1974; Rabin 1977).

Henry suggests that many researchers who have written about aging evaluate old age using an inappropriate middle-age frame of reference. Middle-aged people who feel that it is important *for them* to be productive and involved with other people may assume that an elderly person who is no longer productive or involved must feel depressed or lonely because that is how *they* would feel. They fail to realize that a person's needs, aspirations, and values may continue to evolve and that elderly people have their own goals and agendas.

Henry describes how the TAT can be used to assess the extent and the quality of ego involvement with the outer world. He cites evidence from longitudinal studies using the TAT which indicate that, as people shift from middle to old age, they disengage and move, ". . . from an *active, combative, outer world orientation* to an *adaptive, conforming and abstract inner world orientation.*"

9. *Edwin S. Shneidman (1962).* A basic principle in apperceptive methods, such as Murray's (1943) TAT and Shneidman's (1949) Make-A-Picture Story Test, is that stories told about pictures can furnish meaningful insights into the personality of the story teller. This selection provides a modest empirical test of that premise. The author, Edwin Shneidman, who was both a President of the Society and a Klopfer Award winner, assures us that this, his 1962 Presidential address, was inspired by the picture you find included. After reading this allegory, if you have no hypotheses about the personality of the author, you should seriously consider entering another field.

Shneidman fantasizes that the outer figures represent the patron saints of the idiographic and nomothetic traditions, with "St. Herman" binding them together. He then discusses the theoretical underpinnings of projective techniques. He argues that many of the concepts and categories utilized in personality assessment will be better understood if they are thought of as belonging to what we might now term "fuzzy" or overlapping sets rather than to discrete, mutually exclusive categories. For example, instead of asking if a test is valid or invalid, we should inquire, "How valid and under what circumstances?" For further exploration of the meaning of validity and how it differs from clinical utility, see Shneidman (1959) and Meehl (1979).

10. *Walter G. Klopfer (1968).* Walter Klopfer, who served as Editor of the Society's *Journal* for many years, received the Bruno Klopfer Distinguished Achievement Award posthumously. In this characteristically brief paper, which he delivered to the 1968 International Rorschach Conference in London, Klopfer deplores the tendency for regarding the psychoanalytic, idiographic (European) style as being incompatible with the more empirical, nomothetic (American) approach. Reviewing tests ranging from the Sentence Completion to the Rorschach, he describes how all are, to one degree or another, influenced by situational and contextual as well as personality factors. Projective tests, he maintains, are not magical devices that probe the persona, but stimuli with known values that elicit samples of behavior which correlate with other behaviors, thereby helping clinicians make valid predictions.

Anticipating concerns raised in subsequent selections, Klopfer notes that some psychologists discount the value of assessment. Clinicians who are convinced that their favored method of treatment is a panacea, whether it is behavior modification, client-centered therapy, or orthodox analysis, have little use for assessment and diagnosis. Klopfer, however, reiterates his belief that projective and other tests, used in conjunction with other sources of information, will help less rigid clinicians predict behavior and determine the best intervention to be used with each individual client.

11. *Marguerite Hertz (1970).* Marguerite Hertz was among the first psychologists who attempted to place the Rorschach on a sound psychometric basis. This was evident in her early explorations of Rorschach reliability, her efforts to obtain normative data on various Rorschach response characteristics, and her periodic assessments of the empirical status of the Rorschach. In her "Great Man Award" address, which is included in this volume, Hertz addresses some of the same basic concerns regarding the scientific status of projective techniques that were considered by Maria Rickers-Ovsiankina in her 1943 Presidential address. However, while Rickers-Ovsiankina wrote at a time of general optimism regarding the status of personality assessment, Hertz faced burgeoning disbelief in the validity of projective techniques and skepticism regarding their theoretical assumptions.

In this important paper, Hertz describes how, as part of the social ferment of the period, many psychologists were challenging traditional assumptions regarding the role of the clinician. For a variety of reasons, as Walter Klopfer noted in the previous selection, the basic value of attempting to diagnose or classify deviant behavior or understand its etiology was being questioned, and the validity of psychological tests was disputed. While Hertz focuses on projective techniques in this paper, the validity and usefulness of structured personality instruments and individual intelligence tests were also being challenged during this period. Response sets, lack of discriminant validity, and cultural, ethnic and social class bias were among the criticisms. As we have seen, these concerns led many to doubt the continued viability of psychological assessment and the value of the Society.

Hertz acknowledges the many criticisms of personality assessment, and discusses the changes that have taken place in her lifetime. She describes recent research on the Rorschach, and, citing a host of studies, she defends the validity of projective techniques when used appropriately. Like Krugman and Walter Klopfer, Hertz maintains that projectives are merely one source of data that must be integrated with other available information, including the setting and the situation. Diagnosticians and researchers alike, she states, should be trained in the broad fundamentals of psychology as well as in the intricacies of their assessment tools. In a particularly prescient remark, she suggests, "It may well be that our attention should be directed to the area of cognitive styles." Rather than abandoning the enterprise, she concludes that the times call, ". . . for intensification of effort, for greater vigor and for daring innovation."

12. *Paul E. Meehl (1979).* By 1979, when Paul Meehl delivered his Klopfer Award address, the Society had completed its ecumenical evolution from the Rorschach Institute to the Society for Personality Assessment. Given the threats to the whole enterprise of personality assessment noted by Hertz, it was past time for all those who believed in the importance of psychodiagnosis and personality assessment to unite and stop the squabbling among the advocates of projective and structured tests, clinical and statistical prediction, and idiographic as opposed to nomothetic research. In this paper Meehl first reflects on some of those debates, noting, as had several previous recipients, that many of the points of contention were more apparent than real, and that the adversaries actually shared many basic assumptions about the importance of personality assessment.

In the main body of his presentation, Meehl discusses the nature of classification and its role in science. He notes that the search for and use of latent entities, such as types or syndromes, has declined in psychology in recent years as new schools of therapy have minimized their importance. Despite the power of mathematical and statistical clustering techniques, no viable diagnostic categories or syndromes have been found in either medicine or psychology by formal clustering methods. Meehl offers eight reasons why diagnosis has benefitted more from clinical insight and acumen than from statistical methods of discovery, and suggests ways this situation might be alleviated.

13. *John E. Exner (1980).* In the early 1950s, John Exner began his personal Rorschach odyssey, visiting various centers of Rorschach activity and meeting with the founders of the different Rorschach schools. Like a latter-day Darwin, Exner found that the seedlings germinated by Rorschach had taken root and flourished in the fertile soil of the New World, but over the years divergent species had evolved, each with its own group of adherents. He noted, ". . . one could argue that there were five Rorschachs instead of one, or even more if the foreign proliferations of Rorschach's work were included."

To deal with the multiplicity of Rorschach approaches and their psychometric shortcomings, Wayne Holtzman, who received the Klopfer Award in 1987, devised a new inkblot test in which respondents gave a single response to each of 45 blots. The Holtzman Inkblot Technique features a quantitative scoring system that synthesizes features from the five major systems (Holtzman et al., 1961).

Rather than create a new instrument, Exner worked to improve the existing Rorschach. In this Klopfer Award Address, Exner, who would later serve as President of the Society, reports that he first formulated a scheme in which he would bring Samuel Beck and Bruno Klopfer together to resolve the differences in their approaches to the Rorschach. Unfortunately, they ". . . had not communicated with each other for essentially 20 years . . ." and declined Exner's invitation. However, Klopfer and Beck, along with Hertz, Piotrowski, Rapaport, and Schafer, individually assisted Exner in his efforts to understand their respective approaches. Subsequently, Exner integrated what he felt to be the strongest features of the several schools into his own comprehensive system.

Exner's system, which has been widely accepted, paved the way for renewed research on reliability and the development of norms. In his paper in this volume, Exner presents data on the stability of certain Rorschach patterns among children indicating that their responses are formulated in a very short period of time, based on the interaction of a limited number of personal responses styles with aspects of each person's private world. Exner's study illustrates how tasks such as the Rorschach, the TAT, and the Holtzman Inkblot Technique can be used to provide unique and significant information about cognitive processing as well as personality functioning.

14. *Irving B. Weiner (1983).* In earlier addresses, Krugman (1939), Rickers-Ovsiankina (1943), Walter Klopfer (1968) and Marguerite Hertz (1970) had commented on the status of psychodiagnosis and personality assessment at various periods. In her 1970 paper, Hertz called attention to the crisis of confidence regarding personality assessment. In his Klopfer Award Address, which we have included in this volume, Irving Weiner, who has served the Society as President and currently as Editor of the *Journal,* continues this trend. Examining the field a decade later, Weiner finds the diagnostic and assessment enterprise in the 1980s to be healthier and more viable than it had been earlier.

Weiner observes that psychologists in the 1970s were eager to explore a variety of new roles and career options which had recently opened. Whereas assessment seemed to be a traditional and somewhat stultifying occupation, these newer roles appeared to offer more power, prestige and autonomy. By the mid-1980s, in Weiner's view, psychodiagnosis and assessment were once more respectable. This was especially true in certain areas of application such as health psychology, pediatric psychology and geropsychology. Psychologists realized that personality assessment complemented behavioral assessment. It had also become evident that situational influences interacted with personal predispositions or traits to determine behavior. Moreover, a number of new and revised assessment techniques had put the enterprise on a sounder empirical basis. Weiner optimistically concludes that: "Continued careful research on psychodiagnostic methods and the expert application of psychological test findings in clinical consultation should sustain a bright future for psychodiagnosis and its practitioners."

15. *Richard H. Dana (1984).* Whereas the last several selections addressed a number of the problems besetting personality assessment in the 1970s and 1980s, Richard Dana, a former President of the Society, uses his Klopfer

Award Address to advocate the development of "a unique, human-centered paradigm for research, training, and practice." Dana strongly advocates that psychology ". . . provide the relevance and social concern in research which will render our research efforts directly applicable to the services we provide."

How does one go about fostering humanism in an increasingly impersonal and technological society? Dana suggests that training programs should utilize certain "megatrends," broad cultural forces, that are to be found in current society. The counterparts of these trends in personality assessment are: (a) superempiricism, a high technology orientation which leads in part to computer-generated reports; (b) a biopsychosocial perspective which results in a broad, multivariate approach to assessment; (c) person-centering, with greater participation of the client in the assessment process and individualized training modes tailored to the needs of the student; (d) population-specificity, such as cross-cultural and gender-specific assessment; and (e) self-assessment, in which the client is collegially involved in the evaluation process. Based on these and similar megatrends in professional psychology, Dana envisions an idealized clinical training program designed to foster a human science foundation for professional psychology with trainers and trainees sharing equally in the process.

16. *Sidney Blatt (1990).* Sidney Blatt, another former President of the Society, received the Bruno Klopfer Distinguished Contribution Award during the Society's Fiftieth Anniversary year. In his Award Address, Blatt returns to the early concerns of Krugman (1939), Rickers-Ovsiankina (1943), Kutash (1955), and Beck (1955) on how projective techniques in general, and the Rorschach in particular, can be integrated with the mainstream of psychological theory and research. He notes that, in any age, scholars are limited by the theoretical models that are available at that period. In the 1920s, psychology focused on sensation and perception, stimuli and responses. Cognitive processes were considered too subjective for scientific study, so it was natural for Hermann Rorschach to regard his inkblot task as falling into the realm of perception.

Although the perceptual model has been useful, Blatt argues that some of the most interesting Rorschach phenomena, such as the movement response, are not perceptions (because the blot is not moving) but mental constructions based on perceptual experiences. Thanks to the cognitive revolution in psychology and the work of scholars such as Werner (1948) and Piaget (1954), Blatt maintains that it is now possible to use the Rorschach and TAT, ". . . to develop methods for evaluating cognitive processes and the structures of mental representation from an individual's responses to relatively ambiguous stimuli."

Blatt delineates certain parallels between cognitive psychology and psychoanalysis. Both are amenable to the analysis of mental structures, and in both there is a concern for how latent or unconscious factors unique to each person alter and shape their individual views of reality. Projective techniques such as the Rorschach and TAT can contribute important insights into the association of ". . . cognitive processes with personality organization and psychopathology . . .", according to Blatt. He further suggests that we will eventually need new conceptions of psychopathology that go beyond manifest behavioral symptoms as a framework for evaluating individual differences in development of cognitive schema and structures.

As we conclude the first 50 years in the history of the Society for Personality Assessment, it is evident that much has been accomplished, but that even greater challenges will be encountered. The conclusion reached by Blatt in his Klopfer Award paper sets the stage for personality assessment in the years to come: ". . . we are at the threshold of a new era in personality assessment, one that holds the potentiality for beginning to appreciate more fully the fascinating complexities of the human condition."

REFERENCES

Ames, L. B. (1974). Calibration of aging. *Journal of Personality Assessment, 38,* 507-519.

Beck, S. J. (1955). Personality research and theories of personality structure. *Journal of Projective Techniques, 19,* 361-371.

Beck, S. J. (1972). How the Rorschach came to America. *Journal of Personality Assessment, 36,* 105-108.

Bellak, L. (1954). *The Thematic Apperception Test and the Children's Apperception Test in clinical use.* New York: Grune and Stratton.

Bellak, L. (1958). Henry A. Murray: An appreciation. *Journal of Projective Techniques, 22,* 143-144.

Blatt, S. J. (1990). The Rorschach: A test of perception or an evaluation of representation. *Journal of Personality Assessment, 55,* 394-416.

Carr, A. C. (1971). Society for Personality Assessment: The way to go. *Journal of Personality Assessment, 35,* 203-240.

Cronbach, L. J., & Meehl, P. E. (1955). Construct validity in psychological tests. *Psychological Bulletin, 52,* 281-302. [Reprinted in Megargee (1966).]

Dana, R. H. (1984). Megatrends in personality assessment: Toward a human science professional psychology. *Journal of Personality Assessment, 48,* 563-579.

Exner, J. E. (1974). *The Rorschach: A comprehensive system* (Vol. 1). New York: Wiley.

Exner, J. E. (1978). *The Rorschach: A comprehensive system (Vol. 2). New York: Wiley.*

Exner, J. E. (1980). But it's only an inkblot. *Journal of Personality Assessment, 44,* 563-576.

Farberow, N. L., & Little, K. B. (1970). Society for Personality Assessment: Which way to go? *Journal of Personality Assessment, 34,* 468-469.

Frank L. K. (1939). Projective methods for the study of personality. *Journal of Psychology, 8,* 389-413.

Hammond, K. R. (1954). Representative vs. systematic design in clinical psychology. *Psychological Bulletin, 51,* 208-211. [Reprinted in Megargee (1966).]

Hathaway, S. R., & McKinley, J. C. (1967). *Minnesota Multiphasic Personality Inventory: Manual for administration and scoring.* New York: Psychological Corp.

Henry, W. E., & Cumming, E. (1959). Personality development in adulthood and old age. *Journal of Projective Techniques and Personality Assessment, 34,* 384-390.

Hertz, M. (1970). Projective techniques in crisis. *Journal of Projective Techniques and Personality Assessment, 34,* 449-467.

Holt, R. R. (1958). Formal aspects of the TAT: A neglected resource. *Journal of Projective Techniques, 22,* 163-172.

Holtzman, W. H., Thorpe, J. S., Swartz, J. D., & Herron, E. W. (1961). *Inkblot perception and personality.* Austin, TX: University of Texas.

Klopfer, B. (1957). Psychological variables in human cancer. *Journal of Projective Techniques, 21,* 332-340.

Klopfer, W. G. (1968). The metamorphosis of projective techniques. *Journal of Projective Techniques, 32,* 403-404.

Klopfer, W. G. (1974). The Rorschach and old age. *Journal of Personality Assessment, 38,* 420-422.

Krugman, M. (1939). Out of the inkwell: The Rorschach method. *Rorschach Research Exchange, 4,* 91-100.

Kutash, S. B. (1955). The impact of projective techniques on basic psychological science. *Journal of Projective Techniques, 19,* 453-469.

Meehl, P. E. (1979). A funny thing happened to us on the way to the latent entities. *Journal of Personality Assessment, 42,* 564-577.

Mischel, W. (1968). *Personality and assessment.* New York: Wiley.

Murray, H. A. (1943). *Thematic Apperception Test Manual.* Cambridge, MA: Harvard University Press.

Piaget, J. (1954). The construction of reality in the child. [Translated from the French by M. Cock.] New York: Basic Books. [Original published in 1937.]

Pichot, P. (1984). Centenary of the birth of Hermann Rorschach. [Translated from the French by S. Rosenzweig and E. Schreiber.] *Journal of Personality Assessment, 48,* 591-596.

Rabin, A. I. (1977). Enduring sentiments: The continuity of personality over time. *Journal of Personality Assessment, 41,* 564-572.

Rickers-Ovsiankina, M. (1943). Some theoretical considerations regarding the Rorschach method. *Rorschach Research Exchange, 7,* 41-53.

Rickers-Ovsiankina, M. A. (1977). *Rorschach psychology* (2nd ed.). Huntington, NY: Krieger.

Rorschach, H. (1921). *Psychodiagnostik: Meth-*

odik und Ergebnisse eines Wahrnehmungs-diagnostichen Experiments. Berne: Bircher.

Rorschach, H., & Oberholzer, E. (1923). Zur Auswertung des Formdeutversuchs fuer die Psychoanalyse. *Zsch. f. d. ges. Neur. u. Pschiatr., 82,* 240–273. [Translated as: The application of the interpretation of form to psychoanalysis. *Journal of Nervous and Mental Disease,* 1924, *60,* 225–248; 359–379.]

Rosenzweig, S. (1944). A note on Rorschach pre-history. *Rorschach Research Exchange, 8,* 41–42.

Shneidman, E. S. (1949). *The Make-A-Picture Story (MAPS) Test.* New York: Psychological Corp.

Shneidman, E. S. (1962). Projections on a triptych; Or, a Hagiology for our time. *Journal of Projective Techniques and Personality Assessment, 26,* 380–387.

Spielberger, C. D., & Piotrowski, C. (1992). Profile of the membership of the Society for Personality Assessment: Comparisons between 1987 and 1990. *Journal of Personality Assessment, 58,* 423–429.

Weiner, I. B. (1983). The future of psychodiagnosis revisited. *Journal of Personality Assessment, 47,* 451–459.

Werner, H. (1948). *Comparative psychology of mental development.* New York: International Universities Press.

Out of the Ink Well (The Rorschach Method)

MORRIS KRUGMAN[1]

The title of this discussion has been borrowed, of all places, from an animated movie cartoon series, popular at about the time Dr. Hermann Rorschach was experimenting with ink blots and writing the *Psychodiagnostik*. This series of cartoons was called "Out of the Ink Well," and usually began with a picture of the artist opening an inkwell in preparation for drawing. To his consternation, little black animal and human-like figures would rush out of the bottle, cavort around for a while, ultimately to be rounded up after considerable trouble, and swept back into the ink well. This would then be tightly corked, while the artist breathed a sigh of relief. Like so many other parallelisms between the movies and life, the little demons released by Rorschach were not ultimately rounded up and returned to the bottle, where, safely corked, they lived happily forever after. On the contrary, they still are cavorting merrily, not only in the locality where they were released some nineteen years ago, but all over the world.

Certainly, Rorschach did not invent the ink blot. Long before he was born there were in existence elaborate systems for exercising the imagination by means of ink blots. Nor was he the first to conceive of the possibility of ink blots as media for exploring personality, for, as early as 1895, Binet and Henri suggested that they be used for studying various traits, especially visual imagination. In the next four or five years, four well known and often quoted studies by Dearborn, Sharp, and Kirkpatrick, were published. In the first edition of his "Manual of Mental and Physical Tests," published in 1910, a year before Rorschach began his work with ink blots, Whipple reviewed these studies in some detail, and described his own standard series of 20 blots, constituting his "Test 45," which, he stated, could be purchased from Stoelting and Company. This was probably the first instance of uniform blots that could be obtained for wide experimentation.

The availability of Whipple's blots spurred experimentation in that area tremendously. Three studies by Pyle, one in 1913, and two in 1915 followed. Pyle used the ink blot responses as associations which gave him important clues for studying individual differences. He found age, sex, racial and intellectual differences in the number of responses. Following Pyle's reports, two important studies were published in England, in 1916 and 1917 by Bartlett and by Parsons, respectively. These workers, apparently benefiting from the published reports on ink blot experimentation then in existence, carried the technique much further. Bartlett was probably the first to introduce color and shading. Both Bartlett and Parsons went beyond the earlier efforts to study only, or mainly imagination by means of ink blots, and speculated as to differences in intelligence, as manifested by the responses; differences in approach, as determined by attack on the whole blot as against small details; differences as to background, vocation, interests, etc. that influenced the responses. Content, likewise, was analyzed, and the groupings were not far from Rorschach's later divisions.

I have done no more than mention the early workers with ink blots because they are treated in some detail by

[1]Presidential address of the First Annual Meeting of the Rorschach Institute, Inc.

several writers: by Whipple, in the various editions of his classic manual, beginning with the 1910 edition, by Tulchin, in an article in the *Rorschach Research Exchange*, published early this year, though written in 1925, and by Beck, in 1932, in the monograph on the *Rorschach as Applied to the Feebleminded*.

In retrospect, progress in the use of ink blots clinically and experimentally in psychology was regular: (from 1895 to 1917: Binet, Dearborn, Sharp, Kirkpatrick, Whipple, Pyle, Bartlett, Parsons, in chronological order.)

How much Rorschach was aware of these studies is difficult to say, since nowhere, to my knowledge, did he mention them. Rorschach's work overlapped much of the early work with ink-blots, since he experimented with them from 1911 to 1921. Even though the germs of several of Rorschach's later concepts can be found in the early reports, that fact does not detract in the least from Rorschach's genius. Rorschach did not invent ink blots, but he did develop a method of personality study that yields results that are clinically meaningful—a condition which existed in only one other approach, that of the intensive case study. Rorschach's contribution would not have been very important if he had merely improved the method of inkblot experimentation. His contribution is of the utmost importance because he transformed an amorphous, uncertain instrument into a clinical technique, which, in the hands of the trained clinical worker, makes possible not only a diagnosis, or a confirmation of other types of diagnoses, but presents a gestalt of behavior and personality patterns not otherwise obtainable without much more elaborate procedures, and frequently directs attention to deviations from "normality" often overlooked by other techniques. His conclusions were never reached by *a priori* reasoning. Whatever could be validated clinically, was so validated, and whatever could not be, was presented only tentatively. It is a remarkable tribute to the genius of the man that it has been found necessary to change so few of his original concepts. Undoubtedly, Rorschach had more evidence for his conclusions than was presented in the *Psychodiagnostik*—he hints at it in several places. Nevertheless, a first presentation, no matter how brilliant, is expected to be relatively crude. This is not the case with Rorschach's work. In a few instances, norms have been revised for local use, and original concepts have been elaborated, but, in the main, Rorschach's standards are generally employed in these revisions, and his suggestions for obtaining them are used, as, for example, in designating forms as good or poor; details as normal or rare; responses as original or popular, etc. Rorschach, himself, noted many weaknesses in his method, and even outlined procedures for their elimination. Unfortunately, he did not live long enough to do this work. Now, nineteen years later, much of it still remains to be done.

After Rorschach's untimely death in 1922, experimentation with his technique, and its clinical application, was at first most intensive, as was natural, in Switzerland, and, later in Germany. In 1933, Vernon was able to say: "The Rorschach Ink-blot test has been widely used in continental countries as a psychiatric diagnostic method, but it is still little known in England and America." And yet, even in 1933, only twelve years after the publication of the *Psychodiagnostik*, we find published reports of work with the Rorschach in many countries. Foremost among those who attempted to extend Rorschach's work was, of course, Oberholzer, still recognized as the dean of Rorschach workers. Roemer, another colleague of Rorschach, elaborating on Rorschach's work, attempted to build a framework for a dynamic-analytical theory of mental life and personality, and outlined procedures based on Rorschach's work even during the latter's lifetime, but it is only in recent years that students of personality have drifted toward his way of thinking.

A single talk of this kind cannot possibly provide the occasion of a comprehensive history of the Rorschach method. Nor is such a comprehensive review necessary, since excellent summaries and annotated bibliographies by Beck (1932), Vernon (1933; 1935; 1937), Hertz (1935), Piotrowski (1938), and later summaries in the *Rorschach Research Exchange* are so readily available in English. Only a few trends necessary for the continuity of the discussion can be mentioned.

Immediately following 1921, many of the published reports on the Rorschach method dealt with explanation and amplification of the technique, and with the underlying theory. It was not long, however, before the bulk of the published Rorschach literature began to deal with experimental data. . . .

During all this time numerous attempts to validate the Rorschach and to determine its reliability were made. From the purely statistical point of view, the Rorschach has not proven reliable, for several reasons. To begin with, it does not yield a numerical score, so that the correlation of the results of successive administrations of the instrument to the same subjects is not possible. Then again, alternate forms of the test are not yet in existence, so that method of determining reliability is eliminated. The method of split-halves has been used by several investigators, but this procedure is open to question, because it is impossible to equate any five Rorschach cards with any other five, since, as all experienced Rorschach workers will acknowledge, each card in the series usually calls forth characteristic responses not elicited from the other cards. Finally, and most important, determining the consistency with which the same subjects produce the same Rorschach elements on successive administrations is not very meaningful, since, as every beginner knows, the gross and subtle relationships of these elements determines the diagnosis, and not the elements themselves. New techniques for determining the reliability of the Rorschach, therefore, had to be devised. One is that of the "blind" diagnosis, which has not yet been thoroughly applied, although many reputable experimenters offer evidence of rather good consistency of diagnosis among several interpreters of the same Rorschach protocols. Another ingenious device, being employed in a current research by Fosberg, is to administer the Rorschach three times under different instructions: first, normally; a second time, asking the subject to change his responses to make a good impression; and a third time, asking him to make a poor impression. The results seem to indicate that very little change in the personality constellations resulted, whereas a parallel experiment with the same subjects employing a widely used personality schedule the same way showed radically different personality *gestalten* for each of the subjects.

The validity of the Rorschach has likewise not yet been mathematically demonstrated for much the same reasons. Here, too, the "blind" diagnosis, as well as matching techniques are widely used. The literature abounds with testimony from reputable workers in the various schools of psychology and in widely different situations as to the validity of the Rorschach. It must be admitted that testimony, no matter what the reputation of the giver, is not the ideal basis for a scientific approach. And yet, careful examination of the testimony is impressive. Even more impressive is the Rorschach worker's daily experience of constructing a personality and behavior picture of an individual without knowing anything about him except the responses to the ten cards, comparing that picture with what is learned from an intensive study of case material, from a psychiatric examination, from numerous interviews, and from various psychological tests, and not only finding close correspondence, but frequently throwing new light on the personality, that is substantiated on further investigation by other means.

****

In this country, work with the Rorschach began rather slowly, gradually gathered momentum, gained full speed four or five years ago, and is now riding so high that careful workers are becoming concerned about its use, and are attempting to apply the brakes.

Among the more important happenings that stimulated its use in this country were, the publication of the translation of the famous Rorschach-Oberholzer article in the *Journal of Nervous and Mental Diseases*, in 1924, and the introduction of the method the same year to workers in this country by Dr. David Levy. Beck, one of Levy's disciples, soon assumed the leadership among those experimenting with the technique and those using it clinically, although two or three studies using the Rorschach method were reported in the United States before Beck began working with it. Beck acknowledges that his early work was done under the guidance of Levy and Wells. Both Levy and Beck had considerable contact with Oberholzer, so that the influence of the Rorschach-Oberholzer approach in the use of ink-blots in personality study on workers in this country was direct.

Just as Oberholzer's name has been synonymous with the Rorschach test in Europe since 1922, so has Beck's name been associated with it in the United States since 1928. Beginning with a study of the Rorschach, as applied to the feebleminded, in 1930, a study considerably expanded in a report in 1932, Beck has published one, two or three significant reports every year since 1930. In 1937 he published his *Introduction to the Rorschach Method*, the first comprehensive treatment of the Method in English, especially important since no official translation of Rorschach's *Psychodiagnostik* has ever been published in English, although four or five private translations, not widely circulated, are known. In addition to his written reports, Beck was actively expounding the Rorschach technique and describing his work with it at professional meetings. There was hardly a national meeting of psychologists, from about 1928-29 on, that did not have a paper on the Rorschach by Beck.

In the meantime, a new force began to be felt in the American Rorschach scene. Along about 1934-35, a new name began to be identified with Rorschach—the name of Klopfer. Whereas the Rorschach had, for the previous five years, been used mainly by an esoteric group of workers, it suddenly became accessible to a much larger number of qualified psychologists and psychiatrists. Dr. Klopfer formed study groups, organized courses, traveled and lectured all over the country, devised refined scoring techniques, most of them, incidentally, based solidly on Rorschach, Oberholzer and Binder, founded the *Rorschach Research Exchange* in 1936, established the Rorschach at outstanding universities, clinics, hospitals, and research centers, and in 1939, organized the Rorschach Institute, now holding its first annual conference. The *Research Exchange*, in less than four years, has established itself not only among Rorschach workers in this country and elsewhere, but has also made a unique place for itself, by virtue of the significance of its articles, in the more general clinical literature. That the Institute holds similar promise, is attested by the quality of today's program and by that planned for tomorrow.

****

One crude measure of the amount of work done in a given field is the size of the bibliography of the field. I have compiled a list of publications on the Rorschach, exclusive of general articles or books merely referring to the method, that is as complete as I can make it by utilizing every available cross reference in this country and every bibliography obtainable here and abroad. Two hundred fifty one publications are on the list. Of these, 38 appeared during the first ten years, and 213 during the past nine. For the past five years, about as many articles have appeared each year as were published in the entire first ten-year period. Thirteen languages and 17 countries are represented, although 82% are in German and English. Most of the German articles are from Switzerland, although Germany, and, to a lesser extent, Austria, are represented.

Of the 38 articles published during the first ten-year period, 28 were in German, while the other 10 were scattered among five languages. Since 1931 two trends in Rorschach publications have been noticeable: the appearance of articles in new countries, and the very great increase in published articles in this country; 125 of the 129 American titles appearing on the total list have been published since 1931. This amounts to 59% of all publications during the past nine years, but the ratio is much higher if only the past five years are considered.

There are several reasons for the recent growth of Rorschach work in the United States. Some of these reasons are interrelated: the deplorable situation in Europe the past few years has not only rendered experimental and clinical work there relatively unimportant, and therefore, reduced the number of publications, but many Rorschach workers have migrated to this country and are publishing in American journals, or have stimulated others to publish. The arrival in New York of Dr. Emil Oberholzer, the outstanding figure among Rorschach workers, is an example of such migrations.

Another reason for the growth in the United States is the cumulative effect of the writings and oral presentations of the early Rorschach workers, aided by the demonstrated clinical usefulness of the instrument, and by the known support of outstanding psychiatrists and psychologists like David Levy and F.L. Wells, respectively. Finally, two other factors contributed to the recent rapid spread of the Rorschach: the *Rorschach Research Exchange*, and Beck's monograph. The influence of the latter is no doubt considerable, but difficult to measure; the influence of the *Rorschach Exchange*, to which most Rorschach workers and many libraries of universities, clinics, and research laboratories in this country subscribe, can be gauged roughly by the proportion of American Rorschach articles appearing in it. Since its founding, late in 1936, 58 of the 93 Rorschach articles published in the United States, or 52%, have appeared in the *Exchange*.

The growth of the Rorschach in this country, after the first important work was done abroad, is not as unique a phenomenon as would seem at first glance. Several important more or less related fields show similar histories. Wundt and experimental psychology, Binet and mental testing (and ink-blots), Kraepelin and psychiatry, Freud, Jung, Adler, and Rank, in psychoanalysis, and Galton and Pearson in statistics, as well as Rorschach and ink-blots, all bear striking resemblances in that their basic structures were developed in European countries, but much of the building of superstructures, the practical application, or the widespread use, occurred in the United States. An interesting fact in connection with all of these is that in practically every case, a period of 15 to 20 years elapsed between the time of the original work in Europe and the generalized acceptance and widespread use in the United States.

****

What of the present status of the Rorschach Method? In addition to the marked increase in Rorschach publications in recent years, there are numerous other indications of its acceptance in this country and abroad. We find more and more psychiatrists and psychologists adopting it; in many cases, psychologists are not being employed in clinics unless they have mastered the Rorschach; several universities are giving graduate courses in the method; dozens of dissertations dealing with it have recently been written, or are in progress; professional meetings not only have papers dealing with the Rorschach, but frequently hold round tables devoted exclusively to it; the first monograph published by the American Orthopsychiatric Association was Beck's *Manual*; in England, a medal for one of the outstanding studies in psychiatry for 1935 was presented by the Royal Medico-Psychological Association to Guirdham for his article on "The Rorschach Test for Epileptics."

Furthermore, the fields in which the Rorschach method has been extensively applied have increased markedly the past few years. In addition to the usual research uses, the Rorschach is now widely employed by psychologists and psychiatrists and even neurologists, not only for diagnostic, but also for prognostic purposes and for the determination of status at various point during the therapeutic process; it is widely used in education, in child guidance, in vocational guidance, in business and industry, in social work, and in at least one large school system for teacher selection, and is being considered at the moment as an aid to the selection of students by a large medical school. In short, there is hardly an area in which psychology and psychiatry are functioning, in which the Rorschach method has not made an important place for itself.

At this point it should be emphasized, even though that caution is unnecessary for Rorschach workers, that, except in a few instances, the Rorschach does not displace fundamental psychological practices, or even specialized techniques, but rather supplements them. To use the Rorschach in place of a psychiatric or neurological, or psychometric examination when these are necessary, would border on quackery. To use it as an adjunct to these, is to gain insight in many borderline situations and to gain much valuable information, frequently not otherwise obtainable. The exception referred to, in which the Rorschach has practically pushed popular techniques from use in many clinics, is the large group of various "personality tests," employed by psychologists for the past twenty years or more for want of more satisfactory techniques—tests that have usually been found to have high reliability, but practically no validity, when the criterion for validity was not an artificially constructed one, but agreement with other clinical data.

Another example of the acceptance of the Rorschach in theoretical and applied psychology, is found in some of the discussions of the exponents of the newer schools in psychology such as topological and operational psychology, and in discussion of followers of some of the newer approaches to personality study such as projective methods. One of the clearest statements of such an approach is Lawrence K. Frank's article, "Projective Methods for the Study of Personality," in the October 1939 issue of the *Journal of Psychology*. This article deserves much more consideration than can possibly be given here, but one or two excerpts will be quoted. After showing how the physical and biological sciences have advanced from a static concept of living and of inorganic matter, to a dynamic one, because the former failed to account for the behavior or the organizational structure of matter, he states:

"In similar fashion we may approach the personality and induce the individual to reveal his way of organizing experience by giving him a field (objects, materials, experiences) with relatively little structure and cultural patterning so that the personality can project upon that plastic field his way of seeing life, his meanings, significances, patterns, and especially his feelings. Thus we elicit a projection of the individual personality's private world because he has to organize the field, interpret the material and react affectively to it. More specifically, a projection method for study of personality involves the presentation of a stimulus-situation designed or chosen because it will mean to the subject, not what the experimenter has arbitrarily decided it should mean (as in most psychological experiments using standardized stimuli in order to be "objective"), but rather whatever it must mean to the personality who gives it, or imposes upon it, his private, idiosyncratic meaning and organization. The subject then will respond to his meaning of the presented stimulus-situation by some form of action and feeling that is expressive of his personality." (Frank, 1939, pp. 402-403.)

Again, "When we scrutinize the actual procedures that may be called projective methods we find a wide variety of techniques and material being employed for the same general purpose, to obtain from the subject 'what he cannot or will not say,' frequently because he does not know himself and is not aware what he is revealing about himself through his projections." (Frank, 1939, p. 404.)

He then presents examples of projective techniques. Foremost among these is the Rorschach, about which he states:

"The Rorschach ink blots,... are perhaps the most widely known of these procedures. They have been utilized in Europe and in the United States, frequently in connection with psychiatric clinics and hospitals, for revealing the personality configurations and have been found of increasing value.. Insofar as life histories and psychiatric and psychoanalytic studies of the subjects who have had the Rorschach diagnosis are available, the ink blot interpretations are being increasingly validated by these clinical findings." (Frank, 1939, p. 404.)

Other projective methods listed are Wilhelm Stern's Cloud Pictures, play techniques, eidetic imagery, plastics, artistic media like painting, finger painting, drawing, puppet shows, dramatization, the dance, and music. Thematic Perception Methods, and expressive movements of various kinds. In all of these, the purpose is the same—to get the subject to reveal "what he cannot or will not say"—the quotation being from Henry A. Murray.

Thus, the Rorschach is no longer an outcast in psychology, but rather a perfectly respectable, even a leading member, in the highly respected community of dynamic psychology schools.

****

Numerous problems face Rorschach workers who are interested not only in improving the technique, but in preventing its wide use by untrained people and by quacks. Foremost among the problems of improvement is that of more conclusive clinical validation. Individual users by the hundred are convinced of its validity, but there is need to coordinate available results and to sift facts from subjective impressions. One such attempt was begun some years ago, but, to my knowledge, has never been completed, or brought to any conclusive stage. Possibly it is the function of the Rorschach Institute to engage in this task. The same applied to the reliability of the instrument. In connection with validity and reliability, we must remember that statistical means alone will not serve the purpose, since, as Murray, Frank, and others have pointed out, in clinical work we are more interested in the interactions of an individual's many facets of personality with the many aspects of his environment, than in the extent to which any one of his personality traits, if there is such an entity as a trait psychologically, coincides with a statistically derived norm.

Another problem that is frequently discussed in the literature is the of Rorschach standardization and norms. Since certain Rorschach items like F+, D, Dr, d, P and O are, by Rorschach's definition, determined by frequency of occurrence in an unselected population, they must, of necessity, be statistically determined for each major population grouping. To some extent this has been done by Beck, Hertz, and others, and Rickers has compiled, for limited circulation, a collection of scoring samples from fifteen outstanding Rorschach workers. Necessary as this is, however, it is a far cry from the standardization of these few elements to standardization of the entire method. A symposium on Rorschach standardization, held in connection with the 1939 meeting of the American Orthopsychiatric Association under the direction of Dr. Klopfer, showed marked agreement that what was needed was, in the main, clinical validation, although standardization of certain elements was helpful.

Another problem is one proposed by Rorschach himself, in the *Psychodiagnostik*, but worked on only sporadically since—the construction and equating, card for card, of an equivalent set of blots, capable of eliciting for each individual an almost identical gestalt with that obtained on the present set. This becomes more necessary as the use of the test becomes more widespread. Some workers claim that familiarity with the test does not alter the subject's response patterns, but I cannot subscribe to that point of view, although I do believe that the practice effect on the Rorschach is less than on the usual psychometric instruments.

Still another need in Rorschach work is to determine the characteristics of various children's age groups. It is important to know whether Rorschach's criteria for abnormality in adults apply to young children, preadolescents, or adolescents. Work in this area has not been well organized, and there is contradictory material in the literature. Are preschool children negativistic? Should we expect more but poorer whole responses from six and seven year olds, with poor form, DW's, and perseveration, than we get from older children of the same intelligence level? Is age a factor in the number of responses, in constriction or expansion, in the number and type of color responses, movement responses, etc.? Do the same color shock criteria apply to all ages of children? Does the Rorschach show a "normal" adolescent disturbance, and to what extent should this be allowed for in diagnosing pathology in the adolescent? These are a few of the questions for which we do not know the answers. Miss Paulsen's and Dr. Klopfer's papers today on the Rorschach administered to preschool and first grade school children are a beginning of what is needed for all age groups.

There is one further problem that has not received much attention, especially in the literature, and that is the question of limiting the use of the Rorschach to qualified individuals. Beck (1939, pp. 806-807) has issued a warning about this, but most other workers are too involved in their work to pay much attention to it. Beck's five requirements for a Rorschach worker can readily be accepted, with the possible exception of the requirement that having been psychoanalyzed is an essential condition. I would say "desirable" rather than "essential." Certainly, "broad experience in psychopathology," "experience with the Rorschach Test in many clinical groups," and "orientation in the Rorschach-Oberholzer tradition," are minimum essentials for successful work with the method. Beck implies, but does not list as a specific requirement, the need for proceeding from the point where Rorschach and Oberholzer left off, and being thoroughly acquainted with the development of the Rorschach since the publication of the *Psychodiagnostik* and the Rorschach-Oberholzer supplement.

I should like to join Beck in his appeal for extensive and intensive training and experience in the various branches of psychology for all Rorschach workers. It is trite to say that the Rorschach is not a simple psychological test in which one can be specifically trained, regardless of background and experience, to obtain a composite score that has any meaning psychologically. I can claim only slightly more than half of Beck's 13 years of experience with the method, but I am convinced that his implication that a Rorschach diagnosis is only as good as the one who makes it, is true. I feel certain that the members and fellows of the Rorschach Institute agree on this. I believe one of the major results of the organization of this Institute will be the influence its members will exert to prevent the Rorschach from being misused by incompetents or charlatans. To this end, the Institute should exert every effort to avoid the misleading of innocents by permitting them to enter courses in the Rorschach method before they are prepared to benefit from them. Too many courses are now open to any who can afford the fee, without regard to their qualifications. I have heard some say that this is not a serious matter, and takes care of itself, since the method is so complex that the ill prepared cannot use it properly. That is just the point—they cannot use it properly, but they can misuse it, they can make unwarranted diagnoses, and they can mislead people and do damage. I feel certain that the Rorschach Institute will be very influential in keeping the Rorschach on the high professional level it deserves.

****

Such is the story, considerably telescoped, of the little demons out of the ink well. Psychoanalysts tell us there are good demons and bad demons. Let us hope the good ones will continue the influence they have exerted the past nineteen years and the others will be rounded up and returned to the bottle whence they issued.

Some Theoretical Considerations Regarding the Rorschach Method

MARIA RICKERS-OVSIANKINA[1]

In the twenty-odd years of its existence, the Rorschach method of personality diagnosis has firmly established its usefulness. So firmly and so broadly has it been established, that not only psychologists and psychiatrists, but even members of less immediately concerned disciplines like anthropology and education have begun to consider it a professional "must" to be versed in the intricacies of this method. Within the past few years, the technique has even reached into the consciousness of the popular mind by way, for instance, of the news magazine *Time*, and by way even of Hollywood. And when Hollywood has found a pictorial use for the Rorschach method—though perhaps only to toss our cards about—there can be no doubt among either scholars or skeptics that our method has arrived! Thus it would be rather natural at an annual stock taking of Rorschachists to expect nothing but expressions of gratification and of mutual congratulations over the really remarkable progress that our specialty has made, and particularly over the reception given it by the professional world at large.

And yet in the minds of at least some of us, this satisfaction is frequently mingled with a certain amount of dissatisfaction, or concern. The reason for this feeling of concern seems to lie in the recognition of a discrepancy in the relative positions of our practices and our theory. Every scientist, while working on the discovery of specific empirical facts, does so with the ultimate hope in mind, that his findings, however small or even unimportant they might appear at the time, eventually will be incorporated into the larger body of that particular science. And he knows that the realization of this hope depends on whether his findings either fit into some already existing theoretical principles, or whether the discovery of these facts open up new theoretical avenues. Any such new avenues might serve to fill a gap in that particular system of knowledge.

The emergence of new theoretical assumptions of course leads in turn a search for new empirical facts which would be in line with the theory. In short, in every growing science, fact-finding on the one hand, and the development of theoretical principles on the other hand, are closely interwoven. And only the two processes together can make the cycle of scientific knowledge complete. In has been said, facts without theory to integrate them are blind, and theory without facts to back it up is dead.

With these general considerations in mind, let us look at the Rorschach method again. Nobody will deny the magnitude of broadly selected and carefully controlled clinical and experimental data which is now available for this method. And nobody will doubt the indispensable importance of such empirical data for the progress of psychological understanding and for the application of the method. And yet, granting all this, we must ask one very important question: are these empirical data balanced by a similar development on the theoretical and conceptual side? Has our increasing knowledge of the many concrete facts brought with it a corresponding degree of insight into the necessary underlying theory?

We cannot help but answer this question in the negative. By a negative answer, however, we do not intend to imply that all the work in the field has

[1]Paper read in part as the Presidential Address at the Fourth Annual Meeting of the Rorschach Institute, April 29, 1943, New York City.

been devoid of theoretical considerations. We only wish to point out that theoretical and systematic formulations have been lagging too far behind the impressive accumulation of empirical data.

It is not easy to find adequate reasons to account for this situation. One important factor, however, is surely to be found in the origin of the Rorschach method. One can easily venture the conjecture, that if Rorschach had started out to devise a personality test, he would probably have chosen a medium different from ten partly colored inkblots. It will be recalled that his initial objective was a much more modest one, namely to devise a means of studying the imagination of his psychiatric patients. For this specific purpose, the use of indefinite forms, such as inkblots, appears quite logical, and the relation between the problem and the chosen method requires no particular rationalization.

During these studies of "imagination," however, Rorschach hit upon a number of affinities between performance in the test and clinical symptoms. This was a striking finding, and a finding momentous for the future of personality research, insofar as selectivity in the reactions of the subjects became the basis for those Rorschach categories which in the present test constitute the framework of the personality interpretation.

So we see that these fundamental cornerstones of the method are based on purely empirical findings. No theoretical or speculative assumptions regarding the relationship between, for instance, selectivity for either form or color on the one hand, and a certain personality characteristic on the other, were governing the construction of the test. Since these affinities are, however, no chance finding, but have been demonstrated in innumerable studies, the relationship between the test categories and their assigned personality characteristics can hardly be doubted. Such empirically established correspondences between behavior in a test and underlying personality characteristics are useful from a practical point of view. They are convenient diagnostic tools.

As long as the basis for these affinities is not conceived in terms of an accepted psychological theory, however, the general progress of the work suffers in two respects: first, when we meet a case where the expected correspondence is not demonstrable, we do not know how to account for the exception. The second difficulty is a more fundamental and far-reaching one, requiring close analysis. The Rorschach test is a method which assigns to a subject certain personality characteristics on the basis of the reaction of this subject to perceptive material. But what does the science of psychology have to say about the relation between the perceptive selectivity of a person and his so-called higher mental process? Very little!

And more specifically, how much does psychology know about the relation between a person's emotional life, his reasoning processes, his social adjustment on the one hand, and on the other, his tendency to perceive selectively in two or three dimensions, in chromatic or achromatic colors, in fine articulations in form, or in broader areas, and so on. The answer is that we know still less about this problem than about the more general one.

In search of a common theoretical plane to bring the psychology of personality and of perception together, we may begin with either field. The more we know about one of these fields, the easier it will be to effect an eventual rapprochement. So let us begin considering the psychology of personality as it appears in the Rorschach method. One is thereupon faced with a number of problems that deserve to be mentioned.

The Rorschachist finally arrives at a psychological description of the subject's personality through a complex process of inspection of categories their comparison and evaluation. In rendering this final product of the method psychologically meaningful and theoretically sound, recent research in the field of personality has been of considerable influence. For the formulation of problems of structure and organization of personality, the work of Carl Jung (1926) was of initial significance. Later on, Gestalt concepts, to use the term broadly, provided a conceptual basis upon which the various personality traits as obtained from Rorschach categories, could be organized into coherent configurations. Particularly helpful are such concepts of Lewin (1936) as degree of differentiation, permeability of boundaries, rigidity, harmonious or disharmonious structure, and so on.

When working with the Rorschach method, one is invariably impressed with the close interdependence that exists among the different categories. The psychological implications of this observation are at present finding ample support in the growing tendency in psychology to break down the boundaries between various psychological function. It is a rather common experience among psychologists that whatever the sphere they start out to work in, whether learning or perception or motivation, very soon to find themselves within the domain of one or even two other fields. To illustrate more specifically, one has only to think of the evolution recently undergone by the concept of intelligence. From a specifically demarked, rather static faculty, it has been transformed into a variable function, intimately dependent on the general dynamics of the total organism.

In his posthumous publication, *Zur Auswertung des Formdeutversuchs fuer die Psychoanalyse* Rorschach (1923) successfully employed symbolic interpretations of the content of test material. He borrowed this method from clinical psychoanalysis. Since, however, much of the contemporary laboratory research in motivational psychology has been centering around problems of experimental verification of psychoanalytic concepts, the employment of symbolic interpretations has gained validity beyond purely clinical evidences. At the present stage of the test symbolic interpretations are frequently utilized by Rorschach workers. When used with circumspection and competence, such an approach yields gratifying results in the way of opening up insights into central layers of the personality.

By and large, experimental studies have substantiated the psychological validity of psychoanalytic mechanisms. In so doing, they have indirectly lent theoretical support to those aspects of the Rorschach method which relied on psychoanalytical reasoning. Here should be mentioned particularly the work of H. Murray (1938) inasmuch as his systematic formulations of direct and indirect manifestations of psychological variables offer a useful conceptual framework for the presentation of those desires, strivings, and interests of a subject which are borne out by the Rorschach method.

Most approaches to the study of personality seem to choose one of two avenues. They either see the personality picture in terms of definite content, such as objectives aimed at, specifically determined desires, etc. Or they aim at a presentation of the personality from the point of view of its functional properties, such as rigidity or flexibility of a person's mental make-up, the reality level of his desires, and so forth.

In Rorschach's posthumous publication (1923), mentioned earlier, we have skillful demonstration of the potentialities of his method in throwing light upon both these aspects of personality, by combining content with functional properties in the personality picture of the subject. Here we have a significant contribution that Rorschach made to the advancement of the psychology of personality. Yet it is a contribution which is too rarely acknowledge – and is, indeed, too often overlooked.

In turning now to the field of perception, we find the task of establishing connections less simple or obvious. There are some guideposts, however, which help to point the way. A number of studies yield suggestive ideas or promising leads which warrant closer investigation in the hope of finding answers to our problems.

Let us start with the color category. Regarding the symptomatic value of color responses, Rorschach (1921) states: "the interpretation of the color element in perception as representative of affectivity is at present to be considered still an empirically acquired fact, the formulation of which as yet does not satisfy requirements of scientific logic. What is certain is the correlation among these three phenomena: excitability of affectivity, excitability of mobility and the number of color components in the perception." Rorschach was led to this conclusion by the fact that all clinical groups which are characterized by vivid emotionality gave many color responses on the test, whereas people of either stable or depressive moods gave few or none.

All subsequent research is in harmony with these findings. Most recently, Hertz and Baker (1943) gave a detailed statistical analysis of the various relationships between color scores and clinical data as applied to a group of adolescents. This clinically established relationship would gain greater significance if a subject's characteristic reaction to color could be confirmed by a method outside of the Rorschach test.

Such a confirmation was found by Oeser (1932). Following the technique of Poppinga (1931), Lutz (1929), and Scholl (1927), he acquainted his subjects first with a colored geometrical figure. then he presented them tachistoscopically with eight figures of various forms and colors arranged in a circle, the color and form of the initial figure being now split between two of the eight figures. The place in the circle where the form of the initial figure appeared was called the form pole, and the place with the color of the initial figure was called the color pole. Some subjects would consistently pick out the color pole, and others the form pole. For those who saw both poles, the order of their observation was noted. Subjects who attempted to change their pattern of response at will did not succeed. Oeser therefore concludes that "some subjects are always impelled to select a given object from a number of objects by its form, whereas other subjects are impelled to select on the basis of color."

The subjects who reacted color-dominant in the tachistoscopic experiment showed in the Rorschach test a marked preference for color responses, primarily of the CF and C class. The Rorschach records of form-dominant subjects, on the other hand, contain either no color responses or practically only FC reactions. This is a very important finding since it demonstrates that sensitivity to color, as observed on the Rorschach cards will appear in corresponding degrees under much simplified and more isolated experimental conditions.

Similarly Schmidt (1936) was able to demonstrate color versus form dominance in an ingenious adaptation of the phi phenomenon. At first, a colored form was exposed; then at an equal distance from it to the right and to the left, appeared two figures, one corresponding to the color, the other to the form, of the first. The interval of exposure was adequate for the occurrence of the phi movement. According to the subject's dominance, he would see the first figure move either to the right or to the left. I understand that this study is now being followed up by Heider at Smith College. Should his findings correspond to Oeser's, they would represent really significant implications for our problems.

Recently Ruesch and Fensinger (1941) correlated Rorschach data with a subject's color score, as obtained in a drawing experiment. The results show very consistently that a subject who gives many color responses to the Rorschach cards, in drawing will choose a variety of colors and will spread them liberally over the surface;

whereas the Rorschach record with few or no color responses corresponds to a drawing in which not more than one color is used, and that usually merely to mark an outline and not a surface.

In different ways these studies convincingly point to the conclusion that selectivity for form and color in perception and expression is a consistent characteristic of an individual.

Further information comes from the field of child psychology. Stimulated by Kuelpe's work on form versus color abstraction, Descoeudres (1914), Eljasch (1928), Tobie (1927), Volkelt (1926), Engel (1935), Brian and Goodenough (1929) investigated the problem by means of the matching experiment. This usually consisted of presenting the child with two objects differing from a third one in either form or color. The third object was to be placed with the one "just like it." Again in accordance with Rorschach data, all these workers agree that in younger children color abstraction becomes more prominent.

Finally there are indications that of the animals which do have chromatic color vision, the majority can be conditioned more readily in color than in form discrimination. For example, Kroh and Scholl (1926) trained chickens to pick food from a blue triangle, but not from a red circle. When the colors were interchanged, the birds would immediately eat from the circle and not from the triangle. Apes, however, seem to be form abstracters.

Our perception thus does not depend on chance. It rather presents a definite pattern which is consistent with and fundamental for the individual. Color dominance in particular appears to be characteristic of early levels of development, and also of the emotionally excitable adult personality type.

How can this relationship be understood psychologically? We know from the psychology of perception that the perceiving of a separate form is the product of a Gestalt process, consuming energy. Without the activization of these organizational forces, no form perception is possible. With respect to perception of color, however, the situation is different: apart from the fact that color differences within the visual field will demarcate different areas, and thus bring into play the factor of form with its organizational properties, the color perception as such is not correlated to complex processes or articulation and organization. Color experience, when it occurs, is thus a much more immediate and direct sense datum than the experience of form. Form perception is usually accompanied by a rather detached, objective attitude in the subject. Whereas the experience of color, being more immediate, is likely to contain personal, affectively toned notes.

One is reminded of H. Werner's (1940) concept of physiognomic character of certain perceptive data, in which the ego-environment relation is not a purely cognitive one, but rather, as Wertheimer (1925) has emphasized, a conative one. The impression arising from an outside object is not clearly objectified. It contains elements of emotional and striving nature.

It has been frequently observed concerning synesthesia, that it is the emotional tone which constitutes the link between the two sensory fields. Colorblind people are said to recognize colors by their emotional atmosphere. A person born blind, when he became able to see at the age of 18, described his experience of colors in terms of different emotions, such as red being excitement, or purple corresponding to the anxious clammy feeling that one has before a thunderstorm.

The Japanese psychologist, Tatibana (1936), speaks of inherent or intrinsic feeling value of colors. He intends this value to be understood as existing outside of any meaningful associations or spatio-temporal relations. He characterizes this feeling value of colors as directly connected with the color sensation and calls it sensory feeling. Thus he speaks of exciting versus depressing, warm versus cold, light versus heavy colors. Von Allesch (1925), in his study of the aesthetic appearance of colors, frequently found that subjects, instead of giving the called-for description of the presented colors, would respond emotionally. They would use such affectively toned expressions as: aggressive, robust, shrieking, supercilious, powerful, magnificent, crude, gentle.

The vital and significant meaning that colors have in the life of primitive man can be seen from the roles assigned to them in some cultures. For the Zuni, for example, each direction of the compass corresponds to a specific color. Yellow belongs to the South, red to the East, white to the North, and black to the West (1896). A similar color system existed in ancient Mexico. In Japan, purple, blue and green were reserved for the nobility and so used to be considered forbidden colors. India, Tibet, and China have a similar differentiation between colors that are "proper" to wear and those that are tabu (1936). With all this evidence, it thus seems indisputable that the experience of color is linked to a person's inner life in a fundamental way.

It is inherent in the very nature of a test and its implications to arouse personal reactions in the subject. The person unavoidably feels examined, put on the spot as it were. There is thus a certain lability or readiness for emotional, personally toned expressions to be expected in every test situation. If, in addition, the test material happens to confront the subject with blobs of color, it becomes very understandable in view of the above discussion regarding color perception and personality, that people of different temperamental make-up will reveal these differences in their reactions to the colored parts of the Rorschach cards.

A subject of vivid and responsive emotionality will react spontaneously and freely, which leads to a high color score. The emotionally inhibited person will be embarrassed or even shocked by this intrusion of the outside world into his inner regions. Consequently, he will display confusion and attempts at withdrawal, or, in Rorschach terms, the color shock. Finally, the rigid, emotionally restricted type, in his detached and impersonal attitude, will remain unaffected by such elements in perception which do not lend themselves to clear-cut articulation. As a result, his interpretations in the test are not likely to be stimulated by the color on the cards.

The close relationship between the experience of colors and the emotional life of people has of course been recognized by artists for a long time. In the case of the French poet, Bauderlaire (1921), this connection was so intimate that he frequently described emotions in terms of colors, and denoted colors by their emotional content. Goethe, in his *Farbenlehre* (1867), portrays vividly the interplay between the perception of color and the inner mood and feelings of the perceiving individual. He designates yellow as the color of dignity and of joy, and describes it as gently stimulating and comforting. Orange impresses him as piercing and overwhelming. Blue flees from us, but in doing so draws us with it. Purple is disquieting. A deep red is solemn, and a light red signifies grace and loveliness, according to Goethe.

Rorschach himself put considerable weight upon the diagnostic value of the subject's preference for the warm colors (red-yellow) or the cold (blue-green) respectively. Preference for cold colors occurs primarily in people who consciously control their emotions, according to Rorschach. Subsequently research seems to confirm this diagnostic differentiation.

Ruesch and Fensinger (1941) recently demonstrated statistically that the person who gives many color responses favors red proportionately much more than the person whose record contains but few color interpretations. Color dominance thus seems to find its particularly pronounced form in preference for red. One is reminded of the observation of child psychologists that children up to the age of 6 show a marked preference for red over the other primaries. With grade school children, red moves to second place, and with adults to third.

The psychological meaning of this phenomenon gains in significance in the light of some considerations that grew out of experiments in the field of perception. Koffka and Harrower (1931) for instance, on the basis of their research in color vision, have ascribed to red and yellow a somewhat different psychological nature as contrasted to blue and green. In following up the Lieman investigation (1927) of the effect of relative luminosity upon figure-ground relations, they found that colors of short wave lengths mix better with an equiluminous gray background, than the colors of the longer wave lengths. In other words, red and yellow segregate and articulate the surface better than blue and green. Consequently, red and yellow are called hard, and blue and green soft. And, what is of particular significance for us, the hard colors are the ones which primarily tend to have physiognomic character.

Similarly, Goldstein (1939; 1942) was led by his work on brain injury cases to postulate psychological roles for the red and yellow somewhat different from blue and green. Intensive investigations brought Goldstein to conclusions, which lead beyond the filed of psychopathology and appear of significance for our problem. According to him, "a specific color stimulation is, as a rule, accompanied by a specific response pattern of the entire organism." Thus he finds that green facilitates the performance pattern of the organism and makes the performance more adequate, whereas red is favorable for emotionally determined actions and impairs the performance. The speed of voluntary movement is higher in red and yellow light than in blue and green. Judgment of weights, and of spatial and temporal distances is superior under the influence of red illumination compared with green.

On the basis of these, together with a number of other findings and systematic considerations which cannot be discussed here, Goldstein (1939) comes to the conclusion that in general green evokes manifestations that "emphasize the self in contrast to the world and with that render possible the emancipative distance between ego and world." The experience of red, on the other hand, "corresponds to a form of surrendering to the world, to a more passive mode of being 'in' the world, a state of the ego submerged in the world."

Finally Jaensch (1937), quite independently, again reached the same dichotomy of red yellow versus blue green. He finds that all people can be grouped in a way similar to red-green color blind subjects, namely into those more sensitive to the warm end of the spectrum and those more sensitive to the cold end. The warm color dominant subjects are characterized by an intimate relation to the visually perceptible world. They are receptive and open to outside influences. They seem to submerge themselves rather readily in their social environment. Their emotional life is characterized by warm feelings, suggestibility, and strong affects. All mental functions are rapid and highly integrated with each other. In the subject-object relationship, the emphasis is on the object.

The cold color dominant subjects in the Jaensch experiments have a detached "split-off" attitude to the outside world. They find it difficult to adapt themselves to new circumstances and to express themselves freely. Emotionally they are cold and reserved. In the subject-object relationship, the emphasis is on the subject. In short, the warm color dominant subject is Jaensch's outwardly integrated type, the cold color dominant his inwardly integrated type.

Striking correspondences are thus shown in the conclusions resulting from such very different experimental studies concerning the psychological nature of thee warm versus the cold colors. Furthermore, every Rorschachist will recognize in the warm color dominant person, the subject who would give many color responses to the Rorschach cards, and in the green dominant type the color avoiding subject. This correspondence is gratifying, indeed, since it offers the kind of experimental confirmation that we need to integrate the Rorschach method systematically into psychological theory.

Before we proceed to draw our final conclusions regarding the role of color perception in the study of personality, we might stop for a moment and consider a special aspect of the problem that is apt to lead to misinterpretations. In characterizing the perception of color as one that involves immediate reactions of a personal, emotionally toned nature, we have to keep in mind that this is not the only possible response to color. Under certain conditions a subject may take a detached consciously evaluative attitude toward the perceived color. In the Rorschach procedure, this phenomenon has rightly been separated under the category of intellectualized color interpretations.

In an attempt to clarify this problem, Jane Williams Coyne (1942) presented her subjects with rectangular pieces of colored paper on white background. The size of the papers was 1-3/4 x 2-1/2 inches. The colors were matched as closely as possible to the Rorschach colors. The subjects were presented with a list of 15 to 20 sets of adjectives, each set containing three adjectives. They were requested to choose the one adjective in a set which most nearly described their evaluation of the particular color. Each set of adjectives was so constructed that the first word represented a positive emotion, the second was neutral, and the third negative. Thus one set would consist of these three adjectives: stimulating—active—aggressive. The proportion of emotional choices (either positive or negative) was then compared to the subject's color score on the Rorschach test.

The result of this experiment was that subjects with high color scores did *not* choose emotionally toned adjectives significantly more than the subjects with low color scores. Here then we have a situation which calls for an impersonal, consciously evaluative attitude towards the colors. It is not experienced as a test, or as a means of finding something out about the subject. The experimental situation has put the emphasis on the object, i.e., the colors per se. Accordingly no personal reaction or emotional involvement is aroused in the observer. This experiment thus cautions us to remember that a detached consciously evaluative attitude toward color is possible and will occur even in subjects who are color sensitive on the Rorschach test—provided that the conditions call for such an attitude.

After this digression, let us now return to our more general considerations of the color problem, and sum up the discussion of the role of color perception in the filed of personality research. We might say in general, that in some people, particularly in children and in emotionally responsive adults, the separation between the ego and the outside world is less pronounced than in others. This weakness of the outside boundary, as Lewin would say, allows for a rather free interplay of forces between the reacting person and his immediate environment. Such interplay naturally will enhance physiognomic characters in environmental objects which lend themselves readily to it. Colors, particularly the warm (or hard) colors, seem especially provocative in this respect, and thus serve as a good screening device for the degree of permeability of a person's outside boundary.

Here we might just add that for some people of a certain emotional make-up, the haziness or darkness or the Rorschach cards may acquire physiognomic character. When this occurs it usually has something threatening or disquieting about it. One wonders whether Metzger's (1930) work on the total homogeneous field, in spite of some important differences in the setting, does not offer clues for the understanding of the chiaroscuro response. The physiognomic characteristics of the general fogginess of the total field that seems to move toward the subject and oppress him, are certainly very similar to the emotional characteristics of a chiaroscuro interpretation.

Time does not permit us to elaborate on the chiaroscuro or on the other Rorschach categories in more detail. In a quick survey we will thus merely attempt a few suggestions regarding the remaining components of the method. Of necessity these suggestions will have to be considered of an even more tentative nature than our discussion of the color problem. They are not to be interpreted as definitely established relationships, but rather as indications of directions along which it might be profitable to search for an understanding of the theoretical significance of these empirical tools of personality diagnosing.

One more contribution from this domain of psychopathology deserves to be mentioned. Alice Angyal's (1942) tachistoscopic study on "Speed and Pattern of Perception" provides additional proof for our thesis regarding the consistency of an individual's perceptual pattern. More specifically, inasmuch as the perceptual pattern, observed by Angyal, deals with the sequence of performance, it offers gratifying support to the psychological significance of the Rorschach category of succession of responses. Angyal's two poles of reaction to the experiment situation, a rigid adherence to the factual vs. a free and subjective way of dealing with the material, are well in harmony with Levine and Grassi's (1942) differentiation of the blot vs. concept dominant attitude on their graphic Rorschach. This polarity is of course paralleled by the contrast between the coarted and the dilated type in the Rorschach method.

With respect to the various configurations presented by the inkblots, F. L. Wells (1935) has expressed some stimulating ideas regarding the relation between the contrast of the response and the relative organization of the parts of the blot into that particular response. Klopfer has repeatedly stressed the need for a careful analysis of the factors of relative segregation and articulation, that prevail among the parts of the cards (Klopfer & Kelley, 1942). Recently Brosin and Fromm (1942) have pointed out more specifically the Gestalt factors that might be of relevance for this problem. The first step in the direction of actual research in the field was made by Beck (1933). In his "Configurational Tendencies in Rorschach Responses," he has analyzed the problem of organization within the various parts primarily from a statistical point of view.

The movement responses are particularly intriguing theoretically. For the meaning of this category, a theory has been suggested by Binswanger (1923), based upon anthropological observations and formulated in terms of psychoanalytic speculations. F. L. Wells' (1935) suggestion of the similarity between the movement response in the Rorschach method, and the predicate or egocentric category on Jung's association test deserves experimental investigation. The field of perception also offers some suggestions regarding the movement response—such as some of the work on apparent movement, and McDougall's (1929) hint of the correlation between speed of fluctuation in reversible figures and amount of introversion.

In conclusion we might say: The Rorschach method presents an empirical demonstration of a fundamental relationship between the perceptual pattern of a person and his personality makeup. We have tried to point out a few factual confirmations of this relationship from experimental research in perception. Our purpose is to suggest an approach which might lead to the eventual incorporation of the Rorschach method into the general body of psychological theories and principles.

Such an amalgamation seems to us

of importance in two respects. First, it would in a way rehabilitate the field of perception. This field of psychological research has been losing prestige, in part at least because it deals always with universal laws, applicable to minds in general, and thus has no relation to vital problems of understanding and predicting individual behavior. Evidence of the basic role of perception for personality diagnosis, as it is contained in the Rorschach method, however, may thus lend new impetus and life to research in the field of perception.

Secondly, the Rorschach method has an important contribution to make to the science of personality. Contemporary research in this sphere has been proceeding primarily along the lines of the study of large patterns of behavior, such as traits and attitudes. The basis for such investigations usually have been questionnaires and rating scales. In spite of the conveniences or working with these tools, the prediction may be ventured that they have passed the peak of their popularity. The subjective nature of data obtained by such techniques does and always will lay them open to serious criticism from the strict scientist.

In the Rorschach method, however, the situation is quite a different one. Here we have reactions that are not learned—in fact, the subject is not even conscious of the individual pattern of these responses. Material of this kind offers a far more fundamental and conclusive basis for establishing an individual's personality constellation than do subjective evaluations.

In such a pattern of selective perception of an individual we have a form of miscrostructure of his personality. This miscrostructure may be of basis character, and when properly interpreted should contribute a most important clue to a valid representation of the personality. By providing a theoretical basis for this function of the Rorschach method in the field of personality research, one would not only put the Rorschach test itself on a sound basis, but one would at the same time make a real contribution to the science of personality in general.

The Impact of Projective Techniques on Basic Psychological Science

SAMUEL B. KUTASH[1]

The history of science is marked by dynamic revolutions in method which ushered in new eras of progress and discovery. Many of these changes in method resulted from the invention of new instruments and technical tools. On the long list of such inventions which revolutionized so-called scientific methods and made possible new progress are the microscope, the telescope, differential calculus, the spectrometer and devices for splitting the atom. Scientific method is thus an ever-changing dynamic process by which more is learned about the universe and everything in it. Scientific history also shows that there is more than one way in which a theory can be formulated or a discovery made. The method that enabled Darwin to conceive natural selection and its relation to the origin of species was certainly not the same as that which gave the world the current conception of the atom as a sort of submicroscopic solar system. Certainly the sciences of geology, astronomy, paleontology, anthropology, and embryology, for example, are no less scientific because their methods rely more on careful observation with refined instruments, of the earth's crust, the heavens, fossils, men and unborn embryos, than they do on controlled experimentation as in physics and chemistry. Much of science consists in seeing relationships to which most men are blind, and a good deal is based on exact measurement.

A great scientist, Dr. Percy W. Bridgman, Nobel prize winner and Harvard physicist, denies there is any "scientific method" and stoutly maintains that progress in science is just the result of doing "one's damndest with one's mind, no holds barred." Similarly, Dr. Conant asks, "Is there such a thing as a scientific method of wide applicability in the solution of social problems?" (Conant, 1951, p. 7). Professor Einstein also has said that the greatest advances in science are made by those who ask the right questions or study the important problems, not by those who deify method as an end in itself. Turning to the field of psychological science, we quote J. McV. Hunt who said in his 1952 APA Presidential address that "Science has also been characterized as a method, but the variety of things scientists do stretches the connotation of the word *method* almost beyond recognition" (Hunt, 1952, p. 609). He goes on to agree with Conant and John Dewey (1938) that "Science is probably best conceived dynamically as a kind of enterprise or as a complex, highly generalized form of inquiring behavior." (Hunt, 1952, p. 609).

Yet for a long time self-appointed guardians of psychology, as a science, and of so-called "scientific method" in psychology, have placed projective techniques and the approach to the study of personality represented by them outside the pale of scientific method. When projective techniques appeared upon the scene and particularly when they burgeoned during the after World War II they were constantly scrutinized and re-evaluated in the light of psychological science and so-called scientific method, to see whether they fitted in or could be adapted to the older concepts of scientific approach. Statistical techniques which were appropriate in other contexts began to be applied at first uncritically to determine the validity and reliability of the Rorschach and

[1] Presidential Address, Society for Projective Techniques, Saturday, September 4, 1954, Hotel New Yorker, New York City.

other projectives. When these techniques raised problems that could not be investigated by existing notions of scientific method, the problems and the techniques themselves were often placed outside the scope of science and relegated to the realms of art and intuition. Those who deified and still worship method in psychology as applied to projectives paralleled similar situations in the history of science such as the opposition to the discoveries of Galileo, Louis Pasteur and of all scientific pioneers who over-threw existing methods in order to make it possible to investigate new and urgent problems.

In the field of psychology the mind and personality of man and the understanding of human behavior were inaccessible to thorough scientific investigation by laboratory and research methods reified as scientific method until the entrance upon the scene of new holistic approaches to personality such as Gestalt psychology, psychoanalysis, transactional psychology, field theory, and their practical applications in projective techniques. As Hertz pointed out, the Rorschach Method "was born of revolt in the world of psychological thought" which challenged the "atomistic conception of personality" and raised problems of "how to study a synthesis rather than a conglomeration of isolated parts" (Hertz, 1942, p. 529-530). The progress of basic psychological science was arrested and deadlocked by the fact that leaders in the science were saying that the major problems of mind, personality, and complex behavior could not be investigated scientifically because research and experiments could only be designed in a certain way and that any other way was unscientific. The structuralism of Wundt and Titchener failed to "yield solutions to practical problems in spite of all its logical rigor" as recently pointed out by Hunt (1952, p. 132). Projective techniques broke the deadlock by toppling the older so-called scientific method from its pedestal and forcing not only a thorough retooling in psychology but a complete revolution which is now in progress in the research methods of psychological science. At last, we are learning what automobile manufacturers learned a long time ago—that if you want to produce a new and better car each couple of years you have to discard old machines and tools and re-tool the entire plant if necessary—that if you insist on keeping the same methods and tools a deadlock in progress is eventually reached.

Projective techniques have thus turned the tables and made an impact on basic psychological science which may prove to be of the greatest significance for the development of psychology. It is time to evaluate this impact as well as the contributions that projective techniques have made to research methodology in psychology and to the advancement of psychology as a science. Will we be able to say that projective techniques did more for psychological science than psychological science did for projective techniques just as Conant pointed out that "before 1850 the steam engine did more for science than science did for the steam engine" (Bach, 1952, p. 132). The time is fast arriving perhaps when the so-called cult of Rorschach or of projectives has become part of the mainstream of scientific psychology and the objective, two-variable, control group, normative, parametric statistical approach will become the cult of pseudo-objectivity.

Let me raise a problem for your consideration. A few months ago I read over 150 abstracts of research papers submitted for this year's annual program of Division 12 of the APA. I was struck by a rather curious circumstance. Concerning one topic or hypothesis relating to the validity of certain Rorschach assumptions, about a dozen abstracts for papers were submitted. As far as I could determine in ten of the papers the samplings were similarly arrived at and the designs left nothing to be desired. There were experimental and control groups which were equated for such variables as sex, age, intelligence, and educational level, and the papers seemed like good examples of current university sponsored research. Yet the results of some of the studies contradicted almost diametrically the results of the others. There were indeed four different, mutually contradictory conclusions all arrived at "scientifically." Is it possible that the methods which were adhered to in order to stick to the cult of pseudo-objectivity destroyed the Gestalts which were being investigated, and confused rather than elucidated the basic issues? Can it be that prevailing methods that were applicable to other contexts such as in the validation of non-projective tests, fail to recognize the fact that personality consists of a host of complex, interacting variables organized into a Gestalt and that the method of controlled experimentation destroys this Gestalt which is itself part of a larger Gestalt? Is there implicit in the atomistic experimenter's mind the *prejudice* or the subjective, unverified assumption that such variables as intelligence, perception, emotion, introversion, etc., are independent traits that can be isolated and still retain their properties unchanged, rather than that their properties are at least in part taken on by reason of their position in the organized Gestalt or context? Do these psychologists fail to realize that this is like insisting that when you isolate hydrogen from the Gestalt of the compound water, it still has the same properties as it had when it was in combination with oxygen to form water? Are they making the same sort of error that Newtonian physics made when it attempted without modification to apply to the universe, the general laws and approach developed in studying smaller Gestalts—an error which was corrected later by the theory of relativity when Einstein found contradictions which could not be explained or understood by existing, less dynamic scientific approaches? Or is it merely as the adherents to outmoded methods insist that the errors are in samplings and/or the choice of variables to control? Munroe (1945) answered these questions in 1945 when she stated that the Rorschach was the "first really extensive effort to apply 'objectively' in diagnosis and in research those holistic principles to which psychology at large pays at least lip-service today."

May I turn to another paradox! Even though many of the adherents of the atomistic approach to personality insist that projective psychology is unscientific, the perusal of any issue of a current personality research journal or of the abstracts for scientific programs in clinical psychology will verify that the great majority of current studies investigating problems of human personality utilize projective techniques as the major tools. Furthermore, studies utilizing other techniques such as interviews, non-projective tests, questionnaires, and rating scales, are often evaluated in terms of the hypotheses and inferences underlying projective techniques. It is thus incumbent upon us to recognize and detail the influence upon and contribution to psychological science of projective techniques and to arrive at a picture of their impact. In doing this we will be responding to the fond hope expressed by Rickers-Ovsiankina (1943) and her 1943 presidential address when she stated, "Every scientist, while working on the discovery of specific empirical facts, does so with the ultimate hope in mind, that his findings, however small or even unimportant they might appear at the time, eventually will be incorporated into the larger body of that particular science."

In general, projective techniques have influenced psychological science in the following ways:

1) They have made accessible to scientific investigation a host of crucial practical problems not previously susceptible of such study.
2) They have forced modifications in scientific method in psychology bringing it into line with similar methodological advances in the other sciences.

3) They have revolutionized experimental designs in personality research and developed new guidelines for such designs.
4) They have exploded notions previously thought to be scientifically established and elucidated, enriched, or reopened old problems.
5) They have stimulated changes in statistical method and made necessary the introduction of new statistical techniques more appropriate to the important problems for which psychology is seeking solutions.
6) They have added significant data and knowledge to our science.
7) Most important of all, they have made possible the dynamic practical application of holistic theoretical systems and the further development and refinement of psychology theory.

Let us proceed to discuss and illustrate these broad contributions beginning with some of the newer crucial problems not previously susceptible to scientific study. In the day of the personality inventory it was naively assumed that responses to a questionnaire were independent of motivation, unconscious influences, and total personality functioning. Questionnaires and inventories were, of course, easier to handle by the then existing methods of quantification. They had Yes and No answers or multiple choice responses which lent themselves to additive summation of scores and the arrival at a final numerical score which told us little about the complexities of any one person or of personality as an object of scientific study. Norms were arrived at and predictions were based upon norms or comparison with one's fellows rather than individual behavior studied longitudinally. Numerous attempts to establish the validity of these inventories failed. Essentially they permitted only the revelation of small atoms or facets of the personality torn out of their Gestalt and made to appear like independent variables. One could learn whether a person was probably dominant or probably submissive and the degree of probability that he might be one or the other. If we wanted to find out whether he was also emotionally labile and to what extent, either a new inventory or a re-standardization of the old one was needed, preferably the former. Theoretically, any personality trait or even disorder such as neurotic tendency, elation, depression, extroversion, capacity for insight, would need a new scale or test. To get a picture of the total personality was impossible unless the experimenter naively added together the various facets into a hybrid whole that was artificially produced.

This procedure was most unproductive but preserved all of the scientific trappings of susceptibility to quantification, statistically manageable scores, "objective" responses that did not involve the subjective judgement of the examiner, and machine precision scoring. Yet it could not shed light on the crucial problems of how the total personality functions or the dynamics of personality. The hypotheses that its functioning depends to some extent on unconscious motivations, on the field it is operating in, and on past experience, could not be investigated by these instruments. The projective techniques made possible the study of the total personality or aspects of the personality in their framework of the whole and thus opened up the possibilities of predicting human behavior in terms of how people actually function. It is true that certain scores like M on the Rorschach may mean one thing when it is embedded in a certain Gestalt and something else in another Gestalt. But this is in line with similar problems in other sciences. Thus, in atomic analysis, individual atoms may function differently in different fields or even in the same field. Now that the techniques are available for studying the total personality in action, new methods are being developed to handle the question of statistical validity, reliability and the like as we shall see.

Prior to the advent of projective techniques much clinical research by means of tests involved precise quantitative measurements of intelligence and achievement. Correlations were calculated between IQ and achievement quotients and predictions of school achievement were predicted on the assumption that the more intelligent a person was the better he could function in school. Gradually it became evident that many highly intelligent, in fact, superior individuals often failed to achieve in school and these failures were attributed to so-called non-intellective factors, such as persistence, will power, motivation, and the like. Clinicians when confronted with cases of intelligent children who failed to learn began to be less and less concerned with the IQ and the normative approach and more and more with the incidental qualitative aspects of the subject's functioning on tests. Goodenough (1929) developed the concept of scatter as a manifestation of emotional instability. It began to sink in that two children even of the same chronological age with identical IQ's were totally different in their school adjustment depending upon what went into the IQ, how the intelligence was organized and how it functioned as part of the total personality. Similarly, all objective tests which purported to measure by a number any supposedly independent or even dependent isolated variable eventually proved unable to predict for the individual because of the failure to take into account the total personality. Subjective evaluation of the qualitative aspects of a given individual's performance on a test had to be made in an inefficient, makeshift, haphazard way. The clinician had to "sneak it in," if you please, and his most significant observations were often these smuggled in intuitive statements about the subject. Projective techniques made it possible to investigate systematically and on a large scale the dynamic interrelationships between aspects of the personality such as intelligence, emotion, mood, and all the rest and brought these studies within the realm of scientific investigation and evaluation. A new objective methodology based upon holistic principles was thus provided.

With this new holistic approach, tools and tests which were formerly denuded of their inherent possibilities by being boiled down to a number and being made part of a summative score on an intelligence test, such as Binet's original inkblot test, and free association test on the Binet, the copying of square and diamond, sentence completions, completion of a figure drawing, and a host of other subjects took on enriched meanings as in Rorschach, Word Association Test, Bender-Gestalt, Projective Sentence Completion Tests, and the Human Figure Drawing Test. They became instruments for investigating scientifically the rich hidden aspects of personality previously not accessible.

The greatest contribution of projective techniques is perhaps in terms of making possible psychological studies by means of tests, of the nature of various types of psychopathology such as the psychoses, neuroses, psychosomatic illnesses, alcoholism, and other personality maladjustments. By far the largest number and most fruitful studies of these phenomena have been made, utilizing the Rorschach and other projectives. This is true in spite of the fact that many of these studies are open to criticism on methodological grounds. As we shall see, the modifications in methods are being slowly but surely made which will make such studies more scientifically valid in the future. Of special importance is the fact alluded to by Miller that projective psychodiagnostics has been largely responsible for the "revolt against the nosological categories of Kraepelin and Bleuler" (1950, p. 3).

Along with their suitability for studies of personality disturbance and the accumulation of dynamic data concerning psychopathology, projectives have made it possible to attempt to develop tested prognostic criteria drawn from their findings which could later be used to select patients who might respond best to a particular type of therapy or procedure for personality change. Much research is under way to evaluate with projective tests the personality changes which take place during the course of periods of psychotherapy and to study the possibilities of predicting the course of psychopathology. Thus Bradway (1946) developed a group of Rorschach factors which seemed related to the treatability of promiscuous girls and Siegel (1948) found certain Rorschach signs that aid in forecasting children's response to treatment. Studies by W. G. Klopfer (1945) of group therapy and Muench (1947) of non-directive therapy illustrate the use of projective techniques to evaluate therapeutic results but these are merely the beginnings of much needed research in this area even though the progress to date has justified a chapter by Muench in a recent book (1950). Problems such as these are, however, being made accessible to scientific study now that the tools are at hand. As data accumulates, it may be possible by integrating this knowledge with data accumulated by other methods of experimental depth psychology and psychoanalytic procedure, to contribute to integrated theories of psychopathology which will be subject of further scientific study.

Prophetically, Hermann Rorschach (1942, p. 13) described his technique as "a psychological experiment which, despite its simplicity, has proved to be of value in research . . ." Munroe (1945) commented on the increasing use of the Rorschach, not for individual clinical diagnoses, but as an instrument for the investigation of more general problems. She gave as examples Hertz's (1942, a,b,c) studies of personality development in adolescence, Oberholzer's (1944) contribution to the study of the People of Alor (1945), Ross' objective analysis of the psychological components in migraine and neurocirculatory asthenia (Ross & McNaughton, 1945), Hertzman's study of personality shifts and types of reaction in a stress situation (Hertzman et al. 1944; Hertzman & Seitz, 1942) and Piotrowski's (1941) study of prognosis in the shock treatment of schizophrenia. Today, a host of scientific holistically oriented studies made possible by the existence of projective techniques can be cited which have added materially to existing psychological knowledge. Indeed new untapped areas of research such as the analysis of creativity and the study of the general development of personality by time sequence analysis were suggested by Burchard (1952) and Bell (1953) in their presidential addresses. We can only single out a few of the more recent research applications of projectives in some selected areas of psychological science.

For example, a number of problems in the field of action research such as in the study of group tension, morale, conflict, and prejudice have been opened up for more dynamic investigation by the use of projective techniques (Proshansky, 1950) just as anthropological investigations were enriched by Hallowell (1942). Fromme (1941) used projective cartoons and ambiguous TAT type pictures to study opinions on preventing war. Frenkel-Brunswik and Sanford (1945) used thematic pictures for analyzing the personality factors in Anti-Semitic college women and Hartley (1946) attempted to determine the relationship between basic personality traits and tolerance among college students. Sanford and Rosenstock (1952) utilized cartoon-like projective devices in doorstep interviews and concluded that they "can serve a demonstrably useful purpose in personality study." They showed that for the testing of specific hypotheses about personality a researcher may "tailor a projective device to his own specific research needs" and that "such a test has a fair chance of overcoming the commonly encountered difficulty of getting 'right' or 'nice' answers rather than psychologically valid answers to attitudinal items." The uncovering of unconscious motivations in prejudice and political attitudes is a new promising area for the research application of projective techniques. It is not inconceivable that this method could supplant eventually the present public opinion poll techniques. The applications to advertising and motivation research offer unlimited possibilities.

Another area recently illuminated by projective studies is the study of personality factors in physical disease and the interrelationships between emotions and physiological manifestations in psychosomatic illness. Poser (1951), for example, has studied duodenal ulcer patients and Bell, Trosman and Ross (1952) have summarized the use of projective techniques in the investigation of emotional aspects of general medical disorders. They review 63 recent studies with the Rorschach alone: Numerous other studies of amputees, asthma, cardiac conditions, tuberculosis, arthritis, multiple sclerosis, cancer and other general medical problems can be cited.

For many years the field of mental deficiency had been under the sway of the intelligence testing movement to which it had helped to give birth. The emphasis on classification and the artificial distinction between intelligence and personality as if they existed as independent entities brought the early rapid progress in that field to a standstill. Projective techniques and their dynamic qualities have instilled new life into the study of mental retardation to the point where a full chapter is devoted to them in Sarason's excellent book (1949, p. 222). As Sarason states, "The confusion that results from the implicit assumption that these words refer to different things can be seen in the tendency to put one kind of psychological procedure under 'intelligence' testing and another 'personality' testing-as if one procedure is measuring one kind or variety of phenomena not tapped by the other. Although it may be argued that the use of these words has a practical value, the semantic problem is a reflection of an inadequate atomistic theory of behavior which is bound by the compartments which it has prematurely set up . . . . Recognition of the inadequacy of utilizing intelligence test scores for explaining individual variations in behavior can be seen in the increasing attention given projective techniques . . ." Studies with Rorschach, (Werner, 1945, Sloan, 1948, Jolles, 1947), and the TAT, (Kutash, 1943, Sarason, 1943, and Abel, 1945) have revealed the individual personality differences among the mentally defective and given new insights into the nature of mental deficiency. Sarason's conclusions bear repetition when he says that "the defective individual, like the normal one, has fears, anxieties, wishes, and needs which may affect his intellectual functioning in varying degrees . . . whereas Binet gave the defective individual an 'intelligence,' projective techniques have given him a 'personality' (Sarason, 1941, p. 261).

To exemplify further the contribution of projectives in opening up new areas for scientific investigation it may not be amiss to mention Roe's recent studies of the personalities of physical scientists (Roe, 1950) and biologists (Roe, 1949) with the Rorschach test and the interesting finding that biologists are more concerned with form while physicists emphasize three-dimensional space and inanimate movement. She went on to study the personalities of psychologists and anthropologists (Roe, 1955). I leave it to you to ferret out for yourselves what she found. The study of occupational and professional groups by use of projectives promises to revitalize and reorient the fields of vocational guidance and occupational selection.

What are some of the methodological changes stimulated by projective techniques? In the heyday of atomistic experimental psychology, scientific method in physics consisted of experiments in which ideally all variables but one were held constant, the experimental variable was varied systematically, and the observation of the results was recorded in quantitative terms.

From this data generalizations were drawn which made contributions to scientific knowledge. This approach which served well the purposes for which it was devised and answered the problems it was designed to answer was taken over bodily with only slight makeshift adaptation to study problems in psychology. Thus, the problem of human perception for many years was investigated by such controlled experiments and only those aspects of perception could be investigated which lent themselves to this basic "scientific method." According to Gardner Murphy (1954, p. xvii) "a hundred years of research in physiological optics, visual perception, acoustics, tactual and kinesthetic sensitivity, had laid a sound foundation for the understanding of the main tools by which man makes contact with his environment. Emphasis was placed necessarily either upon the physical properties of the environment or the universal laws of perceptual response. Perception was to be understood as a response of living organisms to their environments by way of focused or integrative recognition of what the environment offers." This, however, necessarily limited the scientific understanding of perception and threw little light on the true nature of perceptual distortion and individual differences in perceiving total situations or complex combinations of stimuli. It did not elucidate the problem of what conditions the individual's focusing on specific aspects of the phenomenological world to the temporary exclusion of other aspects. In other words, this "objective method" divorced perception from the total personality of the perceiver and could only be used to study perception of isolated segments of the environment under laboratory or controlled conditions. It could not predict how an individual perceives the world as it occurs in nature.

With the advent of more sensitive instruments, such as projective tests, it became possible to evaluate the interconnection between perception and the total personality of the perceiver which is the way it functions in real life situations. It became possible to design a study such as described in the recent book, *Personality through Perception* by Witkin, Lewis, Hertzman et al (1954). This project studied the basis of space orientation in human beings, supplementing the laboratory and experimental approach by utilizing the Rorschach and Thematic Apperception tests, the interview, the figure drawing test, and the miniature toy play situation. The study showed, by and large, that "particular modes of perceiving are consistently related to particular ways of adjusting." Yet even here the authors were forced to admit that they were "limited to this form of stating their conclusions about how perception is related to adjustment by the fact that the study had a correlational design." This design did not make it possible for them "to obtain direct evidence concerning the manner in which model of perceiving and techniques of adjustment actually develop in relation to each other, in the course of psychological growth. Nor has it enabled these investigators to establish the specific adaptational value of a particular model of perceiving in the total personality economy of each individual. For the first kind of problem a longitudinal study is required and for the second, a study concerned with the individual rather than with group trends. These latter two areas of investigation are now being pursued" (Sarason, 1943, p. 491).

While the Witkin study started in observations of perceptual processes and sought determinants of particular features of these processes in overall psychological structure, others under way, notably those of Klein (1951) and Frenkel-Brunswik (1949), have started with well-worked-out conceptions of personality, and have been concerned with the way in which needs, feelings, and coping procedures are expressed in perception. The new methods stimulated by the projective hypotheses, after all the Rorschach can be viewed as a test of visual perception, have made a beginning to provide, at last, a fuller picture of the true nature of perceiving, and given an improved understanding of man's essential psychological organization. These new insights are establishing scientifically that perception and personality are not separate processes of equal status in the organism but rather that personality subsumes perceiving as well as thinking, learning and so forth—precisely part of the hypothesis on which the Rorschach is based. At last it seems clear that the explanation of the organized character of perceptual experiences lies neither in the structure of the field alone nor in personal characteristics of the perceiver along, but in both. A new scientific method is being devised to study and do justice to perception as part of the Gestalt of personality.

Other examples of modifications in scientific method brought on by projective techniques can be cited. This new approach consists of carefully controlled clinical study not only of perception but judgement, association, learning, retention, forgetting and emotional behavior as they are embedded in and are part of the total personality. In fact, all the old basic problems can now be re-evaluated from this point of view which will give us new understanding of how these personality aspects are organized and interrelated in normal and disordered persons as well as how this organization develops genetically.

In what *specific* ways have projective techniques influenced and in fact revolutionized experimental designs in personality research? Let us take typical ultra-scientific designs of the past and criticize them from the point of new of projective techniques. Then we can point out how they are being improved and can be improved in the interests of further scientific progress. Suppose that someone proposes to standardize or validate a new projective personality test as a differentiator between so-called normals and schizophrenic patients.

The old research design would take an experimental group of, let us say, 200 verified diagnosed schizophrenics and 200 so-called normals and equate them for such factors as, for example, intelligence, educational level, vocational status, socio-economic status, and perhaps other so-called variables. The test would then be administered to each of the subjects by well-trained examiners, each examiner handling the same number of subjects from each group. The mean scores on all of the scorable factors of the test would be calculated, the differences between the means, and the significance of the differences by some test of significance of differences. Then the test would be tried out on a new group of subjects and the significant differences would be used to separate the normals from the schizophrenics for purposes of cross-validation. This looks like a rigorous design but let us examine it more closely.

In the first place, from the organismic or holistic point of view, as soon as you equate schizophrenics to normals for, let us say, intelligence, you destroy the Gestalt of either normality or schizophrenia. We know that the intellectual functioning of schizophrenics is affected by the disorder, and to pick schizophrenics who function intellectually as well as normals is to get a peculiar group of schizophrenics. If the same were done for educational level, vocational status, marital status, and other factors, we would wind up with schizophrenics who make as good educational, vocational, marital, and intellectual adjustments as normals. Would we then be likely to find significant differences between the two groups on the tests? On the other hand, if we matched the normals to schizophrenics we would have extremely poorly adjusted normals. Would we be able to generalize from the results of our study for typical normals or representative schizophrenics? Our best bet then would be to get random samplings of both groups and forget about equating as was done in a recent study involving the Graphomotor Projection Technique (Kutash & Gehl, 1954). Appropriate statistical measures to study the effects of the variables concerned were applied to the data afterwards thus preserving the requirements of retaining the Gestalt.

On a more sophisticated level Hammond (1954) has shown "how the application of traditional, *systematic*, rather than *representative*, experimental design to problems in clinical psychology results in unjustified conclusions." He indicates that both Brunswik (1947, p. 8) and Fisher (1947, p. 88) pointed out that systematic design "is inherited from classical physics" and that "both agree that revision of this procedure is necessary." In another article Hammond (1951) draws the "analogy between the discovery, on the part of relativity physics, of the confinement of traditional physical laws to a limited universe of conditions, on the one hand, and the considerations in psychology that have led to the establishment of representative design on the other." The further comparison could be made between dynamic projective holistic psychology as representative in scientific psychology of what relativity physics represents in physical science. Among the new designs which may more nearly meet the needs of holistic psychology can be mentioned Fisher's *multivariate analysis of variance* and related techniques as well as Brunswik's *representative* design. Several recent studies illustrate the application of these newer designs notably that of Gibby (1952) on examiner influence on the Rorschach inquiry.

Let us examine further the scientific objectivity of those who insist on controlling so-called variables such as intelligence in a systematic design or on equating groups for intelligence.

Is not this based upon the implicit assumption or prejudice that intelligence or the IQ is a variable capable of being measured by an IQ test, the responses to which, the subject may project into as much as and in the same way as in the responses to the projective technique being validated? By what scientific right does such an experimenter accept as established that intelligence is a unitary trait capable of being isolated from the rest of the personality by a quantitative test? Is not this as subjective as an a priori assumption that color responses on the Rorschach represent emotional reactivity to the environment reactivity to the environment? Perhaps we should be concerned by the insidious way in which the cultists of pseudo-objectivity wrap their subjectivity in neat, airtight, statistically refined, controlled experiments to hide from their own conscious awareness and the scrutiny of others the implicit theoretical prejudices that underly their atomistic method. Perhaps the reification of the method is a further step in the defensive system of enhancing their shaky scientific security. This is not to throw a wet blanket on true objectivity which takes into account in experimental designs that Gestalts must not be destroyed and results in what we might call "holistic objectivity."

A good example of "holistic objectivity" is provided in a recent study by Beck and Nunnally (1953) in which they utilized a method, "scientifically dependable, for patterning out the personality as a whole." Instead of using the relatively simple outmoded atomistic statistics of seeing how any one variable distributes within the whole of any one group such as schizophrenics, neurotics, or normals, they used Q-technique to determine how the many different personality variables distribute in quantity in any one person. In their own words, "How much does he respect reality, against how much fantasy which he is using, against how much emotion which pleasurably excites or painfully agitates—

how much of these go to make up a schizophrenic as against a healthy person?" (1953). The applicability of Q-technique to holistically oriented research in schizophrenia is excellently described in the above-mentioned article (1953).

Another example is provided by Holt's (1950) design for validation studies which he has called "systematic study of unreliability" and in which he distinguishes between *phenotypic* and *genotypic reliability*. This method is derived from Horn's (1943; 1950) repeated test technique for treating intra-individual variability in the study of personality.

Let us turn to the business of using parametric statistics based on the assumption of the normal curve which holds perhaps for the IQ but is certainly not applicable to such Rorschach scores as M, CF, or any of the scores. We know that the higher the score on an intelligence test the better, so that mean intelligence represents a real numerical average quantity of intelligence for the particular group under study. We know that too much M in a Rorschach record may be as bad as too little M if not more insofar as schizophrenia is concerned. The mean M of schizophrenics is utterly meaningless as representative of the group tendency. The fact that there may not be a significant difference in mean M between normals and schizophrenics does not in the least prove that it is invalid for differentiating schizophrenics from normals. The distribution of M does not even follow a normal curve but may perhaps follow a J-curve. This is another example of the improper use of a method applicable in its original context but inapplicable to projective techniques.

This leads us to be encouraging fact that as a result of projective techniques and their new kinds of scores or shorthands for noting qualities, new statistical techniques more appropriate to the important problems for which psychology is seeking solutions are being developed. We need only mention nonparametric statistics, P technique, Q technique, inverse factor analysis, statistics for the individual case, and variations of analysis of variance. Statistical methods that can deal with Gestalts and fluctuations within an individual need further development. The clinician, to predict for the individual, cannot use the normative approach which might conceivably permit prediction on the 5 per cent level of confidence. By taking samplings of ten TAT stories on a case if he finds that in the eight stories that have authority figures the hero, all eight times, shows aggression toward these figures, he might be able to predict with almost complete certainty that this subject will be aggressive toward authority figures especially if other data shows that he tends to act out his aggressive needs. More can perhaps be learned about individual behavior by thorough clinical and statistical study of individual cases than by the accumulation of group statistics. In this respect, psychology is more like the science of astronomy in which the experimental method of controlling variables directly can not be applied at all. Yet it is the purest of the natural sciences, and mathematics has been applied most successfully in this science which uses mostly better and better tools for what we might call clinical observation of the universe. Only after such observation are the Gestalts broken down by use of the spectrometer to add more facts about the stars.

The new era of the development of holistic statistics, ushered in by projective techniques and dynamic psychology, has made clinical researchers as well as statisticians aware of the many common statistical fallacies pervading the static applications of the statistics of the past to current dynamic research problems. These have been summarized ably by Cronbach (1949), Schafer (1949) and others. For example, Schafer points out the error in the frequent conclusion drawn "that a statistically established group trend characterizes all the members of the group." He cites the frequent occurrence in the "interpretation of results" sections of published articles of such statements as "alcoholics tend to" . . . . or "schizophrenics are" . . . "when actually the statistics have merely established that *relatively many* schizophrenics or alcoholics show a certain trend." He asks, "What about the remaining members of the group-those who do not show the trend?" and then goes on the point out that "it is arbitrary to assume that a statistically significant pattern captures the essence of group membership."

"A related erroneous assumption is seen when a mild statistical trend is assumed to indicate that all members of the group show the trend mildly . . . By contrast a statement such as the following may be justified and quite scientific, 'If anyone gives a contamination response in the Rorschach test, it is likely to be a schizophrenic who does so, but not many schizophrenics give contamination responses.' In other words, it should not necessarily be assumed that a statistically insignificant difference implies that there is no difference between groups." Schafer also explodes such sacred assumptions as that "the use of a large sample is always desirable since a large sample will cancel out individual differences that might otherwise becloud trends in our data" or that "a score is an adequate micro-unit for research." Munroe (1948) also has commented that, "By and large it seems clear that poor results are obtained when a limited number of the traditional scores (which were never intended for use in isolation) are equated with personality traits without further ado and correlated with external factors. Promising results are obtained when *combinations* of scores are used . . ."

The critique of uncritical use of inapplicable statistical techniques could be multiplied considerably but it is perhaps more fruitful to dwell on the statistical innovations designed to meet the problems raised by projective techniques. That these newer statistical methods can be attributed to the impact of projectives is attested to by Mensh (1950) who states that "as the projective methods became a more prominent tool of the clinical psychologist, still more statistical problems were posed because of the nature of the tests and the data obtained through their use." An outstanding exposition of the need for a new look in statistics was presented in the symposium on Statistics for the Clinician (1950) chaired by Zubin and participated in by Baldwin, Kubis, Kogan, Hunt, Rabin, and Cronbach (1950).

As Zubin (1950) pointed out, "group centered" statistics are giving way to "individual-centered" statistics and as Mensh (1950) reports, "Particularly since the introduction of the projective methods have questions been raised about the normal distribution curve and its application to data obtained by means of such psychodiagnostic devices."

Among the more promising newer techniques of statistical analysis which have been developed are some which originated within the field of projective testing itself such as Rosenzeig's (1950) "method for validating projective techniques projectively" which he has called the method of "*successive clinical predictions*." But statisticians and research psychologists have also risen to the challenge as witness Zubin's (1950) proposal of the need to sample "not only an individual's performance but also to sample his variability," something which the clinician has relied upon in clinical time sequence studies of individual cases. But Zubin (1948) has also developed a series of rating scales classifying response categories into scale steps and applying rating scale techniques in the evaluation of the Rorschach, Levy Movement Blots, the TAT, and Word Association (Zubin and Young, 1948). While the method may have research use it has as yet received little acceptance by other investigators. Cronbach (1948) has further developed blind-matching techniques which he considers able to yield the "types of objective analysis necessary for a thorough validation of a qualitative assessment of personality." This proves to be a highly cumbersome procedure but may have value for research. The contributions of Cattell (1947) in P-technique and of Stephenson (1949) in Q-technique are gaining some acceptance as witness the Beck-Nunnally study previously mentioned. We have already mentioned the methods of analysis of variance and multivariate analyses. There remains to add the applications of the Fisher discriminant function technique (1950) defined by Zubin as one "which serves to integrate a group of variables into a total score such that the maximum differentiation from a contrasted group is effected."

The entire field of scientific psychology is undergoing a metamorphosis under the impact of projective techniques. Notions previously established scientifically in laboratory and controlled experimental situations are found to be invalid when applied to living human material and real life situations. For example, when anxiety brought about artificially in the laboratory by depriving subjects of their expected dinner is compared to real life anxiety as it occurs at the death of a loved one, any conclusions drawn from the laboratory experiment no matter how well designed is inapplicable. Under the impact of projective techniques all existing theories of psychology are being reevaluated and restudied in the light of the total personality in action. Thus, the newest theories of perceptions elaborated by Ittelson and Cantril (1954) and the transactional school on the basis of the Ames Demonstrations stress the individual nature of perception and its dependence on past phenomenological experience. At the East Orange VA Hospital extensive research is now under way using the Ames Demonstrations in conjunction with projective techniques to study such new problems as Perceptual Fluidity and Neuropsychiatric Prognosis. The Development of Perceptual Differentiations as Psychodiagnostic Clinical Tools, and the Development of a New Integrated Theory of Perception in Normal and Psychopathological States (1954).

We are now in the midst of a new era of dynamic scientific psychological progress ushered in partly by the advent of projective techniques which may eventually raise psychology to the status of the other sciences of physics, chemistry, astronomy and biology. Perhaps our science, too, is at last breaking the methodological chains that bound it and emerging to study man's mind and personality by whatever methods prove able to answer the crucial, important problems that confront us. This is particularly important when we think that the decision as to whether to use atomic energy for the destruction of mankind or the establishment of a utopia on earth will be made by human minds and personalities or to use Gardner Murphy's term, by a special brand of "autisms" (1945).

Personality Research and Theories of Personality Structure: Some Convergences

S. J. BECK[1]

I

Three theses form the substance of this, my president's paper, to our Society. One, there is theory as to personality, theory which has crystallized out of the clinically realistic facts of life as investigated by two men of highest genius. It is theory developed in the clinical field. Two, investigation carried on systematically with the Rorschach test and the results as seen through the medium of theory underlying this test are valid when tested by findings independently obtained by clinical method and in accordance with clinical theory. Three, current viewpoints on the logic of science concerning method and design are applicable to the method and design of the investigations referred to in my theses one and two. Or stated conversely the method and theory of the two men I have in mind as well as method and theory in Rorschach investigation are consistent with one another and with a general logic of science. They converge.

Before proceeding with this exposition a word is necessary about the topic of personality in general. When the future historian of psychology comes to write of the years in which those of us here present came of age he may well focus on these years as the period in which the study of personality as a science came of age. He will so write but with reservations, the same that many of you here tonight must be entertaining. Is there a science of the unit personality? One can even ask—the personality, does it exist? Considered philosophically it is a construct by which we mean a figment. It is nothing concrete. No one has ever seen personality. We do say that a man or a woman has personality, as we also say that our cat has it or our parakeet, and as the advertising men assure us, a piece of furniture, or a cigarette, or a pair of bedroom slippers have personality. All of which is only a way of saying that the man, the cat, the piece of furniture, possess certain traits. These are known or are inferred from certain overt manifestations. We reason from these outer data to the underlying construct.

Personality is then a concept, a handy abstract term useful in the study of human behavior. The term unifies. It does this to the overtly observable phenomena which as first seen are disorganized; helter-skelter, confused. It moves us to sift these, to compare and examine them in the light of some large idea meaningful in the field of behavior, to discard some, retain those that fit, and to embrace all within a statement which is also a prediction. All of which is to say that the term stands for a program of research. To the extent that the new experience is consistent with the idea, it all builds up into a theory.

II

And now back to my three theses. One of the two great men to whom I referred above worked in the field of neurology, Hughlings Jackson. He is best known for that description of the epilepsy which bears his name. Jacksonian epilepsy. It is description which makes most satisfying reading to those of us in the habit of looking for evidence as the point of departure for

[1] The thinking here reported grew, in important measure, out of findings obtained in a research, obtained in a research conducted under grants from the National Institute of Mental Health. Department of Health, Education and Welfare; Research Project MH 597, S. J. Beck, Principal Investigator.

reasoning. It is a factual recounting of the overtly observable behavior, relating the observed data to the known facts of the nervous system, with especial reference to the brain; selecting the facts and rationale which make sense in the light of the whole behaving person; resynthesizing these data and behavior and rationale in the light of our knowledge of the brain's function.

The net result is his concept that however disordered the person, it is always a whole person on whom we are looking. The total observed activities-Jacksonian epilepsy, aphasia, chorea, or any of the neurologically caused diseases-this total behavior is the work of whatever whole brain structure is available to the sufferer at the time. A person in a delirium is, by the Jacksonian theory, not one who has lost his reason. He is a person living by as much mental power as is available to him.

> "For the scientific study of maladies of the nervous system . . . . .we must also take into account the undamaged remainder . . .what is left intact of a nervous system mutilated by disease," (Jackson, 1932, p. 411).

Let us exemplify by a patient, say in early stages of senility. Some moderate errors in judgement have only recently been cropping up in his day to day conduct of his business. His personality is judged by deportment, adhesion to social standards, personal self care, and effort at independence, remains unchanged. But the Jacksonian concept there are moderate losses of brain function, moderate pathology within the "highest" brain centers. But in the main he is intact as a psychologic person. He is functioning with the tissue that is without damage.

Consider next a patient in an extensive intoxication, whether the agent be alcohol or some other drug. Critical perception is seriously impaired, judgement is poor, possibly clouded. The illness is obviously more severe or the patient may even be suffering those bizarre hallucinations in which a variety of animals or multicolored little men are playing with or amusing him. The brain damage is that much more wide-spread, with the attendant greater loss of intellectual function. The individual is, however, still capable of enough conscious psychologic activity to experience certain percepts unreal as they are. That is, he is the whole person functioning with equipment represented by his intact layers. In the condition next schematized more brain tissue is inoperative and much less of the psychologic person remains. Possibly the dream moments of sleep, the "noises in a swound" of the *Ancient Mariner* is as much consciousness as is here pictured. Finally there is Jackson's "fourth degree of insanity," presumably the unconscious state in the full epileptic fit or any coma. In Jackson's language, "there are no positive mental symptoms; there is no mind or consciousness."

The queer productions in mental disorder are then activity of still healthy brain tissue.

> "A delusion, however absurd it may be, signifies activities of healthy nervous arrangements," (Jackson, 1932, p. 418).

Again,

> "All mental states, healthy or morbid, are the survival of the then fittest states during activity of what are the highest arrangements at the time," (Jackson, 1932, p. 24).

The damage to the higher layers can not be spoken of as causing the symptoms, as for example, in speech defect. For,

> "Strictly speaking it is simply impossible that softening of the brain can cause any wrong utterances; for softened brain is no brain; so far as function, good or bad is concerned it is nothing at all. I submit that the wrong utterances occur during activity of parts not softened but healthy" (Jackson, 1932, p. 17).

> "The positive symptoms are indirectly caused, or it is better to say, are 'permitted:' they answer to increased activity of lower nervous arrangements, uncon-

trolled by their now exhausted higher," (Jackson, 1932, p. 21).

In language of more current neurology, the damage to the higher layers means the removal of the inhibition. That is one major function of the cortex. It inhibits the "lower" centers, those connected with biologically more primitive behavior including reflex action and autonomic and hence instinctual functions.

Jackson makes it clear also that it is first and last the brain as physical organ which is strictly and narrowly his field of investigation. He is unequivocally explicit on this point:

"It is impossible to study cases of disease of the brain methodically if we confuse psychical states with nervous states. We must be thoroughly materialistic in our method so far as is practicable" (Jackson, 1932, p. 9).

"Consciousness *attends* activity of a certain nervous arrangements, and ceases when those nervous arrangements are *hors de combat,* " (Jackson, 1932, p. 16).

That is, Jackson declines to psychologize. He is a neurologist and limits his exposition to the data in his field. As psychologists we are however interested in his theorizing principally for the aid it lends toward understanding psychologic phenomena. And his thinking can not help being a bridge from neurologic to psychologic theory and specifically in the field of personality. Thus his language

"Figuratively speaking, and yet almost literally, the patient who has undergone dissolution is at once 'less himself', and 'too much himself'; speaking more in detail, he is too little his *highest* self and too much his lower self . . . .We may say that he suddenly ceases to be enough his highest self, and at once or soon, become too much his lower self," (Jackson, 1932, p. 26).

Which is to say that as a person he is now living by less mature patterns. But in saying this we are actually stating the essence of Freudian personality theory. By this theory the previously developed standards, the ego, have lost some or all their effectiveness. The psychologic person is in retreat to an earlier pattern of living. The patient is, in psychoanalytic language, in regression. This is exactly what we are observing in Jackson's "dissolution."

In sum, and it is exciting to realize this, when we are formulating personality structure as derived from the Jacksonian hypothesis, we are at the same time actually talking of the Freudian personality concept. The converse also holds. The data of the one fit into the logic of the other, and *vice versa.*

It is not necessary to into detail here concerning the psychoanalytic hypotheses. Their essentials are well known and in fact Freudian thinking has so far percolated into that of the European and American populations at large as to become part of the folk culture.

This convergence of Jacksonian and Freudian theory is discussed in detail by Grinker (1939). A psychoanalyst who started his career as a neurologist, he has a systematic knowledge of both disciplines. He traces infantile developmental patterns within the framework of Jacksonian logic, discusses neurologic phenomena with the psychoanalytic theory of symptom formation of the dream, of regression, points to implication for learning theory, and relates his reasoning to psychoanalytic ego theory. "It is amazing," he asserts, "how this psychological explanation coincides dynamically with the neurological."

The convergences can in fact be traced throughout the range of psychodynamic pictures. Consider hysteria. In the hysteric painful experiences or ideas are removed from consciousness. The patient carries on now with less mental equipment than before the hysteric attack. Freud's Dora, she whose love affair with its frustrations may be said to have opened the door to psychoanalysis, this young woman would have attacks of aphonia – when her lover was absent from Vienna. On his return she would regain her voice.

In Jackson's language, she was now less than she was before. In the Dora with the behavior pattern which Freud reports some of the functioning which Jackson relates to the highest level of evolution was lost. By the Freudian hypothesis the loss was related to a strongly experienced emotional need. There were certain repressions, i.e. exclusion of certain ideas from consciousness. In Jackson's model, only the upper layer would be affected, and that not to an extensive degree. The patient was intact in essentially all her mental functioning. But the symptoms did show that she had suffered loss similar to that found with neurologic damage.

All of which is not intended as argument that the emotions "caused" the aphonia. To do so would be to make assumptions as to cause and effect in mental phenomena, and their relation to the activity of the brain as organ. It would be a wandering into that *terra incognita* the mind-brain problem. As psychologists we have no more warrant for neurologizing our data than Jackson claimed for psychologizing his. All we can at present say is that the data in each field are logically consistent within the theory of the other.

In another group of neuroses, the obsessive compulsive, the patient is psychologically crippled. He has abilities he can not use. Again the activity of the emotions has so affected him that he is less of his "higher self," than he can be, i.e. not living his life at the evolutionary level which his brain equipment makes possible, as psychological tests clearly show. There is interference with or blocking of the higher functioning centers, those that produce the higher intelligence. But as the centers which differentiate, they are the ones also with which we know values, and which integrate our abilities towards the pursuit of values. This is ego, which is to say that the impairment characterizing these neuroses is impairment of the ego. This precisely is the psychoanalytic theory. Fenichel (1945) generalizes:

> "In all psychoneuroses the control of the ego has become relatively insufficient."

So the losses which in the Jacksonian model would be located in the highest evolutionary levels, where Jackson sees the "finest sentiments" residing, are ego losses.

The behavior manifestations in the two great groups of the "functional" psychoses, the affective and the schizophrenias, can also be understood and hypothesized within the framework of either of the two theories.

In a depression the person can not grasp connections which he formerly could. His field of vision is limited. Thought content and interests are channelized into his personal and anguished preoccupations. The whole functioning person is clearly less than he was before the illness. The oppressive feelings have affected his reasoning ability and his judgement. By the Jacksonian hypothesis the thinking which he produces is that which is possible for as much of his mental ability as the overwhelming melancholy has not hamstrung. The ego-effect equilibrium has been seriously altered, against the ego, with pathologic effects to the person as a whole. And now we are again talking Freudian terminology. The difference is of course that the analysts orient themselves around the patient's personal needs: what in his experience as human being effected the imbalance? Jackson, neurologist *par excellence*, remains impersonal. He is concerned with the function of brain tissue, whatever may be the human needs that agitate the person.

In the manic attack, diametrically different though the patient appears as compared with what he is like in his depression, the structure is the same. The ego-affect balance has shifted, violently. The only, but critical difference is in the quality of the affects. The emotions are in possession of the person. His judgement has fled and with effects contrary to that in the depression. His flighty attention, unchecked flow of speech, exaggerated good spirits, misperceptions of himself, these again are the work of as much of his brain equipment as can still function.

This is what is left to his personality's structure and is the present whole person. The intellectual control of which the patient is known to be capable is lost and the subintellectual processes are liberated. Adult standards which once had been learned are not discarded. The ego is submerged.

Similarly in the schizophrenias the gross distortions of reality, distortions though they are, are still projecting such intellectual functioning as is available to the patient. The fantasies and elaborate delusions are evidence that there is enough intact tissue to fabricate this dream world and the dereistic symptoms. The irrealities permit inference that to that extent the critical functioning of the higher brain centers is suspended. Similarly the clearly inadequate or inappropriate responses tell something of the ebb and flow of the feelings in the patient. The amount of reality distortion, the living in the fantasy, the emotional disorderliness, is a picture again of the net personality remaining in function, or conversely, the extent to which more infantile levels of the personality are again ascendant. This is the whole person presently remaining. In the psychodynamic terms, it is regression. The ego, that capacity to know reality, to discriminate values, has lost stamina, or has fully given up its adult position. But ego, as conscious intellectual activity, is resident in the higher differentiating brain centers according to the Jacksonian hypothesis. So again psychodynamic phenomena can be pictured in the neurologist's design.

A paragraph from Grinker's (1939) paper summarizes the convergences in the two disciplines as seen in the several levels of illness. Thus

> "In the psychoneuroses there is a functional paralysis of the Ego concomitant of cortical activity resulting in the release of autoplastic regressive psychological concomitants of lower level activity to a large extent exteriorized through the vegetative nervous system. In the psychoses regression is deeper both neurologically and psychologically."

Most important with regard to the two clinical theories is that the reasoning rests on overtly observed behavior data, and on much verification. The evidence which has been accumulating these past two generations, and probably longer, lends weighty support to both Jacksonian and the Freudian hypotheses.

III

I have gone to some length in my exposition of these two major concepts, one neurologic and one psychologic, because of the orientations which they provide as to what the whole personality is. Each amounts to being a definition which the "scientific" psychologist can attempt to retrace with his own techniques, his psychological tests. The two theories give him intellectual direction along which to try his gadgets and so to subject the results to the critical checks which he includes in his scientific repertory. Secondly, to the members of this Society, concerned as we are with projective tests and with the potential in such tests for being scientifically valid, Freud's and Jackson's concepts have a more incisive interest. And this is it. Speaking for the one test with which I am most especially acquainted, how do Rorschach test results fit in with clinical theory? Can personality structures obtained with this test be translated into clinical language? Do its findings make clinical sense?

The answers to these questions, whether for the Rorschach or for any other test, can only be given by experiment. The results must verify the reasoning. Furthermore these results must first be interpreted independently and entirely by theory underlying the test. In the case of the Rorschach test we have operated with certain assumptions beginning with the work of Hermann Rorschach himself (1942). What these are has been stated by numerous writers, and two broad principles are emphasized, whatever differences there are among us as to technical detail. One is the generic significance of certain kinds of associations: e.g. the bright colored determinants as projecting out the nuances of the pleasurable emotional experience; shading determinants as arising out of unhappy mood experience; the movement response, that most original and exciting of Rorschach's discoveries, as communicating unconscious needs in the patient, some from dream level. There are the several response categories in the intellectual sphere with what they tell us about the patient's ability to call on his personality resources and to integrate them, to control himself—projecting out ego. In an earlier paper (Beck, 1942) I showed the essential equivalence of these broad Rorschach test significances to personality trends, as well as the possibility of translating the inferences from Rorschach test findings and their interrelations into the constructs of Jackson and of Freud.

The second broad principle in Rorschach test personality theory is that a human personality is multidimensional and that the whole personality as it is seen in function in any one moment is a net product of the interacting psychologic forces composing it. The problems of verification when working with this kind of a test are therefore of two kinds. One is to test out Rorschach's assumptions concerning the generic significance of the component variables in his instrument. Secondary it is necessary to test the validity of the findings for each whole personality: how accurately, as judged by non-Rorschach test formulation, does the instrument describe any one person? Efforts at verification have been going on, beginning soon after publication of the *Psychodiagnostik* (1942) and in mounting crescendo within the past two decades. In the main these have focused on the component variables. Concerning these I shall not now dispute. Much has been written purporting to refute, and much to confirm the claims concerning the generic significance of e.g. color, M, shading, F plus, perceiving wholes or parts of the blots, and the others. The statistics here employed are those of probability, quite appropriately for this much of the problem, the nomothetic approach. But can we apply these statistics to the datum, the human personality, which is an interaction of the forces in these separate variables? to the individual conceived of as a combination term? Since these psychologic forces have the personality value which they do because they are functioning within a whole field of forces—here Kurt Lewin's (1951) concepts come to mind naturally—what happens to any of these variables when one is extracted out of the entire? Are we by sieving them out of the personality dissipating the very phenomena we are interested in studying? As a parallel, there is that simple experiment of our high school physics. We pass a ray of white light through a prism and we see the well-known component colors: violet, indigo, blue, green, yellow, orange, red. Is any of these colors, as extracted through the medium of the prism, the same physical or psychologic event when co-functioning to make the white light ray? Is it not rather necessary to do research on the white light rays as combinations of violet, blue, yellow, red and the others if we want to know how these components function in combination and as the new unit which they compose?

Study of the whole personality sets up a new challenge to statistical science. Fisher (1954) in a recent article points with justifiable pride to the important role which statistics have played in the wondrous growth of science. However, in one sector the advance has been slow. This is in the field of the whole psychologic individual as such. Yet the attempt is being made. For one example of a statistical approach to the human personality, I make reference to the research in schizophrenia in which I am currently engaged. My technique is Stephenson's (1953) Q. I am aware of the critiques that are being directed against this technique and that my results must be taken with the reservations that are dictated by the possible flaws in the Stephenson logic. Still our results, within the range warranted by the method, have the following import for the investigation of schizophrenia and personality in general.

(1) The research used operational or quasi-operational descriptions of schizophrenic behaviors, i.e. it started with the outer "sense data" of schizophrenia.

(2) It subjected these operational statements to the impersonal mathematical treatment involved in correlating and factor analyzing.

(3) When our statistician associates in the research had finished their factoring, we examined the clusterings of traits, i.e. the personality types or patterns that were derived out of the statistical processing. We then found that

(4) We had personality structures consistent with the Freudian personality hypothesis. The ego-affect equilibrium, the degree of domination by "lower" over "higher" processes, the regressive intellectualizing or fantasying, the inhibiting or repressive defenses,—these are the structural configurations we abstracted out of our Rorschach test findings interpreted in accordance with Rorschach test theory. Table 1 shows the conceptual schema by which the persons in our research can be described. These constructs are in psychodynamic terms, these being the terms in which we carried on the research, entirely psychologic. Thus our experiment, in which conclusions are drawn from Rorschach test findings, yields personality constructs congruent with those of the Freudian hypothesis. To the extent that the psychodynamic construct is sound, there is basis for inferring that the Rorschach test logic is founded in fact. Since this logic is built out of the assumptions as to the generic significances of the test's major response categories, these significances appear to be, in so far, supported. Then I point once again to the convergence between the Jacksonian and the Freudian constructs which adds that much spot of comfort to the Rorschach test premises.

IV

Now for my third thesis. It grows out of the thinking, today current and vigorous, concerning scientific method itself. Scientists are inspecting their own methods and as a major task in these inquiries, their own intellectual processes. It is not enough to march starry-eyed in the name of Science. They want to know what they are themselves doing intellectually, the semantic references of the language they use, the possibility of testing these apparent significances, the limit on what can be tested out. It is some of this literature that I want to cite briefly and selectively. We will then see how this

Table 1
Conceptual Scheme of Factors in Schizophrenia*

Theoretical Component	Factor	Level of Manifestation	
A. Defense Organization	I^1	a. Withdrawal	b. Constriction
		c. Pathogenic	(d. Balanced)**
B. Intellectual Functioning	II^1	a. Orderly	b. Disrupted
C. Fantasy Activity	III^1	a. Autistic	b. Regressive
		c. Little or none	(d. Creative potentially)**
D. Social Adaptation	I^2	a. Self-absorption	b. Self-deprivation
		c. Restitutional	(d. Constructive life objective)**
E. Emotional State	IV^1	a. Lability	b. Fixed tone
			(c. Controlled release)**

* Reproduced from the monograph reporting this research (Beck, 1954) by permission of the publishers.

** Levels developed in research following publication of the monograph.

reasoning applies to the clinical theories (Freud, Jackson) and to the Rorschach test experience.

In a paper carrying the title "Science and Complexity" Weaver (1948) brings into high relief the scientific issues which living things present in contrast to those in which the physical sciences have made their progress. The latter prior to about the year 1900 have experimented with two-variable problems which Weaver calls "problems of simplicity." To be sure, as he points out, the physical sciences made possible those marvels which are the commonplaces of our every-day life, the telephone, radio, air travel, high fidelity sound reproduction, But,

> "The significant problems of living organisms are seldom those in which one can rigidly maintain constant all by two variables. Living things are more likely to present situations in which a half-dozen, or even several dozen quantities are all varying simultaneously, and in subtly interconnected ways. Often they present situations in which the essentially important quantities are either non-quantitative, or at any rate eluded identification or measurement up to the moment. Thus biological and medical problems often involve the consideration of a most complexly organized whole," (1948).

The next step was again taken by the physicists. They developed, with the help of the mathematicians, powerful techniques of probability theory and of statistical mechanics, and were now able to tackle "problems of disorganized complexity." In these the "number of variables is very large," but "the system as a whole possesses certain orderly and analyzable average properties," (Rorschach, 1942). That is they deal with probability for large numbers of cases, the nomothetic approaches. Useful as these techniques have been in extracting some of the fundamental laws of science, e.g. thermodynamics, motion of atoms, of the stars, they still leave untouched what Weaver (1948) calls "a great middle region which science has as yet little explored or conquered."

"What makes a primrose open when it does?" he asks in the first of a series of questions all of which lead to his conclusion,

> "They are all problems which involve dealing simultaneously with a sizable number of factors which are interrelated into an organic whole. They are all, in the language here proposed, problems of organized complexity, (Weaver, 1948).

To the student of individual human behavior this is a welcome pronouncement. We have seen our colleagues piling data on data for many decades now. Research reports accumulate in the psychology tomes and this is not to count the countless unpublished researches. The number of journals is ever burgeoning yet the publication lag which these new organs are intended to take up, far from diminishing, is growing at an ever faster rate. And quoting that acid observer of human life, Eccelesiastes, "of making many books there is no end." Yet all these data piled on data are not yet knowledge. The fault has been tersely stated by von Bertalanffy (1949):

> "Science is not a mere accumulation of facts; facts become knowledge only when incorporated into a conceptual system, (von Bertalanffy, 1948)."

Too many facts, too much data actually hamper the discovery of theoretical schemes, he notes a bit further.

There has been thus much unorganized accumulation, and psychology had at its inception as a science been limiting itself to problems of simplicity. Fascinated by the successes of the physical sciences it imitated them and kept its nose to the grindstone of the two variable experiment. More recently it has been climbing out of this confining channel and daring to come to grips with what looked like problems at Weaver's second level, those of disorganized complexity.

Meanwhile it develops that we are really fascinated with still another question, the one that Weaver (1948) asks, why does the evening primrose open when it does? And we ask further what is happening when you or your neighbor sees a primrose just opened up? or smells it? What is this total human experience? And the multiple others that are so human. This is that third level in Weaver's exposition, that of organized complexity in which many variables interrelate to issue into the observed whole.

Psychology in the strictest scientific sense has so far been sterile in this field of whole personality theory. The two fruitful concepts that I have described above, those of Freud and of Jackson are in neither instance product of the laboratory or of the academic hall. It is a philosopher of science, one who has much devoted himself to the problems confronting psychology, Feigl, who points to what he calls the "regionalism" of psychological theories and to the small success which the theorists in psychology have so far had in their search for a higher integration.

Feigl (1951) is himself apparently not pessimistic in his outlook for psychology. His paper, entitled "Principles and Problems of Theory Construction in Psychology," is a critical examination of the problems which psychologists need to cope with in relation to personality. He sees our time as ripe for an "Anschluss" between theories emerging in the different disciplines.

> "Analogical or abstract models of the Freudian or Lewinian type will from now on have to be appraised in terms of the isomorphism they attain with the corresponding structures and processes certified by the physiological approach. There is no question that the mythological fictions as well as the hydraulic models of psychoanalytic theory have been immensely fruitful heuristic devices. Similarly, it may be admitted that Lewin's topological and field theoretical concepts have stimulated not only a certain way of talking in the psychology of motivation but also a great number of highly original and significant experimental investigations. But from a critical methodological point of view there are serious doubts as to whether these types of theorizing amount to more than a tentative groping for the laws and concepts which will ultimately have to be provided by the molecular approach," (Feigl, 1951, pp. 206-207).

Most relevant to my present thesis is his exposition of "individual facts" as "subsumed under empirical law." To this I juxtapose his discussion of "dispositional properties" as explanatory and his transition "from surface traits to source traits or factors in personality psychology." In this pointing up of surface traits and source traits he is offering what I see as theory helping us to understand what happens in any of the investigations in personality to which I have referred in this communication. Jackson (1932) starts by describing the overtly visible motor discharges of epilepsy, or aphasia, or chorea, or a paralysis. These are the surface traits. From them he infers processes going on in certain areas of the brain, the source traits. In Freud the symptom is the surface trait-blushing, boasting, aggression, sexual impotence, intellectual disturbances. From these he reasons to the psychologic dynamics: repression, conversion, identifications, projections, and the others; i.e. the source traits. In the Rorschach test we see the person associating with the varieties of response categories, wholes or details, or rare details, color, shading, movement, i.e. the surface traits. We reason from these to certain affective and intellectual source traits.

Now it is only in so far as investigations by two of the three or by all three methods confirm one another that the inferences from surface traits to source traits can be considered to have validity. Unless so we are just bandying so many long scientific words that inflate our egos, words that are only "verbal magic and verbal sedatives," (Feigl, 1951, p. 202). He notes in this context that "to anchor our concepts and constructs in the data of observation, should in this age of modern science be so banal and obvious as to be superfluous," (Feigl, 1951). This is an axiom which one should hardly need to repeat today. Yet, I digress at this point to say that it is, unfortunately, very necessary. Much Rorschach test interpretation is sheer verbalism and giving in to the seduction of magic. The primitive rules we learn in our first weeks in the psychology laboratory are blithely disregarded when it comes to using the Rorschach test. The temptations are no doubt great, it is so easy: only inkblots. So one may shut his eyes and interpret as a laying on of hands or a speaking with tongues, or what have you. And so long as Rorschach or other personality testing disregards the basic rules or verified method, so long will they yield results that will elicit raised eyebrows from our colleagues in psychology.

Returning to the source traits: these are not yet the whole personality. They are the source processes (whether neurologic or psychologic) that produce the surface traits. Investigating at this level, we would still use the nomothetic approach and rely on the law of probability. We are dealing here with the generic processes, whether affective or intellectual. That is, we are still at the level of unorganized (rather than disorganized) complexity. But in any person the processes do interact, and configure into the whole as unit system. Here we are dealing with the organized complexity of Weaver: the primrose that opens; or you or I smelling the primrose.

In any event, here we are again, after Jackson viewing the individual as he functions with the net total of brain function available to him, and inhibited or permitted; and after Freud in the net equilibrium of ego affect forces, released or controlled, and thirdly in that balance of psychologic stresses which we see projected in a Rorschach test protocol. Table 2 shows that convergences in synopsis.

This then is my third thesis—the convergence of a logic of science with the theories inherent in the two clinical approaches and that in the Rorschach test. My own conclusion from these convergences is that it is possible to have a scientific approach to the study of personality, one consistent with clinical theory and with scientific logic. The psychologist is to be sure today between the Scylla of being too much scientist, and throwing the personality into the sea; or the Charybdis of promising everything in predicting a personality course, having thrown away the scientific rules which are his pilot wheel and so not steering at all. However, Feigl (1951) well summarizes the situation:

> "The only thing psychologist can do in molar behavior studies is to steer a middle course between recklessly issuing promissory notes and overcautiously but

Table 2
Personality Structure in Human Behavior and in the Rorschach Test in the Light of Theory. Overview.

	In the field of behavior	In the Rorschach test
The raw data	The manifest phenomena in life generally; clinical; experimental.	The scored variables of the test (W, F+, M, C, and the others.)
The source forces (or traits, Feigl)	The separate psychologic processes: affective, intellectual.	Projected affective and intellectual traits.
The individual as whole system	The interaction of the processes in the unit personality; or organized complexity (Weaver).	Personality theory. Higher- lower brain levels (Jackson). Ego-id (Freud). Field forces (Lewin). Balance of psychologic stresses

> unfruitfully restricting themselves to purely operational procedures. They need not apologize for being unable to provide strict operational definitions for every concept used. Molar behaviorism cannot avoid these ambiguities and indeterminacies. A strict one-to-one correspondence of indicator variables and intervening variables can be achieved by arbitrary definition—but the severely limited success of the prediction and explanation of behavior on this basis shows convincingly that we must search by whatever means available for a more complete frame of concepts and laws. It stands to reason that this can only be achieved through the method of existential assumptions, i.e., through the introduction of hypothetical constructs," (Feigl, 1951, pp. 199-200).

This states for me the frame of reference within which I see the psychologist most fruitfully working the field of personality. Also, we have the constructs,—those of our two clinical theorists. Each had a sharply comprehended scientific objective and states it explicitly. I cite Jackson again

> "What we call the scientific investigation of insanity is really an experimental investigation of mind; and in this regard the slightest departures from a person's standard of mental health are to be studied" (Jackson, 1932, p. 4).

And,

> "We require for the science of insanity a rational generalization which shall show how insanities, in the widest sense of the word, including not only cases specially described by alienists, but delirium in acute non-cerebral disease, degrees of drunkenness, and even sleep with dreaming, are related to one another. Dreaming is for such purpose as important as any kind of insanity . . . We have to find some fundamental principle under which things so superficially different as the diseases empirically named hemiplegia, aphasia, acute mania, chorea, melancholia permanent dementia, coma, etc. can be methodically classified," (Jackson, 1932, pp. 4-5).

Freud sums up his general hypothesis even more tersely and with all clarity:

> "The division of mental life into what is conscious and what is unconscious is the fundamental premise on which psychoanalysis is based; and this division alone makes it possible for it to understand pathologic mental processes, which are as common as they are important, and to coordinate them scientifically," (Freud, 1927, p. 9).

In a word, the concepts which guided Jackson and Freud were intended by them to be consistent with a general philosophy of science. But concepts can only be tested out with tools. Rorschach's test I see as such a concrete tool which enables us to break up the personality into its component elements, much as the prism breaks up the light ray, at the same time that it still leaves for study the personality itself, whole.

Psychological Variables In Human Cancer

BRUNO KLOPFER[1]

During the eight years from 1939 to 1947, when I served as Director of the Rorschach Institute before it blossomed into the Society for Projective Techniques, I faced many difficult tasks, as Dr. Bellak so friendly hinted, but never before one as difficult as this, presenting a presidential address. This task is especially formidable in terms of tradition; if you think back to the first years of our organization, for instance, the very first presidential address was Morris Krugman's "Out of the Inkwell"; the second was Marguerite Hertz's "Twenty Years After," shortly after that Marie Rickers presented her address called "Some Theoretical Considerations Regarding the Rorschach Method." These papers are even now classics among the 3,000 publications on the Rorschach method which have accumulated since then.

As Dr. Bellak pointed out, five authors of such presentations are here in the room and make me feel very anxious as to how my presentation will compare with theirs.

It is quite natural to expect from presidential addresses more than just an interesting talk; more than just some interesting material. All these presentations were characterized by a gleam in the eye of the speaker who told of wide horizons, of wise overviews of a large sector of the field.

Following my non-conformist tradition I felt, oddly enough for my usual point of view, that I would rather start this presidential address from a specific piece of research.

Those of the present former presidents who have presented some research material, like, for instance, Theodora Abel with her Chinese records used it as a point of departure for a large theoretical consideration. I hope the selection I have made will also serve as a departure into wider horizons. But I will leave it to you to judge the significance of what I have to say.

The beginning of this project goes back about seven or eight years. A couple of physicians at the Veterans Administration Hospital in Long Beach, California—the head of the cancer department and a biophysicist who worked very closely with him—got interested in some extensive research work with cancer patients in what we nowadays might call the symbiosis between the cancer patient and his cancer. They left aside all the difficult problems connected with the genetic aspects of cancer, and concentrated on one very well circumscribed problem, namely, the mysteries of the growth rate, the rapidity or slowness of the growth of cancer. This has been observed as a problem for many, many years and there are indications that there is something peculiar about it.

This problem has even what you might call a sentimental angle. Very often physicians have observed that the cancer seems to be particularly successful in some of the patients whom they appreciate most as human beings.

There may always be a little retroactive halo effect that you feel a person was worthwhile when he dies, according to the Latin principle "de mortuis nil nisi bonum"—not to say anything bad about the dead—but still there is quite some evidence that this is not only a sentimental illusion.

There are indications, for instance, that in mental hospitals cancer has a much harder time than outside. Not only is cancer proportionately slower growing among schizophrenics, but the schizophrenics seem to live much more comfortably with their cancer than

[1] Presidential address delivered at annual meeting of Society for Projective Techniques, August 31, 1957, New York, N.Y.

other people do. I don't know whether there are exact statistical data, but this is a general observation that seems pretty well established.

In order to investigate this problem scientifically, the first thing to do was to objectify the concept of the rate of cancer growth. How can you say, or where do you draw the line in order to say that a cancer is fast or slow in growth?

Now, these two physicians, Dr. Frank Ellis and Dr. Phillip West,, used a fairly simply way of approaching this knotty problem. They got hold of all available U.S. statistics about the life duration of cancer patients. It is well-known that this depends first on the kind of cancer from which a person suffers. For instance, acute leukemia, which takes mostly children as its victims, is probably of all cancers the most rapid type, while on the other hand cancer of the breast is not only least terrifying because it is most susceptible to surgical removal, but, even besides that, seems to be one of the slowest-growing cancers.

So, first of all, if you want to decide whether a cancer grows slow or fast, you have to decide it for each type of cancer growth separately.

It seems, if you take these U. S. statistics as a basis, that there is a certain distribution of longevity or survival time for each type of cancer. You determine for each cancer how many people are still alive who suffer from this cancer from the time when it was discovered (which is uncertain in many cases), in one year, in two years, in three years, in four years, in five years, and so on. What they did is simply to take a crude measure for separating slow and fast cancer growth by determining for each kind of cancer the time period in which only 25 percent of the patients with this particular kind of cancer had died. Then they determined the second point—when 75 percent of all patients with this particular cancer had died and only 25 percent were still alive. They decided to sacrifice, in an effort to objectify the concept of fast and slow kinds of growth, 50 percent of all possible cases and exclude from their research all cases whose time of death fell between the 25th percentile and the 75th percentile of duration of survival.

They decided that anybody who dies earlier than the first 25 percent of the patients with a specific cancer had unquestionably a fast cancer growth; and anybody who is still alive after 75 percent of all patients with the same type of cancer have died showed slow cancer growth.

This takes care, also, of one other factor which may or may not have a strong influence on the cancer personality picture, and that is the age of the patient. There are certain types of cancer with a very specific age distribution, for instance, acute leukemia. Thus you compare each patient with his own age group. In those cases where the cancer seems to be rather without a specific age distribution, it seems likely that age doesn't seem to be decisive.

The next point was, how do we go about finding out whether this medical fact—that they had a fast or slow-growing cancer—could be related to personality.

The whole research project and a great deal of the original data are published in a book which has the same title as my talk, "Psychological Variables in Human Cancer," which was published in 1953 by the University of California Press.

My own contribution to that book consists of three pages in one place and one page in another. I am therefore not repeating what I have already published, because all that I published were a few preliminary remarks in a symposium we had in October of 1953, without having had an opportunity to work over the data on which these preliminary impressions were based.

I may say, just for the sake of exactness, that I did talk once before in February 1956 at the Northern California Chapter of the Society for Projective Techniques about his material, and it was a very interesting discussion where Dr. Harrison Gough reported about some very meaningful parallel results with other psychological tests in TB patients. But first I have to tell you how I got into the whole business myself.

In connection with this research two our Ph.D. candidates wrote their dissertations. They used other techniques but also collected Rorschach records of these slow and fast cancer patients. Then a routine situation developed which I have come across quite a number of times. They had the Rorschachs on these cancer patients and they didn't know what to do with them.

Since I was coming at that time every week, later every two weeks, as a consultant to this particular hospital, they said, "Well, you come here anyway. You could do some work. Why don't you spend an hour and a half of each visit and have a look at these Rorschach records?"

The only approach I know to such a problem is a direct empirical one: "All right, let's get started. You pick me three records of patients who have fast-growing cancers and three records of patients with slow-growing cancers and I will look at them and see if I see any difference."

I looked at these six records in one our first sessions and I got some ideas in what way they might be different from each other. In the second half of my presentation, I'll discuss what this way was, so I won't go into it at this moment.

We had used up six patients for this preliminary study and then I looked at the Rorschach records of twenty-four patients blindly. I knew they were cancer patients, to be sure. I knew, also, their sex and age. They were all men, except one, by the way. But that is all I knew. I also did not know what kind of cancer they had. Interestingly enough, that wouldn't have made much difference to me because I didn't know enough about it when we started this research.

I can give you very simply the results of this experiment, if you want to call it that. I may say, by the way, that among these twenty-four cases, there were not only postdictive cases, there were also three or four newly arrived cancer cases where none of the doctors could foretell whether they would be fast or slow. So there we made real predictions not postdictions.

Out of the twenty-four patients I postdicted or guessed correctly that nine of these twenty-four had a fast-growing cancer. I also guessed correctly that ten of these twenty-four had slow-growing cancer. I could not decide which it was in one case. And in each case I made two mistakes; two fast-growing cancers I called slow and two slow-growing cancers I called fast.

The statistics showed that this could not have been a pure chance result. (Chi-square is 6.042 corrected for continuity; $P < .02$).

Now, we had one other criterion to use, that of life or death itself. Five years ago all this work had gone on, just recently I got the idea, "Now let's see what happened to these patients in the meantime." You understand that whether they are still alive or not does not determine whether there was a fast or slow-growing cancer because if a patient has lived beyond the 75 percent of his quota, even if he dies, which we all eventually do, he still remained a slow-growing cancer patient. But if any of these patients are still alive we are sure that they were in the slow-growing group. As a matter of fact, in December 1956, of the ten whom I had predicted or postdicted correctly as having slow-growing cancers, four were still alive and none of the others were living.

I can give you some other figures about the experiment. The MMPI was also used for such postdictions. In 44 cases, 21 were correctly identified as fast-growing cancer, 13 correctly identified as slow-growing; five of each group wrongly identified. It is a larger group of people, therefore the statistical significance is on a .001 level as far as MMPI is concerned. (Chi-square = 12.356)

In fifteen cases we had postdictions from the Rorschach and the MMPI.

Eleven of these patients were correctly recognized by both the Rorschach and the MMPI; two were incorrectly recognized from the MMPI, correctly from the Rorschach; two correctly recognized from the MMPI and incorrectly from the Rorschach; and only one case of the 15 mis-diagnosed by both techniques.

These figures are supplemented by two later experiments, if you want to call them that. Last October at the M. D. Anderson Hospital in Texas a most interesting research conference was called of about forty psychologists and physicians from all over the United States, all of whom were actively engaged in cancer research from the psychological point of view. They asked me at the conference to perform the same experiment with two of the patients at the hospital there, this was a particularly ticklish experiment because they had then only melanoma patients in their research files and slow-growing cancers are very rare in this group. One of my faculty colleagues was present also at this experiment and I don't think he was so much impressed by what I did, but he was impressed by the reaction of the other thirty-eight people. He happened to be in charge of our research seminar so he asked me whether I would be willing to stick my neck out in front of 150 students and 50 faculty colleagues. So I said, "Chop it right off." They selected three cases again from the files of the Long Beach Hospital whom I had not seen before and I identified all three correctly. In these subsequent experiments I therefore identified correctly four out of five.

You may assume no matter how I did it, whether I did it by ESP or anything else, that this might be an interesting result in itself. What could it mean? If anybody, no matter by what means, can, merely from a Rorschach record, say whether a person's relationship to his own cancer is such that the cancer grows fast or that the cancer grows slow, what possible inference can you draw from that?

As far as I can see, there is only one possible inference, if we in the light of the statistical significance agree that this is not just a fiction but a real fact. However, in order to discuss that with you I have to explain to you first how I did it, or at least how I think I did it.

In order to perform this job I turned back to a conceptual scheme which had been slowly crystallizing in my mind for about two years preceding this experiment. This was the first time that I actually used this scheme as a research tool and I felt very much reassured by it.

I called this peculiar pseudo-statistical or quasi-statistical scheme, with my disrespect for nomenclature, "The Pathway of Diminishing Ego Strength." Assuming we had some kind of instrument with which we could accurately measure anybody's ego strength and we applied it to a random sample of a large population, let us say a million people—as long as we don't have to do it we can be generous—we could rank them from the person with the greatest ego strength all the way down to the person with the least ego strength. Then we take this long line of a million people and fit it into a scheme of two axes pictured in Figure 1.

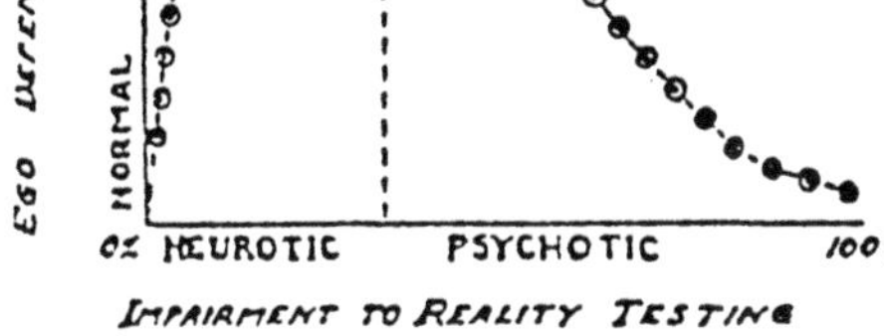

FIGURE 1.

The vertical axis represents the amount of vital energy each of these people consumes in the defense of an insecure ego (level of ego defensiveness).

Quite arbitrarily, from the point of view of this concept we grant generously to everybody that he can show 50 percent of the maximum amount of ego defensiveness and still have a normal adjustment.

People who use less than 50 percent of whatever vital energy can be invested in ego defensiveness are located from O to A and people who use more than half of the available amount of vital energy for ego defensiveness are above this point, "A".

At this point we have to make an important distinction between "adjustment" and "ego" defensiveness. Below point "A" the two concepts are practically indistinguishable. Above point "A" we'll find many people who show an excellent outer adjustment—the very people who give rise to the sentimental aspect of our problem—but who pay too high a price in ego defensiveness for such achievements. Along with these well adjusted, but insecure people we find between point "A" and point "B" all kinds of overtly neurotic people.

The horizontal axis of the illustration represents loyalty to reality. How faithfully does a subject adhere to reality as it is, or how deficient is his reality testing? In this scheme we can describe the degree of impairment of reality testing from complete loyalty to reality to the point where there is no more real contact with reality.

Now, the zero point in reality testing and ego defensiveness in the scheme (where both axis cross) is an utopian point. It would locate those people who can take reality absolutely unflinchingly, without any need to defend their ego, without ever getting afraid of it. There are no such people, you know that. But theoretically we can say this is "the ideal type."

You could line up from this ideal point all the people who don't overinvest in ego defensiveness, whom we call normal. They can afford to be quite loyal to reality. They don't have to distort reality. Then we come to the point in our long line of persons from the strongest to the weakest ego to people who do overinvest in ego defensiveness. The illustration shows that you can invest a good deal in ego defensiveness and still stay pretty close to reality.

At point "B" we come to the point of diminishing returns. If you approach the point where you have invested all the vital energy you can in ego defensiveness, something gives way. Usually I say it's like the principle of butter and cannons. If you overinvest your economic strength in armament then you run out of butter. It seems a point where the overinvestment in ego defensiveness makes it impossible to retain loyalty to reality. You get a pretty sharp break where loyalty to reality diminishes rapidly. Strange as it seems, at that point where the ego structure starts to crack, suddenly the amount of vital energy invested in ego defensiveness diminishes.

At point "C" we come then to the strange phenomenon of people who are really quite sick but on a superficial look at their Rorschach records you have the feeling, "Oh, they are not much more uncomfortable than a fairly normal person." From about this point on in the scheme there is no longer anything to defend; the ego becomes dissociated and no more systematic effort in defensiveness can be recognized.

This is nothing but a schematization of something which I think everybody knows. There are limitations to the scheme that I want to point out. I don't think it fits more than 80 percent of possible subjects.

Let us take just one possible large exception. There are various kinds of people whom I always describe as having a "floating island" ego. They have shallow roots for their ego. Hypomanic people, psychopathic people, and a number of other categories form this group. When they get under great stress, symbolically speaking their ego seems to pull up its roots and floats on the tide. They float away. And when the stress is over they settle down again and are the same as before. You don't have the feeling their ego becomes fragmented, as in the other cases. But most of the normals, neurotics, and psychotics, I would say about 80 of any hundred people, would fit somewhere into this scheme.

We have to make one more step. One of the reasons why I used these two particular components of ego functioning, the general level of ego defensiveness and reality testing, is probably that these two components are relatively clearly reflected in Rorschach records. The general level of subjectively-felt discomfort in dealing with the emotionally loaded stimuli of shading and color seems to be a good yardstick for the level of ego defensive investment.

The more a subject shows any of the myriad kinds of discomfort in handling, in using, or not using shading and color, the more subjective discomfort you see, the higher you have to rate him on ego defensiveness. And, if you investigate the form level, the qualitative aspects of the whole thought process, you can determine how far from the ideal point of loyalty to reality the subject is.

When I looked at these first six preliminary experimental subjects there was no question that every one of the people with the slow-growing cancer was, in his level of discomfort, below his line, A-C. And even though none of them was clinically a psychotic, they had developed a relationship to reality which you can only describe with the simple phrase, "They didn't give a damn." Their whole attitude was, "Why should I care?" and they were very sloppy in the organization of their responses. They changed and shifted around in their responses. They didn't have the very bizarre kind of responses which you find in many schizophrenics but, in comparison with the kind of intelligence which the whole Rorschach showed, they were not making any effort to be loyal to reality. They were all to the right of point "B" and at the same time they remained below line A-C in terms of ego defensive investment.

And the three fast cancer patients were all in the quadrant A-B without any question. They were all people who tried very hard to be loyal to reality and paid a terrible price for it.

This is the first hint of what the sentimental aspect of the whole problem is about, why a "prince of a fellow" dies so fast from cancer. It may not indicate whether these people were "good people" or not. It may simply indicate what price these patients, for whom the doctor always feels extremely sorry, had to pay for being "good"; that they overinvested too much ego defensive energy in their attempt to be good and loyal.

I can only say that my errors were mostly in this area between point "B" and point "C." In other words, in our clinical nomenclature we would have to say these were all people, whose fragmented ego defenses placed them somewhere between psychosis and neurosis.

According to my conceptualization, you couldn't do better than chance in this quadrant B-C because you could never tell whether the beginning fragmentation of the ego defenses has reached a point where the ego has practically given up defending itself, and allowed the psychotic coping mechanisms prevail, or whether the "scar tissue," figuratively speaking, of these fragmented ego defenses create the kind of discomfort which uses up vital energy even faster than a well-compensated, well-functioning character neurosis.

If we leave this out for a moment, it seems that the chances of guessing correctly, if you are sure that a person belongs in this quadrant A-B or that the person belongs below this line A-C, is extremely high.

Let me add that fortunately among our samples we have also two patients who belong in quadrant O-A, people who were amazingly well adjusted not just in a superficial behavioral sense, but amazingly relaxed, amazingly mature.

I know one of these people personally. She has had Hodgkin's Disease now for over twenty years and occasionally she gets sick again but responds very quickly to X-ray treatment. She is a very extreme case in this category.

I had a very interesting experience last night. I met there one of my colleagues and we talked about whether he wants to come here tonight and listen. Then he said, "You know that I am a cancer patient." I said I had no idea. I hadn't seen him in quite a few years. He developed a very severe intestinal cancer five years ago, which was unfortunately not recognized. He says the doctor, when he went to him and talked about his complaints first, said to him, "Oh that's psychosomatic." He said. "I'm a psychologist myself. I know what it is, it feels different." He went on a trip and he almost didn't make it home because the cancer had developed to such an extent that he nearly died on the way. He was immediately operated when he came home and this is now five years ago and as far as he can tell there is no new metastatic development. And this is a man who I would say, from the way I know him, is about as undefensive as I know any of my colleagues to be.

As I mentioned earlier, among the twenty-four cases which formed the basis of our original research project were four "misses" as far as the predictive or postdictive task of the Rorschach technique is concerned. In one of these misses the Rorschach record gives the impression that the patient had a slow-growing cancer while the medical indication put him clearly in the "fast" category. The rather dramatic course of events in this case may be more instructive than any examples we have covered so far. Therefore, I am inserting here the report of these events as given to me by one of the patient's physicians, Dr. Philip West, in a personal communication.

> "Mr. Wright had a generalized far advanced malignancy involving the lymph nodes, lymphosarcoma. Eventually the day came when he developed resistance to all known palliative treatments. Also, his increasing anemia precluded any intensive efforts with X-rays or nitrogen mustard, which might otherwise have been attempted. Huge tumor masses, all the size of oranges, were in the neck, axillas, groins, chest and abdomen. The spleen and liver were enormous. The thoracic duct was obstructed, and between 1 and 2 liters of milky fluid had to be drawn from his chest every other day. He was taking oxygen by mask frequently, and our impression was that he was in a terminal state, untreatable, other than to give sedatives to ease him on his way.
>
> "In spite of all this, Mr. Wright was not without hope, even though his doctors most certainly were. The reason for this was, that the new drug that he had expected to come along and save the day had already been reported in the newspapers! Its name was "Krebiozen" (subsequently shown to be a useless, inert preparation).
>
> Then he heard in some way, that our clinic was to be one of a hundred places chosen by the Medical Association for evaluation of this treatment. We were allotted supplies of the drug sufficient for treating twelve selected cases. Mr. Wright was not considered eligible, since one stipulation was that the patient must not only be beyond the point where standard therapies could benefit, but *also* must have a life expectancy of at least 3, and preferably 6 months. He certainly didn't qualify on the latter point, and to give him a prognosis of more than 2 weeks seemed to be stretching things.
>
> However, a few days later, the drug arrived, and we began setting up our testing program which, of course, did *not* include Mr. Wright. When he heard we were going to begin treatment with Krebiozen, his enthusiasm knew no bounds, and as much as I tried to dissuade him, he begged so hard for this "golden opportunity," that against my better judgment, and against the rules of

the Krebiozen committee, I decided I would have to include him.

Injections were to be given three times weekly, and I remember he received his first one on a Friday. I didn't see him again until Monday and thought as I came to the hospital he might be moribund or dead by that time, and his supply of the drug could then be transferred to another case.

What a surprise was in store for me! I had left him febrile, gasping for air, completely bedridden. Now here he was, walking around the ward, chatting happily with the nurses, and spreading his message of good cheer to any who would listen. Immediately I hastened to see the others who had received their first injection at the same time. No change, or change for the worse was noted. Only in Mr. Wright was there brilliant improvement. The tumor masses had melted like snow balls on a hot stove, and in only these few days, they were half their original size! This is, of course, far more rapid regression than the most radiosensitive tumor could display under heavy X-ray given every day. And we already knew his tumor was no longer sensitive to irradiation. Also, he had had no other treatment outside of the single useless "shot."

This phenomenon demanded an explanation, but not only that, it almost insisted that we open our minds to learn, rather than try to explain. So, the injections were given 3 times weekly as planned, much to the joy of the patient, but much to our bewilderment. Within 10 days he was able to be discharged from his "death-bed," practically all signs of his disease having vanished in this short time. Incredible as it sounds, this "terminal" patient, gasping his last breath through an oxygen mask, was now not only breathing normally, and fully active, he took off in his plane and flew at 12,000 feet, with no discomfort!

This unbelievable situation occurred at the beginning of the "Krebiozen" evaluation, but within two months, conflicting reports began to appear in the news, all of the testing clinics reporting no results. At the same time, the originators of the treatment were still blindly contradicting the discouraging facts that were beginning to emerge.

This disturbed our Mr. Wright considerably as the weeks wore on. Although he had no special training, he was, at times, reasonably logical and scientific in his thinking. He began to lose faith in his last hope which so far had been life-saving and left nothing to be desired. As the reported results became increasingly dismal, his faith waned, and after two months of practically perfect health, he relapsed to his original state, and became very gloomy and miserable.

But here I saw the opportunity to *double-check* the drug and maybe too, find out how the quacks can accomplish the results that they claim (and many of their claims are well substantiated). Knowing something of my patient's innate optimism by this time, I deliberately took advantage of him. This was for purely scientific reasons, in order to perform the perfect control experiment which could answer all the perplexing questions he had brought up. Furthermore, this scheme could not harm him in any way, I felt sure, and there was nothing I knew anyway that could help him.

When Mr. Wright had all but given up in despair with the recrudescence of his disease, in spite of the "wonder drug" which had worked so well at first, I decided to take the chance and play the quack. So deliberately lying, I told him not to believe what he read in the papers, the drug was really most promising after all. "What then," he asked, "was the reason for his relapse?" "Just because the substance deteriorates on standing," I replied, "a new super-refined, double-strength product is due to arrive tomorrow which can more than reproduce the great benefits derived from the original injections."

This news came as a great revelation to him, and Mr. Wright, ill as he was, became his optimistic self again, eager to start over. By delaying a couple of days before the "shipment" arrived, his anticipation of salvation had reached a tremendous pitch. When I announced that the new series of injections were about to begin, he was almost ecstatic and his faith was very strong.

> With much fanfare, and putting on quite an act (which I deemed permissible under the circumstances), I administered the first injection of the doubly potent *fresh* preparation—consisting of *fresh water* and nothing more. The results of this experiment were quite unbelievable to us at the time, although we must have had some suspicion of the remotely possible outcome to have even attempted it at all.
>
> Recovery from his second near-terminal state was even more dramatic than the first. Tumor masses melted, chest fluid vanished, he became ambulatory, and even went back to flying again. At this time he was certainly the picture of health. The water injections were continued, since they worked such wonders. He then remained symptom-free for over two months. At this time the final AMA announcement appeared in the press—"nationwide tests show Krebiozen to be a worthless drug in treatment of cancer."
>
> Within a few days of this report Mr. Wright was re-admitted to the hospital *in extremis*. His faith was now gone, his last hope vanished, and he succumbed in less than two days."

Mr. Wright's Rorschach record was obtained before his transformation from optimism to pessimism took place. It reflects the picture of a personality with what I called previously a "floating island ego organization." This is reflected in his actual behavior and the great ease with which he followed first the suggestions of the drug advertisement and later on the deliberate experimentally motivated suggestion of his doctor without any sign of defensiveness or even criticalness. His ego was simply floating along and therefore left all available vital energy free to produce a response to the cancer treatment which nothing short of miraculous.

Unfortunately this situation could not last since it was not reinforced by any deep-rooted personality center with a long-range point of view which could have counteracted the catastrophic effect of his disappointment about the drug. To use a symbolic analogy, while he was floating along on the surface of the water under the influence of his optimistic autosuggestion or suggestion, he was transformed into a heavy stone and sank to the bottom without any resistance at the moment when the powers of this suggestion expired.

This analogy with the body swimming in water could also be used to express the whole core of our hypothesis figuratively (what we described previously as ego defensiveness): It could be described as a fear of life or death or both. Just as a person who is afraid of the water has a hard time learning to swim, so has a person who is afraid of life or death a hard time to fight against cancer. One can only utilize the carrying power of water optimally if one gives oneself trustingly to this element and then uses all acquired skills of moving around in water to maintain oneself and get to where one wants to go; thus the cancer patient has to have a deep-rooted confidence in life and an attitude to death which is not colored by terror but considers it simply as one of the forces one has to contend with in order to conduct a successful fight against cancer. The superficial success of Mr. Wright was also due to lack of ego defensiveness but could only last as long as reality testing could be avoided.

There are many other aspects to this material. One of the things I dream about is to go after all these patients given up by physicians and then "cured" by Christian Science practitioners. To study a number of these people who actually had metastasizing cancer and were cured would be an extremely interesting project.

Now I can come back to my idea, what it means; if there is any such connection between either the ego organization or the personality organization of the patient and the rate of cancer growth. The only possible explanation I can think of—but maybe you can think of others—is in a symbiotic relationship between the patient and his cancer. If a good deal of the vital energy the patient has at his disposal is used up in the defense of the insecure ego then the organism seems not to have the vital energy at his disposal to fight the cancer off and the cancer has easy going. If, however, a minimum of vital energy is consumed in ego defensiveness, then the cancer has a hard time making headway. This is the only explanation which makes sense to me.

Now this seems to me extremely important, as a symbolic expression of the change in our psychosomatic thinking. Psychosomatic medicine started with an attitude that we wanted to find psychological causes for somatic events. Any attempt to follow the idea through with philosophical rigor and scientific exactness leads into difficulties. We would probably almost say today that the whole question of causation of somatic events by psychological factors in the literal sense of the word was probably the wrong question.

I would say that even in the whole philosophical problem of soma and psyche the same is true. The answer, however, is not an empty kind of parallelism. I think the most sensible terminology, even though the book which has been published about it has used not very convincing examples, is the concept of synchronicity by C. G. Jung. I leave it to you to follow this line of reasoning and develop it. I am very much impressed with this particular piece of research because it points so strongly in that direction.

One other theoretical aspect I want to mention in closing. When I published my first English book in 1942, "The Rorschach Technique," at the end of the foreword I expressed the pious hope that even though we didn't have, at that point, a personality theory, usable as a scientifically developed tool, we shouldn't put all our projective techniques on the shelf and wait hopefully until somebody presented us with a workable personality theory; that in using projective techniques we will slowly but surely come to a crystallization of a usable personality theory; that the development of a personality theory and the practical application of projective techniques have to go hand in hand, and the one cannot wait for the other.

I would say that this research, if anything at all, has very strongly confirmed and strengthened my belief that this is the way it will be.

Henry A. Murray

AN APPRECIATION

LEOPOLD BELLAK

In these days in which the nation searches the state of its intellectual resources, it would be worthwhile for the Federal Government to make available a grant for the study of the personality of Henry A. Murray.

For Henry Murray is a creative man: This can hardly be news about the father of the most important native American personality test. Though his "Explorations in Personality," is also a classic, I don't think that his personality theory, as expressed in the "Explorations" is sufficiently appreciated in the U.S.A. It has seemed to me that it has attained more importance in some European countries, notably Scandinavia, and will yet have a renewed impact here. His was a perceptual theory of personality long before the rest of the academic community saw any of the systematic experimental values of psychoanalytic concepts. Psychoanalysis might still profit from Murray's need-press schemata or from his systematization of the concept of projection. It might be difficult tothink of even one other psychologist who could have organized the psychological section of O.S.S. when Murray did: One must remember that clinical psychology hardly even existed then as a concept. Murray had the psychoanalytic training, the experimental knowhow and above all the flexibility and vitality to create whatever the circumstances called for.

What the dynamics of his early life were that engendered such spirit we do not know; his later training in varied fields obviously contributed: After Groton and Harvard College, an M.D. from Columbia in 1919, supplemented by an M.A. in Biology. A surgical internship at Presbyterian Hospital from 1920-22 was followed by research at the Rockefeller Institute and a Ph.D. in Biochemistry from Cambridge University in England, in 1927; and after that to Morton Prince, the Harvard Psychological Clinic, psychoanalytic training under Franz Alexander and Hanns Sachs, to mention the barest outline (which, for instance omits his contact with Carl Jung; that too left its imprint). This background may help make intelligible the organismic nature of his personality theory: it was often thought that the picture of a schema of need and press looked like an organic chemical compound.

All this does not necessarily make Henry Murray the easiest person to be with: to start with, it is difficult to keep pace with him, be it walking or thinking. Particularly the latter process is rapid, nearly bubbling, accompanied by the exhilaration of "Aha" experiences, and bewildering: especially to a Graduate student who would like to get his thesis firmly circumscribed and reacts with anxiety to a constant flux of ideas; alas, the process which Kris has called "regression in the service of the ego" can be observed in awesome proportions in Henry Murray; after a while one may plot an "r" for the excursions—not without having sweated some.

There is the curious admixture which Jones had observed in Freud: sometimes an easy credulity, too much open-mindedness, and then the sharp testing. I think it's probably just a form of regression in the service of the ego of very gifted people who can let themselves go more freely than others. That Murray is deeply imbued with an almost mystical need to search is evidenced by his life-long interest in Moby Dick—that romantic American version of the Faust theme. The Harvard Psychological Clinic Annex is called the Balleen, and an imprint of the mighty whale serves often as Henry Murray's informal signature.

There are frozen faced men who, with impeccable judgment, are ever ready to guard against the smallest error in irrelevant issues and who meet with a total lack of imagination every problem of importance. In short, Henry Murray is not such a man.

If the picture of Henry Murray is not complex enough so far, add to it the fact that he had been voted the most popular lecturer at Radcliff year in and year out, and could attain the same distinction with any other female group extant. Add also the fact that he had made the Harvard Psychological Clinic a jewel of a Goldcoast claustrum behung with old prints, letters from the world's great; he instilled it with the freest and easiest spirit (among a slew of rugged individuals) that can be found anywhere. Then, add to this a boyish figure and a willingness to help; an often very conservative element, not without some traces of Boston's Beacon Hill's aristocratic notions; an easy social footing with many prominent people and probably all the gifted ones, and a first-name relationship to the tobacconist of many years acquaintance; he never wears a winter coat, probably supports Harvard at least as much as it supports him, has never held office in any professional society, possesses courage and an immaculate prose—and you have a small part of the man that is Henry Murray.

On his 65th birthday: Gaudeamus igitur . . .

Formal Aspects of the TAT—A Neglected Resource

ROBERT R. HOLT

An often—encountered fallacy is the statement that "the Rorschach is a test of the structure of personality, the TAT a test of its content." I have even seen a question on a preliminary examination for the Ph.D. in clinical psychology, which required the student to accept and justify such a statement. The trouble with this formulation is that it is incomplete; it is a half-truth, which would read just about as accurately the other way around. For certainly research and clinical practice in recent years has shown that Rorschach content can teach us a great deal about strivings, preoccupations, conceptions of self and of others, and other "content" aspects of personality. The purpose of this paper is to present arguments and facts to support the position that much can be learned about the structure of personality from the TAT, primarily from a study of its formal aspects.

Actually, the point is not specific to the TAT. As we have progressed from the era of "psychometrics" to that of diagnostic evaluation and assessment of personality, our conception of tests has changed. In its original meaning, a test was (or was intended to be) a quantitative measure of a specific psychological variable. Thus, it was reasonable to approach any new instrument by trying to narrow down its sphere of relevance as much as possible. As psychologists learned to use projective techniques and related methods they began to grasp the fact that they were dealing with what Cronbach calls "wideband" instruments: not tests of precise functions, but devices that elicit broad, characteristic samples of behavior in more or less standardized ways. And it has become gradually clearer that records of such behavior could be subjected to almost as many different kinds of analysis as there are theoretical propositions about personality.

Therefore it has become inappropriate to criticize a projective technique for not having an agreed-upon scoring system, even though some people still reject the TAT on these grounds. There can be no one set of scores for an instrument like Murray's, which draws forth such a rich and multidimensional output. Rather, there can be as many different scoring systems as there are types of variables that may be discovered in it.

Methods of clinical assessment like TAT, Rorschach, interview, autobiography, play sessions, etc., have in common that they pose a task that cannot be satisfied by a simple adaptive act, as can an arithmetic problem. Rather they confront the subject with a requirement to produce something from himself in as creative a way as possible, yet within the guiding framework of some general adaptive requirements. Thus, as compared to free association, the TAT requires that the subject attend to the picture, interpret it with a degree of realism and produce a story with a certain structural features. It is far from an "unstructured" requirement, just as the pictures themselves are mostly rather clear in their major import, but there are enough degrees of freedom so that the subject can express countless variations on the basic themes that are suggested (e.g., parent-child relations) and can meet the adaptive requirements in his personal idiosyncratic ways. The usual clinical interview poses a similar kind of adaptive requirement with plenty of leeway for personal expression, and most other projective techniques likewise. Whether we choose to attend to content themes or to the formal properties of the performances depends in each instance on us, the interpreters, not on the material: The question is whether or not we have the conceptual lenses that enable us to see a person's defensive style as well as his resolution of the Oedipus complex when we interview him about his parents, or study his Rorschach or TAT responses. Human productions of this degree of freedom and richness can always be analyzed for formal properties as well as for content.

When we approach any clinical material, then, including TAT stories, we can conceivably direct our attention towards any of its infinite number of aspects, and must choose on some basis. Our choice is determined usually, either by a theoretical notion or by a practical requirement. As we shall see shortly, it makes a good deal of difference to the usefulness of a set of variables just what theoretical or practical considerations the psychologist has in mind. When we draw a general distinction between form and content, however, we are orienting our analysis of data towards different spheres of personality. For the same general distinction can be made in the realm of personality itself. Consider for a moment how we reach conceptions like need for aggression, introspectiveness, or reliance on reaction formation, as personality variables. We do so by generalizing from many particulars of just the kind we find in projective tests. Is it not likely, therefore, that we should be able to generalize best about the particular needs, sentiments, identities, conflicts and personal-historical themes in personality from the content of responses to assessment? By the same token, if we mean by structure of personality persisting regularities in the *how* rather than the *what* a person thinks, feels, wants, strives, etc., we can find the particulars from which structural generalizations are made by attending to the ways he copes with the demands of a TAT as well as a Rorschach or a WAIS.

Murray and Morgan were primarily interested in producing an instrument by which they could study the dynamic aspects of personality, which were the ones that mainly interested them. Consequently, Murray concentrated on developing a scoring method that focussed on content–needs, press and themas. But he had builded better than he knew. The TAT was so designed that is struck a happy balance between freedom and control; not only was it an unrivalled source of dynamic hypotheses, but it allowed a useful variety of formal features of performance to emerge at the same time. It remained only for persons who were mainly interested in the structure of personality to exploit the structural resources of the test performance.

So far, I have been using the terms *form* and *content* as if their meaning were perfectly obvious and did not need definition. Indeed, the distinction between manner and matter, or style and substance, is as old as criticism in the arts. But when you get down to specifics, it is not so easy to say just what the defining principles are, and where dividing lines should be drawn. Unambiguous examples come readily to mind: when we single out the fact that the little violinist in Card I likes his instrument and enjoys playing, we are surely attending to content. When we take note of the fact that the story is neatly finished without the examiner's having to intervene or prod, it is certainly a formal feature that engages our interest. Consider, however, a general variable like Adequacy of Hero—is this an aspect of content or of form? It touches closely on a feature of plot; surely part of the substance of a story is the success of the hero in achieving his own goals. But note that we are not talking about any particular story, nor any particular way of being adequate: one subject might get a rating for a story in which a religious man succeeds in mastering his impulses so he can successfully contemplate the kingdom of heaven, and another could get the same rating for a hero who succeeded in killing his rival for the possession of a woman. Such a generalized property of content seems worthy of being kept separate from the thematic material of the usual, concrete kind. Another way of looking at it is to ask *What interference we draw* from the abstracted part of a story. If it has been caused by and enables us to infer the presence of some value, attitude, purpose, preoccupation, or type of present or past personal relationship, it should be considered content.[1] In this case, however, the fact of consistently adequate heroes suggests primarily an inference about ego-strength: the capacity to delay impulse and strive successfully for long-range goals, sustained by self-confidence. By this token, the general quality of stories referred to in the variable, Adequacy of Hero, can be considered a formal aspect.

Concretely, we might make the distinction as follows: Let us take a story in which the hero, a student of the violin, enjoys the instrument, works hard to perfect his artistry, and becomes a great virtuoso. The fact that the hero succeeds in this particular way enables us to make a *content* inference: strong need for achievement. But the general fact of adequacy, taken together with the success of heroes in other stories in reaching other, non-achievement goals, leads to the *formal* inference of ego-strength.

In what follows, therefore, I shall use content in this sense: particular meanings referable to analogous meaning-contents in the teller's own life. It is convenient to define formal aspects residually, as everything else about stories except content, since it is hard to do it any other way, just as it is remarkably difficult to produce a useful definition for the term, personality structure.

SOME HISTORY[2]

There have been two main approaches to formal features of the TAT: test-centered and person-centered. From almost the beginning of TAT work, some people have recognized that there *were* formal aspects to the performance and that they were being neglected by Murray and Morgan's content-oriented approach. In 1940, Frederick Wyatt began elaborating a system of formal aspects, proceeding largely from a logical by story-centered approach and covering such qualities as the following (see also Wyatt, 1947).

1. Linguistic analysis (e.g., type-token, adjective- verb ratios).
2. Modes of presentation (e.g., general sentiment of the story, major emphasis of presentation, setting in time and space, quality of plot, development of the story, introduction of figures, character if imagery, etc.).
3. Comprehension of stimulus (e.g., relationship of figure and background, details utilized, shock-like effects, etc.).
4. Subjective reactions (e.g., expressions of like or dislike as to the stimulus, explanatory remarks and comments).

He and Marianne Weil applied these categories to the TATs of 11 *Ss* who were being intensively studied at the Clinic at that time, rating their stories as objectively as possible on these dimensions. They then performed a syndrome analysis, emerging with clusters of co-varying formal aspects, and correlated both the syndromes and the original variables with the many rated variables of personality that became

[1] Incidentally, K. M. Colby has coined the word *meantent* (a condensation of *meaning* and *content*) to stand for all these matters, because it is a little awkward to speak of the "content of personality."

[2] This historical sketch is far from complete, and omits mention of some TAT workers who have published research on formal aspects (e.g., Balken and Masserman, G. Lindzey) or whose published method of interpretation includes considerable use of formal aspects (e.g., M. Stein, S. Rosenweig). But the fact is that the great majority of TAT interpreters have emphasized content almost to the exclusion of formal features. For example, of the 15 "experts" included in E. Shneidman's *Thematic Test Analysis*, the great majority worked almost entirely with content (M. Arnold, B. Aron, I. Eron, R. Fine, W. Joel & D. Shapiro, S. Klebanoff, S. Korchin, J. Lasaga, P. Symonds, R. K. White), a few made some use of formal aspects (L. Bellak, J. Rotter & S. Jessor, H. D. Sargent), while only A. A. Hartman in addition to myself used formal features extensively. Hence the title of this paper.

available from the Diagnostic Council in 1941.

The results were so disappointing that they gave the whole cause of formal aspects a setback. The correlations were meager, did not fall into meaningful patterns, and suggested that the features of TAT performance under study were not determined to any large extent by important dimensions of personality.

In retrospect, it is possible to see two reasons for the failure of this pioneering effort: first, the selection of formal variables was made on rational rather than clinical grounds—it grew out of an attempt to catalogue all major aspects of the stories rather than to find measures of important aspects of the persons who told them—so that many of the myriad possible formal aspects were not used. Second, the set of personality variables in use at the Clinic was Murray's (1938) latest revision of the system described in *Explorations in personality*; and though it was by far the most imaginative, broad and comprehensive set of personological variables in existence, it did have a weakness: in the realm of personality *structure*. The system had after all grown up in the same fertile brain that had produced the TAT and the need-press approach to its analysis. Murray's first and most dominant interest was in motivation: the current needs, the fantasy themes and the residues of infantile experience that determined the goals for which men strove in reality and in dream. He did not ignore structural components, such as defense mechanisms, traits and abilities; these were all studied and rated. With the exception of the general area of introversion-extroversion, however, Murray was not deeply concerned with these features of personality and his approach to them was more summary, less differentiated and less founded on extensive clinical observation than was his orientation to dynamic aspects of personality. Therefore, the structural personality variables that probably determined the formal features of the TAT were relatively neglected, and so could not be discovered in Wyatt's study. It remained an open question whether such undiscovered causes might have large significance.

The other main figure whose approach to what he called the *variables of form* was an essentially story-centered one is William E. Henry. In his recent book, *The analysis of fantasy* (Henry, 1956), a chapter is devoted to these variables, and in his case studies one can see the sensitive and imaginative ways he uses them in the actual analysis of the TAT. A listing of Henry's main variables of form shows their relatedness to Wyatt's and their origin in the study of logically possible features of the stories themselves. In addition, however, the list also clearly shows that some variables originated in a deliberate attempt to find analogs of Rorschach scores.

1. Amount and kind of production (e.g., length of stories; amount of introduced content; kinds of introduced content; vividness and richness of imagery; originality vs. commonness of imagery; rhythm and smoothness of production; interruptions of story production; variations in all of these from story to story).
2. Organizational qualities (e.g., presence of the four basic parts of the story; level of organization; listing, description of relations, imaginative elaboration; coherence and logic; inclusive whole concepts; manner of approach to central concept; variations in these).
3. Acuity (e.g., of concepts; observations and their integration).
4. Language usage.

Aside from the fact that he worked with a slightly different set of variables than Wyatt, Henry achieved some success with formal features for several reasons. I do not mean to be snide when I say that one reason was that he did *not* begin by putting his variables to a rigorous statistical validation, as Wyatt did. With a clinical instrument, it is undoubtedly wise— perhaps even necessary—to subject the method to intensive clinical trial and development first, and only after this informal process of revision and hunch-forming to test hypotheses or look for correlates. At any rate, Henry did develop his system in the more usual clinical fashion, while subjecting it to indirect tests (Henry, 1947) which seemed to support its general validity.

In my judgement, Henry's variables are an improvement over Wyatt's, but they still leave something to be desired. They do not get at aspects of personality that are as clinically significant as one might wish.

The other approach, which by contrast might be called person-centered, was followed by Rapaport (1946) and Schafer (1948). They began by giving the TAT to patients of all kinds, in a diagnostic, not a research context. They approached the study of the stories with definite ideas about certain features of personality structure—particularly the defenses and signs of their decompensation. Notice in the following partial summary of their findings (from Rapaport, Gill & Schafer, 1946) that Rapaport organized his variables by the aspect of personality or pathology they refer to, not in terms of the stories themselves.

Affective lability: exclamations, interference of affects with story production, the content shaped primarily by affective response to the picture.

Depression: paucity of production, over-elaboration or perseveration of the theme of happiness vs. sadness (verging on content).

Obsessiveness/compulsiveness: circumstantial descriptions of pictures, fragmentation with doubting, intellectualizing, awareness of own thought processes, compulsive criticism of picture, pedantry.

Paranoid trends: deducing motives of E, elaborate inferences, perceptual distortions, cryptic statements.

Schizophrenia: over-elaborate symbolism, bizarre or delusional qualities, peculiar verbalization or story development, vague generalities, disjointed or mixed-up organization, arbitrariness, continuation of same story from one picture to another.

Schafer (1948) has added a number of other formal features to this list, formed in the same way. In his book (Schafer, 1948), he lists for example formal aspects that are found in character disorder: factitiousness, attempts to shock the examiner, over-casual attempts to shrug off emotionally touching topics, etc.

A FEW DATA[3]

No one will have any trouble seeing that the Rapaport-Schafer approach to formal aspects is the one that seems most fruitful to me. Shortly after I first learned it, I began work with Lester Luborsky and David Rapaport on a research project in which we were trying to learn how to predict competence of psychiatric residents during their training (see Holt & Luborsky, 1958). We tried various tests, and of course the TAT was one of them. We decided to see how well various specific aspects of content, and general formal features of the stories, could be used in this predictive task (as well as aspects of Self-Interpretation; see Luborsky, 1953). Consequently, we set to work collecting such indicators (or as we called them cues) and looking for them in TAT stories from selected samples of residents who were judged by their supervisors and by their fellows to be the best and the worst of the first group of residents.

Going over the 20 sets of stories from good and poor residents, I tried to list all of the formal features that distinguished the two groups; these

---

[3] The research reported here was supported by the Veterans' Administration, the New York Foundation, and the Menninger Foundation, and was carried out in collaboration with Dr. Lester Luborsky.

were the nucleus of a manual that ultimately grew to a single-spaced typed document of 54 pages. This manual grew by a process of applying the variables to various sets of stories, rewriting, adding qualifications and examples to sharpen the discrimination of better and poorer residents. The manual was organized, following Rapaport, in terms of various features of personality thought to be relevant to functioning as a psychiatrist.

The manual was then subjected to its first real cross-validation when the stories of 34 applicants to the class that entered the Menninger School of Psychiatry in 1948 were analyzed blind. Then at the end of the first year of work by the men who were accepted and entered the school, we got their supervisors' ratings of their over-all competence as psychiatric residents (the criterion). The predictor was the *cue-sum*, the total number of times each positive variables was recorded as present in one of 12 stories told by a subject, minus the number of times negative variables appeared in his stories. This score correlated significantly with the criterion, at around .40 ($p<.05$),[4] the score from the content manual did at least as well, and the sum of cues from the two together correlated approximately .60 ($p<.01$) with our preliminary criterion! This figure was obtained by including two men who had dropped out of psychiatry and assigning them minimal criterion scores, a somewhat dubious procedure; when they were omitted and when a final criterion was available after the men had finished their three years of training, the correlations with supervisors' evaluations of psychiatric competence for the remaining 32 men were not nearly so exciting: for the Formal manual .24 (n.s.); Content .31 ($p<.05$); total, .38 ($p<.01$). By that time, however, we had already revised the manuals in light of the findings on the first cross-validation, and were well launched on a second.

In this final predictive study, the N was nearly twice as large: 64. The manuals had been brought to a condition of high polish, and were applied blind once more, this time during the course of a design too complicated to go into here (see Holt & Luborsky, 1958). Our criterion measures were as good as could be obtained; measures of Overall Competence had an internal consistency of better than .90 ($p<.01$), and were based on close contact with a man's actual psychiatric work.

Three psychologists applied the TAT manuals to the dozen stories told and written by the subjects. Unfortunately, there was not enough time for careful training of the other two raters in the use of these highly judgmental variables, and the degree of agreement in scoring was poor. The coefficients of observer agreement for the cue-sum from the Formal manual were .42 ($p<.01$); .34 ($p<.01$); and .23 ($p<.05$)—all significantly better than chance, to be sure, but by no means adequate for reliability.

It should be no surprise, therefore, that in this second cross-validation the scoring of only one judge, who had written the manual, retained significant validity as a predictor of general psychiatric competence. His (my) cue-sum correlated .22 ($p<.05$) with Overall Competence as judged by supervisors, and .25 ($p<.05$) with the same criterion variables as judged by a man's peers (a sociometric criterion). Though this was a meager result, there was hardly any cross-validation shrinkage (from .24 (n.s.) to .22 $p<.05$), while the validity of the Content manual, no matter who scored it, regressed to zero.[5] If we look at validity not in

[4] One-tailed tests are used throughout to test directional null hypotheses.

[5] This time the validities of the two manuals were not additive, as they had been in the first validation; the total cue-sum for both manuals correlated positively but insignificantly with the criteria. The content manual was quite reliably scored, but had no validity in either this study or in the study of labor mediators.

terms of correlation but in practical terms, of hits and misses through taking men who scored about a critical point in the earlier study and rejecting those who scored lower, we find that the formal manual in my scoring held up quite well: there were significantly fewer misses than would be expected by chance ($p=.02$, one-tailed test), and there were only 4.5 per cent extreme errors (predicting top performance for a man who was inadequate, for example), which is significantly better than the base rate of 18 per cent ($p<.05$).

An additional result gives a clue to the indifferent success of the formal manual's cue-sum as a predictor of Over-all Competence. The formal cue-sums of two judges correlated over .30 ($p<.01$) with Supervisors' Evaluations of *Spontaneity vs. Inhibition*. This aspects of psychiatric residents' behavior was not as relevant to ratings of general competence as many others (criterion evaluations of Spontaneity correlated only .63 ($p<.01$) with Over-all Competence; only two others of the 14 specific criteria correlated less with this, our principal criterion). Consequently, the reserved, quiet, self-contained man who did well in his psychiatric work might have been erroneously rejected if the formal manual had been put into operational use.

So far, we have been talking about the group of formal variables as a whole. Let us look at them individually in some detail.

First, the formal aspects that ended up by having little validity as predictors of psychiatric competence. (This does not necessarily mean that they are not valid indicators of the constructs they were supposed to measure, for in some instances, the latter turned out to be less relevant to psychiatric work than we had thought.) *Comments on the mood, spirit, or connotations of the picture*: this was included as a measure of Cultural Wealth, a variable that in the end had only a slight and tenuous relationship to the criterion. A negative cue, *Vulnerability to unpleasant mood of picture* (a measure of Inadequate Emotional Control), was not scored very often and did not differentiate well. *Expressions of intense inadequacy feelings* (a sign of low Self-Confidence) did not get scored more than once or twice, and so could not demonstrate any validity in this study; we had earlier seen clear manifestations only in men who left the field of psychiatry. A cue to poor Clarity of Thoughts—*Vagueness, overgeneralization, or disjointedness of organization*—did not work, probably because it was not scored strictly enough, for mild degrees of this quality are pretty widespread, even in men who turn out to be quite adequate psychiatrists. Stereotypy of Thought is another personality variable that showed very little relation to the criterion of competence in this sample; one of our measures of it, *Stereotype of story or content*, had no validity. The other *Originality of Story*, did quite well; in my scoring, for example, this one cue correlated .26 ($p<.05$) with Over-all Competence and .27 ($p<.05$) with Diagnosis.

But to return to the less successful cues: *Arbitrary story developments* seemed to be a measure of Emotional Inappropriateness, but did not work very well—probably again because it was not scored strictly enough. I still feel that arbitrary turns of events, forced and unprepared endings, and the like, are good indicators of a lack of sensitivity and appropriateness in emotional expression. *Sensitive descriptions of cards vs. perceptual distortions*: this cue was one of our main measures of Perceptual Sensitivity, a variable that was completely unrelated to the criterion. Apparently the kind of interpersonal sensitivity needed in psychiatry is unrelated to sharp vs. distorted observation of test pictures. Finally, I thought that *Self-references* indicated low Self-Objectivity, which was a relevant enough variable. But although in earlier samples, self-reference remarks had been given predominantly by the poorer prospects, this cue did not work in our final sample.

The list of formal variables that had continuous validity as predictors of psychiatric competence throughout the various trials is not large. The following tended to discriminate better from poorer residents in the scoring of at least two of the three judges in both validity studies, though only my scoring of Originality correlated significantly with Over-all Competence. *Originality of story* also tended to correlated from .23 ($p<.05$) to .26 ($p<.05$) with several specific aspects of proficiency. Indicators of Psychological-Mindedness were also good—*Degree of characterization of figures* in story, and especially *Complexity of motivation or of interpersonal relationships* in story. The former had no significant correlational validities, but the latter predicted Spontaneity vs. Inhibition ($r=.29$; $p<.05$). Genuineness vs. Facade was measured by signs of *Facade*: pretentiousness, pollyannaish concealment of conflicts, or ungenuine behavior by hero (acceptable to teller). Finally, *Evidences of zest and enthusiasm vs. automatism or repetition compulsion* held up fairly well, but did not correlate well with the criterion rating of Spontaneity vs. Inhibition, though it was supposed to be a measure of Adequate Emotional Control.

We also rated *Adequacy of Hero* on most of the cases, though it was put back into the picture after the final predictive study had begun and so was not added in with the sum of formal cues. Taken alone, however, it had even better validity. One other judge scored it as well as myself; our coefficient of agreement was .78 ($p<.01$), which is not bad. In my scoring, it correlated .31 ($p<.01$), with Over-all Competence (Supervisors' Evaluations, $N=53$) and .23 ($p<.05$) to .28 ($p<.05$) with four other criterion variables. As scored by the other judge, it correlated significantly only with the residents' evaluations of competence in Management (.30; $p<.01$) and ward Administration (.33; $p<.01$); my scoring correlated .28 ($p<.05$) with this last criterion, too. It seems reasonable to assume that the self-confidence measured by this TAT variable is particularly useful in running a psychiatric ward smoothly.

So much for the data from the selection of psychiatrists. Finally, I want to cite some further validating data from an independent and quite different study.[6] I had a visit in 1954 from a psychologist at the New York State School of Industrial and Labor Relations, Henry Landsberger, who was planning a study of the personalities of labor mediators. He wanted to use projective techniques including the TAT, and having got wind of the fact that I had developed a method of scoring Formal aspects for the selection of psychiatrists, wanted to try them out on his labor mediators. Rather skeptical that anything would come of it, I nevertheless lent him a copy of the manual and worked a little with Dr. Joan Havel, training her in the scoring of the categories, which she did for him.

A while later, I was quite surprised to hear from Dr. Landsberger that he had completed the testing of 18 labor mediators, and had gotten independent criterion evaluations of their work from people who were closely acquainted with it. With his kind permission, the principal results of the TAT scoring are presented in Table 1. (See also Landsberger, 1956).

Although the sample is small, there are ten significant correlations in this little table indicating relationships of some size. It is almost embarrassing to report such good validities from another study, when my own failed to produce any correlations as large. But it is encouraging that in general the variables correlated best with criteria the meaning of which was closest to

[6] I am very grateful to Dr. Henry Landsberger for permission to cite his findings. Dr. Landsberger adds a caution that the various criteria he used were intercorrelated as were the TAT scores, so that there are strictly speaking not as many independent results as one might think at first glance. He is also working on a cross-validation of these findings.

Table 1
Validities of Formal Aspects of TAT Against Criterion Ratings of 18 Labor Mediators
(Landsberger's study)

TAT Variables	Criterion Ratings					
	Over-all Competence	Originality of Ideas	Intellectual Grasp	The Mediator as "One of us"	Liking for him	Control of Feelings
Stereotypy of Story and Sentiments	*.42*	*.51*	*.41*	.39		
Emotional Inappropriateness	.35			*.41*	.25	.35
Genuineness vs. Facade	*.49*		.29	*.52*	*.50*	.46
Complexity of Motivation	*.42*		.25	*.44*	.37	.24

Note: Italics indicate significance at the 5% level.

them. Thus, *Stereotypy of story and sentiments* correlated best with Originality of Ideas, while the three remaining variables (all of which bear on a person's capacity for interpersonal relationships) correlate best with the interpersonal aspects of mediators' work, expressed in the criterion variable, The Mediator as "One of Us."

In addition to the variables listed in the table, *Vagueness and overgeneralization, Characterization,* and *Originality* were also used, but without significant findings. Two other criterion variables were correlated with the formal aspects scoring but without any significant relationships. It seems odd that *Stereotypy of story and sentiments* should work so well for mediators and not *Originality*, whereas the opposite was true for psychiatrists. Perhaps the difference is that we distinguished between *good* and *bad* originals in the psychiatric study, giving negative scores for stories the originality of which was due to psychopathology, whereas both good and bad originals were scored positively in the study of labor mediators.

CONCLUSION

Test variables of the kind described here are suitable primarily for construct validation (Cronbach & Meehl, 1956); the data given here constitute the beginnings of an attempt to establish construct validity for a few formal aspects of the TAT. The approach of construct validity is slow, and one cannot expect high correlations. If the figures cited here were taken literally as the only basis for paying attention to formal aspects of the TAT, most clinicians might well be forgiven for deciding that they are simply not worth the effort.

Projective techniques have not yet reached the state of development, nor have research methods for validating them, where we can give up that treacherous but indispensable crutch, clinical experience. As I have used the TAT over the years and as I have tried to teach it, I have become more and more convinced that not what is told but how it is told can teach us most about personality, particularly in its structural aspects. Certainly in diagnostic testing we can be of most assistance to the referring psychotherapist, psychiatrist or psychoanalyst by concentrating on personality structure rather than by trying to reconstruct development or interpret symbols. This is not to deny that we can learn a great deal from content; but if the TAT had only its formal aspects to offer us, this vigorous off-spring of a great psychologist would still be indispensable for psychodiagnosis and the experimental study of personality.

Personality Development in Adulthood and Old Age

WILLIAM E. HENRY
and
ELAINE CUMMING

It is self-evident to us all that changes in those attributes of persons normally called personality do indeed occur in the years subsequent to early adulthood. Yet the discovery and clarification of the particular nature of these personality events seems to remain a difficult task. This difficulty may stem in part from our general conceptions of personality as a characteristic of persons which shows the most marked changes and development only in the pre-adult years. We are inclined to think, not without some justification that personality becomes "established"—and by this we seem to mean "fixed"—rather early in life; by five years of age possibly, of by the end of the developmental trials of adolescence, depending upon our theoretical preferences, or upon the particular aspects of personality at which we choose to look. It may also be that we are partially blinded to changes after adulthood by our own middle-age-determined bind to the verities and stabilities of middle class life. In spite of these possible personal or theoretical resistances to the notion of describable personality changes in the later years of adulthood, we all are aware that such changes do occur—at least in other persons.

I should like to call attention first to the possibility of certain conceptions in our views of old age which may lead us to see that age-group more in terms of its similarity to middle-age than in terms of attributes inherent in old-age itself. In review, I will suggest that our conceptions predispose us to use the middle-age status as a model of desirable social and personal development, and hence to see any deviation from this model as negative and undesirable. This may perhaps result in a failure to conceive of old-age as a potential developmental stage in its own right, having features qualitatively different from middle-age.[1]

Our thinking about old age might be described in terms of several themes. The first of these is the theme of middle-age and middle-class bias. Understandably enough, we are inclined to set the standards of behavior of this group as the model for the elderly. It has been noted before that studies dealing with issues of morale and personal adjustment find lower-class persons systematically lower in morale than middle-class persons. We also find ourselves using as indicators of morale for the elderly such questions as "Do you feel useful to those around you?", interpreting the response "No" as an indicator of lowered morale. Feeling useful is certainly an appropriate middle-age virtue, especially to those involved in family life. The implication of higher morale stemming from service to others also appears to be a highly functional middle-class at-

[1] The work which I will describe is the result of the research being conducted by the Committee on Human Development of the University of Chicago by a group of persons of which I am only one. This is the Kansas City Study of Adult Life financed by the National Institute of Mental Health. The study is under the direction of Robert J. Havighurst, Bernice L. Neugarten, with myself as Principal Investigator. The Director of the research is Dr. Elaine Cumming. The work on the sociological and social interaction aspects is centrally that of Dr. Cumming, assisted by Dr. Lois Dean and Mr. David Newell. The theory of disengagement, which constitutes the central axis of this paper is the conception of Dr. Cumming and has been presented by her in another section of this Convention. I will focus today on the personality aspects of this project and report work undertaken by Dr. Louis C. Schaw, Dr. David Gutmann, Miss Jacqueline Rosen under the direction of Dr. Bernice Neugarten and myself.

tribute. What remains unclear is whether the older person should and does feel the same bind in this respect as does his younger counterpart.

A closely related second theme is the assumption of continual expansiveness. We place considerable emphasis, in our own lives, upon keeping up our activities and contacts. Our presumption is that such continued participation in the events of the social world is also a necessary and desirable condition of adequate adjustment beyond the middle years. Thus we advise the older person to continue to develop new interests and new contacts, to replace such interactions as may disappear through retirement or death of associates. This logic seems entirely sound if we have in mind the development more characteristic of the years before middle age, in which an extension of knowledge, experience, and interaction indeed seems appropriate to the eventual goal of active family and social participation in middle age. When the goal and endpoint is, however, death, the model of continued expansiveness seems less appropriate and somehow to ignore the retrenchment and eventual removal from the social nexus of interaction involved in this approaching endpoint.

A third theme deals with the quality of interpersonal relations in the later years. We do assume some change in these relations yet appear to expect that the aged continue to desire instrumentality, that competence in the active management of the environment so valued in the middle years. Thus "feeling wanted," as well as "feeling useful" appear to us as desired attributes of the aged. In a society where in the older years being useful to others is not inevitably linked to being adequately cared for, it would seem more logical to anticipate a desire to be valued not for being useful, but for *having been* useful, for a history of successful instrumentality.

In this model of active, rich, outgoing, satisfying and useful relations which we appear to hold of older persons, it seems odd that we choose to withhold the assumption of active sexuality. While it is clear that we are ambivalent about whether or not sexuality should or should not be present in the older person, a fourth theme would appear to assume its absence. This is, of course, contrary to Dr. Kinsey's findings, who, while he suggests no marked activity, does clearly indicate that the rate of declining sexuality in those years is a rate no greater than that starting after the peak years of adolescence.

The interaction of these various themes seems to imply that old age is not a state into which we move, a state possibly having its own unique attributes, but rather that it is a period of moving away from some previous and more desirable period—"the prime of life" or the "years of usefulness." From this we can only infer that we see the middle-age state as much preferable to the old-age state, and that to retain indefinitely its features constitutes successful aging.

An alternative model of aging would seem to us to have to take into account the possibility of some attributes qualitatively different from those of the middle years and, in particular, that one special "behavioral" feature of age, the inevitability of death. I should like now to state such an alternative theory—a restatement of a theory of disengagement proposed by Dr. Elaine Cumming and stemming from the Kansas City Study of Adult Life. In overview, we see the aging individual as changing gradually from a state of full engagement with the world around him (middle age) to a state of disengagement from it (old age). This process should have aspects similar to the developmental tasks or focal conflicts of the earlier years, at least in that it may be thought of as occurring typically in several stages. If this proposal is reasonable, we would imagine a series of steps somewhat as follows.

Stage one must involve some changes in the perception of time. It is said that the young person never really believes that he will die. This first stage must bring with it some realization of the mortality of life. The thought must occur that time is not infinite. One characteristic of this changed perception may well be the end of the habit of measuring time from birth on and a tendency now to measure it by the distance from our death. Loss of enthusiasm for some kinds of activities and involvements may be the result of this feeling that time is running out and hence must be apportioned according to some principles—saving money becomes less important than traveling, the time required to paint the living room would be better spent in reading. The hidden agenda come to the fore—agenda put off perhaps during the long years of socialization when we learned how to delay personal gratification in exchange for the accomplishment of something others expected of us. It may be the abandonment of the faith that everything is possible because life is long which constitutes the first step in disengagement.

The second stage of disengagement may be concomitant with the vision of the briefness of life, or it may follow shortly after it. It is a shift in saliency between the inner and the outer world. This may in some take the form of religious concerns. In others it may take the more general form of asking oneself what one really is and has been. In whatever format, it would appear to be a stage in which introspection and the contemplation of the inner thoughts begin to replace concerns with outer world demands.

A sharpening of the sense of the shortness of time may be the third stage. Here the thought "time is finite" becomes "time is running out." One of our respondents reports: "I used to read very rapidly when I had all the time in the world left, but now that I am old, I piece my books out, a little each day." He seems to have attached the passage of time to the reading of books and has so arranged it that his life will last as long as his supply of reading matter. A crucial element of this sense of the ending of time seems to be a redefinition of the self as less bound into the surrounding network of social interaction including an anticipation of being more distant from persons nearby. This is in a sense a practicing of loss through a sense of already being disengaged from immediate relationships.

We believe that this sense of social separation is accompanied by a restructuring of the boundaries of the ego—in particular a reduction in object cathexis. This may occur in both the sense of a constriction of ego boundaries which leaves fewer objects in direct contact with the ego and in the sense of a shift in the order of involvement so as to place a higher priority on some kinds of objects as opposed to others.

We would see both of these effects occurring at the point where the psychic investment turns from outside to inside.

In stage five there occurs an actual curtailment of direct contacts with other people—the movement anticipated in the previous stage. This stage is one in which the number of hours of each day spent with people is reduced, even though the number of categories of associates—friends, colleagues, relatives, neighbors—may remain the same. Contrary to general expectation, we think the older person experiences some rewards, rather than loneliness or despair, in this inward turning. As well as finding pleasure in this re-experiencing of the inner life, the aging person may also find new rewards in quite casual contacts which he did not find in the past. He will find himself more responsive to undemanding contacts with comparative strangers, and less interested—unless dependent upon them for food and shelter—in becoming involved in a close and binding way with his own relatives.

It is at this time in his life cycle that the aging person can for the first time since childhood afford to be carefree. With the thinning of his ties of obligation to others, he can gratify some of his more personal desires and ignore some of the harsher strictures of social life. In a study of the deliberations of juries by James and Strodtbeck, Miss James comments that it is the older and the younger people who reach the most lenient verdicts. It is the middle-aged persons, bound to the task of keeping society's rules, who reach the harshest ones. One woman encountered in our study told us that she had returned to work when her children left home, not because she needed the money, but because there they told her just what she was required to do. She remarks that this is much easier than the responsibilities of community organizations she formerly had. "Let the young women worry about the community," she said. "I don't even want to give advice to the young girls I work with, so I don't even eat with them—it's so nice to be free." As Lady Astor, at 80, regrettably not one of our subjects, is quoted by *Time* magazine as saying, "I used to worry about being old. I thought I wouldn't be able to do the things I'd want to do. Now I find I don't want to do anything after all."

This all suggests that the very old person is free to die because he has long since withdrawn himself from the on-going stream of life. In his last years he may pick up old trains of thought, and while enhancing those aspects of living that are immediate and have no consequences, turn back to the thoughts of his own past to relive those older enduring and now undemanding relationships. As one old lady says: "I do so love to be alone. I can think then."

Finally, the movement in extreme old age, readiness for death, leaves the aged person almost totally preoccupied with inner states and with the most instantly gratifying of outside contacts. His pleasures reside in meals, outings, and in friendly, undemanding companionship. In general, he displays behavior characteristic of one who has withdrawn his investment from the world around him and reinvested it in himself.

If the old person faces a crisis appropriate to his age, it may be that of accepting or rejecting the past which supplies the content of his inner life. As Grotjahn (1955) comments: "The task of integrating one's life as it has been lived and the final acceptance of one's own death are problems of existence. To deal with them is the great task of old age. They are essentially different from the tasks of infancy, childhood, adolescence, and maturity."

This process of disengagement involves changes of a social and of a psychological nature. The arguments and data related to the social interaction side of disengagement are presented by Dr. Cumming in her paper at this Convention (Cumming et al., 1959) and elsewhere (Cumming, 1960). I have presented this overall theory here in order that you may more clearly envision the context within which we believe personality changes occur.

The first group of hypotheses which we have which appear to suggest personality changes with age related to the theory posited above are those stemming from a study of younger and middle-aged persons. This is a study conducted quite independently of the Kansas City work principally dealt with here. It involved the Thematic Apperception Test responses of three groups of men employed in administrative positions in business—one group with a mean age of 30 years, one 40, and the oldest group with a mean age of 50. The method of this study is based upon a system for describing and grouping dominant thema and is described elsewhere in a monograph by Schaw and Henry (1956). In this analysis emphasis is placed upon three central elements of personality reflected in the TAT:

1. *The nature of their view of the outer world*—that is, the assumptions regarding the characteristics of people and situations around them.
2. *The nature of the assumptions regarding their own inner world,* that is, their view of the techniques and resources they can

bring to bear upon the solution of outer world problems or the attaining of their personal needs and desires.

3. *The nature of the interaction* proposed between these two worlds and the outcome of this interaction.

For our purposes here, I may briefly summarize our findings. It is apparent, first, that these three groups of men do indeed show changes in these attributes that appear to be related to their differences in age. In particular, the *thirty-year-old* group displays a substantial agreement and consistency in their view of the outer world as achievement-demanding, in their agreement to follow assertively the cues provided them by that outer world, and by their confidence that whole-hearted devotion to these achievement demands will result in the successful accomplishment of their personal ambitions. Thus their preoccupation with inner world contemplation is minimal, their conflict over possible routes of action is minimal as is their discharge of affect and emotion, since their techniques of relating themselves to self-simplified outer world goals are direct and efficient.

The *forty-year-old group* tends to view the world outside them far more in terms of potential conflictual elements and attempt their solution through the utilization of introspection and inner resources. The aim of these problem solutions seems to be an effort to reestablish a sense of personal integrity through a reexamination of their inner drives and goals and a concomitant questioning of the outer world achievement demands — demands which to the 30's seem so right and reasonable. In this situation the direct awareness of their own emotion and affect becomes heightened.

The *fifty-year-old* group continues, as did the 40's, to experience outer world events as conflictful and demanding, yet appears to find a resolution in immediate experience. They move to a heightened involvement with abstract integrative systems with which they preoccupy themselves as an instrument of avoiding specific commitments to action. As in the 40's, increased personality differentiation and complexity occurs. However, in the 40's this complexity appears to serve the ends of integrating inner and outer world to the end of adequate problem solution, whereas for the 50's these processes suggest a compartmentalization within an increasingly isolated inner world.

These findings tentatively suggest the possibility of describing personality changes with age in terms of established personality integrations undergoing rephrasing under the necessity to adjust to internal and external changes. The consistency with which these changes appear in these data suggests that in middle maturity normal working business men experience a need for the reconsideration of established personality patterns. If these factors do indeed constitute an age trend, the rephrasing leads away from the possibility of finding immediate and satisfactory resolutions in terms of the 30-year-olds' conflict-free active mastery, and suggests a movement of energy into an internalized form of passive mastery of an ideal abstracted inner world—a world of their own creation, governed by their own rules.

The basic nature of this principle of change appears to be a movement from an *active, combative, outer world orientation* to an *adaptive, conforming and abstract inner world orientation*.

A further test of this proposal is provided by some parts of a study undertaken by Dr. David Gutmann. Dr. Gutmann's study is based upon TAT material from a group of men ranging in age from 40 to 71.

In a preliminary examination of subjects Gutmann proposed a system of five personality types which appeared to account for the major personality variation found within the sample. In order to submit to examination the question of the relation of these types to age, he composed a larger sample of

145 subjects covering a 40 to 71 year age span and coded each record in such a manner as to disguise their age. He then analyzed each record in terms of its fit to the five personality types and subsequently decoded them and arrayed them by age against type. This permits an estimate of the occurrence of each type by age and a statement of trends with age.

The types in question are themselves arrayed along a continuum analagous to the principle of change appearing in the first study described above—a continuum from the *active, combative outer world orientation* to the *adaptive, conforming inner world orientation*. For the sake of simplicity in presentation, I shall merely identify these as type I through V, it being understood and I and V represent the extremes of this continuum and II, III and IV represent intermediate steps. There is in these types no assumption of adjustment or maladjustment, though such a relationship may appear upon subsequent investigations. Thus a predominance of types I and II suggests a group of persons actively involved in relating themselves to the world of outer events. A preponderance of types III, IV, and V suggests a movement away from such outer world involvement and an increased emphasis upon internal, self-oriented events.

Before the relation of type to age was tested for significance, one further analytic judgment was made. Each case was judged to be either an *Externalizer* or an *Internalizer*. This judgment was made, again blind for age, on the grounds of a series of predetermined criteria related to the extremes of the outer world to inner world orientation discussed earlier. On the theory that personality change, if it appeared, would be clearer if related to initial overall personality type, the cases were examined within each overall type, that is, the Externalizers were examined for the relation of age to type, and then the Internalizers. In the Externalizers we find a relation of types to age which on a Chi Square method is statistically significant at beyond the .01 level. This clearly suggests an overall trend with age in the direction of increased preoccupation with inner world events and an increased isolation from outer world stimulation. At the same time it implies a reduction in the assertive combative elements and an increase in conforming passive mastery through inner life contemplation. In the Internalizers an identical trend is found, though significant at between the .02 and .05 level of confidence. This slightly different confidence level may be an artifact of the sample, and may indeed reflect a tendency for those who are basically more prone to Internalization to change less noticeably—even though still in the direction of increased internalization. Combining the group shows the same trend significant at the .02 level.

These data are in effect clinical judgments which may or may not be reproducible by another person. We are now in the process of investigating the reliability with which these judgments may be made. However, Dr. Gutmann (1959) has already devised a system of scoring, in a more objective fashion, certain elements of TAT stories which reflect, or so we believe, the same psychologic issues embodied in the types. The first test of this system, when related to age in the same sample of subjects, shows developments paralleling the shift in types already seen. These changes are significant at the .05 level when we divide them by three age groups, and at the .001 level when we deal with only the bottom and top third (Gutmann, Henry, & Neugarten; 1959).

These data appear to us to suggest the same kind of disengagement from the social nexus of interrelation posited by our overall theory. They would appear to contain one element in addition to the increased interiority required in that theory. That element is the seeming reduction in active to passive modes of problem solution which accompanies the shift in saliency from the outer to the inner world.

In another quite independent study, Miss Jaqueline Rosen has undertaken to examine age changes in personality in the same basic sample of cases. Her sampling permits attention to categories of class, and sex, as well as age. Cases were again rated blind for all these sample components, each index being rated separately to avoid the possible halo effect of one index upon another.

The issues dealt with stem from reflections upon Zygmunt Piotrowski's discussion of the Rorschach M-response but should not necessarily be seen as a test of that concept.

The issues may be roughly called estimates of ego energy and divided into

1. Estimates of the *extent of involvement of ego in outer world events.*
2. *The qualitative nature* of these involvements.

The *ego involvement* issues are measured by two scores:

1. The number of introduced figures in stories. Here the logic proposes that it requires more spontaneous ego involvement to burden a story with figures not actually pictured in the stimulus than to compose a story dealing only with the picture figures.
2. The presence in a story of any element of content involving "conflict" or "controversy." By this it is meant the introduction of any reference to issues requiring decision, choice, self-denial, argument—the introduction of any reference to issues requiring decision, choice, self-denial, argument—the proposal being that it requires more ego involvement to do so than is required to either merely describe and enumerate or to compose a plot completely devoid of such impeding or controversial points. This applies whether or not the story is negative or positive in tone.

The *quality of ego energy* is measured by two indices:

1. The rating of emotional intensity, based on an estimate of the extent to which any affect states described actually play a role in the story.
2. A count of whether the activity described is assertive rather than passive.

These four indices once decoded and distributed by age, sex, and social class were submitted to an analysis of variance. Neither the social class nor sex components account for any significant proportion of the variance in any of these indices. Age, however, does.

All four indices show significant declines with age, the breakpoints differing somewhat.

1. The ego involvement measures both decline, the count of posing of conflict and controversy breaking between 40 and 50, and the count of introduced figures holding up until between 50 and 60.
2. The quality of involvement indices also shows declines with age, the shift from assertive to passive affect occurring between 40 and 50, and the intensity of affect declining progressively but showing significant differences only when comparing the 40's with the 60's.

These results, framed in somewhat different concepts, appear to us to strengthen the definite shift toward internal preoccupations and to passive techniques of problem mastery seen in the material presented earlier.

When seen in the light of our overall theory of disengagement, these personality changes seem consistent with, and a necessary accompaniment of the gradual process of disentangling the self from the network of mutual responsibilities, social interactions, and strong object cathexis so characteristic of the middle-age years.

I have not dealt as yet with the crucial question of how these developments in the psychological and social aspects of older age relate to issues of morale and of successful adaptation to the demands of deriving for oneself a state of mind consistent with a personal universe shrinking both from inside and from without.

We do, however, have some, as yet insufficient, evidence of that accompanying sense of passive enjoyment and that sense of isolation without desolation which our theory proposes. We also have an Index of Morale, reliable in its derivation and independent of social class factors, which we hope will be the key to those relationships. Now I can only report that those individuals who are age-inappropriate in terms of the developments described—whether among our middle-aged or our old-age subjects—tend to be those of low morale. We do imagine that it will turn out that there will be, within the overall framework of this disengaging trend, more than one style of aging positively correlated with high morale.

If any major portion of the findings of this research can be substantiated in parallel investigations, we believe that we do indeed have evidence of developmental demands characteristic of old age and qualitatively different from the developmental stages of childhood, adolescence, and adulthood. If so, the central axis of this stage is the process of disengagement— which serves as the mechanism for integrating one's life as it has been lived and the final acceptance of the reality of death, as Dr. Grotjahn has commented—and as a logical parallel of Erik Erikson's (1959) focal conflict of this age, ego-integrity versus despair, and of the psychological modality of that period, "To be, through having been to face not being."

Projections on a Triptych; or a Hagiology for Our Time[1]

EDWIN S. SHNEIDMAN

While roaming aimlessly through a large and wonderful museum recently, I came upon—in a dim cul-de-sac apart from the main gallery—a particularly fascinating triptych. Its three panels, each with the representation of a sainted figure, instantly caught my eye. Being in a reverent mood, it captured my interest, and I, having that day an active spirit that was susceptible to random stimulation of this kind, found my imagination excited by its mysteries. The presentations in this short paper are, in part, a result of the ruminations initiated by that triptych.

In that I aspire to deal with some abstractions in this paper, I shall, for purposes of contrast, begin by being specifically concrete, that is, by showing you that very same triptych, which, to use a euphemism, I "borrowed" from the museum at a moment when my favorite guard, who happens to wear a hearing aid, had momentarily turned his back. Permit me to add that I fully intend to return it at the earliest possible opportunity. Here it is. (See Figure 1).

Looking at the triptych, you will notice that the left panel depicts St. Carl Gustav, patron of printing. He is the special saint of ink and printers' tools. His domains of benign influence include workers with ordinary and special inks, bottled ink, spilt ink, and, of course, ink blots. He is concerned with printers' types of all sorts, including daguerreotypes, linotypes, and archetypes. He is the protector of the special graphic arts, and thus one can refer to him as the saint of the idiographic. We shall have more to say about him.

The panel on the right is, as I hope you can see, one of St. Icarus. He is the saint of the air, of breezes and of gales. He is especially endeared to baloonists and those of us who purchase insurance policies in airline terminals. His interests include all things gaseous and aerial: hurricanes, cyclones, vacuums, winds, flat tires, pneumatic drills—all of pneumatics, and he is therefore often called the saint of the pneumathetic, which, as you well know, is usually mispronounced as nomothetic.

The middle, and perhaps most important, saint is St. Herman. He was an early divine who is noted for his preaching among the mountains and near the lakes, and is known to have died an untimely death after delivering his ten tablets—each remarkable for its ambiguity—to an eager world. Those of you who are versed in the history of our Society know the story well. But I have not indicated what he is saint of. In that this aspect of his character is crucial to the development of my theme, I shall hold this secret for awhile until a more auspicious moment for the revelation of his complete identity.

We have, at this point, partially identified our complement of these extraordinary personages. In this fruitful triptych we have the saint of the idiographic, the saint of the nomothetic, and the saint of aspects as yet unknown. Now our task is to see in what directions our own projections on this brief hagiology can lead us.

Let us begin with the saint of the nomothetic. Notice, in the figure on the right, the elegance, exactitude and precision of his garb. There is an

[1]Presidential address delivered at the annual meeting of the Society for Projective Techniques, St. Louis, Missouri, August 31, 1962. This paper was written while the author was a U.S. Public Health Service Special Research Fellow (1961-1962), at the Department of Social Relations, Harvard University, studying with Dr. Henry A. Murray.

FIGURE 1

apocryphal story that the book that he is holding contains tables of random numbers; another story holds that it is much more organized and is filled with mean heights and weights, average IQ's, median M's and W's and so forth, for every major country in the world, divided, of course, for sex and pathological diagnostic category. His sermons are a joy to hear. Maybe not a joy exactly, but they are remarkably distinct and clear. He never says a sentence except that he takes pains to say it exactly the same way on another occasion. He can be depended upon—for that. It is said that he speaks an elegant Coptic but there are very few of us who can apply what he says to the pressing problems of our everyday lives. Some of us would, to confess it outright, trade some of his precision and reverence—and it might be added that his reverence seems to be for his precision—for a little more that is practical and relevant to the activities of ordinary (and extraordinary) human living. His published summarization, in Latin, of the average proportions of the fifty cathedrals in our country was inexplicably impressive, but in our secret hearts we would have appreciated more his discussing with us — in vulgate—how to put the roof on our own church. His concern with all of God's creatures is remarkable, but, lamentably, almost to the exclusion of his interest in man. For some reasons (wondrous to speculate on), he is especially devoted to the dog and the rat, although he has also been known to keep pigeons. For him, the proper study of mankind is math. But, withal, we are happy to say that we have many good friends among those who are devout members of his parish.

On the other hand, our idiographic saint has, as one might suspect, something of a different personality. It is said that on more than one occasion he has refused to take up a collection because he did not believe in aggregates. In his long walks through the country-side with his neophytes he will often divine the meanings of cloud formations in such a way as to border on the miraculous, but he does not (or cannot) tell exactly how it is done, and it has been noted (no doubt only by disaffected detractors) that he has, more than once, made rather different pronouncements to rather similar situations. Inasmuch as all of his interpretations seem so sensible and meaningful, this unforeseen plethora of riches introduces the embarrassing problem as to which of his quite different prescriptions to believe. It might be added as an aside, that a hurried consultation with our nomothetical saint did not resolve the dilemma, for he was able to supply us only with information about cloud formations in general, how they varied as to season, altitude, and potentiality for precipitation. Our idiographic saint sticks pretty closely to humans, and seems especially interested in the confessional. He appears to believe that every situation is absolutely unique, and, even further, that some situations are more unique than others. He has great self-confidence and undiminished zeal in relation to his own beliefs. Once, for example, he was asked if he believed in baptism. "Believe in it?" he is reported to have replied, "Why Good Lord, man, I've seen it!" He is very diligent by nature, and has been known to devote himself for days and weeks to the study of the written biography of a single individual, feeling that if he understood this one person he could thereby know something of great importance about the particularities and universalities in every man. It can be added that even our nomothetic saint is fond of him but thinks that he is hopelessly (but romantically) muddle-headed, and tells him so. In light of this last fact, it is somewhat difficult to understand why, when one of the brothers of the nomothetic saint suffered from phobias and nightmares, he sent him, for counsel, to his idiographic colleague. The ways of the world—and of saints—are marvelous to behold and oftentimes impossible to fathom.

At this point, the big question in my mind is whether or not we must limit our choice between these two side panels. There seem to be some whose words would rather imply that we must. But you will note that when these esteemed persons ask us to choose between these two—the clinical and the actuarial—we are able to do just that (and to ameehliorate the situation), not by picking one *or* the other as they would seem to imply that we must (and indeed they even suggest which one we ought to choose), but by selecting a position *in* between the two side panels. This type of choice permits us to avoid a totally unnecessary dichotomy and allows us to concentrate on the *quality* of the conceptual nature of our normative or individually-oriented enterprises.

As a small addendum, one can note too that the dichotomizers, it turns out after further thought, may not have been correct even in their initial premise regarding this polarity, for we see that Michael Polanyi, in his *Study of Man,* reminds us that Windelband (who, in 1894, thought up these notions in the first place in order to distinguish between the apparently unique character of historical events and the seemingly repetitive character of events in the natural sciences) did "not say that the field of reality can be divided into the subjects of nomothetic and idiographic knowledge," but rather said something quite different, namely that these two are forms of knowledge, and are, so to speak, simply "two logically distinct parts of all knowledge." Logicaly, there may be other logical positions.

Further, we can note that other conceptualizations of these different emphases of approach have been formulated. That most eminent Professor of Philosophy, the late Morris Cohen, in his review of Dewey's *Essays in Experimental Logic,* insightfully combined philosophers and scientists and then described two main species of either, as follows: "Among philosophers as among scientists we may roughly distinguish two types that may be called the mathematical and naturalistic. The mathematicians excel in grasping some fruitful idea and elaborating it with such a perfection or finality of form that humanity is compelled, through sheer admiration, to strain the facts to make them fit these perfect forms. The naturalists, on the other hand, are more eager to observe the actual facts in their naked natural state. They love accuracy more than elegance. That philosophers can write with their eye on the object of their observation rather than on the symmetry of their final system, careful readers of Aristotle and Kant know full well. Nevertheless, the prevailing temper among philosophers has been the mathematical one; for all the great men of science whose achievements have stirred the human imagination, from the days of Euclid and Archimedes down to Copernicus, Galileo, and Newton, have been mathematicians. It was only in the middle of the nineteenth century, and most notably in the case of Darwin, that men of the naturalistic type succeeded in impressing humanity with results of the first magnitude."

The general point that we wish to make at this juncture is this: rather than to argue the relative merits of the idiographic or nomothetic approach (or to decide the merits of an approach in terms of whether it is essentially idiographic or nomothetic), it would make much more sense to inquire about the "goodness" of the conceptualizations. If poor concepts abound, neither idiography nor nomothetics will be fruitful: if rich concepts are present, it may not then be critical whether the enterprise is primarily one or the other, in that the quality of the concepts may superordinate the label.

A brief personal digression may be

useful here. As some of you know, I have, for the past year, been at Harvard University enjoying the great pleasures of talking to and listening to a number of their illustrious professors in such varied fields and disciplines as social relations, psychology, philosophy, human development, public health, public administration, psychiatry, etc. In casting my mind back over the memories of this year's experience, I have taken delight in thinking *ad hominem,* characterizing each of these eminent teachers in terms of a famous historical personage. Thus, in the contemporary Harvard scene, in the departments I have mentioned, I have found one professor who espouses a Cartesian point of view, one who is a present-day Plutarch, one who attempts to emulate Ebbinghaus; there is a Leibnitz, a Mahan, a deTocqueville, a Breughel, a Linnaeus, and so on. Now, in line with the *ad hominem* approach, one is not precluded from making personal comparisons among these worthies. But how? It seems to me that the most relevant dimension is one of *timeliness.* Did not Aristotle himself say that it is the mark of an educated man to know the degree of precision (referring to both observation and report) that is most appropriate to each state in the development of each realm of knowledge? And, if one may quote a Yale man in this context, do we not have the dictum of F. S. C. Northrop "that to talk about scientific method apart from specification of the specific stage of inquiry for a given type of problem is . . . meaningless"? Who then, *in our field,* are for our time and who are anachronistic? Who are most appropriate, useful, meaningful in terms of the paramount scientific needs of our time? One must first ask, what are these needs? Is it not true, as that great modern-day Harvard Linnaeus—who believes that psychology is the scientific study of *man* and that "the marked deficiency in our supply of ordered knowledge about compound types of normal human beings is that psychology in its anxious, importunate determination to become an accredited experimental science, skipped the basic naturalistic stage of careful observation, description and classification which has constituted the first chapter in the development of all other sciences that deal with different varieties of entities"—has said that it is most appropriate for psychologists at our present stage of development to be "man-watching naturalists"?

For those of us who feel more comfortable with the identification and status that accrues to a party label, who have been debating between conservative idiography and radical nomothetics, the banner of liberal personology—with its specific humanistic orientation—has a great deal to recommend it. The personologist selects from both extremes. He is not content to know some few pre-selected facts about many people, or many facts about only one person, but rather he aspires to investigate intensively several people—paranormal, normal, supernormal—seeking what is common to all, present in some, and unique to each, all the while keeping his inner eye open for new groupings, new families or idiosyncracies, new human complexes. The personologist is bold enough to modify the traditional courtroom oath: he swears to investigate the individual, all the individual, but stops short of limiting himself to nothing but the individual, for he includes the individual in his natural habitat and in his pacific and stressful dyadic relationships. Further, the personologist uses—or feels free to select among—all the available psychological tests that meet his purposes of immediate observation and subsequent classification. He feels equally free to invent and construct new devices, instruments, techniques and procedures as the situation and the terrain demand. He is concerned as much with the creative analysis of conversations within the social hour as of consultations within the therapy hour. He searches out opportunities to engage in bold theoretical reflections as well as in rigorously sophisticated researches; he tries to direct himself away from the trivially clear and the clearly trivial. These flexibilities of approach, taken together with his goals (of studying human subjects in meaningful ways) may permit him to ford swollen streams of consciousness, cross chasms between dichotomous bluffs, avoid jungles of mazes, traverse deserts of scientific aridity, and get over mountains of information—on the long march to the promised lands. He is, as you can see, an adventurer as well as a pioneer.

I wish to reiterate my belief concerning our optimal primary orientation. We are not atomic physicists, not Boolean algebratists, not experimental biologists, not particulate physiologists, not symbolic logicians—but rather we are, or ought to be, man-watching naturalists.

Our prayer is for more modern Linnaeuses and for more Linnaean attitudes in all of us. It seems that we, in sheer sibling-emulation of sister sciences have shown unnecessary celerity in trying to close the doors of our incompletely constructed taxonomic barns. The great difference between us and some of the physical and other biological sciences is that they have their cows and sheep and horses inside the barn, counted and classified, whereas our barn is both somewhat empty and the clusterings of the inhabitants are definitely confusing. Along with the nonsense of locking the barn door after the horse is stolen is the equal foolishness of freezing the shape of the incubator before the unhatched chickens are counted.

The Board of Trustees of the Society has, as part of its on-going responsibilities, given serious thought to the useful extension of the role and scope of the Society. One of the suggestions seriously entertained was that of redesignating our organization as the Society for Projective and Assessment Techniques. The idea has considerable appeal, but I am still bedeviled by the feeling that I do not satisfactorily know how our subjects project, or how we, as psychologists, assess. I might almost be tempted, if this were the beginning of my tenure rather that its conclusion, to propose instead that we consider calling our group the Society for Paradigmatic Techniques. Such a designation might be more accurate and more challenging, for one of the ways that we might face our reality is by recognizing that much of our reality is abstract.

What does it mean to believe in paradigms? For one thing it means that we abandon our belief in many of the melancholy Santa Clauses of contemporary psychiatry and clinical psychology. These not-so-happy mythical figures masquerade under such names as alcoholism, delinquency, schizophrenia, suicide, homosexuality, and so on. The Santa Claus belief is that all adults are either homosexual or heterosexual—that all cases of schizophrenia—whatever that is—are hebephrenic, catatonic, paranoid, or simple (sometimes complicated with such modifiers as sub, latent, pre, incipient, borderline, chronic, acute, pseudo, etc.). We all know that schizophrenia has been variously divided into two types, six types, four types; that schizophrenia has been thought of as metabolic (Kraepelin); paleological (Arieti); ego deficiency (Alexander); emergence of the archaic (Jung); habit disorganization (Meyer); projection of repressed homosexual desires (Freud); etc. And even this brief recitation omits the more recent notions of schizophrenogenic mothers, autonomic balance, psychotic plasma, reticular formation, and the drug of the week. Clearly, we cannot treat and cure until we can achieve understanding; clearly, the need is to set aside conceptualizations of little usefulness and to strive for powerful concepts and for viable taxonomies.

One additional illustration (of the near-uselessness of some of our current keystones) may suffice. This example has to do with suicide. In regard to "suicidal" aspects of personality, what we do currently is to measure our Rorschach, TAT, Blacky, MAPS test, Szondi, House-Tree-Person and anamnestic protocols against the criteria of "non-suicidal" versus "suicidal"—the latter sometimes being further subdivided among commit, attempt, and threaten,—often overlooking whether our subject did, is, will, won't; often gainsaying all the complexities of the individual's belief systems about death, hereafter, rebirth; often neglecting his particularized ways of reasoning and his idiosyncratic logical styles; often ignoring his special need systems and his individual constellation of press; often forgetting that he is engaged in dyadic relationships of great variety and nuance; often closing our eyes to a multiplicity of possible unique psychodynamic ferments and ego organization; often side-stepping the issues of ego-passivity and ego-activity. Such delinquencies of omission seem to be part and parcel of our most honored current enterprises. For my part, if I know anything about suicidal phenomena it is that the present-day crude classification (or assemblage of gross categories) is essentially confusing, if not downright obfuscatory. This is one reason why some of my own efforts in this field in the past year have been directed toward the attempt to develop new classifications and fresh models to embrace many behaviors now loosely labeled as suicidal. Very briefly, I have been concerned specifically with such concepts as cessation, termination, interruption, and continuation, particularly the variety of "orientations towards cessation" which can be conceptualized in terms of the individual's intention—but this is not the appropriate setting for an explication of those thoughts. However, it is appropriate to remark that classifications of observed and elicited phenomena under these (and other relevant) rubrics would be a necessary beginning to meaningful understanding—and ultimately to preventing, controlling, predicting, treating—these now only dimly understood self-destructive and other-effecting behaviors.

I hope that I have made the point—really two points are implied: one, that in our field there is no *ding,* only data; and two, that, further, we know no pure-color data, only hypothesis-saturated data. We have no choice—regardless of our personal intolerance for ambiguity and our concomitant need for structure, reliability, precision, elegance, pseudo-certainty—but to subsume our professional lives under the purview of hypotheses, analogies, paradigms, and constructs.

It would appear, at first thought, that what I am saying is that individuals in clinical psychology and psychiatry have to deal primarily with the methodological problems attendant to *construct* validity. But, even on this very issue, let us see what our second thoughts contain.

We all know the proposal regarding types of validity so lucidly enunciated by the APA Committee on Test Standards in 1952, a classification which included predictive validity, status validity, content validity, and congruent or construct validity. (There is a new committee presently at work on this formulation, addressing itself to a remodeling of this decade-old formulation).

Our re-reflections about construct validity might lead us to reaffirm its crucial role in our enterprise, but as we examine the concept itself we might well conclude that it contains two major shortcomings. The first is that the phrase "construct validity" might turn out to be an interesting contradiction in terms. It is, if you see what I mean, like saying "untestable truth," or "debatable fact," or "transient verity," or "unsubstantiated belief," or "unreal reality." That is to say, to conceptualize in terms of construct validity is tantamount to stating that one insists that the phenomena under investigation correlate high with ideas that one somehow trusts and with taxonomies, usually implicit and unverbalized, whose ordering of the universe into apparent phenomena (implied by the taxonomy) one has unconsciously or uncritically accepted as either optimal or real.

A second major shortcoming latently contained in the concept of construct validity is the possible general confusion between validity and other types of verifiability; that is, the danger of assuming that an explication of types of validity exhausts the topic of "truth." The propositions within contemporary psychology appear to be amenable to division among a relatively few major different degrees of confirmation, conceptual buttressing and/or empirical verification. Thus, within psychology, there appears to be a certain range, containing perhaps no more than three or four more-or-less similar degrees of precision of prediction and exactness of repeatability (ranging from unprovable to plausible) compared with the larger number of precision-uncertainty positions within the totality of sciences and disciplines. Recognizing this, we should, in our activities and pursuits, be continuously committed to correcting our speculations, insofar as is possible, against facts and data. Further, we may have to extend our thoughts about psychological truth not only to include the notions of degrees of certainty, precision, and completeness, but also to encompass the concepts of espousal, proof, and maximum verifiability, along with the ideas of validity. One implication of this is that a classification of types of validity (which might well include something akin to construct validity) would be only one sub-section in a large array of several ways of cognizing our findings and taking our data to our bosom.

It needs to be added that the outmost reaches of verifiability which any data can possess may be set by the theoretical notions with which they are identified. In this sense, it may be that the maximum possible "validity" of the Rorschach technique, for example, as most of us who use it currently conceptualize it, may be somewhat less (but certainly not one whit greater) than the present veridicality status of the psychoanalytic personality concepts (like super-ego control, latent homosexuality, regression in the service of the ego, etc) which currently give the Rorschach technique its theoretical vitality and its intellectual permissiveness.

If "validity" is a concept that we wish to preserve, it may be most useful at this time to employ a straightforward description of each particular study in terms of a rather simple common-sense classification of (a) validity from *whom* (describing the subjects, the examiners and the judges in terms of the variables deemed to have major relevance); (b) validity for *when* (in terms of future variables or prediction, past variables or postdiction, or more-or-less present variables or what I call paridiction); (c) validity for *which* (in terms of either factual variables or inferred variables); (d) validity for *what* (in terms of the stimuli which were employed and the continua or dimensions along which it is believed that those stimuli are deployed); and (e) *how* validity was established (in terms of the statistical and other manipulative procedures employed). This brief spelling-out of the process for each study would increase initial understanding and facilitate replication by making explicit the concepts (in the stimuli, in the personnel, in the situation, etc.). It would underscore one main point of this presentation: that we recognize the abstract and essentially paradigmatic quality of our constructs.

Retrospecting over our brief trail, it would appear that we have attempted to build markers at four separate points. They are these:

1. The current view of the psychodiagnostic field as idiographic or nomothetic is unnecessary dichotomous, limiting our vision to the two side panels and focussing our attention away from the center ring of contemporary thought.

2. Whether idiographic, nomothetic, or whatever, most of our psychological realities are concepts—constructs, metaphors, analogies, paradigms.

3. Some of us have greater need for certainty and structure than others. One way of seeking to achieve certainty is by way of validity, and that type of validity which apparently has most relevance for the psychodiagnostic enterprise is construct validity. But the concept of construct validity may itself imply a contradiction in terms in the sense that one cannot have nonreality (constructs) and certainty (validity) as part of a single encompassment. The concept of construct validity may reflect too much of the nomothetist's need for preciseness at the expense of relevance.

4. It is believed to be axiomatic that before one can meaningfully and efficiently treat, predict, help, one has to understand, and, further, that the heart of understanding depends upon meaningful taxonomy or classification. Our great current need is for multiple viable classifications. In relation to this orientation, the position of the personologist has much to recommend it. This position holds that psychologists should be "man-watching naturalists," finding, describing, and systematizing the multifarious individual and social behaviors of their fellow human creatures.

But we have yet to talk about St. Herman. What kind of a saint is he? What is he saint of? Here was a mystery indeed. Permit me to share with you the process whereby this puzzlement was solved. By examining the painting carefully, I discovered that there were, on the podium in the middle panel, two small silver coin-like objects. Accordingly, I took the triptych to a Professor of Classical Numismatics—an elderly Englishman whose hobby was the coining of phrases—who, to my great delight, identified each of those two objects as a denarius, that is, a Roman coin worth exactly ten cents. In light of the fact that there were two of them, he suggested that the figure in the panel be called the Saint of the Pair o' Dimes! And so he is: the saint of analogies, allusions, allegories, abstractions, models, patterns, conceptualizations; the saint of if as-if then but-then! He is, I propose, the patron saint of our Society.

As a last thought, I wish to state that the Society for Projective Techniques should make haste slowly by manifesting autonomy, initiative, integrity, maturity, at its own rate; and that this rate should be set at a pace which is consistent with its own nature, its own ego, its own needs, its own development, and its own identity.

Saints preserve us!

The Metamorphosis of Projective Methods[1]

WALTER G. KLOPFER

Summary: Early approaches to projective methods emphasized the use of unstructured materials as stimuli designed to elicit symbolic material within a psychoanalytic framework. Current theorizing concerning projective methods emphasizes the multi-level nature of test behavior and the unique role that projective methods play in the assessment armamentarium.

When projective techniques were first popularized in the United States in the late 1930s they received a very mixed reception. Those American practitioners who had been trained in the psychometric tradition were extremely ill at ease with techniques that seemed to demand so much in the way of clinical judgment and qualitative appraisal. Even the so-called 'scores' used in connection with the Rorschach apparently lacked psychometric reliability and other desirable characteristics.

On the other hand, projective methods were warmly welcomed by those American psychologists who were more psychoanalytically oriented. This was because personality assessment, from a psychoanalytic point of view, emphasized the 'basic' personality. Basic herein implies a focus upon factors of which the subject was not consciously aware. Early advocates of the projective approach described their techniques as x-rays of the personality and imputed a sort of magical quality to them which would enable the assessor to detect the 'true' characteristics of the individual in spite of any attempt on the part of the subject taking the test to bring ego-defenses into play in an effort to deceive the examiner. Early research on the Rorschach, such as that of Fosberg (1938) seemed to lend some credence to this assumption.

Since that time a vast literature concerning the validity and predictive efficiency of projective techniques has grown up in the United States. Regrettably, much of this has been partially or totally ignored in the European literature. In many of the German journals, for example, a kind of polarization is described in which there are the *good* guys and the *bad* guys. The good guys are psychoanalytically oriented, use subjective methods of appraisal, deplore the use of probability statistics, and espouse the ideographic approach to personality assessment. The bad guys, on the other hand, use objective and empirical methods, couch their findings in quantitative terms, and tend to favor the nomothetic approach. Within this kind of polarized dichotomy, much of the research conducted by American psychologists on projective methods has been written off as irrelevant, inappropriate, and worthless.

However, in the viewpoint of the present writer, projective techniques do not have to be regarded either as a shibboleth to be refuted or defended, or a panacea which will enable the diagnostician to put aside all other tools. Rather, they are a necessary, but not sufficient means for understanding both the individual personality and the characteristics of groups. As the profession has gone forward in its increasing sophistication regarding projective methods, the latter have been more clearly defined on a continuum in terms of what they measure. Tests with a good deal of structure, like sentence completion methods, for example, seem to depend for their value mainly upon the cooperation of the subject taking the test. They can be interpreted simply as structured interviews, requiring the subject to answer questions just as he would if he were asked directly; or, the subject can assume a more spontaneous stance and thus reveal aspects of his personality of which he may not be consciously aware. Tests of the thematic variety, as graphically documented in a book by Murstein

[1] Based in part upon a paper presented to the International Congress of Rorschach and Other Projective Techniques on August 5, 1968 in London, United Kingdom.

(1963), are not clearly related to material of which the subject taking the test is unaware. Rather, the material obtained by means of the Thematic Apperception Test (TAT) is, as Leary (1957) termed it, 'preconscious,' or privately symbolized. Leary has postulated a level which he calls the "unexpressed unconscious" which deals with needs the individual may possess, but which are not expressed in projective tests. Thus, there is suggested the possibility that even the expression of a psychological need on a projective test may imply a certain readiness on the part of the person being tested to bring the need close enough to awareness so as to be able to verbalize it and communicate it to the examiner administering the test.

Another important kind of research which has bearing on our theoretical model is that kind which deals with the stimulus properties of the test itself. For example, Klopfer and Borstelmann (1950) in regards to the Szondi Test; Suczek and Klopfer (1952) in regards to the Bender-Gestalt; and Baughman (1959) in connection with the Rorschach, have all demonstrated quite convincingly that the results of projective tests are not only a function of the subject taking the test and what he projects into the situation, but also a function of the test itself and its stimulus-demand properties. A recent tendency on the part of persons investigating the Rorschach Test, has been to investigate both the cards and selected responses by means of the semantic differential method developed by Osgood, Suci, and Tannenbaum (1957).

Indeed it would appear that projective tests, having lost their apparently magical potentialities for revealing all important aspects of the personality, are becoming sufficiently differentiated from each other so that specific aspects of the personality can be illuminated as the psychologist desires it. There are, of course, those psychologists, especially in the U.S. whose system of assessment and psychotherapy completely obviates the necessity for utilizing projective methods. Included in this group are the enthusiasts of behavioral modification as a means of adjusting people with emotional problems. Since their method seeks only to identify the symptoms that the individual consciously would like to have eradicated, they are not interested in causes, and any attempt to probe more deeply into the personality is obviously not necessary. Thus, the behavioral modifiers can get along without projective techniques. Another group of practitioners who can do without them are the client-centered psychologists who do all of their counseling without regard for either the patient's past or the aspects of his motivation of which he himself is unaware. Within this frame of reference, any knowledge of the patient which the patient does not himself freely and consciously render to the therapist, becomes undesired and undesirable. Still a third group of practitioners who do not require projective techniques as part of their armamentarium, are those psychoanalysts who are so convinced of the universality of dynamics as described in the early literature that they fail to see the need for any individual evaluation of personality. Thus, if one were to be convinced that all people with marital problems have unresolved Oedipal complexes, that all persons with paranoid schizophrenia have latent homosexuality, etc., there would be little need to determine the truth or falsity of these hypotheses, as they would be, rather, certainties. Thus, it can be seen that projective techniques can be cast aside on many pretexts. Of course, the same individuals as described above who would relinquish the need for projective methods might also very well be able to do without objective methods of personality assessment, interviews with family members, or other aspects of the diagnostic process.

Thus it appears that the individual who is left with the need for projective techniques is the clinical psychologist, who really experiences an intense need to understand each individual who comes across his professional path as an entirely new problem in evaluation. He would probably want to know something about his public image, as determined from his way of influencing those around him, and from his personal and work history. He would also want to know on what bases the individual made cognitive judgments about himself as gleaned from interviews or other sources of self-report; and he would certainly not want to ignore the individual's motivations insofar as he was barely or not at all aware of them. Thus, projective techniques become identified as the major source of information concerning this last aspect of the assessment approach. In a recent survey of the research literature on the Rorschach Test conducted by the present writer (Klopfer, 1968), it was discovered that the content of the test seemed to lend itself more readily to predicting observable behavior, than other aspects such as formal scoring. Perhaps this is because the personality areas that were of interest to Rorschach and Jung are no longer part of the concern of the clinical psychologist engaged in the assessment procedure. The kind of typologizing which characterized the early part of the century was related to the atmosphere of somatotyping and pigeon-holing which was typical of that era. There was much faith in the propostion that once a few objectively verifiable facts could be determined about a given individual, that all else would follow, and that predictions concerning other areas of functioning could be made with great accuracy. Perhaps the reason that Rorschach content is gaining impetus as a predictive device is because we are now trying to predict what the individual will do and say and not whether he will be identified as a member of a certain class or type on the basis of some other test procedure. Thus the matter of predictive efficiency is more highly valued today as a criterion of validity than is the concurrence of one test interpretation with another.

In conclusion, the theorist of today considers a projective test as a stimulus with known properties, which interacts with a perceiving subject, and produces certain verbal or graphic results. As far as projective test behavior has known correlations with other kinds of behavior, it is possible to save time and effort by predicting from one situation to another. Furthermore, the projective test situation since the individual is unable to control his responses consciously, is more likely to reveal aspects of functioning which are socially undesirable, and possibly ego-alien. However, projective test behavior cannot be considered as revealing the entire personality in view of the absence of any adequate evidence that either conscious self-report or observable behavior measures the same level of personality functioning. Rather, the projective test has now become one of the important elements of an assessment procedure, rather than either a trivial one or the sole one of significance; thus, the psychologist utilizing the projective test is like one of the three blind men who is viewing the elephant: when he puts his material together with the rest, he might be able to estimate the nature of the beast and give it a name. With this new realistic frame of reference, projective techniques have developed a new following and a new surge of interest in their use.

Projective Techniques in Crisis [1]

MARGUERITE R. HERTZ

"We know ourselves so little that many think they are going to die, when they are well."
Blaise Pascal, Pensées XXV, 1670

The projective methods which but a few years ago were greeted with hopeful acceptance, today are so embroiled in controversy that it may be said that they are in crisis.

Their underlying theories and hypotheses are called deficient and invalid; their methods are termed unreliable, and their research and application are declared irrelevant. In short, we are told there is no need for their being.

The predominant behavioristic trends in our field contend that there is no need to explain human behavior. Indeed there are even some who claim there is no need to understand human behavior at all. All that is required is ability to modify it. Hence, we should have no concern either with the dynamic aspects of disordered behavior or with its etiology. From such reasoning, the conclusion follows that there is no need for our diagnostic tools.

Furthermore, the emergence and rapid development of community psychology with its focus on community social systems and community institutions, make it unnecessary to be concerned with the understanding intrapsychic systems. Again it is argued that there is no need for the traditional clinical skills or diagnostic techniques.

This assault on the validity of our being and the need for our services has produced confusion in our ranks marked by divisiveness and acrimonious debate to the extent that Adelson (1969) finds chaos among us and Zubin, Eron, & Schumer, (1965) refers to it as anarchy.

Those who themselves employ the projective techniques ask with growing frequency such questions as: Is our theoretical position sound? Have our preparations been adequate? Is our research worthwhile? Are our services relevant and effective? These are the questions which reveal a sense of inadequacy, tension, restlessness and dissatisfaction.

These phenomena are, however, not peculiar to the field of the projective methods. They may be found in the entire field of diagnostic techniques. In fact, they characterize what is happening in clinical psychology generally. Clinical psychologists everywhere are questioning not only their traditional modes of functioning but more fundamentally, the value and the relevance of their efforts.

The chaotic state in which we find ourselves must be understood in terms of the reasons behind it. These include the new demands which are made upon us adding to our traditional burdens, and our own differences in theoretical posture, methods of study, definition of goals and areas of activity.

The accelerated tempo of technological change has given us new instruments for the self-destruction of all mankind. The atom bomb and missiles, germ and chemical warfare, all contribute to the urgency with which man must devise new means of promoting international understanding. Clinical psychology must make its contribution.

On the domestic scene, increasing violence, massive destruction of property, revolt against authority and drug addiction create new demands from us for appropriate contributions.

[1] Address delivered, Society for Projective Techniques and Personality Assessment, September 3, 1970, Miami, Florida.

Newer developments in education, its function and its methods also demand the attention and effort of the psychologist.

The advent of an affluent society offers more opportunity for leisure and for us, creates the problem of utilizing that leisure.

In the individual, we still have the traditional problems to deal with but they appear in new settings and new forms. In addition, new and more clearly perceived phenomena challenge us,—alienation, lack of direction, identity diffusion, feelings of futility and powerlessness, and reactions to the contradictions in our system of values.

Employment is no longer merely a matter of providing jobs. We now face the challenges of underemployment and displacement by the computer and automation.

All these problems and more contribute to the urgency with which we must seek for preventive techniques and programs.

Such new demands asserted with such urgency are enough in themselves to explain a large measure of confusion if not panic among us.

Our chaotic state can be explained in part also by the divergences in points of view, disagreement as to methods of study and investigation, and diversity as to goals, purposes and areas of activity, all born of varying conceptions as to the proper subject matter of psychology.

Those who embrace the dynamic psychologies think in terms of the subjective aspects of psychological experience, — with perception, feelings, motives, attitudes, values, conflicts and the like. They think of these as intervening variables which enter between the stimulus situation and the individual's behavior.

Those who are behavioristically inclined tend to recognize only that which can be observed objectively or publicly. They claim that only such can afford legitimate data for psychology. Although some, neobehaviorists and stimulus-response psychologists for example, accept mental phenomena as intervening variables, they nevertheless restrict their focus to objectively observed behavior.

We debate this issue extensively because it influences how we think and how we function. Do we study only that behavior which is directly observable? If so, is our phenomenological approach outmoded and unscientific?

This is especially important for those of us in clinical work who try to understand behavior problems. If we rely only upon overt behavior, we may overlook or even misinterpret the real meaning behind it. As Zubin (1967) has emphasized, the behavior we observe may well be epiphenomenon, only distantly related to the etiology of the disorder.

This general divergence as to what are acceptable raw data expresses itself in the projective field. With the Rorschach, for example, it raises such questions as whether differentiation should be made between the percept and the verbal form in which it is transmitted. Should analysis be restricted to overt and verbalized behavior? In evaluating responses, how much reliance should we place on a subject's introspections?

There are many who restrict themselves to the verbalizations of the subject in the interest of objectivity. On the other hand, others view overt behavior as clues to the content of the intrapsychic realm. They find it necessary to get below the surface and study the inner experiences and the subjective feelings of the individual as he interacts with his special and unique life situations. They utilize not only the subject's introspections but their own clinical intuitions.

This creates another problem among users of projective methods, i.e., the extent to which we should express our findings in terms of specific behavior.

There are many who restrict their reports to a description of personality dynamics. They hesitate to indicate how the tendencies noted will manifest themselves in overt behavior. They talk of latent dispositions which may emerge under certain conditions. At best, they express their inferences as to overt behavior as tentative hypotheses.

On the other hand, others insist that the area of interest is behavior. If the behavior cannot be specified, our efforts are not helpful.

Of course, most clinicians agree that it is our business to describe and, if possible, explain behavior. Sometimes we can and do predict manifest behavior from projective material alone. Where, for example, we infer compulsive defenses from Rorschach data, it is not difficult to indicate the kind of behavior to be anticipated.

As clinicians, however, we are aware that behavior is the product of the interaction of innumerable underlying determinants. Thus, a variety of behavioral reactions may be generated by either harmony or conflict among certain aspects of personality. Therefore, from projective material alone, it is not always possible or wise to predict specific behavior.

Years ago, Schafer (1954) discussed this problem in detail. He pointed out that most diagnosticians use batteries of tests which in combination permit more specific descriptions of overt behavior. More recently Klopfer (1968b) demonstrated how productively the integration of data from a number of projective techniques can contribute to the clinical case study.

Further, if projective data are analyzed in conjunction with life history and the situational and social context, we are able often to specify the probable form which behavior will take.

Thus, inferences made from projective data depend upon how much we know about the individual, especially about his needs and drives, the nature and success of his coping operations, and his whole experiential background, all in the light of the requirements of reality.

Therefore it would appear that there is no real difference between the views expressed. If we base our reports on projective data alone, more often than not we can make only tentative hypotheses as to manifest behavior. If, on the other hand, we incorporate in our analysis all the information we have about the individual, we are better able to talk in terms of specific behavior.

Another basic divergence of far-reaching consequence is the difference of opinion concerning origin and development of behavior. There are those who tend to emphasize the existing properties and predispositions of the individual which impel a given response to environmental stimuli, while others stress the predominant influence of the situation and the social and cultural milieu. This difference in emphasis persists despite the general agreement that personality and the behavior which it manifests, must be viewed as a complex interplay among inner dynamic and outer situational, social, and cultural forces, in the context of development and change.

In the past, clinical psychologists and certainly the users of projective methods, have concentrated on intrapsychic dynamics to the exclusion of social and cultural variables. There has been a reaction against this emphasis and a swing of interest to the situation and the social and cultural milieu in which behavior occurs.

This is due no doubt to accumulating evidence which shows that the environment affects and even determines the quality of an individual's adjustment and his susceptibility to behavior disorders. Indeed certain behavior disorders have been found to be rooted in the social and cultural systems in which the individual participates.

The trend certainly has been accelerated by the behaviorists' insistence that behavior is environmentally determined. Perhaps we are indebted to them for reminding us of the importance of the situation and conditions in the immediate environment. Certainly the emphasis in the environment has been strengthened by the current concern with group behavior, community problems, and social change. Indeed the environment has become so important that a new discipline of environmental psychology has emerged (Wohlwill, 1970).

The trend today, then, is to overemphasize the impact of the situation and social and cultural conditions upon personality, behavior and psychopathology to the neglect of their intrapsychic aspects.

This trend influences the interpretation of projective data and their use in research. For example, in evaluating the quality of an individual's adjustment or in prognosticating his susceptibility to a given disorder, many fail to give due consideration to the social and cultural factors which help shape the individual's ability to withstand stress, and which affect his tolerance for deviancy and influence his choice of defense mechanisms.

Yet there are even some who would view the introduction of such data as contaminating.

Furthermore, the norms which we have established and accepted also reflect in their nature and quality, the consequences of our divergencies.

The need of normative frames of reference is generally conceded and the use of those norms which are readily available is general. But we disagree as to the extent to which norms should be related to cultural, subcultural and ethnic groups (Gleser, 1963, Lindzey, 1961).

Some psychologists feel that environmental and cultural factors have a differential effect on the responses themselves. They affect for example his interpretation of the test situation, his attitude toward tests, his abilities, his experiences, all of which influence his test responses. Hence appropriate normative data must be amassed and utilized in the interpretation of a record.

We are told for example that where a protocol shows patterns reflecting hostility and aggressiveness, such traits may be in conformity with the norms indigenous to the immediate reference group which supports adherence to certain standards of conduct and penalizes deviations from them. To this extent, these patterns are normal and adaptive. This does not mean of course that the individual will show behavior which is adjusted to the norms of the large community.

There are many diagnosticians who believe that we must have both general norms for the larger community and norms specific to a reference group. Then we should be able to determine patterns which reflect traits shared by a particular subculture and those which are uniquely relevant to the individual. Further, we should be able to determine traits which deviate from expected norms of the larger group, making the individual maladapted to the larger community.

It is contended that this procedure and this point of view would enable us to define goals of intervention more realisically and to make better use of the intervention methods at our disposal.

This group therefore insists that appropriate normative data must be amassed. We must have multiple norms.

We find then considerable divergence among us. We seem to lack norms of the kind which many believe we should have but we have norms which many feel on occasion are being misapplied.

The position we take on the relative contribution of personality and environment to the projective responses of individuals with divers social and cultural backgrounds, definitely influences our interpretations and our research with projective data. For example, there are many today who believe that the norms which we have developed for middle class white children are being applied improperly to the records of children from the lower classes and from different ethnic groups. Indeed, I am not sure that even the norms which we use today are appropriate for middle class white children, adolescents and adults. Conditions affecting American life are different today from what they were years ago when Beck and I developed Rorschach norms for various age groups. We know there have been dramatic changes in modes of thinking, emotional expressiveness, levels of frustration, values, methods of coping, and the like. It may well be that the norms we have developed may have to be reevaluated and adjusted.

This problem of the relative influence of personality and environment on projective responses also causes some to question the use of "blind diagnosis" both in the clinic and in research because such use ignores relevant environmental data.

Again some question the use of sign batteries because they fail to indicate the complex interplay of personal and environmental variables which elude the formal scoring system. Indeed many of us question whether any projective data can be interpreted meaningfully unless weighed in the context of the immediate situation and the social-cultural milieu.

Most basic of all, however, are our differences concerning our roles and functions.

Until recently, most clinical psychologists would have been content to describe our functions as including description, explanation, understanding, predicting, and modifying behavior. Most would have agreed that underlying these, is the search for knowledge.

Today, this is not entirely true, for there are those who would minimize if not exclude, understanding the full background of behavior and in this sense they discourage the acquisition of knowledge.

If as some contend, behavior is merely response to environmental stimuli, the individual's inner life has become irrelevant. Hence, it is pointless to try to understand its etiology. Diagnosis is unnecessary.

But if, as others contend, behavior reflects not only environmental stimuli but also the individual's inner life because his intrapsychic processes give his response its special form and character, etiology remains of tremendous importance, and for this, the tools for diagnosis are essential.

Most users of projective techniques insist that understanding is basic to all our other goals. As Polanyi (1964) says the aim of science is explanation through understanding.

Diagnosis is necessary, they add, because it is an indispensable prelude to treatment if we aim to select the best possible procedure from the multitude of intervention modalities now available. Additionally, it is necessary if we are to determine the depth of a disorder and whether any intervention is indicated.

Thus, the two points of view. If we harken to one, we shall abandon one of our functions, the search for etiology. If we heed the other, we shall preserve it.

Even among those who admit the need for diagnosis, it appears that techniques for the diagnosis of the group, the neighborhood and the community at large are more important than the traditional diagnostic methods for understanding individuals. Additionally, even when dealing with individuals, the pressures for quick solutions are so urgent that diagnostic techniques are ignored and treatment is attempted directly.

Accordingly, we witness an alarming change in goals and in direction of interest; from understanding and diagnosis to intervention, be it psychotherapy, behavior modification, or group therapy.

In contrast, another contention would add rather than subtract another function, service to society and to the community, a demand recently extended to include social action and political activity.

Numerous psychologists feel that we have not responded to new needs and we have not moved fast enough into new areas. They complain that we concentrate on traditional problems because they fit our methods and mode of thinking, making both our service and our research irrelevant.

On the other hand, there are those who think that we have moved too fast into new areas by attacking community problems, group behavior and social change without adequate preparation. These claim that we have become overly involved to the point that we are forgetting our chief function as psychologists, the search for knowledge. Indeed there are some who fear that our diversive activities may retard our basic scientific development.

While most clinical psychologists agree that it is imperative to serve society and the community with our special competencies, some question the extent to which this includes social action. For example, should the clinical psychologist help people gain power and use it, as has been done in some community service projects (Bloom, 1969)? It is not clear to some of us how scientific detachment can be reconciled with partisanship. To say the least, this is a radical departure from our traditional goals.

Still another expression of our difference is our difficulty in deciding what kind of training we should require of our professionals, if we need them at all. In the light of the many services the clinical psychologist is called upon to perform, what should be the model of internship? Should there be a general model or numerous specialized models? What basic knowledge must he have and what basic skills must he develop, whatever be the model or the setting in which he operates? Where do the projective methods fit in?

This has generated considerable difference of opinion in our ranks. It appears to be the position of many universities that if diagnosis is irrelevant, there is little need to spend time giving training in diagnostic methods. Therefore they are not interested in developing competence in the traditional clinical skills. Nevertheless, students are placed both in hospitals and in clinics where such skills are needed.

Again there is a demand for community services which is being answered by placing students in community settings. Yet few institutions are training their students in community programs or giving them community organization skills. In fact, in many community programs, clinical psychologists are participating in all kinds of activities for which they have no background and no prior training (Bloom, 1969, Goldenberg, 1969).

To solve manpower shortages, many advocate the use of semiprofessionals or nonprofessionals trained in specialist oriented subdoctoral programs in clinical psychology (Arnhoff & Jenkins, 1969; Cowen, Gardner, & Zax, 1967; Guerney, 1969; Knott, 1 69). Indeed, a wide variety of services is being performed by persons with no professional qualifications. Such services include the traditional work of the psychologist, work related to diagnosis, administration, consultation, training and research. We are told for example (Bloom, 1969) that nonprofessionals are trained in six months to direct clinical services to patients in a state mental hospital, mothers on welfare are engaged in therapy, a school janitor conducts a therapy group for disturbed children, and discharged patients conduct other therapy groups. When questions as to the effectiveness of their respective performances are raised, we are told of the apparent satisfaction of their supervisors, hardly a scientific evaluation.

Although success in delivering clinical services by semiprofessionals and nonprofessionals is thus reported, the fact remains that projective techniques cannot be employed to their fullest potentialities by those who lack broad scholarship, intensive training, and varied experience.

As to methodology, we disagree on how data are to be gathered and how data are to be manipulated. Shall emphasis be placed upon objectivity to the point of ignoring the subjective? To what extent shall we place quantitative measurement in the forefront? What should be the role of psychometrics and computerization?

These questions have been debated in the literature (Hertz, 1963, Watson, 1959). It seems sufficient to point out at this time that evidence accumulates that objective data have their subjective aspects (Rosenthal, 1966, 1967) and subjective data may be rendered objective (Hathaway, 1959; Hertz, 1963; Watson, 1959; Wyatt, 1967).

In clinicial procedures, most dynamic psychologists agree that inclusion of subjective variables in the interpretation is indispensable. They make possible richer, more specific understanding of problem behavior and in this way contribute to the accuracy of our diagnoses.

Of course dynamic psychologists are aware of the limitations and uncertainties of subjective judgments. It is difficult to conceptualize, specify and measure the more nebulous dimensions of the inner world of the individual. Despite the fallibility of human interpretation, however, clinicians are confident that the interpreter with knowledge, training and experience can develop the necessary skills to penetrate the inner world of the individual (Holt, 1961, 1967; Klopfer, Ainsworth, Klopfer, & Holt, 1954; Schachtel, 1966; Schafer, 1954).

Further they believe that with appropriate design, clinical data can be objectified and can be used productively in research (Hertz, 1963; Holt, 1961, 1967; Neuringer, 1967).

On the other hand, there are those who insist that the standards and methods used in psychometrics should be applied to clinical data (Block, 1962; Holtzman, Thorpe, Swartz, & Herron, 1961). To be acceptable, they say, clinical data must be reliable, meaningful and valid according to psychometric standards.

It is difficult for some to understand how rigid standards of validation and psychometric methodology can be imposed upon subjective data without prejudice to their inherent value. They therefore question whether this can or should be done (Hirt & Kaplan, 1967; Holt, 1967).

Even if subjective variables were beyond quantification, they would not lose their significance. Those who in the interest of objectivity would accept only a quantifiable evaluation of behavior and who insist on actuarial methods of personality assessment, sometimes fail to keep in mind that statistical analyses are not immune to errors which are introduced by those subjective variables which are involved in the gathering and manipulation of data.

Indeed, we should all remember that even without quantification, research can be fruitful and that even with it, it may be sterile. Elaborate statistics are not in themselves enough to establish the validity of an hypothesis. While computers can simplify our labors, subjective considerations inevitably play their part in determining what the task shall be and with what the computers are to be fed. A computer remains only a helpless machine, until provided with a master, even with his subjectivity.

We have many reports that computers can scan, select, process and make decisions once they are fed adequate data on problems (Ross, 1968). Thus atlases for medical students have been published (Thomas, Ross, & Freed, 1964, 1965) where individual and group Rorschach responses are listed in terms of key words for each card, area, position, and content. Again Piotrowski (1964) has developed a computer which examines Rorschach scores for diagnostic signs and writes interpretations. We point out that the computer gives what he has put in, — his scores, his signs, his programs, and his subjective evaluations.

In our judgment, we do not as yet have sufficient data on the complex and intricate patterns of scores, situational context and socio-cultural influences for computerization of the Rorschach or any of the other projective methods. Nor have we arrived at the stage where we can translate clinical experience and intuition into digital computer language.

There is no reason to believe that the computer will replace the clinician or that our problems will be solved without clinical participation, however subjective such participation may be.

Parenthetically I would like to make some observations on the assertions of our behavioristically oriented colleagues who challenge the usefulness and the validity of clinical testing and dismiss it because of its extreme subjectivity (Mischel, 1968). They find their methods more objective. They focus on specific problem behavior, determine specific objectives in the attempt to change that behavior, and select certain procedures to implement their objectives, which may be repeated by others.

As Klein and her colleagues have pointed out so well (Klein, Dittman, Parloff, & Gill, 1969) whether they know it or not, they still employ clinical procedures. They make clinical inferences, for example, when they evaluate the problem behavior which is to be modified and when they select the specific conditions in the environment which must be handled. They utilize clinical intuition when they evaluate progress in the process of their therapy and in the management of their patients.

Most therapists agree that empathy is a vital quality in the therapist. Some suggest that this empathic understanding of the cognitions and the feelings of the patient must be coupled with an ability to communicate this to the patient. Rogerians refer to this as "congruence" and view it as a precondition for effective therapy. It may well be that the reported success of many of the behavior therapies may be due not so much to the special techniques themselves as to this phenomenon of "congruence" which involves clinical skills and intuitive ability on the part of the therapist, talents which many behaviorists deride.

The controversy concerning the comparative success of the actuarial and the clinical methods of prediction should also be mentioned. It is a controversy which despite the evidence of its moribundity, persists in refusing to die (Gough, 1962; Holt, 1958, 1970; Lindzey, 1965; McReynolds, 1968; Meehl, 1954, 1965; Sawyer, 1966; Zubin, 1966).

Although Meehl (1954) in his now famous monograph, found after a review of the literature, that the evidence preponderated in favor of actuarial prediction, he was countered by others (Holt, 1958, 1970; Lindzey, 1965) who pointed out the flaws in Meehl's analyses and the inadequacies of his approach. Furthermore, Meehl later tempered his own extreme position, and in 1959, himself identified circumstances in which the clinician may function better than the actuary. Others (Lindzey, 1965; Zubin, 1966, Zubin et. al., 1965) have shown also that there is no true dichotomy between actuarial and clinical predictions and that, depending upon the nature of the problem and the criterion to be predicted, each has its own place. Despite the paucity of evidence that clinical prediction fails to match the success of actuarial prediction, the controversy still persists and the clinical is judged on "failures." As a corollary the projective methods which are often involved in the clinical studies, are termed invalid as tools of prediction.

In the limited time at my disposal, it is impracticable to exhaust the entire litany of our differences. Nor is it practicable even to list all their sequelae. A number of them have been touched upon and their effects upon diagnostic techniques have been suggested.

I would like to add that all these and others have been exacerbated by fragmentation within our own ranks and by our isolation from other branches of science and other disciplines.

While admitting that the emergence of new knowledge creates need for specialization, we must recognize even greater need for interaction. It may well be that with better lines of communication among our subspecialists and between our profession and others, we might have strengthened our projective methods by incorporating appropriate findings from other areas of psychology and we might have avoided over-focus upon a single point of view. It may well be true also that we might have benefited from greater familiarity with, for example, what the geneticists or the sociologists are finding. Thus much overstatement might have been avoided.

But not all our differences are avoidabe. Some are inherent, for dissidence "is the badge of all our tribe." Theories frequently equal in number those who formulate them and often all who think produce their own opinions. Differences as such are neither new nor disturbing. What is noteworthy is the turmoil in which we differ because it reflects our inner conflicts.

Shall we cling to that which is familiar to us or modify or even reject it? Shall we adhere to, abandon or alter our traditional standards, methods, and values? Shall we remain within our present school or escape to the new? To what extent will our response be merely an appeasement of our critics?

There are among us those who have become hypercritical of themselves and over impressed with their failures and inadequacies, basking in Wordsworth's "luxury of self-dispraise." Some are tense, restless, dissatisfied and frustrated. In panic, they become hyperactive and like the fictional horseman, they "dash off in all directions," seeking quick and easy answers, avoiding diagnosis, embracing temporary solutions, attacking problems with inadequate preparation, and undertaking work for which they are not fitted.

Some project blame for their inadequacies upon the "foreign houses" in which they have to operate or the "inferior position" in which the psychologist must function on the "psychiatric team."

And some become disillusioned, withdraw and become alienated. They are dissatisfied with their own orientation but they cannot accept the newer modes of thinking and functioning. As a result they have no psychological roots, no theoretical anchorage, and no psychological standards and traditions to sustain and direct them. May we question whether the contemporary clinical psychologist is threatened with a kind of anomie?

Some among us, however, retain both composure and serenity and stand their ground. They evaluate the contemporary furor realistically. To them there is much which has been proven to be both valid and useful, and this they strive to preserve and retain.

Calmly they intensify their efforts to make projective methods more relevant, more productive and more effective. They refuse to join the generation of dilettantes. They persist in being clinical psychologists with a theoretical foundation provided by psychological tradition.

Their efforts have made our procedures with projective methods in the clinic more sophisticated. Scoring, for example, has become less mechanical and gives consideration to the various qualitative nuances of response. Analysis has come to incorporate many situational and motivational variables in the testing situation. The general level of psychological maturity, adaptation, adjustment and social competency is stressed rather than mere diagnostic categories and pathology. Without minimizing weaknesses, they focus more on strengths in looking for assets pointing to potential competence and effectiveness (Beck & Molish, 1967; Hertz, 1969; Kaplan, Hirt, & Kurtz, 1967; Mucchielli, 1968; Schafer, 1954).

In research, in the last two decades alone, they have added supports to our theoretical foundations and thus have given both research workers and practical clinicians ample guides from which to choose, in their use of projective methods. We have only to read Holzberg's chapter in Rabin's review of projective techniques (1968) to appreciate the extent of concern with the problem of relating psychological theory to the projective methods. Indeed, today research with projective methods contributes to the development of psychological theory.

There has been progress in research on projective methods themselves and also on their application (Singer, J., 1968).

The stimulus attributes of projective material have received much experimental attention. In addition, innumerable studies contribute to knowledge of the influence exerted by the conditions and the context which obtain in the testing situation and the nature of the interaction between the subject and the examiner. These too have been amply reviewed (Masling, 1960; Murstein, 1965; Rabin, 1968a; Zubin et. al., 1965).

As to our techniques we have made considerable advance in administration, scoring, and interpretation.

In the Rorschach, for example, progress has been made in scoring form quality. New and revised frequency lists have been published (Beck, Beck, Levitt, & Molish, 1961; Beizmann, 1961, 1966; Hertz, 1970). The Mayman form-level scoring method has been shown to have unique value in qualitative analyses of Rorschach protocols (Lohrenz and Gardner, 1967). Responses of medical students to both the individual and Group Rorschach have been recorded (Thomas et. al., 1964, 1965). In addition, dimensions of categories for analyzing responses to the Thematic Apperception Test have been established by many investigators (Atkinson, 1958; Henry, 1956; Holt, 1961; Lindzey, Bradford, Tejessy, & Davids, 1959; Murstein, 1963; Zubin et. al., 1965).

Again, in the area of Rorschach, innumerable studies show content analysis to be important in research and in practice, stressing its diagnostic and predictive potentialities. Research has focused for example on various summary scores, scales, and configurations, many of which combine content analysis with qualitative features of response and conventional Rorschach patterns.

Mentioning only a few, we have indices for gauging hostility and anxiety, primary and secondary thinking definiteness and permeability of bodily boundaries, levels of maturity in object relations, and cognitive deviancy, all well reviewed by Haley, Draguns, & Phillips, 1967. Added to these we now have scales to measure repressive style (Levine & Spivak, 1964), and regression in psychosis (Neiger, Slemon, & Quirk, 1965). Manuals for scoring communication defects and deviances for both the Rorschach and the TAT have been developed, primarily for application to parents of schizophrenic patients but they may be applied productively to many other groups (Singer & Wynne, 1966).

Many studies have contributed to understanding the relation between certain personality variables and behavior, as for example the color and shading responses in the Rorschach. Studies have concentrated on investigating the validity of many projective hypotheses.

Projective methods have contributed to knowledge of cognitive processes and cognitive complexity (Fulkerson, 1965; Schimek, 1968; Witkin, Dyk, Faterson, Goodenough, & Karp, 1962), developmental and genetic levels (Hemmendinger, 1960), achievement (Atkinson, 1958; Murstein, 1963; Skolnick, 1966; Zubin et. al., 1965), anxiety (Goldfried, 1966), aggression and hostility (Megargee & Cook, 1967; Murstein, 1963, 1965; Townsend, 1967), acting out (Brown, 1965; Hammer, 1965; Piotrowski, 1965; Shore, Massimo, & Mack, 1964; Weissman, 1964), impulse-control balance (Holt, 1966), conformity (Smith, 1967), empathy (Mueller & Abeles, 1964), ego process and ego strength (Frank, 1967; Meyer & Caruth, 1965), and ego-impairment and ego adaptation (Kaplan, 1967). In addition, projective methods have given us some insight into imagination (Singer, J., 1968) and creativity (Dudek, 1968; Feirstein, 1967; Hersch, 1962; Rawls and Slack, 1968; Rogolsky, 1968). They have added to our knowledge of coping and defensive operations (Grebstein, 1967; Haan, 1964; Schimek, 1968).

Research workers continue to study the predictive potentialities of various projective methods and the effectiveness of clinical judgment based on projective data. For example, studies continue to accumulate pointing to the potentiality of Klopfer's Prognostic Scale to predict improvement (Butler & Fiske, 1955; Cooper, Adams, & Cohen, 1965; Endicott & Endicott, 1963), the effectiveness of diagnostic judgments and the validity of some of our interpretations (Fisher, 1967).

Utilizing projective methods, research workers have contributed to our understanding of a variety of psychological problems including issues in child development and education. For example the Rorschach has been used to study developmental changes with age (Ames,

1966; Coleman, 1968; Hayworth, 1968), emotional disturbances in children (Francis-Williams, 1969; Hall & Abramson, 1968), the impact of maternal deprivation on conceptual development in young children (Taylor, 1965), and adolescence and adolescent problems (Offer & Offer, 1968; Propper, 1970). Again projective methods have contributed to our understanding of school readiness and to a variety of educational problems (Ilg, Ames, & Apell, 1965).

Projective methods have also been used to study the aged (Ames, 1960, 1966; Eisdorfer, 1963; Oberleder, 1967; Rosen & Neugarten, 1960).

Research has likewise encompassed many aspects of psychopathology. For example, investigators have been especially active in recent years in exploring schizophrenia (Beck, 1965, 1967; Kantor & Herron, 1966; Singer & Wynne, 1965a, 1965b; Weiner, 1966). Again many studies have demonstrated the value of the Rorschach in detecting suicidal risk (Cutter, Jorgensen, & Farberow, 1968; Daston and Sakheim, 1960; Hertz, 1965; Neuringer, 1965; Sakheim, 1955).

Additionally, many studies have employed projective methods as research tools to explore delinquent behavior and other forms of social malfunctioning (Ichimura, 1966; McNeil, 1962; Megargee, 1966a, 1966b; Pati, 1966; Piotrowski, 1965; Purcell, 1965; Selosse, Mazerol, & Jacquey, 1967; Weissman, 1964).

In the industrial field, the applicability of some of the projective methods is also revealed by many current studies (Baruch, 1967; Grant, Katkovsky, & Bray, 1967; Kinslinger, 1966; Korman, 1968; Piotrowski & Rock, 1963).

Again the usefulness of projective methods in the attack on social, cultural and ethnic problems is suggested by several studies (Levy, 1970; Levy & Kahn, 1969; Reissman & Miller, 1958).

Racial studies are beginning to make their appearance (Ames & August, 1966; Ames & Ilg, 1967; Hall & Abramson, 1968; Megargee, 1966a; Williams, 1968).

Finally, problems of mental health are now included in the area of our research. For example, measures of prediction of mental health based on the Rorschach Prognostic Rating Scale (Endicott & Endicott, 1963), on certain Rorschach adjustment patterns, (Gaylin, 1966) and on the primary process scoring index (Benfari & Calogeas, 1968) appear to have considerable validity.

Mention should be made of the application of projective methods in the culture-personality area (DeVos, 1965b, 1968; DeVos & Hippler, 1969; Honigmann, 1960; Lindzey, 1961). Despite the multiple difficulties involved in applying any kind of tests in this area, many studies utilizing projective methods have made substantial contributions to our knowledge of a wide variety of cultural groups. For example recent investigations have been reported for African children (Weinberg, 1968), adult Indians (Prabhu, 1967), Thai peasants (Phillips, 1965), Alaskan Eskimos, (Preston, 1964), the Mountain Arapesh (Mead, 1968), Japanese (DeVos, 1965a; Takahashi & Zax, 1966), Japanese Americans (Caudill & DeVos, 1967; DeVos, 1966), Apaches (Boyer, Boyer, Hayao, & Klopfer, 1965, 1967; Boyer, Boyer, Klopfer, & Scheiner, 1968) and a host of other groups.

Again exciting new developments in the making, are to be found in a number of creative modifications of some of our projective techniques.

The Holtzman Inkblot Test has been devised to satisfy those who feel that the traditional Rorschach Method has psychometric limitations (Holtzman et al., 1961). Considerable experimental and clinical work is going forward. As yet clinical application is not extensive but an entire new field of research has been opened.

Many other projective methods devised for special purposes are being utilized with considerable success (Rabin, 1968b). Especially exciting are those devised for the study of interpersonal patterns and problems such as various forms of Conjoint Family Assessment (Bauman & Roman, 1968; Bodin, 1968; Dudek, 1969; Levy & Epstein, 1964; Loveland, Wynne, & Singer, 1963), and the Consensus Rorschach (Cutter, 1968; Singer, M., 1968; Wynne, 1968). These are utilized in innovative ways to compare communication and behavior patterns from group to group and from individual to individual, and to predict relationships between couples and between members of families.

These are only a few of the recent developments in our field.

True, our contributions have had their shortcomings, many documented in the literature (Exner, 1969; Fisher, 1967; Gleser, 1963; Hertz, 1963; Klopfer, 1968a; McReynolds, 1968; Rabin, 1968a), in discussions which have included such topics as appropriativeness of raw data, criteria used in validating basic hypotheses, norms applied, population samples studied, score-oriented procedures, control of stimulus material, insufficient attention to examiner and situational effects, and their statistical manipulation. Additionally, we may comment that our efforts have not been organized, systematized or well planned.

Neither our shortcomings, however, nor our difficulties justify the current mood of discouragement. Our brief review of recent research points up not only the problems in the field but also the promise for the future of projective methods, for it reflects variety, strength, vigor, and movement as we come to grips with many controversial issues.

Discouragement is unwarranted also when we view what is happening in historical perspective.

We have never enjoyed unanimity. We have always differed in respect to points of view, definitions of psychology, and as to methods of study and investigation. This is not the first crisis in the history of clinical psychology.

I myself have lived through many crises. I have seen doctrines and methods which were enthusiastically accepted, rudely rejected with the passing of time, only to reappear again. The phoenix is not an unknown bird among clinical psychologists. Many of our doctrines have re-arisen from their own ashes.

As a student, I had to memorize lists of instincts according to McDougall, Thorndike and a host of others, only to learn later that no self-respecting psychologist should even use the term "Instinct." But around the 1940's instincts came back into fashion with Tinbergen's work on lower organisms (1951). Later the years brought more modifications until today, we talk of primary drives, libidinal drives and energizing bases of human behavior, being careful to avoid the word "instinct."

In the early 1930's when behavioristic attitudes were current in American psychology, I joined in excommunicating mental phenomena and in insisting that only the objectively observable can furnish the proper data of science. I, too, thought that an individual's responses were mechanically subservient to the control of conditioned stimuli.

Suddenly, in crisis, I found myself reacting against this form of behaviorism and I became involved in gestalt psychology with its emphasis on dynamic wholes and interrelationships and its phenomenological approach. I vigorously revolted with others against atomistic procedures especially the so-called objective tests, rating scales and inventories which studied personality and behavior piecemeal. I became interested in the newer tools for personality evaluation and adopted the projective methods which came into being as an antidote to the psychometricians who were unable to handle important aspects of personality such as motivations, emotions and thoughts and psychopathology. I joined other workers in developing projective methods and in applying them to a host of problems. With others, I soon found that many of us were over-optimistic and soon our unbridled enthusiasm was replaced by a more realistic view as to what projectives can and cannot do.

With a host of others, I embraced psychoanalysis. I grew comfortable in understanding behavior in terms of psychodynamic processes. Then in crisis again, the revolt against psychoanalysis carried me with it and I joined those for whom ego psychology was the new faith.

In today's crisis I find that mental phenomena are banished again and that phenomenology is out. A new kind of behaviorism reigns, focusing on the behavior of the individual in the specific situation, and a new discipline develops concentrating on the group, the community, and the culture.

I now witness a new rebellion, this time against projective methods with the demand that we return to the methods of the psychometrician, the very methods against which we revolted years ago.

You can understand then when I say that all these happenings give me a feeling of familiarity. Borrowing from the French, I think I suffer from *déjà pensée,* the current ideas seem familiar, *déjà entendu,* the voices sound familiar, and *déjà vu* the scenes appear familiar. But these are not illusions; they all have really happened before. For we have travelled in circles.

Of course, with the accumulation of knowledge and with the acquisition of new procedures, changes are inevitable. We all know that theories, methods, and therapies, when subjected to the scrutiny of time, are modified. Perspectives are broadened to meet new conditions, new developments, and new knowledge. My point, however, is that doctrines enthusiastically accepted at first, may be subsequently rejected with equal vehemence, only to reappear in more acceptable form.

Further, controversy is not new. There has always been what Dunnette (1966) calls "fads, fashion and folderol" in psychology. There have always been adherence to extreme views, rigorous partisanship, and exaggerated notions of simplicity. There have always been particular doctrines or methods which are enthusiastically advocated, often without historical perspective and without critical evaluation of alternative methods. What we witness today has its precedents. The shifting back and forth, however, the fluctuations, even the regressions are not unwholesome. They do not forbode the dissolution of clinical psychology nor the scrapping of projective methods. Rather they reflect critical evaluation, necessary experimentation, and expansion of horizons. Even what many of us consider regressive tendencies may well be "regression in the service of" our discipline, in the sense that attempts are now made to revive that which was valuable in the past, merge it with the new, and experiment with new and creative methods in order to meet current needs.

Historical perspective gives us a deeper understanding of what is happening today. It should inspire more caution and humility in those who think that their methods are the only methods. It should help those of us who are anxious and confused to see our position in its true light. It should give us not only direction and purpose, but even more important, challenge.

The challenge remains, to try to understand behavior and to try to treat behavior disorders. To answer each challenge we place our hope in the growth of scientific knowledge of the nature of human behavior. Such growth can come from the search for the "why" behind that behavior.

This means that diagnostic skill is part of our job and with it, the task of fashioning and improving its tools. Thus, neither the diagnostician, nor his tools have lost their reason for being.

In the diagnostic field, we need more sharply formulated questions, further refinement of techniques, and more creative ways to handle old problems. We need to attack some of the new problems to which I have already referred.

Our chief task, in my judgment, is more extensive and systematic study of the special significance of situational and cultural factors which differentially influence test responses. Another need is for more systematic study of the subjective aspects of our methods and the qualitative features of projective responses, so as to achieve greater objectivity and empirical validity.

Still another major task before us it to study the clinical judgment process itself, i.e., the mode in which subjective judgments and clinical cues combine to produce the inferences we make. How do we perceive, code, and combine projective data to produce our diagnoses, our predictions and our prognoses?

It may well be that our attention should be directed to the area of cognitive styles. Research indicates that people differ in their styles of processing and organizing their observations of environmental data and their cognitions about others. Possibly, then, we should focus on individual differences among judges in modes of perceiving others. In research studies with the projective methods, in which clinical judgments tend to be unreliable and of low validity, the reason may be found in the differences among the judges in their modes of perceiving.

In addition, it is necessary for the diagnostician and the research worker who uses projective methods to be a broadly trained clinician. He must have a fundamental grounding in psychology and intensive training in assessment which is the basis for the development of clinical skills so vital in practice and research. Even those clinicians who do not use diagnostic procedures and who specialize in psychotherapy, behavior therapy, consultation, or community psychology cannot understand or help others without some knowledge of intrapsychic dynamics and of the patterning of defenses and the interpenetration of motives, thought and affects which we get from diagnostic procedures.

In addition, the diagnostician must have a fundamental grounding in social processes, social and community organization, social change and crisis. It is only with such background that the psychologist can develop the ability to integrate all the data furnished by the projective methods and weigh them with contextual and environmental factors for the purpose of diagnosis and prediction.

Finally, there must be a receptiveness on the part of all of us to interdisciplinary activity and effective communication and collaboration among us in our subspecialties.

These are therefore times for intensification of effort, for greater vigor and for daring innovation.

I have sought herein to explain the current chaotic turmoil in the realm of the projective techniques in terms of the urgency of new and pressing problems which confront us added to some of the differences among us in respect to theoretical posture, methods of study and diversity as to goals and areas of activity.

I have sought to describe the impact which all these have had upon the clinical psychologist.

I have ventured a brief appraisal of our labors in the last two decades. I have tried to evaluate our situation in the perspective of history.

Finally, I have touched upon the needs which confront us.

In all, I have aimed to have us know enough of ourselves to be able to accept Pascal's reassurances that we should not think that we are going to die, when we are well.

A Funny Thing Happened to Us on the Way to the Latent Entities

PAUL E. MEEHL

I daresay some of you — especially those of my age group — were surprised to find the Bruno Klopfer award bestowed upon a notorious dustbowl empiricist whose modest claims to fame include a wicked book on actuarial prediction (Meehl, 1954) which I am currently struggling to up-date, and the advocacy of cookbook interpretation for the most widely used of structured personality inventories, the MMPI (Meehl, 1973d). I must confess that I was pretty surprised myself. But on reflection, I concluded that your outfit (which traces its ancestry to the old mimeoed *Rorschach Research Exchange*) showed scholarly integrity and good taste. For the record, you can't pin the Minnesota Multiphasic Personality Inventory on me, as I was an undergraduate during its development. The Minnesota lore is that McKinley wanted it, Hathaway built it, and Meehl sold it — not a bad summary of the situation! The eminent contributor for whom this award is named was known to me, although not well, because back in 1947, I went off first to Michael Reese to learn some Rorschach with Beck and followed it a couple of months later by going to Bard College where Klopfer was doing a workshop.

My first publication, "The dynamics of structured personality tests" (Meehl, 1945), replied to a paper by a distinguished contributor to projective techniques, Max Hutt. While that polemic was overly optimistic, it was, I think, an important contribution for its time. It urged a more sophisticated way of looking at verbal items, more like the way we listen to psychoanalytic material or responses to inkblots, but linked to a more atheoretical blind external criterion keying than I now defend. Those old polarizations between structured and projective methods are weaker today, and I think this is partly because all of us have undergone some disillusionment with the power of our favorite assessment methods. The younger clinicians are less test oriented, whether structured or projective, than was my generation. Part of this comes from concerns about reliability and validity and the often depressing results of validation studies. But I think some of it comes from a greater skepticism about the usefulness of inferences concerning latent entities in favor of a greater shift toward purely behavioral, dispositional analysis. I suppose I play a rôle here, both in the emphasis upon empirical keying and in my views on actuarial prediction, which downgrades the usefulness of mediating forecasts via structural or dynamic inferences. There is a philosophical point here which I would still press, namely, that in the other sciences, powerful predictions can be mediated by theoretical constructs only when two conditions are met (Meehl, 1973a). First, the theory is well worked-out and well corroborated, having high verisimilitude, as Popper calls it (1962, 1976); secondly, there exists a powerful technology of measurement. Since we meet neither of those conditions in clinical psychology, we should not be surprised to find out that our predictive powers are limited.

Students have commented on an ambivalence in my writings on assessment, but I like to think that this is reality based. I do not dispute the powerful influence on me of cultural factors, such as the accident of Minnesota geography. But I was first attracted to the field by reading Karl Menninger's *The Human Mind*, and my cognitive passions were mobilized by psychoanalysis. I find it hard to imagine what kind of psychologist I might have become had I been born and raised in San Francisco or New York City, but it was

Part of this article was presented at a meeting of the Classification Society, Gainesville, Florida, April 10, 1979.

cheap and convenient to go to the University of Minnesota where I was exposed to behaviorist and measurement-oriented super-objectivists like Donald G. Paterson, Starke R. Hathaway, William T. Heron, and B. F. Skinner. Despite this education, in my 1954 book on prediction, a page count shows that even including the pro-actuarial results in the empirical chapter (and after all, I am not responsible for how those studies came out), by far the larger part of my text defends the clinician's special powers of psychodynamic inference against the claims of Lundberg, Sarbin, and others that he's nothing but a second-rate computer. I had analysis partly with a Vienna trained analyst and mostly with one trained at Columbia under Rado (I may say that Nunberg, Ackerman, and Helene Deutsch are among my psychoanalytic grandparents), and after doing a couple of controls, I then practiced a mix of psychoanalytic and rational emotive therapy which I continue today. It would be surprising if a person with that life history didn't show some ambivalence about clinical inference!

While this talk is about cluster problems, psychoanalytic inference is not without relevance, as I need hardly remind a group interested in projectives. Most objections I hear from my behaviorist anti-Freudian colleagues seem to me beside the point, focussing on the legitimacy of unobservable entities, operational definability of terms, reduction of psychodynamic to learning concepts, or the problem of mapping into physiology. All of these I view as red herrings (Meehl, 1970). The big problem about psychoanalytic inference is contained in Fliess' attack on Freud at their last meeting at Achensee in 1900, when he told Freud that "the thought-reader merely reads his own thoughts into other people." Freud, who, right or wrong, usually knew pretty much what he was up to and what the scientific stakes were, immediately perceived that this attack went to the jugular. If that was what Fliess really believed, he should throw the just-published parapraxis book into the wastebasket; and that Achensee "congress" was the last time the two men ever met. The critical problem about psychoanalytic concepts is precisely here. It is the epistemological or methodological problem of the inference, rather than any of those other side issues commonly mentioned. The shift in psychoanalytic therapy away from reconstructing the past, and even from the interpretation of dreams, to moment-to-moment handling of the transference, and the ascendency of two powerful therapeutic competitors, namely, rational emotive therapy and behavior therapy, have lessened the clinical importance and, I fear, the intellectual interest of psychoanalytic therapists in this epistemological problem. But students and colleagues still ask me, "Meehl, you have always been interested in psychoanalysis. How come you haven't ever published any quantitative research on the psychoanalytic hour itself?" They don't seem to believe me when I say straight forwardly, "Because I don't know how." And, alas, I don't think anybody else does either.

But it is not inference from dreams, associations, expressive movements and parapraxes of the kind we make in the psychoanalytic session that I want to discuss with you here. Rather, I want to consider another kind of inferred, latent entity allegedly underlying human behavior and experience, namely, the inner structures or states — if you like, the genotypic traits and types — that psychologists have searched for using correlational methods. The paradigm case of factor analysis I am going to bypass, partly because I am not sufficiently expert and have only conducted a few factor analyses in my career, although I may say that the few I have done were more illuminating than I had anticipated, having been taught at Minnesota that factor analysis was pretty much a waste of time. If the rotation problem can be solved nonarbitrarily, which is doubtful, I think one of the main problems that will persist in factor analysis is the conceptualization of the obtained factors. There is here a highly subjective interpretative feature present, comparable in quality, and I fear sometimes even in amount, to that which obtains in psychoanalytic interpretation of the patient's verbal material. I co-authored a paper some years ago on an approach to reducing that subjectivity of factor interpretation, which we thought was rather clever at the time, but which seems to have dropped into the bottomless pit and this talk gives me a chance to recommend you have a look at it (Meehl, Lykken, Schofield, & Tellegen, 1971). Briefly, what we showed is that using not test data, but therapists' ratings as our raw material, to be correlated and factored, then if one presents skilled clinicians with a randomly chosen half of the phenotypic traits showing high loadings on a factor, and these clinicians, after independently characterizing the factor's psychological nature, have a meeting in which they thrash it out and settle on a christening of the factor; then if you present a set of such factor names to a new batch of clinicians who do not see the original half of the items and whose task is to match the remaining half of the items with the factor names, you achieve almost a perfect correct identification. We didn't expect it to come out this well, but since it did, we have been surprised that nobody has picked up the method subsequently.

It has taken a too long and rambling introduction to get around to my main focus here which is not the inference to psychodynamic entities from psychoanalytic session material nor from projective tests, nor the identification and interpretation of dimensions underlying a battery of ratings or psychological test scores, as in multiple factor analysis; but the inference to *types* or *taxa*, entities of a categorical rather than dimensional kind. Detecting these taxonic entities has been the traditional aim of the methods called cluster analysis, and the field has undergone a tremendous publication explosion within the last decade. (I belong, for instance, to an organization called the Classification Society that was originally dominated by plant people, bug people, and statisticians, and had only a half a dozen psychologists at its first meeting in 1970. Our profession now numbers about a third of the membership.) I want, in the remainder of my remarks, to make, forcefully, a point about cluster analytic methods that we have been reluctant to face. It goes without saying that in science as in psychoanalytic therapy, if a problem is not faced, it can hardly be solved. In the latter portion of my remarks I will say something about some current efforts of my own and my former student, Robert Golden, now at Columbia, to solve one important subclass of the cluster problem. What follows is an expansion of some remarks I made as a member of a panel on the proposed revision of DSM-III at the Classification Society's April (1979) meeting in Gainesville. Readers unfamiliar with the current situation in cluster analysis and numerical taxonomy may sample the intellectual ambiance of the Classification Society in Sokal (1974), Hartigan (1975), or Sneath and Sokal (1973). An excellent brief exposition for psychologists is found in Blashfield (1976), and see also Blashfield (Note 1), Blashfield and Draguns (1976), and Blashfield and Aldenderfer (1978).

I shall not offer here a rigorous general definition of 'true type' or 'taxon' or 'entity,' for which taxometric rather than continuous factor analytic methods are appropriate. I have concluded that such a general definition cannot be given except implicitly, via the mathematical formalism itself, together with references to dichotomous etiology that are problematic and not defensible within my time constraints. Roughly, then, I mean by a 'type' or 'taxon' a class entity having a nonarbitrary basis of categorization, that is, not simply a conjunction of attributes that one might impose conventionally for some useful communicative or administrative purpose, but a class of persons that really belong together, a classification punchily expressed by the metaphor that we wish, as Plato said, "to carve nature at its joints." Seeking a more rigorous (mathematical or causal) definition of a "true taxon" convinces me that taxonicity is itself not taxonic, but a matter of degree. Some of you might want to read my paper in the *Journal of Medicine and Philosophy* (1977) on some quantitative meanings of specific etiology and other forms of strong influence, and a forthcoming book on taxometrics by Dr. Golden and myself (Golden & Meehl, Note 2). While a genetically determined disease entity, such as Huntington's or (as I believe) schizophrenia, and manic-depression provides the clearest examples of causal taxonicity, we should not equate that notion with the medical model, or even with genetic etiology. Any kind of type or syndrome, however produced, that has a sufficiently strong knitting together, statistically and causally, is a taxon. For instance, consider Freud's early hypothesis that the specific etiology of hysteria is a passively experienced prepubescent sexual trauma involving genital stimulation with affects of fear and disgust predominating, whereas the obsessional neurosis springs from a similar sexual experience, but with enjoyment, aggression, and activity initiated by the subsequent patient. That would have been a perfectly good taxon, even though it had nothing to do with germs or genes. 'Indigenous fascist' is a perfectly good taxon, as is 'Stalinist,' 'Freudian,' or 'behaviorist.'

It seems odd that what purport to be objective, quantitative methods of classifying mental patients have not been conspicuously successful, although the effort goes back at least a half century. I don't wish to commit overkill, but I do aim at a confrontation. We have here a mind-boggling fact: No accepted entity in psychopathology has owed its initial *discovery* to formal clustering methods, whether those invented by psychologists, biologists, or statisticians. In fact, I know of no agreed-upon instance where taxometrics has been mainly responsible for definitively *settling* a controversy about an already "noticed" syndrome, e.g., as to its existence if disputed, its specific etiology, whether it should be sub-divided, or subsumed under another accepted category as a *forme fruste*, and so on. If I am wrong in this strong negative claim, it should be easy to refute me. The thesis is historical, and one clear counter-example will suffice. In organic medicine, physicians succeeded in identifying hundreds of disease entities long before Pearson invented chi square or the corrlation coefficient. Even in psychopathology, recent advances in the genetics of major psychoses such as schizophrenia and the distinction between the bi-polar and uni-polar affective disorders have relied hardly at all upon formal clustering methods. Instead, researchers have moved forward by improving the verbal specification and the objective recording of the behaviors that were traditionally looked at by psychiatrists and clinical psychologists. For example, the recent work on bi-polar and uni-polar affective disorders showed that the single objective symptom 'agitated pacing' yields a nearly perfect discrimination between unipolar and bipolar depressions when the diagnosis is based upon the previous history of the patient or the patient's family for a manic attack (Depue & Monroe, 1978, pp. 1004-1005). Or with respect to schizophrenia, researchers have not said, "If we start with a big mess of correlations of everything with everything, will such a thing as schizophrenia emerge from the mess?" but instead, "Conjecturing that schizophrenia is a disease entity that has objective reality, how can we refine the way in which the interview is conducted and observations recorded so as to study its heritability?"

It seems to me that this historical observation is important. We can't explain the ability of medicine to identify disease entities by saying that all medical syndromes are tightly knit, which they are not; or by referring to pathognomic signs, that are rare in organic medicine, probably as rare as in psychopathology. The existence of external validating criteria in the form of specific pathology and etiology help (Meehl, 1973e, pp. 284-289), but hundreds of entities were identified before the specific etiology and pathology were known. So this is a puzzle about the history of medicine, and I think somebody should look into just how they managed to do it without any fancy statistics. I have some hunches, such as the fact that in medicine we focus on a small number of powerful indicators rather than a large number of weak ones such as regularly practiced in the classical psychometric model, and that medicine does not start, so to speak, blindly entering a huge matrix of intercorrelations among patients or variables. The physician hasn't said, "Look, we have hundreds of people coming into this outpatient clinic sick in a lot of different ways with a variety of complaints. Let's concoct some ingenious formula or index for putting together their symptoms and then try to extract truth out of the mess." Instead, the physician has seen a small number of patients with certain striking configurations and writes a description of this which immortalizes him with an entry "Fisbee's Syndrome" in Dorland's Medical Dictionary. Conjecturing that there is such an entity as Fisbee's Syndrome and postulating that underlying any statistical order of symptoms, complaints, course and response to treatment, there is some strong causal factor within the individual, we try to improve the identification of Fisbee's Syndrome versus everything else. This leads to a rather different kind of research strategy from the statisticizing of a large can of worms.

Some believe that the main reason our methods haven't been earthshakingly successful in psychopathology is that the model is wrong, that there aren't any entities analogous to measles, mumps, and cholera. I don't believe that for the major psychoses, for the psychopath, and for one or two of the neuroses. The question is fundamental: Why do we want to classify anyway, instead of merely predicting useful dispositions, such as response to a drug? I am unaware of any proof that it is statistically profitable to sort people into taxa or groups or types or species if there aren't any real types to be discovered. Is the procedure merely imposing our arbitrary order for an alleged economy in description? We often talk about this kind of economy, but I must confess I've never understood what we mean. From the standpoint of clinical handling, it seems unlikely that a taxometric procedure would be better than a purely dimensional one. Given a finite set of indicators that are correlates of some disposition such as response to group therapy or differential reaction to two anti-depressants, why mediate transition from predictors to predicand via a taxon? I am not enough of a mathematician to give a general formal proof, but I submit the following rough and ready argument against such an arbitrary imposing of taxonicity on dimensional facts: Given a half dozen facts about a patient such as certain Multiphasic scores, items from Mental Status and life history, we want to predict whether he will respond to Elavil. We can combine the predictors in some simpler linear form — Goldberg, Dawes, and Co. would say even unweighted standard scores! (Dawes, 1979; Dawes & Corrigan, 1974; Goldberg, 1965; Wainer, 1976) — or, if you think it's configural, using a function-free actuarial table as advocated by my colleague, Lykken (1956) (Lykken & Rose, 1963). In the classification approach, I first move from the predictors to the taxon, with statistical slippage, and then from the taxon to the drug response, with some more statistical slippage. Why would that be a profitable endeavor, especially if the taxon has no reality, but is only in the statistician's head?

Doubtless I disagree with many of you on a philosophy of science issue, in that I am a scientific realist rather than a fictionist or instrumentalist. For me, the purpose of taxometric procedures is to carve nature at its joints, to identify the real underlying taxonic entities whose conjectured existence motivates a classification rather than a dimensional approach. As Ernest Nagel says, the difference between realist and instrumentalist is usually only philosophical and without impact on their work as scientists. But sometimes it makes a difference in one's research strategy. In the *Medicine and Philosophy* paper, I set out a dozen meanings of 'strong influence,' formulable mathematically and metatheoretically. The three or four "strongest" are easily identifiable as influences that would in organic medicine be called 'specific etiology' (cf. Meehl 1973b). Examples: A necessary and sufficient condition, such as the Huntington gene; or a necessary but not sufficient condition, as the gout genotype; or a threshold value, as in a deficiency disease below a certain minimum dietary input. Somewhat weaker is the case where a causal variable is the most powerful one everywhere, such as caloric intake in nonglandular obesity. I see the basis for a nonarbitrary taxometric approach as causal, which I realize is controversial. Unless I hypothesize a quasi-dichotomous causal factor, historically or latently generating the pattern of interpatient resemblances, I doubt I should be doing a classification job rather than a dimensional analysis in the first place.

When "true taxon" denotes a conjectured specific etiology, we replace the usual statistician's reference to "assumptions" by neo-Popperian "auxiliary conjectures." These hypotheses, while auxiliary to the main substantive theory of interest, are still factual claims rather than mere conventions for data manipulation (Meehl, 1978, pp. 818-821). They constitute a part of the whole network of scientific hypotheses and are falsifiable. But they may not be subject to *direct* falsification, as in an auxiliary assumption of homogeneous covariances or linear regression. They may be falsifiable only by falsifying indirect, remote consequences. This is true of several consistency tests that Robert Golden and I have devised. I believe that consistency tests of a postulated latent causal model are imperative in taxometric investigations. In my paper on Popper and Fisher just cited, I develop this thesis and point out that the reason consistency tests are not labelled as such in sciences like chemistry, astrophysics, and molecular biology is that they are used ubiquitously, taken simply as a basic process of respectable science, (do two or more numerical procedures lead to the same inferred answer?) so they don't have a special name (Meehl, 1978, p. 829). A taxometric procedure in psychopathology which has to begin and end by saying, "If the reader is willing to assume with us that..." is weak. Even if it happens to carve nature at its joints, the investigator and his readers have no way of knowing whether it has in fact succeeded in doing that. Fisher said, in criticizing systematic plots like the Knut Vik square, that we want not merely to have a small error, but to have an accurate estimate of error. The analog to this methodological demand in classification is that we want not only to have a search method which will detect the true entities underlying the phenomena, but we want to have auxiliary methods which tell us whether we have succeeded in that detection. If twenty people are guessing how far it is to the moon, it doesn't help if one of them is right on the nose unless we have some way of telling which one he is! Again, I am not enough of a mathematician to give a rigorous formulation of the difference between a consistency test and a main estimator of a conjectured latent quantity, but it could be done first round in terms of the relation between number of equations and number of unknowns. An expression of equality that is not an algebraic identity, or one stemming simply from the formalism itself such as integrating a differential equation, but an equality in which the expressions on the two sides contain variables that are assigned numerical values from our taxometric search procedure, should be satisfied within allowed tolerances. If the equality between these two expressions is not a mere identity, but flows as a theorem from suitable postulates formulating the conjectured latent causal model, then it can serve as a consistency test when we plug in the numerical values and see whether they fit. If they don't, either something is wrong with the model or we have had an unfortunate sampling error, despite the model itself being substantially correct. I do not see much point in doing significance testing here because (other than my general distaste for the significance test tradition, Meehl, 1970, 1978) we already know that the substantive theory as stated in the formalism is literally false. All theories are false, and for a neo-Popperian, it's a question of how much verisimilitude the formulation has. Suitable conventions concerning tolerances are preferable to showing a statistically significant difference from the idealized model, which will always happen if the sample is large enough and the measures sensitive.

I take this opportunity to urge (as I did at the Classification Society) something that, while involving some risk of the taxpayer's money, is pretty sure to be informative. I propose a large scale study of the presently available taxometric search methods. Methods would be chosen on the basis of some combination of their current popularity and the plausibility of their mathematics, given the metatheoretical position that we want to carve nature at its causal joints rather than just lump people together administratively or for an alleged economy of description. I take that "realist" view partly because I don't know how the rules of the game for such a study could be written on a nonrealist, fictionist view that all cluster methods ever do anyway is impose our desire for order upon the world, that is, they don't discover entities, they invent them. I am not interested in inventing entities. As I once said in an argument with my friend Gardner Lindzey about fictionism in psychoanalytic theory, if there isn't any Santa Claus, then it isn't he that brings the presents! One would include methods that rely on very different latent structural models in the postulates employed in their formalism and in the algorithm of their search and weighting method. One would also want to try methods that are similar but differ in some interesting respect. I would, given my prejudices, prefer methods that rely upon a moderately strong causal model rather than methods of which nothing could be said except they represent one more ingenious way of combining a bunch of differences or distances in a phenotypic space. (I think that a physical scientist would find the exercise of ingenuity in concocting distance measures and cluster algorithms a bit odd, but I won't press the point. I hasten to add that I am not pointing the finger pharisaically at others, having committed similarity index concoction myself!) I would give high weight to the existence of consistency tests, and if there are otherwise promising or popular methods which do not presently have consistency tests available, some preliminary efforts should be made to derive them. I suspect that there are a lot of potential consistency tests around which, because of the lack of emphasis upon this aspect of the problem in the classification tradition, nobody has bothered to derive. After such a preliminary screening of taxometric methods by a combination of intuitive plausibility, similarities and differences, current popularity, and the derivability of consistency tests, we could compare the methods on three broad fronts. First, we select taxon or species instances from several domains of the biological and social sciences, dispersing the qualitative characters of domains and emphasizing loose clusters that are known to reflect a truly dichotomous causal origin. For example, nobody disagrees that multiple sclerosis is different from tabes dorsalis or that mumps is different from scarlet fever. We try disease entities where we have an external criterion provided by pathology and etiology, ranging over neurology, pediatrics, internal medicine, and so forth. We do the same for suitable examples in entomology, botany, geology, and the like. For each instance, the requirement is that we have a syndrome of indicators of only moderate tightness (there is no point, as my philosopher friend Feigl says, in cutting butter with a razor), but we have an independent criterion (such as tissue pathology or causal origin or what kind of rock something is found in) that specifies what it means to carve nature at its joints.

We employ two or three dozen such pseudo-real problems, "real" in the sense that there are biological entities being measured and clustered, but "pseudo" in the sense that the taxon and its membership are known to us independently of the cluster search method. We are asking whether we *would* get the right answer if we lacked access to the independent objective criterion (Golden & Meehl, Note 3).

Use of pseudo problems with a known real answer over various areas of the life sciences is desirable because neither analytical derivations nor Monte Carlo methods can quite simulate the features of irregularity and discontinuity and so on which we find in the world of real taxa. The most plausible behavioral examples would be those in behavior genetics. For instance, there are now something like 120 clearly identified Mendelizing mental deficiencies which would present a nice problem because on the behavior side, it would be surprising if studying patterns on subtests of intelligence tests results would succeed, whereas combining these with some of the nonbehavioral pleiotropic effects found in these conditions, e.g., skin markings, developmental malformations of the ears, or whatever, might be quite powerful. From the purely behavioral side, things get a little tougher, but even there, one can think of examples. For instance, a cluster method that fails to discriminate active dues-paying members of the John Birch Society from similarly zealous members of the Socialist Workers Party would not appear to be very promising! We might confine this first domain to situations commanding quasi-universal agreement among informed persons that a real taxon exists.

Secondly, extensive Monte Carlo runs combining various latent parametric situations and a wide range of sample sizes should be conducted, an important part of that procedure being to study how well consistency tests detect sample results as untrustworthy, as giving the "wrong answer." Using four consistency tests as successive hurdles that a sample must "pass" to be acceptable, Golden and I were able to detect every single "bad" sample (one giving poor taxonic parameter estimates) in 600 Monte Carlo runs, at the expense of only 6% false alarms (Meehl, 1978, Table 1, p. 827). The Monte Carlo runs should include situations where there is no taxon but in which various dimensional relationships could produce a pseudo taxonic situation. The question here is, can the method be fooled into finding types when there aren't any?

The third sector is problematic but, I think, still worth doing. Here we apply the methods in contexts where there are real problems, where some expert agreement exists that there is a taxonic entity, but there is persisting disagreement as to what are strong indicators. For instance, another clinician and I might be in complete agreement as practitioners and as scientific researchers that schizophrenia is real, an entity having something to do with genes and not merely society's wickedly labelling people of strange life styles. But we might disagree as to the importance of a given symptom, such as anhedonia. There are many such questions around, both in psychopathology and in nonpsychiatric medicine. For example, I gather that there is still not universal agreement in medical genetics as to whether the juvenile and the adult forms of diabetes involve a different locus or simply a question of the juvenile patient being less adequately protected by polygenic modifiers. There is dispute as to whether malignant hypertension represents simply the upper end of the distribution of blood pressures in otherwise normal young persons, or does that suspicious "bump" or "tail" reflect a taxonic entity whose frequency in the population is not sufficient to generate a visible bimodality but only a skewness. (See, e.g., Murphy, 1964; Wender, 1967; Meehl, Lykken, Burdick, & Schoener, Note 4.) Do certain taxometric methods help clarify such situations? Are the more clarifying methods the same ones that show up well in the Monte Carlo runs, and in the pseudo-problem runs with a known true dichotomous etiology?

The hope would be to identify taxometric procedures that consistently "work" in that they give the true answer or help us to reach consensus about a plausible answer on currently active scientific problems. If no methods consistently work, we could at least scrutinize the mathematics and conceptual underpinnings that correlate with a tendency to work better. It could be that nothing works, but I can't believe that. More probably different methods will work for different kinds of situations. But I think we should be able to generate latent structures which tell us something about certain minimal conditions that a method should possess if it is likely to give the right answer. If nothing consistent showed up, that would be discouraging; but it would be enlightening.

If I permit myself to play diagnostician and prophet, attempting to say what's the matter with the social scientist's search for latent entities via the received cluster methods, I would identify several features of our approach that are individually damaging and jointly have made us so largely unsuccessful. Some have already been alluded to in the preceding text, but I want to pull them together here. Note that each of them contrasts with organic medicine, where without high powered statistics, entities have been identified with conspicuous success. First, we lack an independent criterion that corresponds to the internist's pathology (and, when known, etiology). About that lack, there is nothing we can do. If a syndrome in psychopathology is not caused by a germ, and does not involve tissue pathology (in the usual sense of Virchow), so that, at most, anything "anatomically haywire" is a matter of CNS fine structure, the psychoclinician is permanently disadvantaged. But I repeat that organic medicine succeeded in identifying numerous disease entities prior to Koch's postulates, which date in the 1880s, and even prior to the development of scientific "pathological anatomy" as it used to be called. Secondly, instead of starting out with a huge battery of miscellaneous indicator variables, not chosen with a taxon of interest in mind, we should rely on clinical experience and sketches of causal theory to identify a relatively small number of potentially powerful taxon indicators. Thirdly, it may be better strategy to think in terms of Taxon X versus everyone else, and then subsequently to research Taxon Y versus everyone else, studying conjectural entities one at a time, tailor-making indicator domains to the focus of interest, instead of the social science tradition of an almost blind statistical scanning of heterogeneous dispositions hoping that cluster statistics will be enlightening. (Our focussing on this strategy is one reason, aside from proper modesty and scientific caution, that Golden and I lay no claim to having "solved the cluster problem," despite our growing confidence that we have "solved" what might be called the *conjectured taxon problem.*) Fourthly, we want qualitatively diverse indicators, not devices all of the same sort which are heavily saturated with methods or instrument variance (a policy I violate myself later in this paper). Fifthly, a few strong indicators minimally correlated are, as the history of medicine shows, better than many weak ones with variable correlations. Sixthly, the cluster algorithm ought not be arbitrarily concocted but should reflect our conjectures, however primitive, about the underlying causal structure. Seventh, it is undesirable to employ procedures that will always give a clustered result, as true of many popular cluster methods, in that they always end up slicing the phenotypic pie regardless of whether a true taxonicity exists; and, furthermore, two different methods that each guarantee to slice the pie may (sometimes surely will) slice it in different ways. An investigator who adopts his favorite cluster algorithm because his teacher believed in it or because he happens to have a canned program around is proceeding in a way that it is perhaps not uncharitable to describe as whimsical. Finally, I cannot emphasize too strongly the desirability — I, myself, would be more inclined to say the necessity — to develop consistency tests sufficiently strong that a taxometric search procedure can "flunk" them. I mean that one may appear to succeed in identifying a taxon, but the internal quantitative relationships of the data force him to admit that something is very wrong with the inferred situation and so he cannot rely on the deliverances of the method.

Simple conventional statistics (like indicator phi-coefficients) can yield odd results that ought to make us worry about statistical identification of taxa. For example, I have concocted a simple paradox by considering four diseases, the first three of which have clinic population base rates equal at .30, and the fourth one a base rate of .10. We consider symptoms *a, b, c, d,* through *i,* the first disease D_1 producing symptoms *a, d, e,* the second one D_2 symptoms *b, f, g,* the third one D_3 symptoms, *c, h, i.* The fourth entity D_4 — which we haven't discovered yet — invariably produces the triad of symptoms *a, b, c.* There is nothing bizarre about such a configuration, and in fact, if anything, it makes life easy for the "search statistician" by involving only four disease entities, with indicators infallible as exclusion tests (one-way pathognomicity, cf.Meehl, 1973c, pp. 208-211; 1973c, pp. 230-231). Would we discover the new disease entity, D_4, using one traditional procedure, R-correlating everything with everything in a big symptom matrix? The answer is that we would not. Constructing simple four-fold tables from these proportions will quickly convince the reader that the three phi-coefficients for symptoms (*a, b, c*) taken pairwise are all *low-negative* (−.25). Only if the clinician pays attention to the triplet (or, if you like, the conditional probability of *c* given conjoint presence *ab,* and similarly for the other two divisions) will he "notice" that the syndrome of D_4 exists. I do not suggest that this is a typical state of affairs, although I see no reason to think it extremely rare, the numerical assumptions not being outlandish. My point is a general methodological one, namely, the fact that such a thing can happen ought to make us nervous about identifying taxonic entities by calculating phi-coefficients on a big symptom matrix.

In this kind of example, a relatively simple detection procedure seems to work, comparing the incidence of symptom triads, tetrads, and higher conjoint patterns with expected values based on simple probability multiplication. But the number of patterns gets big quickly with increase in indicators, and I have not yet worked out the general mathematics rigorously.

I think we have to face the fact that the deliverances of traditional cluster methods have, by and large, been disappointing in psychopathology. Not to sound overly pessimistic, let me conclude by summarizing briefly some recent research of Dr. Golden and myself which attempts, we do not yet know how successfully, to draw on the lessons of experience and philosophy of science. I have been interested in the diagnosis of pseudoneurotic schizophrenia, and even more, Rado's "compensated schizotype." Being one of the minority still betting on a dominant gene theory, I realize that unless very low penetrance is abused as a fudge factor to defend that theory from refutation by the concordance data, it is necessary to identify the non-psychotic schizotype with respectable accuracy for genetic statistics. That includes identifying those patients in a mixed psychiatric population who receive some other nosological label (such as anxiety neurosis or reactive depression) but who are, in the eyes of Omniscient Jones, really schizotypal because their psychopathology is mainly attributable to the causative influence of the specific dominant schizogene. You will have to put up with my using the MMPI as behavior data, not because I see it as God's gift to the clinician, but because we have a large data bank at Minnesota that permits the kind of statistical manipulation required. I would prefer to have behavior ratings, soft neurology, soft cognitive slippage, and other qualitatively diverse data, as urged in my earlier remarks. The first methodological point is to avoid the flabby procedure of psychologists and sociologists, showing that there is some feeble difference between two groups. Nor do we want to rely mainly upon external criterion keying, (despite Meehl, 1945!), since if there were a satisfactory criterion permitting a numerical statement of the valid and false positive rates for MMPI items or scale cuts, that criterion would be the one to use in testing a genetic model. We want numerical estimates of item parameters, and of the hit rates attained by items and item patterns, or scales and scale combinations. We don't just want to say the schizophrenics differ from the manic-depressives, or the males differ from the females, or inpatients show more bizarre items than outpatients, or any of that kind of feeble "statistically significant" business. We want to estimate the base rate of schizotypy—a *number*—in the clinical population, and to determine the valid and false positive rates of the items (singly and collectively) so that for any given patient showing a pattern, we can assign a Bayes Theorem probability that he does or does not belong in the schizoid taxon. Verbally explained, what we want to do is have the best of both worlds by combining some features of the dustbowl empirical keying approach with the bootstrapsing approach via item patterns, and relying upon the consistency tests to tell us if we have failed in our endeavors despite generating a phony success. We begin by a crude item analysis of the MMPI 550 item pool, using formal diagnosis of schizophrenia against Minnesota standardization normals. This is only to get our foot in the door by finding a set of potentially powerful indicators. That is, we begin with the formal psychiatric label attached, but we do not continue reliance on it in our subsequent manipulations. (Of course, later, in testing a genetic model, we must return to this formal nosology, because the identification of carefully diagnosed schizophrenic probands is necessary in studying the incidence of subclinical schizoidia in family members, to test a dominant gene hypothesis of the schizotaxic defect.) Secondly, we make use of crude content validity, based upon extended experience (some forty years of psychotherapy practice, including thousands of hours in the treatment of schizoid and schizophrenic patients.) I have some faith in my clinical judgment and attempted to identify items in the MMPI pool that were relatively schizo-specific, and yet not mainly psychotic schizophrenia, reflecting the accessory symptoms. We are reassured to find a high agreement between Meehl's content validity intuitions, and the empirically discriminating items. We then consider the mixed clinical population of psychiatric patients who were not formally diagnosed schizophrenia nor organic brain disease or affective psychosis. We have left a heterogeneous collection of psychoneuroses, character disorders, psycho-physiological reactions, marital problems, and the like. One knows from clinical experience, as well as a few statistical studies that in such a miscellaneous group of patients, there is a subset who, if followed over time, will develop a florid schizophrenia. Looking at it from the other ("input," causal) side, foster persons at high genetic risk for schizophrenia although they have about the same 12% diagnosis of clinical schizophrenia as they would if reared by their own mothers, more often show other kinds of neurotic, pseudoneurotic, or character anomalies (Heston, 1966; 1970). On a dominant gene hypothesis, in order to reach the theoretical 50%, one has to consider those persons as unrecognized schizotypes in varying degrees of pseudoneurotic or pseudopsychopathic decompensation. I am not reasoning circularly, but in the context of discovery, the theory tells you what to look for, and how to look. Having identified the provisional pool of indicator items by reliance on formal diagnosis, we now apply our taxometric procedure to bootstraps ourselves into an identification of good indicator items, estimates of the base rate, valid and false positive rates, and so forth. Let me sketch out three taxometric bootstraps procedures briefly, and refer you to our recent paper (Golden & Meehl, 1979) for details. I hope I can convey the essential ideas without tables or equations, because they are basically quite simple. Replacing the significance test orientation by the mental set "wherever possible, estimate point values," we proceed as follows: Some years ago, I proved some theorems based on the fact that the covariance of two fallible indicators of a taxon has a maximum value for a 50/50 taxonic mix (Meehl, 1973c; Note 5; Note 6). This is a useful theorem in bootstrapping from fallible indicators of a conjectured latent taxon, because we can simply plot the covariance of two of the indicators as a function of the third. If it behaves as predicted, starting out near zero and going through a maximum somewhere in the middle range of the third variable and then declining to zero again, we conclude that the latent model is as conjectured. Further, we infer that the class interval on the third indicator variable for which the observed empirical covariance of the first two has its maximum, is the one which is below the intersection of the two latent frequency functions (what I call the *hitmax interval*, as cutting at that interval maximizes the hit percentage). From the observed (yz)-covariance in the hitmax interval of x, we can compute the product of the latent taxon mean differences on y and z. Using this product $(\bar{y}_a - \bar{y}_n)(\bar{z}_s - \bar{z}_n)$, we obtain a quadratic in the latent interval schizotype-rate p_i, and solving that quadratic in each x-interval we infer the latent schizotype frequencies, adding them to get the total schizotype-frequency and the taxon base-rate. (Statistical bootstrapping, properly done, *can* cook up knowledge out of ignorance!) Meanwhile, the computer has drawn the latent frequency functions, so we can solve for latent hit-rates achieved by the hitmax cut. Finally, we use Bayes' Theorem to classify the patients individually as schizotypal or not. Notice that we estimate a hit-rate despite having no criterion! (See Dawes & Meehl, 1966; Meehl, 1973c, pp. 216-217; Note 5, pp.

37-44) The "Super-Bootstraps Theorem" is counter-intuitive and totally ignored in the psychometric literature, but it could theoretically be a source of greater power in research on fallible indicators of latent taxa. This is especially likely in behavior genetics, where a non-behavioral pleiotropic effect could be discerned as quasi-infallible by using the Super-Bootstraps Theorem on a behavior syndrome whose component indicators possess only moderate validity.

Secondly, it can be shown that the hitmax cut is approximately located, within an interval error at most, by a sliding cut which maximizes the difference in the proportions of patients above and below the sliding cut who ring the bell on a candidate item. Beginning with a set of potentially good items one identifies strong items, tests them for consistency, rejects those that are most inconsistent with the model, thus creating a new sliding cut scale, and iterating until the system settles down, that is, until the valid and false positive rates, hitmax cuts, and inferred latent base rate of schizotypy are all numerically coherent. Thirdly, conjecturing an approximately normal distribution for the latent taxon and the latent extra taxon class, one can use a kind of cut and try procedure, that minimizes discrepancy between the observed and theoretically predicted values when we *arbitrarily* assign base rates, means, and standard deviations. Here again, we have no criterion. We consider a model supported if there exists an assignment of the latent values which gives an insignificant (or very small) chi square to which the discrepancies move in an orderly fashion, as we approach the optimal choice of latent parameters. Using these three non-redundant methods, we arrive at an estimate of the validity of each selected indicator and of the estimated latent base rate. We get some faith in our results partly from the fact that the base rate estimated by these three independent methods is about the same, and that it is about the same as an antecedently recorded base rate. Some of you will be shocked by this value, but I guessed around 40% are unrecognized schizotypes in such a mixed psychiatric population. If the taxometric corroboration of my 40% clinician's guesstimate is sound, that is an important and disturbing finding. It suggests that a rather large batch of schizotypal patients are being non-optimally treated, and research results in psychotherapy, pharmacology, diagnostic reliability, and genetics are likely to be fuzzed up or even uninterpretable due to the undetected presence of that many schizotypes. We are reassured to find that the estimated validities of items found by the three procedures generates a predicted degree of agreement between them by pairs that is close numerically to the observed values. Further corroboration is found by showing that the MMPI profile of the group thus identified as schizotypal is very similar in pattern to a VA group diagnosed "anxiety neurosis" who subsequently developed florid schizophrenia on follow up (Peterson, 1954a, 1954b).

Summary

Inferred latent entities, whether those of psychoanalysis, factor analysis, or cluster analysis, have declined in value for many clinical psychologists, both as tools of practice and as objects of theoretical interest. Behavior modification, rational-emotive therapy, crisis intervention, psycho-pharmacology, and actuarial prediction all tend to minimize reliance on latent entities in favor of purely dispositional concepts. Behavior genetics is, however, a powerful movement to the contrary. As regards categorical entities (types, taxa, syndromes, diseases), history reveals no impressive examples of their discovery by cluster algorithms; whereas organic medicine and psychopathology have both discovered many taxonic entities without reliance on formal (statistical) cluster methods. I offer eight reasons for this strange condition, with associated suggestions for ameliorating it. Adopting a realist instead of a fictionist approach to taxonomy, I give high priority to theory-based mathematical derivation of quantitative consistency tests for all taxometric results. I urge a large scale cooperative survey of taxometric methods based on

Monte Carlo runs, biological pseudoproblems where the true taxon is independently known, and live problems in genetics, organic medicine, and psychopathology. An empirical example of taxometric bootstrapping and consistency testing was presented from my own current research on schizotypy.

But It's Only An Inkblot

JOHN E. EXNER, Jr.

Abstract: The nature of the Rorschach is discussed using data from three temporal consistency studies with children of different ages, plus two other studies in which the retest reliability question was approached by experimental manipulation. It is postulated that the test response reflects the basic psychological styles or response tendencies that have developed within the personality, plus representations of the more private world of the person. The challenge for interpretation and research is to differentiate which of the test elements reflect each of these features, and to determine how they merge to create the response during a very brief time interval.

It was not really difficult deciding on a title for this address, for it was provoked by some recently processed data, and in many ways reflects my own perspective about the Rorschach after having progressed through a rather long journey of use and research with it. I first laid hand to the Rorschach blots nearly 30 years ago. I felt, on that occasion, as if I were to be suddenly privy to all of the wonders of the psychological world. At that time, assessment, or psychodiagnostics as it was called, was the forte of the clinician, and I had eagerly awaited the "laying on of hands" that would permit me into the inner sanctums of the mind. Thus, that first experience was awesome, but to my surprise nothing happened. There were no bells, no peals of thunder, and I seemed no more knowledgeable for my experience. Nothing had happened by osmosis. And more surprising, my first Rorschach teacher, a lovely Swiss lady, Marti Meyer, seemed to regard the test much more matter of factly than I expected; and much more conservatively in her approach than I had been led to believe from Rorschach lore. My text was *Psychodiagnostics* (Rorschach, 1921), and I also found myself a bit disappointed that it was such a small book, and because it failed to speak to the magic of the *ego* and the *id*, and the myriad of intrapsychic conflicts that, as rumor had it, could be discerned from this miracle test.

But it was not long thereafter, working with various supervisors during externships, that I began to hear the magic. I learned of the father card, the mother card, a sibling card, and a sex card, and of course, I learned to differentiate phallic from vaginal symbols. During those early months of studying the test I was in a kind of "dynamic glory." During that time, I also had a brief but somewhat tutorial exposure to David Rapaport, who reinforced for me all that I knew to be true, using the brilliant conceptual framework that he was developing concerning ego psychology. But the faculty of my university, Cornell, were rather conservative and quite demanding, and not as open to all of the psychoanalytic propositions as I had become. In the irritating way that professors seem to have, they kept demanding justification, and many an eyebrow was raised when I would attempt to meet a challenge for proof with a quote from my newfound authority. Among others, they insisted that I read Beck, and then compounded my confusion by forcing Klopfer on me. Having first read Rorschach, then Rapaport (Rapaport, Gill, & Schafer, 1946), then Beck (1944, 1949), then Klopfer and Kelley (1942); I found myself puzzled about which course pointed toward truth. And the matter became more complicated when Schafer's beautifully written work on psychoanalytic interpretation came before my eyes (1954).

During that period of no more than one year, I never really asked myself, "What is this test?" But my mentors seemed devoted to forcing that question on me. Three of them, Frank Freeman, Howard Liddell, and T. A. (Art) Ryan insisted that I devote more time to Beck. I am not certain why, but I believe that they perceived Beck to be the most conservative of the group, and they even went to the extreme of arranging for me to journey to Chicago to spend some time with Beck during the following summer. It was an inspiring experience for me, for Beck was a warm, sensitive, and inspiring man who gleefully loved to talk about the test. And during that relatively brief time in his presence he warned me never to neglect the origins of the test, even though by that time he was also strongly commited to an analytic framework and displayed a remarkable mastery in nursing the contents. In that same summer, I became immersed in reading Klopfer's new book (Klopfer, Ainsworth, Klopfer, & Holt, 1954) and tried to discuss it with Beck but learned quickly that his interests were in other directions. I later discussed that experience with my committee at Cornell and Freeman decided that some time with Bruno Klopfer would add to my education. Consequently, it was off to California the next summer. It was also an awesome experience. Bruno Klopfer was a gigantic personality, charismatic as a person and phenomenal as a teacher. Not so much because of what you learned, but because of what you saw unfolding before your eyes, his sensitivity and his remarkable ability to mass tiny cues into a seemingly full understanding of a person.

After those two summer experiences I was sure I had "been to Mecca." I was more convinced than ever that those 10 blots held the key to the psychological world of people, and while I still really did not understand the test, like many of my day I persisted in the belief that it was, indeed, an x-ray of the mind. But again, the faculty of my university were not as enthusiastic as I and continued to "pull hard on my reins." Whenever I was certain about the nature of relationships between fathers and sons, husbands and wives, or brothers and sisters, I was challenged. And when I was convinced about how a person perceived their world and how they defended themselves, I was challenged. These challenges took two forms. One came from my clinical colleagues who assured me that treatment and not assessment would be the wave of the future, and so why worry about inkblots. My experimental colleagues kept harping for proof, often pointing to an increasing number of publications concerning Rorschach failures. The word was out. The test was neither reliable nor valid, and in the eyes of many, had little more utility in the clinical setting than a set of Tarot Cards. And, unfortunately, many of the ciriticisms that accumulated concerning the test were quite legitimate. Many clinicians truly believed in the magical x-ray quality of the test and often rendered speculations about people, purportedly from the test data, that would go well beyond the renderings of even the most creative artist. One feature that contributed to the problem was the fact that those using the test did not do it in the same way. My earlier experience with Rapaport, Beck, and Klopfer had left indelible marks on my psychological brow about this; and I had also gradually become aware that Beck and Klopfer had not communicated with each other for essentially 20 years, during which time three other significant Rorschach people, Rapaport, Hertz, and Piotrowski had "gone their own way" with the test. Unfortunately, few of us recognized the truly vast differences that existed among them, nor the impact of those differences on both research and interpretation.

In 1960, I began to develop a delusion of grandeur concerning Beck and Klopfer, namely, that because each had been so kind and generous to me during my student years and in our continued correspondence, that each might be willing to meet. In my fantasy, I would assume the role of a monitor while they discussed their differences with the objective of some reconciliation from which a "consolidated front" might evolve that could be used to fend off some of the outrageous slings and arrows that were being cast at the test. Unfortunately, both declined to participate in my grand scheme. I say unfortunately because each had so much to offer and I continue to harbor the belief that a dialogue between them might have captured many concepts for which we are still searching. Even though they declined, each encouraged me to study and write about their differences and agreed to support that effort wholeheartedly, and they did, as subsequently did Rapaport, Hertz, and Piotrowski. Unfortunately, Rapaport died early into the project so that much of his personal input was not to be. During the next seven years I devoted most of my free time to the literature of these people, and to many journeys to California, Chicago, Cleveland, and Philadelphia trying to cull out the positions of each, and at Beck's suggestion, even spent some time in the Rorschach Archives in Switzerland to better understand the historical perspective from which each of the approaches had evolved. It is important to add that there is no way to fully acknowledge the warmth and generosity that each devoted to the project. Not only were they eager to clarify their own positions, but also shared many personal and private bits of history to aid in helping me to gain a more complete understanding of their work with the test.

As more and more information accumulated it became easier for me to understand how many of the criticisms about the test had originated, and how some, indeed, might be justified. When the manuscript, later published as *The Rorschach System* (Exner, 1969) was complete, I arranged for it to be sent to Beck, Klopfer, Hertz, Piotrowski, and Schafer, mainly to insure that there was no historically incorrect material and to receive some reassurance that I had presented their positions fairly and objectively. Klopfer was the first to respond. He was very complimentary about the work, suggested one or two minor changes, and then added a sense of disappointment about the fact that I had drawn no conclusions. Two days later, I had lunch with Beck and heard almost the same commentary, including the sense of disappointment that I had drawn no conclusions. I was also disappointed, for I had failed to find any great solution to what, by that time, I had conceived as the "Rorschach Problem." What I had found was that there were five clearly different approaches to the 10 blots, often subtle, but generally so different that one could argue that there were five Rorschachs instead of one, or even more if the foreign proliferations of Rorschach's work were included. Obviously, for me, the Rorschach lost some of its magic during this lengthy project; but it was Klopfer and his striking sensitivity who put me in a new direction. About eight weeks after my conversation with him concerning the manuscript we discussed our mutual disappointment about the lack of a conclusion in the book, and he said, "but maybe you should look further." His suggestion became something of an internal challenge and I decided to pursue the matter further; and that was the beginning of what is now called Rorschach Workshops, formed originally to research each of the systems more completely for issues of reliability and validity. Ultimately, the logic of integrating empirically defensible features became obvious (Exner, 1974).

The notion of integration really did not occur for nearly two years, during which we floundered about trying to test out different aspects of each of the systems. I now suspect that had I listened carefully to the records of five- and six-year-old children, I might have started with the test more objectively than I did as a graduate student, and that our research effort might have begun differently. Which brings me to the title of this address, "But it's only an inkblot." It really is only an inkblot! That is one of the most common first comments or responses to Card I given by five- and six-year-olds. That answer, or variations on it, such as, "An inkblot," or "A splotch of ink," or "A mess of ink," or "I know how to make these," etc. constitute 207 of 500 first comments or responses given by 210 fives and 290 sixes, drawn from both nonpatient and psychiatric populations. And they are correct. Whether it is a function of correctness or the simple honesty of the child, these two groups give the "right" answer more frequently than any other groups. It is only an inkblot. But when the "right" answer is delivered, we do not accept it. Instead, we encourage and even demand that the subject make it into something else. And we get responses. But is not really a bat or a butterfly. It is not blood, or two dogs, or two people. It is not a skin, or a rug, or a flower, or witches, or crabs. There is no face, no wings, no body, no legs, no smoke, no water, no fur, no heat, and no sadness. It is just an inkblot. But as people convert that inkblot, they do truly see all of these things and many more. To date, after having coded more than 5,000 protocols card by card, by location, which involves about 100,000 answers, we have recorded more than 8,000 *clearly* different responses to the 10 blots. I do not mean one person reporting two waiters carrying something and another reporting two people dancing. In those instances, the content is essentially the same, but rather one person reporting two people dancing whereas another reports two dogs in a circus act to the same blot area. Those are different responses. But it is still an inkblot. It is not people dancing, or two dogs in a circus act. And that seems to be indicative of the nature of the test.

When the subject is forced to convert the ambiguity of the blot into something else, that is to violate reality, an intriguing complex of psychological activity is stimulated. It is a truly remarkable process that permits the game, "Blotto" from which Rorschach really derived many of his ideas, to become sort of a test. As we understand this game-test more, the yield is substantial, but not in the context in which I was originally taught the test. The figures have no universal meaning. That has been demonstrated in many studies, the most recent of which, and possibly the most well designed was by Wallach (1978). There is no father card, nor mother card, nor sibling card. Much to the chagrin of many there isn't even a sex card. Each figure has contours, most of which are not very precise and consequently can be translated in a variety of ways, and the process of that translation forms both the strength *and* the mystery of the test. How does the translation take place? How can something as simple as an inkblot provoke the idiographic mediational activity of the person. As some answers to these questions have unfolded it has been necessary to reevaluate our concepts about the test. It is not really an x-ray to the mind. Were that true it would be delightful, but in reality, the data of the test provide a glimpse of how the individual works with the world, or that part of the world that is less precise.

Rorschach apparently sensed this, although information available to him was far more limited than is now the case. Certainly, he was intrigued with the Helmholtz concept of an "apperceptive mass" and he tried to use that concept in understanding the differences in response that he obtained in his samples. During the past 40 years, beginning about 20 years after Rorschach's death, there has been a great deal of contention that the feature of "projection" constitutes the primary basis of Rorschach responses. That is probably not true. Certainly, the feature of projection plays an important role in the Rorschach, just as it might in an interview, or responses to a sentence completion, or an apperceptive test, or even in some parts of intelligence tests, but the main or primary feature of the Rorschach answer is created by the "routine" psychology of the person, or stated differently, the manner in which the person has been accustomed to dealing with stimuli, and especially those stimuli that require translation and decision operations. People develop psychological habits, and as aging occurs those habits, or styles, or tendencies are prone to occur with a greater frequency as decision making or problem solving situ-

Table 1
Correlation Coefficients for Two Testings with Two Groups of Children, One Group Retested After 24 Months, and the Second Group Retested After 30 Months, Compared with Retest Data for 100 Adults Retested After 36 to 39 Months

Variable Description		First Test Age 6 Retested After 24 Months $n = 30$		First Test Age 9 — Retested After 30 Months $n = 25$		100 Adults Retested After 36-39 Months	
		r	r^2	r	r^2	r	r^2
R	Responses	.67	.45	.61	.37	.79	.63
P	Popular Responses	.77	.59	.74	.59	.73	.53
Zf	*Z* Frequency	.55	.30	.68	.46	.83	.69
F	Pure Form	.51	.26	.69	.48	.70	.49
M	Human Movement	.48	.23	.62	.38	.87	.76
FM	Animal Movement	.49	.24	.60	.36	.72	.52
m	Inanimate Movement	.13	.02	.09	.01	.31	.10
a	Active Movement	.86	.74	.81	.66	.86	.74
p	Passive Movement	.42	.18	.29	.08	.75	.56
FC	Form Color Answers	.38	.14	.34	.12	.86	.73
CF+C+Cn	Color Dominant Answers	.27	.07	.35	.12	.79	.63
Sum *C*	Sum Weighted Color Answers	.41	.17	.58	.34	.86	.74
Sum *SH*	Sum of All Grey-Black and Shading Answers	.08	.01	.29	.08	.66	.43
Percentage-Ratios							
L	Lambda	.18	.03	.39	.15	.82	.68
X+%	Extended Good Form	.84	.71	.86	.74	.80	.64
Afr	Affective Ratio	.51	.26	.79	.62	.90	.81
3*r*+(2)/*R*	Egocentricity Index	.78	.61	.74	.55	.87	.77
EA	Experience Actual	.19	.04	.45	.20	.85	.73
ep	Experience Potential	.20	.04	.57	.32	.72	.52

ations arise, and this tendency to become more and more consistent is reflected in Rorschach behavior quite well.

Numerous temporal consistency studies on the Rorschach have been reported for adults, and illustrate that the majority of variables included in the Comprehensive System are very sturdy over various time intervals ranging from seven days to three years (Exner, Armbruster, & Viglione, 1978; Exner, 1978). The most extensive of these involved the retesting of 100 nonpatients after a three year interval. Retest correlations ranged from .90 for the Affective Ratio to .66 for the Sum of all grey-black and shading answers. Today, I would like to share with you some additional data about this consistency that may signal something about when it develops in the younger person.

The voluminous literature of developmental psychology illustrates that extensive changes occur with the youngster during relatively short intervals. Thus, we would not expect the sort of temporal consistency in Rorschach behavior to exist in children as it does in adults, but at the same time, as the child grows older, some features of a "developing" consistency should appear among the data.

In our first study (Thomas & Exner, Note 1) two groups of children were retested after relatively long periods. One group consisted of 30 nonpatient children tested first shortly after entering the first grade. It consisted of 17 females and 13 males all between the ages of six years, two months and six years, five

Table 2
Correlation Coefficients for Two Testings for Two Groups of 25 Subjects Each With the Second Test Occurring Seven Days After the First

Variable-Description		25 Adults		25 Eight-Year-Olds	
		r	r^2	*r*	r^2
R	Responses	.86	.74	.88	.77
P	Popular Responses	.84	.71	.86	.74
Zf	Z Frequency	.88	.78	.91	.83
F	Pure Form	.68	.47	.79	.62
M	Human Movement	.81	.66	.90	.81
FM	Animal Movement	.63	.40	.75	.56
m	Inanimate Movement	.28	.08	.49	.24
a	Active Movement	.91	.83	.91	.83
p	Passive Movement	.84	.71	.86	.74
FC	Form Color Responses	.93	.87	.90	.81
CF+C+Cn	Color Dominant Responses	.82	.68	.89	.79
Sum *C*	Sum Weighted Color	.85	.72	.88	.77
Sum *SH*	Sum Grey-Black Shading	.51	.26	.70	.49
Percentages-Ratio					
L	Lambda	.73	.54	.82	.68
X+%	Extended Good Form	.88	.78	.95	.90
Afr	Affective Ratio	.93	.86	.91	.83
3r+(2)/R	Egocentricity Index	.91	.82	.94	.88
EA	Experience Actual	.83	.69	.85	.72
ep	Experience Potential	.62	.39	.74	.55

months. Ten examiners were used with none collecting more than four protocols. These children were retested after approximately 24 months, shortly after they entered third grade by 10 different examiners, with none collecting more than three records. The second group consisted of 25 nine-year-olds, 14 females and 11 males, tested for the first time while they were in the fourth grade, and retested approximately 30 months later. Eight examiners were used for both testings, with no examiner taking more than seven of the 50 protocols or testing the same child twice. The retest correlations for these two groups, plus those for the 100 adults retested after three years, are shown in Table 1.

These data reveal that the nine-year-olds do tend to have slightly higher retest correlations for several variables than the sevens, but in only three instances (X+%, Active Movement, and Populars) are the correlations similar to those for the adult group. In those three instances, all groups have substantially high retest correlations. When the two groups of children are compared, a similar diversity exists for many variables. They are quite similar for four more variables (*R*, *FC*, *m*, and the Egocentricity Index), but are quite disparate for 12 of the 19 variables. These findings should not be surprising in light of the expected development that should occur for each of the groups over a two or two and one half year period. The disparity between the groups might have been greater if the differences in ages had been greater. They are separated by only three years. These somewhat low retest correlations do not necessarily reflect on the validity or utility of the test with children, but do indicate that data collected at one point in the developmental process may not predict very accurately what the Rorschach data will be like after a significant interval. However, the data do not indicate whether children would display greater consistency over a much shorter interval. Retest data for adults, where the second test was administered after only seven days showed remarkably high correlations (Exner, 1978). A similar study was completed to determine if the same might be the case for children (Brent & Exner, Note 2).

Twenty-five third-grade students, ranging in age from eight years, two months to eight years, eight months were retested after seven days. Twelve examiners were used, six for each testing, with none collecting more than five records. The results of this study are presented in Table 2, which also includes the retest correlations for 25 adults retested after seven days that have been reported earlier.

The retest correlations for each of these groups are remarkably similar, with nearly all being very high. Whereas the data presented in Table 1 indicates that the Rorschach, when used with children, will not be very stable over long periods, these data indicate considerable consistency over a brief interval. The remaining question concerns the stability of the test data for intervals of less than two years, but more than seven days. Obviously, a large sample longitudinal study would be required to address that issue with precision, however, some added information may be gleaned from a third study (Alinsky & Exner, Note 3).

This investigation involved the retesting of two groups of 20 subjects each. The retest occurred during a period of 260 to 290 days after the first Rorschach administration. In each group, 10 of the 20 subjects were drawn from black or hispanic urban populations, while the remaining 10 subjects in each group were drawn from white, suburban populations. Included in the selection criteria, in addition to parental consent, were the provisos that each child was performing adequately in school, and that none had a psychiatric history. The 20 subjects in the first group ranged in age from seven years, two months to seven years, seven months at the first testing, and all were in the second grade. The 20 subjects in the second group ranged in age from 15 years, three months, to 15 years, eight months at the first test, and all were in 10th grade classes. Twenty-two examiners were used to collect the 80 records, with none taking more than five, and none retesting the same subject. The correlations for these two groups, retested after approximately nine months are shown in Table 3.

The findings for these two groups indicate a much greater stability of scores among the 15-year-olds as compared to the sevens. In fact, many of the correlations for this older group are very comparable to those obtained for adults retested after three years. This suggests that many of the personality features represented by Rorschach variables are stabilizing, or have stabilized by this mid-adolescent period. Conversely, the seven-year-old group reflects a substantially greater disparity of scores at the retest. Only 6 of the 19 variables have truly high retest correlations (*R, P, F,* Active Movement, X+%, and the Egocentricity Index). This should not be surprising in light of the many rapid developmental changes that occur among sevens.

The composite of these three studies renders information that should be useful to Rorschach interpretation with children. First, and most obvious, the data reaffirm that children do, indeed change over time in their Rorschach behavior, and that the younger the child, the more change may be expected. Therefore, it would be very erroneous to assume that test findings developed from a record of a younger child can be used as indications of "things to come." Second, that as subjects age into mid- or late adolescence, the likelihood is greater that the results will reflect a more stabilized psychology. And third, and possibly most important, is the fact that the retest correlations for the X+% are consistently high for all groups in all of these studies. This not only suggests that perceptual accuracy appears to stabilize early, but clearly contradicts the often heard interpretation of a low X+% in

Table 3
Correlation Coefficients for Two Testings for Two Groups of Younger Subjects, Each With the Second Testing Occurring Approximately Nine Months After the First Testing

Variable-Description		First Test, Age 7 — Retest After 9 Months $n = 20$		First Test, Age 15 — Retest After 9 Months $n = 20$	
		r	r^2	r	r^2
R	Responses	.71	.50	.80	.64
P	Popular Responses	.88	.77	.83	.69
Zf	Z Frequency	.62	.38	.79	.62
F	Pure Form	.82	.67	.74	.55
M	Human Movement	.64	.21	.82	.67
FM	Animal Movement	.53	.28	.70	.49
m	Inanimate Movement	.06	.01	.17	.03
a	Active Movement	.77	.59	.85	.72
p	Passive Movement	.39	.15	.64	.41
FC	Form Color Answers	.28	.08	.81	.66
CF+C	Color Dominant Answers	.46	.21	.71	.50
Sum-*C*	Sum Weighted Color	.37	.14	.70	.49
Sum *SH*	Sum of All Grey-Black & Shading Answers	.11	.01	.48	.23
Percentage-Ratios					
L	Lambda	.24	.06	.76	.58
X+%	Extended Good Form	.86	.74	.83	.69
Afr	Affective Ratio	.61	.37	.89	.79
3*r*+(2) *R*	Egocentricity Index	.70	.49	.86	.74
EA	Experience Actual	.23	.05	.73	.53
ep	Experience Potential	.18	.03	.64	.41

the record of a child as being attributed to the fact that he or she is only a child. This finding coincides very well with normative data reported earlier (Exner, 1978).

There are two other studies that I would like to share with you that seem to bear directly on this issue of reliability or temporal consistency of the test. The first was conducted by Hulsart (Note 5), and was designed to assess the stability of the major structural variables under a retest condition in which severely disturbed children were encouraged to "improve" their performance. This study used 55 children, between the ages of 11 and 15, who were drawn randomly from inpatient and daycare populations of a children's psychiatric unit. All were screened for intellectual deficiency and neurological involvement. They were randomized into two groups of 27 and 28 subjects each, and administered the test by one of eight examiners, none of whom were aware of the purpose of the study and all used a standard procedure of administration, with the exception that each subject was instructed to give two responses per card. The retest occurred two days later, with each subject tested by a different examiner. The retest was introduced to one group by the project coordinator who told each subject that the staff, including the professional regarded as the most "significant other" for the child, had reviewed the findings of the first test and reached the conclusion that while the subject did well, all agreed that the subject could render a better performance and, "We'd like to give you a second chance at this test so that we can see the very best you can do." The retest was introduced to the control group by simply noting that the test is always administered twice as a standard part of the routine of the facility.

The results indicate no significant differences for any of the major structural variables for either test, between or within the groups, even though many of the retest answers given by the experimental groups were different than those delivered in the first test. These findings, though intriguing, raised several issues. The subjects were seriously disturbed and possibly the instructions to the experimental group were too ambiguous and/or too threatening. The key word, *best*, might have been interpreted in a variety of ways; or it is possible that the severe pathology present could have been an overwhelming variable that inhibited any significant alterations in performance. These issues provoked a new design which involved nonpatient children as the target population (Thomas & Exner, Note 5).

Sixty nonpatient eight-year-olds, 30 male and 30 female, were recruited for the study from four third grade classes in the same school district. They were randomized into two groups of 15 males and 15 females. Each subject was tested twice, with each test being administered on a school day, during regular class hours, but none during the play periods. Ten examiners were randomized across the 60 subjects so that no examiner tested any subject twice, or more than four subjects from a single class. Each examiner collected 12 records. None of the examiners were aware of the nature of the study, assuming that they were collecting data in a routine reliability investigation. The retest was completed on the third or fourth day after the first testing. The subjects had been recruited through their parents and school officials for participation in an examiner training program, and told that the records would be taken as a matter of practice for the examiners. Thus, each subject anticipated being tested at least twice. No additional information was provided to the 30 control subjects except to note that a different examiner would be used at each testing. The 30 subjects in the experimental group were specifically instructed to give *different* answers in their second test. This was explained to them using the premise that examiners tend to hear the same answers over and over, and that their training would be improved by hearing different kinds of responses. All examiners used the standard procedure for administration, *except if* they had to encourage a subject because only one answer had been given to Card I, the standard prompting, "I think if you'll take your time and look a bit longer you find something else too" was lengthened to include, "...and I hope that you'll find at least two things in each one."

The retest correlations for the two groups are shown in Table 4. It will be noted that the correlations for the experimental group are very similar to those for the control group for 10 of the 13 individual variables and 4 of the 6 percentages and ratios. The main differences between the two groups occurs for the frequency of *pure F* responses, with the experimental group giving significantly more in the second record; inanimate movement, with the experimental group giving significantly more in the second test, and the Sum of the grey-black and shading responses with experimentals giving significantly fewer of these answers in the second test. The differences between the groups for these three variables creates the differences for Lambda and the Experience Potential. It is also interesting to note that the retest correlations for the control group are remarkably similar to those previously illustrated in Table 2 for the 25 eight-year-olds retested after seven days.

Another important set of data to be examined in this study concerns shifts in the directionality of five ratios that are important foundations of interpretation. Data from the retest of 100 nonpatient adults, retested after three years, revealed very little change in directionality for that group in four of the five ratios (Exner, Armbruster, & Viglione, 1978). Results from this study, for each of the five ratios, are shown in Table 5, and are very similar to those found in

Table 4
Correlation Coefficients for Two Testings of Two Groups of Eight-Year-Olds, Retested After Three or Four Days, With the Experimental Group Instructed to Give Different Answers in the Second Testing

Variable-Description		Experimental Group $n = 30$		Control Group $n = 30$	
		r	r^2	r	r^2
R	Responses	.81	.66	.89	.79
P	Popular Responses	.76	.58	.84	.71
Zf	*Z* Frequency	.89	.79	.87	.76
F	Pure Form	.59	.35	.81	.66
M	Human Movement	.91	.83	.89	.79
FM	Animal Movement	.78	.61	.75	.56
m	Inanimate Movement	.27	.07	.48	.23
a	Active Movement	.94	.88	.90	.81
p	Passive Movement	.82	.67	.87	.76
FC	Form Color Responses	.91	.83	.89	.79
CF+C+Cn	Color Dominant Responses	.83	.69	.87	.76
Sum *C*	Sum Weighted Color	.88	.77	.85	.72
Sum *SH*	Sum Grey-Black Shading	.44	.19	.71	.50
Percentage-Ratios					
L	Lambda	.67	.45	.82	.67
X+%	Extended Good Form	.84	.71	.94	.88
Afr	Affective Ratio	.92	.85	.91	.83
3*r*+(2)/*R*	Egocentricity Index	.90	.81	.93	.86
EA	Experience Actual	.84	.71	.88	.77
ep	Experience Potential	.38	.14	.70	.49

the long-term adult study.

Both the experimental and control groups tend to remain very stable for directionality in four of the five ratios. Only 8 of the 60 subjects, and only three controls, changed direction for the *Erlebnistypus* (EB) when a criterion of a two or more point difference between ΣM and ΣC is applied, and of 32 of the 60 subjects showing directionality in both tests, *only one*, a control subject changed direction. Similarly, 48 of the 60 showed at least a one point difference between *EA* and *ep* in both tests, and *only one*, a control subject changed direction. Forty-five of the 60 showed at least a one point difference between active and passive movement in both tests, and *only* two, both experimental subjects, changed direction, and 47 of the 60 showed a difference of one point or more between *FC* and *CF+C* in both tests, and only one changed direction. The greatest frequency of shifting direction appears in the Experience Base (*eb*), in which 21 of the 60 subjects showed a directionality in the second test that is the opposite of the first, with 15 of those changes occurring among experimentals. This is not surprising, as four of the six variables that constitute the *eb* have the lowest retest reliabilities of all variables under normal retest conditions with nonpatients. These include *m*, *V*, *C'*, and *Y*.

A very important issue in this study is whether the independent variable was effective, that is, did the subjects in the experimental group follow the instructions to give different answers when taking the test for a second time? This was evaluated by comparing frequencies of "same" and "different" answers, with the criterion for a "same" answer defined as, any response with identical content to that given in Test 1, using the

Table 5
Test-Retest Frequencies for Two Groups of Eight-Year-Olds Concerning Five Ratios, with *Z* Values Concerning Change in Directionality

Ratios	Number Showing Direction In Both Tests		Number Showing No Direction In Either Test		Number Showing Direction In Both Tests Who Changed Direction		Number Showing Direction In Only One Test		Total Changing In Second Test		*Z* Value	*p**
	Exp	Con	Exp	Con	Exp	Con	Exp	Con	Exp	Con		
EB	17	15	8	13	0	1	5	2	5	3	7.9	<.001
eb	19	23	0	3	4	2	11	4	15	6	1.8	ns
EA:ep	26	22	1	3	0	1	3	5	3	6	7.7	<.001
a:p	24	21	2	4	2	0	4	5	6	5	5.5	<.001
FC:CF+C	22	25	2	3	1	0	6	2	7	2	5.1	<.001

Note: Directionality is defined for *EB* as two points or more and for all other ratios as one point or more.
* One-tailed.

same or nearly the same location area. In other words, a response of two men fighting to the Popular area on Card III would be considered the same as two men working at night, given to the same area, even though the second answer might include the additional determinants of *C′* or *Y*. Conversely, if the answer in Test 2 were two women dancing, that response would be considered different than the Test 1 response. Data concerning the replication of identical or nearly identical answers are shown in Table 6. These data indicate that the two groups gave about the same number of responses in each test, but much more important to the issue here, the experimental subjects do appear to have followed directions. They repeated only about 14% of their Test 1 responses in Test 2, while control subjects repeated about 86% of their Test 1 answers. These findings seem to support the proposition that a consistency will exist in the perceptual-cognitive operations of a person even though some of the manifest behaviors are altered.

Collectively, these five studies seem to offer considerable information about the reliability of the test when used with younger subjects over various time intervals. Adding these findings to those already reported on the retest reliability with adults seems to make it practical to suggest that past claims that the Rorschach is of limited use because of reliability problems have, at least, been overstated.

On a different level, the accumulated data on the temporal consistency of the test offer some intriguing "food for thought." First, they tend to reaffirm something that we've known in psychology for quite some time, namely that the human tends to be quite consistent in his or her operations or habits, but more important for purposes here, that the Rorschach is one way of gaining information about those habits. Second, it is quite exciting to find this test stability occurring even though much of the verbiage, from which these consistent scores are derived, is altered significantly. In other words, even though we tell someone not to do something, he or she tends to do it anyhow if it is an integral part of their psychological system. While this is not necessarily a new revelation for psychology, it does help to understand the test better. If the earlier question, "what is this test?" is resurrected, the answer is a bit clearer. It is a set of stimuli which, under a given instructional set, provoke into operation many of the "natural" psychological features of the individual that have formed or are forming; or stated differently, it provokes the response tendencies or styles that will ultimately be

Table 6
Total Number of Responses by Card Given by Each of Two Groups of Eight-Year-Olds Plus the Frequencies and Percentages of Answers That Were Repeated in the Second Testing

Card	Experimental Group $n = 30$				Control Group $n = 30$			
	Total *R* Test 1	Total *R* Test 2	Repeated Answers	%	Total *R* Test 1	Total *R* Test 2	Repeated Answers	%
I	63	66	4	.06	60	62	51	.85
II	61	63	7	.11	64	61	56	.87
III	58	62	6	.10	61	57	49	.80
IV	51	57	9	.17	49	54	42	.85
V	39	34	7	.17	44	47	38	.86
VI	47	44	8	.17	51	48	46	.90
VII	52	50	10	.19	55	51	49	.89
VIII	63	65	9	.14	59	60	53	.89
IX	41	39	6	.14	46	44	43	.93
X	73	71	11	.15	69	65	51	.73
Totals	548	551	77		558	546	481	
Means	18.26	18.36	2.56	.14	18.60	18.20	16.30	.86

Note: Repeated answer defined as identical or near identical content to same or near same direction.

among those features that mark the person as a personality. I do not mean to cast aside the notion that the test is also a projective instrument, for obviously that would be foolish. Each protocol is also characterized by its own idiography and is often rich in unique verbiage that is exclusive to the person who delivers it. This material is often quite valuable to interpretation and should not be neglected in research. In fact, the challenge to both the interpreter and the researcher is to sort through the features of the response with the objective of identifying those that illustrate the basic psychological styles or habits of the person as differentiated from those that permit a glimpse into the more private and personalized world of the subject. Some of us have been prone to make this differentiation using structural data to identify the former, and content to address the latter. But this may be an approach that, while useful for the moment, neglects some of the breadth of data available, and particularly the issue of how these features merge to provoke the final decision of what answer, selected from many available, will be delivered. A more useful understanding of that merging process requires that research be extended more directly to the events that occur between stimulus exposure and response.

For years, most of us using the test have faithfully recorded first reaction times, even though the research on that feature has been very equivocal. But there probably is something there. Our problem is that we have been timing the wrong thing. The mean reaction time to Card I, for 525 nonpatient adults is 5.78 seconds ($SD = 2.11$). Thus most first answers occur between 3½ and 7 seconds. If a response occurs in an interval of less than three seconds, some tend to think of it as representing a potential for impulsiveness; but is it really? In some 300msec, the scan of the eye may criss-cross the blot many times, and many pauses occur long the way. Figure 1 is a crude facsmilie of the eye scan of a 20-year-old nonpatient male to Card I for the first 250 to 350msec. It has been reconstructed from videotape and thus, has the flaw of imprecise timing, but the interval represented is not less than 250msec or more than 350msec. It encompasses most of the blot and raises the issue that the entire stimulus input may conceivably occur in less than 1/20th of the time span be-

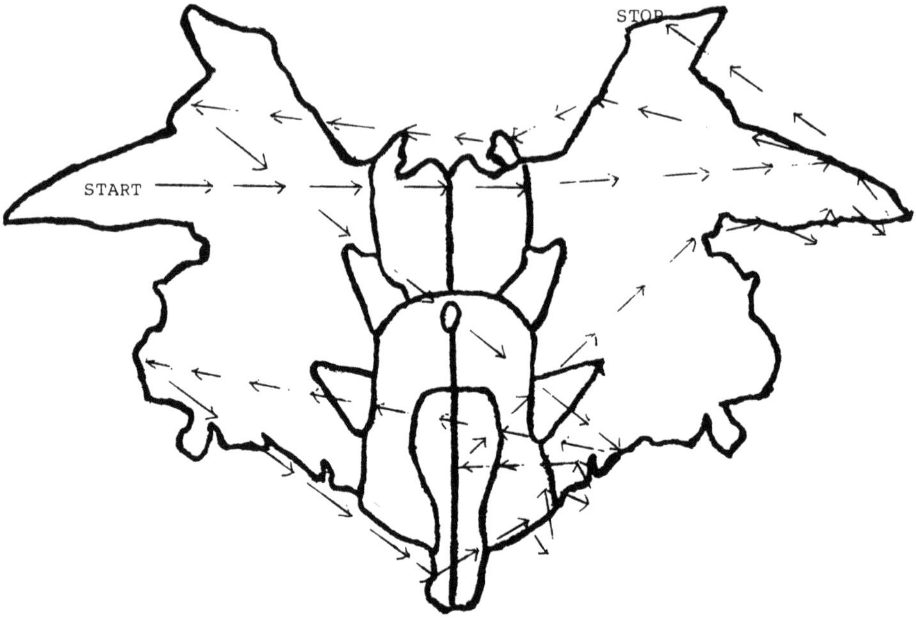

Figure 1. Eye Scanning Activity of Card I by a 20-Year-Old Male During an Interval of Between 250msec and 350msec After Exposure.

tween exposure and response. What happens during the remaining 19/20ths of that interval. How do the formed response styles merge with the more personal psychological world of the individual in creating potential answers, and the final decision about which answer to deliver? Because the test stimulates these processes, it also holds the potential for being part of the laboratory from which those answers can be derived. And if we can find those answers, we will surely be able to perform better in the service of others. I am optimistic that we can, for after all, that kind of searching for truth concerning people is what we are all about.

The Future of Psychodiagnosis Revisited

IRVING B. WEINER

Abstract: Convergence among theoretical perspectives in clinical psychology during the last decade has moderated many earlier disputes concerning the worth and propriety of personality assessment. Survey data indicate that traditional psychodiagnostic methods continue to be widely used and taught. New directions in professional practice, especially in relation to health and forensic concerns, are providing increasing opportunities for clinical psychologists to find rewarding roles as expert diagnostic consultants.

In 1971 I was invited to give a colloquium at a major university with a highly regarded clinical psychology program. The faculty in the program were concerned about their students' lack of interest in learning about psychological testing, and my task was to present the positive case for psychodiagnostic assessment. This was to include dispelling doubts about the worth and propriety of psychodiagnosis and explaining why clinicians should strive to become competent diagnosticians.

This was not an easy task in 1971, which was a low point in the history of psychodiagnosis. Psychodiagnosis can be defined as the clinical use of psychological tests to facilitate personality assessment. As such, it was under heavy attack when the 1960s drew to a close. The emergence of behavioral approaches in psychology had seriously questioned the value of personality assessment. Mischel (1968) and Peterson (1968) had argued in influential books that clinicians who want to predict behavior reliably should stop trying to infer personality characteristics from test responses and instead concentrate on constructing test situations that provide representative samples of the behavior to be predicted.

Concurrently, the emergence of humanistic approaches was challenging the morality of using psychodiagnostic instruments for classification purposes. The writings of Maslow (1962) and Rogers (1961), stressing the unique individuality of each person, had led many psychologists to feel (a) that what is true about people is only how they experience themselves, not anything shown by an external evaluation, and (b) that attempts at classification, whether according to personality traits or dimensions of behavior, are dehumanizing procedures that strip people of their freedom and dignity.

I prepared a paper for the colloquium that reviewed and responded to these criticisms, affirmed the clinical and research utility of psychological testing, and summarized available data on the use and teaching of psychodiagnostic methods. The paper appeared in the *Journal of Personality Assessment* in 1972 under the title "Does Psychodiagnosis Have a Future?" On being invited to give this address, I thought it would be fitting to update that paper and revisit the future of psychodiagnosis — especially since the last decade has been a period of vitality in psychodiagnosis that has moderated many earlier disputes, expanded our knowledge and brought growing numbers of psychologists into rewarding roles as expert diagnostic consultants.

Moderating Theoretical Disputes

In contrast to some earlier periods of sharp and not always civil debate among clinical psychologists of different persuasions, a fairly ecumenical spirit has been afoot in recent years. Surveys by Garfield and Kurtz (1977) and Norcross and Prochaska (1982) reveal that a substantial number of clinicians regard themselves as having an "eclectic" theoretical orientation. Most of these eclectic psychologists embrace some synthesis of diverse theories, and most other clinicians who identify themselves as committed to one primary theoretical orientation are nevertheless willing to indicate secondary orientations that also influence their professional work.

As I have elaborated elsewhere (Weiner, 1983), this openness of most clinicians to others' views means that reliable data and demonstrably effective strategies are more likely than in the past to receive their just due, regardless of the theoretical frame of reference in which they emerge. The waning of parochial dogmatism in psychotherapy has been illustrated in recent books and articles by Garfield (1980, 1982), Goldfried (1982a, 1982b), and Wachtel (1977, 1982) and will not be our focus here. As far as psychodiagnosis is concerned, earlier disputes have been moderated both by a less contentious spirit and by significant substantive advances as well.

With respect to distinguishing between traditional and behavioral assessment, for example, we have come a long way from some previous views that traditional methods are inferential and hence unreliable, whereas behavioral methods are representative and hence accurate (Goldfried & Kent, 1972; Weiner, 1983). Most workers in the field have come to realize that inferences can rarely be avoided in clinical assessment, regardless of the approach one uses, and are not necessarily disadvantageous. What all clinical assessors must do, whatever their approach, is first to monitor the extent of inference involved in getting from client responses to personality description and behavioral predictions, and second, to limit themselves to conclusions that can be justifed on the basis of sound concepts or solid empirical data.

Thus, behavioral assessors can seldom find a perfectly representative situation in which a client's behavior will provide unequivocal answers to complex assessment questions. Instead, they usually must contrive situations as best they can to elicit reasonably reliable behavioral data samples, and in recent years behavioral assessment has come increasingly to consist of clinical interviews, personality inventories, self-report measures, and role-playing exercises — each of which requires inferential processes to yield conclusions about real-life behavior outside of the assessment situation. Moreover, as behavioral assessment has matured and prospered, and especially as it has been influenced by cognitive perspectives, many of its proponents have begun to address not only what people can be observed to say and do, but also what kinds of feelings, fantasies, expectations, and beliefs they seem to harbor (Ciminero, Calhoun, & Adams, 1977; Goldfried, 1983; Hersen & Bellack, 1976; Kendall & Hollon, 1981; Landau & Goldfried, 1981).

Over time, then, behavioral assessment is coming to stand less as a critic of traditional assessment than as a complementary approach, dealing with similar conceptual and psychometric issues and exerting a constructive influence on how best to deal with these issues. If anything, as far as I am concerned, these advances in behavioral assessment have enriched psychodiagnosis in the clinic and the laboratory, rather than detracted from it, and they are likely to continue doing so.

One case in point is the care that has been taken in some quarters to identify features of traditional clinical tests that may elicit representative samples of behavior. Recent developments in Rorschach testing, for example, distinguish between two distinct components of subjects' responses: one component that involves problem-solving behavior on a perceptual-cognitive task and therefore provides a reliable representative index of problem-solving behavior in other situations, and a second component that reflects some projection in dealing with an ambiguous situation and hence yields speculative hypotheses about the subject's underlying attitudes and concerns (Exner, 1983; Exner & Weiner, 1982, Chap. 1; Weiner, 1977).

Turning to humanistic approaches, most clinicians have come to recognize that abuses of personality assessment resulting in erroneous or discriminatory classifications do not reflect any inherently dehumanizing features of psychodiagnostic instruments. Good clinical testing pays as much attention to how people are different from each other as to how they are alike, and there is no compelling reason to regard accurate assessment of a person's assets and limitations as necessarily damaging to him or her (Appelbaum, 1976; Sugarman, 1978). To the contrary, some clinicians writing from a humanistic point of view have suggested ways in which interpersonal interaction can be enhanced through assessment procedures, especially if they are used as part of a therapeutic encounter and clients are involved in the evaluation of their test responses (Craddick, 1975; Fischer, 1970, 1973).

Beyond these matters of theoretical rapprochement, psychodiagnosis has gained considerable status within psychology during the last decade by virtue of extensive research that has expanded normative and validating data on existing clinical tests and introduced promising new measures as well. A short and far from comprehensive list includes the following: new revisions of the Wechsler scales for both children and adults (Wechsler, 1974, 1981); the development of the Kaufman Assessment Battery for Children (Kaufman & Kaufman, 1983); the formation of the Halstead-Reitan and Luria-Nebraska batteries for neuropsychological assessment (Boll, 1981, 1983; Golden, 1981); continued refinements of the MMPI (Butcher, 1979; Gynther & Gynther, 1983) and the introduction of Millon's (1982) Multiaxial Clinical Inventory; improved psychometric foundations for the Bender Gestalt (Lacks, in press; Tolor & Brannigan, 1980); and the development of the Comprehensive System for Rorschach assessment (Exner, 1974, 1978; Exner & Weiner, 1982) and cumulative evidence of the reliability and validity of this instrument (Parker, 1983). To this can be added such important books tying psychodiagnosis to the basic facts and theories of psychology as Lezak's (1976) *Neuropsychological Assessment*, Maloney and Ward's (1976) *Psychological Assessment*, Palmer's (1983) second edition of *Assessment of Children*, and the revised edition of Rickers-Ovsiankina's (1977) *Rorschach Psychology*.

At the same time, notions that behavior is situation specific, and that personality characteristics that lend continuity to behavioral styles therefore do not exist to be measured, have been laid pretty much to rest under a heavy weight of reason and evidence. Today's mainstream psychology views how people act as a complex function of their abiding dispositions to behave in certain ways and the nature of the situations in which they find themselves. This contemporary interactional perspective makes ample room for the assessment of personality traits to figure prominently in the exploration of human behavior (Endler & Magnusson, 1976; Rorer & Widiger, 1983; Wachtel, 1973). Atkinson (1981) has recently made this point in no uncertain terms: "It is time to drag assessment of personality into the mainstream of scientific motivational psychology and a commensurate developmental psychology" (p. 117).

Teaching and Use of Psychodiagnosis

A widely held view on the future of psychodiagnosis at the time of my 1972 paper was that it didn't have one. Numerous impressions and some data were leading many psychologists to conclude that psychodiagnostic tests were being discarded by practicing clinicians and were disappearing from the curricula of graduate training programs. Despite the theoretical rapprochements and substantive advances in psychodiagnosis during the 1970s, serious doubts about the value and viability of traditional clinical assessment procedures continued to be expressed. Thus, journal articles of the last several years have told us that psychodiagnosis is losing status in clinical psychology (Bersoff, 1973; Ivnik, 1977); that "psychological testing... is declining as a viable component of clinical psychology" (Cleveland, 1976; p. 317); and that "psychologists have all but given up on traditional assessment procedures" (Lewandowski & Saccuzzo, 1976, p. 17). A frequent theme in these articles is that, if there is any vestige of respect left to clinical testing and any remaining hopes for its survival, they are vested in objective measures that can be interpreted actuarily, and not in projective instruments or measures that rely on clinical judgment.

I have always had difficulty finding data to justify such gloomy prophecies, and I still do. Let me mention briefly some of the key studies in this regard and then share with you some new and not yet published data on the teaching and use of traditional assessment procedures.

First, with respect to the use of psychodiagnostic instruments, reports from community mental health centers, outpatient clinics, and college and university counseling centers document frequent use of traditional tests for intellectual and personality assessment (Piotrowski & Keller, 1978; Sell & Torres-Henry, 1979; Stevens, Yock, & Perlman, 1979). Even in counseling centers, where testing focuses primarily on instruments related to vocational planning, three traditional psychodiagnostic measures — the WAIS, the MMPI, and the Rorschach — are among the 10 most frequently used tests. Among individual clinicians, a survey by Wade and Baker (1977) of APA Division 12 numbers revealed that 83% of the 236 respondents used tests with their clients, and 72% used test results at some stage of their treatment work. These clinicians were spending about 15% of their time each week in assessment activities, and over 85% believed that clinicians should know at least one test well.

Second, with respect to the teaching of assessment, there has been and continues to be strong feeling on the part of internship directors that students coming to them should receive better and more extensive preparation in psychodiagnosis than their graduate programs provide (Russ, 1978; Shemberg & Keeley, 1974: Shemberg & Leventhal, 1981). In a survey by Garfield and Kurtz (1973), 89% of internship directors responding agreed moderately or strongly that "all clinicians should be well versed in diagnostic testing." When Petzel and Berndt (1980) asked internship directors to indicate three kinds of courses they would most like to see on an applicant's transcript, the kinds of courses most frequently mentioned by their 90 respondents were courses in psychodiagnostic assessment. Skills in psychological testing are also listed among the most important requirements for students in school psychology and master's level clinical programs (Clair, Osterman, Kiraly, Klausmeier, & Griff, 1971; Smith & Soper, 1978).

Third, with respect to the place of projective techniques in the present and future of psychodiagnosis, a survey by Levy and Fox (1975) of employers who had posted positions for clinical psychologists found that 91% of 334 settings responding expected their job applicants to have testing skills, and 84% expected these skills to include projective techniques. Brown and McGuire (1976) asked community mental health agencies and hospitals which tests they used most frequently for personality assessment. In order, the six most frequent measures indicated by 118 responding settings were Rorschach, DAP, TAT, HTP, Bender, and MMPI — the first four of which are projectives. The clinicians surveyed by Wade and his colleagues, when asked which tests they would recommend that clinical psychology students learn, mentioned the Rorschach most often, followed in order of frequency by the TAT, WAIS, MMPI, Bender, WISC, picture drawings, and sentence completion — the first two and four out of eight being projectives (Wade, Baker, Morton, & Baker, 1978). Consistent with these findings, Levitt (1973) reported that 80% of a sample of practicum directors felt that it was important for practicing clinicians to master projective techniques, and Ritzler and Del Gaudio (1976) learned that 94 of 100 responding APA-approved doctoral programs were teaching their students the Rorschach, and 81 were placing major emphasis on it in their assessment courses.

And now for some current, unpub-

Table 1
Percent of Clinical Settings Using Ten Psychological Tests

Test	1961[a]		1971[b]		1983[c]	
	%	Rank	%	Rank	%	Rank
WAIS	72	6	93	1	90	1
MMPI	65	7	77	6	85	2
Bender Gestalt	86	4	91	3.5	82	3
Rorschach	93	1	91	3.5	81	4
TAT	88	2.5	91	3.5	76	5
WISC	62	9	75	6	71	6
Peabody PVT	—	..	49	13	69	7
Sentence Completion	49	13	70	8	69	8
HTP	56	12	66	9	69	9
DAP	88	2.5	79	5	68	10

[a]From Sundberg (1961), based on 185 settings.
[b]From Lubin, Wallis, and Paine (1971), based on 251 settings.
[c]From Lubin, Matarazzo, and Larsen (Note 1), based on 221 settings.

lished findings, that colleagues have been good enough to share with me. First, Bernard Lubin has recently repeated his previous survey of test usage in the United States, published in 1971, which had repeated an earlier survey published by Sundberg in 1961. Table 1 shows the frequency with which tests were mentioned as being used in 221 clinical settings, which included psychiatric hospitals, community mental health centers, mental retardation centers, counseling centers, VA hospitals, military settings, and private practice; data from the two previous surveys are included for comparison purposes.

These results reflect continued widespread use of psychodiagnostic instruments, although with some change in rank order. Most notably, the MMPI has become relatively more widely used, moving from sixth to second place, while the Rorschach and TAT have dropped slightly. However, before these or any other data in Table 1 are interpreted to confirm a decline of projective testing, two other facts must be noted. One, apparent from the table, is the small number of percentage points that separate the MMPI, Bender, and Rorschach. The other, in supplementary data reported by Lubin, is that patterns of test usage vary across clinical settings. For example, neither the Rorschach nor the MMPI is among the 10 tests used most frequently in mental retardation settings; the MMPI has more widespread use than the Rorschach among counseling center and military settings; and the Rorschach is mentioned more frequently than the MMPI as a test used in psychiatric hospitals, community mental health centers, VA hospitals, and private practice settings.

Second, in two very recent surveys directors of clinical programs have been asked once again about their current practices in psychodiagnostic training. Donald Leventhal (Note 2) reports that, among 93 responding directors of PhD programs, 97% require training in psychodiagnostics, 87% require at least some training in projective techniques, and two-thirds require two or three courses in psychological testing. Chris Piotrowski (in press) finds that APA-approved doctoral programs in clinical psychology place equal emphasis on projective and objective assessment in their coursework and concludes from reports of 80 respondents that "The projected demise of psychodiagnostic testing as purported in recent years seems to have been premature."

Present and Future Directions in Clinical Psychology

The future of psychodiagnosis is of course tied to the directions of clinical psychology as a science and as a profession. The history in this regard is familiar and has been stated frequently (Blatt, 1975; Holt, 1967; Korchin & Schuldberg, 1981; Rosenwald, 1963; Weiner, 1972). Clinical psychology emerged as a profession with a formal doctoral training program after World War II and through much of the 1950s took psychodiagnostic assessment as its primary applied function. Growing interest in conducting psychotherapy began to replace or at least accompany diagnostic testing as a leading career interest among clinical psychologists during the 1950s, and this evolution was furthered during the 1960s by the leadership of psychologists in advancing a wide variety of intervention modalities, including group and family therapy, behavioral methods, and community mental health approaches. With so much else for them to learn and do, clinical psychologists began to devote less of their time to mastering and conducting psychological test assessment. This trend was fueled by widespread personal experience that newer roles offered more prestige and autonomy, and hence greater professional satisfaction, than merely providing test results in an ancillary way for other people to use in performing the "real" clinical work of treating patients.

For many clinical psychologists, however, the bloom never went off the psychodiagnostic rose. They found that, if they brought their specialized skills in personality assessment sensitively to bear in resolving difficult diagnostic questions that other professionals were unable to answer with other means, they could gain considerable respect, autonomy, and satisfaction as expert consultants. Currently, some newer trends in the profession of clinical psychology are promising to bring increasing numbers of clinical psychologists into the rewarding role of expert diagnostic consultant, where they will find psychodiagnostic skills an asset that is valuable to them and valued by others.

One of these trends is the growing interest and professional involvement in the broad field of health psychology. This includes such specialized areas as neuropsychology, pediatric psychology, geropsychology, and health enhancement, the expansion of which is reflected in such signs as topical books, specialized journals, divisions and sections of APA, and funding support. A common feature of these newly emerging areas of professional emphasis in clinical psychology is that *providing necessary interventions* is often a less challenging and prestigious activity than *being able to determine what kind of intervention is indicated* — which is a question of differential diagnosis frequently referable to some form of personality or behavioral assessment.

Another trend is the expansion of forensic psychology. Many clinicians have become interested in matters of litigation and jurisprudence, and, interested or not, increasing numbers of practitioners are being asked to give opinions on questions of child custody, competence to stand trial, criminal responsibility, impaired functioning, and suitability to work in law enforcement. In this area as in health psychology, the more highly esteemed professional function is not *doing* whatever should or must be done, but *helping to decide what would be best to do.* Once more, the role the clinical psychologist serves is that of expert diagnostic consultant, and sophisticated psychodiagnostic assessment can contribute substantially to filling this role.

Revisiting the future of psychodiagnosis in 1983 has thus been a pleasant task, and certainly easier than defending its future was in 1972. Continued careful research on psychodiagnostic methods and the expert application of psychological test findings in clinical consultation should sustain a bright future for psychodiagnosis and its practitioners.

Megatrends in Personality Assessment: Toward a Human Science Professional Psychology

RICHARD H. DANA

Abstract: Societal megatrends have assessment counterparts — superempiricism, biopsychosocial perspective, person-centering, population-specificity, self-assessment — which are used to examine the contemporary status of professional psychology. A human science approach to research, training, and practice can exemplify a profession that acknowledges these megatrends. The nurture of competent professional psychologists requires a reinvestment in Boulder Model ideology, a human science that is shared with consumers on the basis of values which communicate caring and understanding.

We each elaborate a few major themes that expose a personal presence within our professional lives. Perhaps once in a lifetime comes a self-indulgent opportunity to make a statement that fuses public and private selves with the values which sustain both domains. This paper is concerned with megatrends. A megatrend is a new shibboleth to reframe our perceptions of ourselves and our profession on the canvas of a changing society. Assessment megatrends are larger than reality, ground rather than figure, and easily overlooked in a frenetic agglomeration of new tests. Nonetheless, assessment megatrends provide some contemporary themes for our profession. By listening to these themes we may address issues that have been raised by critics. An elaboration of these themes within our training programs would be reflected ultimately in research and services since they evidence increasing concern for a new paradigm.

It has long been my belief that professional psychology must develop a unique, human-centered paradigm for research, training, and practice. A human science approach can provide the relevance and social concern in research which will render our research efforts directly applicable to the services we provide. This paper uses assessment as a vehicle to introduce and convey the sense of this human science approach and to present an example of how training in professional psychology can be articulated within this idiom.

Prepared for presentation at the meeting of the American Psychological Association as recipient of the 1984 Distinguished Contribution Award of the Society for Personality Assessment, Toronto, August 25, 1984.

Grateful acknowledgement is made to Brian Bolton and Ted May, Alpha and Beta psychologists, respectively, for careful commentary on this paper.

Societal Megatrends

With thanks to John Naisbitt (1982), I borrow both the idea and the substance of some of his 10 megatrends as referents for this paper (Table 1). Briefly, we now inhabit an information society in which public access to information and rate of knowledge acquisition continues to increase. Because the impact of technology is impersonal, we are beginning to acknowledge that simultaneous nourishment by infusion of a personal ingredient is vital to our human well being: high tech must be accompanied by high touch. As we move toward a world economy with long-term planning for species survival, we rediscover a grass roots, participant democracy with decentralization and local problem-solving much as Cronbach (1975) envisioned. Self-help with networking to augment effects leads to multiple options for individuals.

Recently, Ted May and I (1984) restated some of these megatrends in the general culture as they applied to professional psychology (Table 1): access to knowledge, rehumanization, a preventive ethos, metaprofessionals, self-help, and changing population demographics. An information society fosters immediate access to accumulating research content and applications. For example,

Table 1

Megatrends Identified by Naisbitt, in Professional Psychology, and Personality Assessment

Naisbitt	Professional Psychology	Assessment
Information society	Access to knowledge	Superempiricism
High tech/high touch	Rehumanization	Biopsychosocial perspective
World economy	Preventive ethos	Person-centering
Long-term planning	Metaprofessionals	Population-specificity
Decentralization	Self-help	Self-Assessment
Self-help	Changing population demographics	
Participant democracy		
Networking		
South		
Multiple options		

university libraries which despair of ever having complete holdings even in limited areas now can provide routine online access to our research literature, including data bases and document retrieval (Perry & Dana, in press). New opportunities for self-education are one consequence of tapping into existing programs and data bases. Moreover, any individual with a home computer has potential access to educational resources for problem-solving. Public availability of information that was once restricted to professional persons suggests that consumer awareness can result in more realistic expectations for high quality services and greater ability to identify competence in professional practices.

Rehumanization implies a reinfusion of energy into relationships as antidote not only for the increasing impersonality of our social institutions, but the relative unavailability of caring in contacts between professional persons and their clients. As we leech the human element from our technology-based transactions, it is mandatory to focus on quality and personal investment in day-to-day professional applications.

We have painfully learned that tertiary intervention is an endless ritual that can misdirect and obligate our humanity. We ameliorate human misery by fostering endurance and the courage to prevail in the face of intrapersonal blight, interpersonal fiasco, and daily hassles. A preventive ethos, however, is emerging which can increasingly focus attention on planning for a social climate in which quality of life and self-directed lifestyles are feasible for more persons. A new generation of metaprofessionals, paraprofessionals, and lay persons have already popularized this preventive ethos on an individual basis by making holistic health components available to the general population. These persons now provide strong competition for orthodox professional psychologists.

From modest beginnings, the self-help movement in this country has grown to encompass not only a group focus that can multiply scarce treatment resources, but has become a touchstone for new learning and shared access to information (Rodolfa & Hungerford, 1982). No longer do persons feel any exclusive reliance on experts for technical knowledge — knowledge which was unavailable to consumers in an earlier generation. There is a new sense of confidence in applying this knowledge to personal life. In addition, there is public recognition of the limitations of knowledge and/or services provided by the professions. Self-help can also provide a constructive aegis for a growing cynicism regarding quality of services, costs of services, and motivations of service providers.

Finally, the changing population demographics attest to burgeoning of non-white political power, affluence, and acknowledged contribution. Jesse Jackson has made clear in universal idiom that these persons now have the political power to implement social change. Some cultural values of minority persons as contrasted with the dominant culture are communion/cooperativeness as distinct from autarky/competition, person priority as opposed to task priority, and relaxed versus rigid time scheduling. An infusion of these values into the larger culture can foster an augmented humanity for all citizens. The question for minorities is no longer one of simply obtaining a fair share of material goods, but the desire to be part of a society whose values are responsive to human needs.

Megatrends in Personality Assessment

During the last year several reviews have delineated areas of concern which can be summarized by assessment megatrends. Berg (1984) examined nonpsychometric, structured interview assessments which use the interpersonal context as a source of hypotheses relevant to ego functioning, objective relations, and interpersonal dynamics. Dana (1984-a) suggested new assessment domains that include personality disorders, stress and coping, modernity and acculturation, psychological health, and self-assessment. Assessment training should require competence across an adequate repertoire of instruments and demand cross-cultural sophistication for fairness to minority groups. In the 1984 *Annual Review*, Lanyon provided a comprehensive 3-year evaluation of assessment literature. He found an emphasis on normal personality and specificity of psychological disorder within a behavioral/social learning perspective. These trends have encouraged a clear division into theoretical study of personality structure and practical assessment of psychological problems. Smith and Allen (1984) perceived a declining investment in assessment, particularly diagnostic testing which they attribute to professional identity conflicts. By way of remedy, they suggested a consultative role for psychodiagnosticians. Weiner (1983) scrutinized a 10-year period between two of his own reviews. He described a complementarity of traditional and behavioral approaches, an enhanced interpersonal interaction of assessor/assessee, and a more adequate research base with norms, validation, and new measures.

The contents of these assessment reviews provide the basis for identifying several assessment megatrends: a) superempiricism; b) biopsychological perspective; c) person-centering; d) population-specificity and e) self-assessment. Table 1 juxtaposes these assessment megatrends with megatrends that apply to the general culture and to professional psychology. The purpose of this table is to acknowledge the reiteration of societal themas within our professional microcosm.

Superempiricism

Superempiricism refers to the high technology orientation that results in a proliferation of self-report tests with computerized scoring and interpretation. A research basis is now a prerequisite for assessment devices and their applications. The provision of a comprehensive research basis includes new instruments for restricted measurement purposes. These self-report tests have assumed priority for most assessment purposes. Projective techniques such as the Rorschach (Exner & Weiner, 1982), the TAT (Dana, in press-a), and the Bender-Gestalt (Lacks, 1984) require a normative basis for validation as psychodiagnostic instruments if they are to retain their relative frequencies of usage.

Computerized assessment has been available since the 1960s and there were eight reviews of MMPI automated systems in the *Eighth Mental Measurements Yearbook*. However, one reviewer of these systems (Butcher, 1978) indicated that automated assessment was "little more than an art... disguised as a science" (p. 617). He warned that these reports cannot substitute for clinical judgment, are dependent upon relevant demographic data, deify partial truths, and are largely lacking in system validation. Now — in 1984 — each *Monitor* issue is crowded with competing advertisements that extol computer services for many widely used instruments and for some frankly esoteric instruments as well. One vendor offers services for 14 different objective tests, and even the Exner and Piotrowski Rorschach systems have available services. The software to enable individuals/agencies to generate their own reports is also readily available.

Since computer-generated reports are extremely variable in quality/accuracy and their economy and availability leads to practitioner dependency, there is need for continued development of standards for providers. Interim standards, available by 1966, were targeted at vendors rather than consumers. In addition to monitoring consumer use of automated assessment, practitioners need training in ethical use of computer services and software programs. Moreover, research on system validation is mandatory. Demonstrations that compare automated reports on single clients while documenting the clinical astuteness of particular vendors (e.g., the Caldwell Report) are insufficient for high technology assessment.

There are also new practitioner domains — health psychology and clinical child psychology — that have emerged directly from empirical foundations. In health psychology, for example, separate symptoms can be delineated, measures devised for particular at-risk medical populations, and assessment accomplished that is exclusively for goodness-of-fit with specific treatments (Dana, in press-b).

In addition to new clinical populations, all persons are now potential consumers for assessment services. Health hazard appraisal provides actuary based feedback on health risks as a result of completing a questionnaire. Holistic health appraisal uses assessment to describe individual status on components of "wellness" (Shuffield & Dana, 1984).

Biopsychosocial Perspective

Assessment domains and process are now being conceptualized using a systems approach — the biopsychosocial model. This model is replacing the univariate model with a multivariate frame of reference for health status. The biopsychosocial model uses a natural systems hierarchy, a continuum that ranges from molecule, organelle, cell, tissue, organ/organ system, nervous system, person, two person, family, community, culture-subculture, society-nation, to biosphere (Engel, 1980). While these components are interdependent, the focus of attention historically has been on one component at a time. It is necessary to identify the constituent components as well as the systems characteristics of each component.

There have been applications of this model in medical speciality areas, including psychiatry, a variety of published case studies, and the development of a Patient Evaluation Grid (Leigh & Reiser, 1980) for simultaneous reference to dimensions (biological, personal, environmental), contexts (current, recent, background), and interventions (short term, long term). Physicians and other health professionals are being trained to use this model in providing health care, although not without some resistance (Beitman, Williamson, Featherstone & Katon, 1982). Research applications for specific areas (behavioral medicine, medical anthropology, psychiatry) and populations (the aged, Native Americans) are already being described (Kleinman, 1983; Lazarus & Weinberg, 1982; Marburg, 1983; Reiser, 1980; Schwartz, 1982).

A biopsychosocial application to assessment has already been made (Pancratz & Taplin, 1982). A first decision consists of identification of the system or systems (biological, intrapersonal, interpersonal, family, small group, society). Screening occurs for functioning of each system, a tentative priority of systems is established, and validation by additional assessment data confirms a final priority ranking of systems. A second decision pertains to identification of a perspective for intervention-curative, learning, or growth. These authors clearly describe some pitfalls encountered in any search for contextualization of the individual within a multidimensional frame of reference.

Engel (1980) has stated that the biopsychosocial model includes "the patient and his attributes as a person, a human being" (p. 536) and uses data from an ongoing human relationship. This model is thus a potential vehicle for high touch in medical practice and health care. In professional psychology use of this model can promote competent and ethical practices that are increasingly person-centered. We can make better use of sophisticated and systematic assessment procedures because the focus is on the person rather than on behaviors or symptoms — data that is level-specific. The possibility of confounding causes for symptomatology are minimized by elucidation of levels and an eventual linkage of assessment outcomes with treatment alternatives becomes more feasible.

Person-centering

Person-centering in assessment practice is both complex and subtle, an attitude toward assessees predicated on values which define human relationships. Existence in a world of impersonal institutions with chronic and life-threatening hazards can be awesome and result in feelings of powerlessness, fatalism, and alienation. High technology and superempiricism create dependency upon science. We have learned to perceive other persons through cognitive assessment spectacles which objectify, fragment, and inevitably distort. The data may then be reconstituted or interpreted by comparison with norms to provide a nomothetic evaluation. High technology assessment requires a counterbalance by what Naisbitt (1982) has referred to as "high touch," an infusion of personal relevance by an enriched relationship that includes consent with understanding for participation, shared process, and influence on outcome. I will try to clarify "enriched relationship" by describing contexts that include shared process, projective technique usage, service, and training.

Shared assessment process. By way of personal parable, Rick Murphy and Paul Griswold were student assessors who inadvertently discovered a research deception by a role-playing Rorschach assessee (Dana, Dana, & Comer, 1972). Since that time I have been acutely aware that anything less than complete honesty in assessment practice or research obfuscates the intent of the process and may even compromise the value of the data. As a result I believe in sharing the decision to assess, the process of assessment, the data which contribute to an evaluation, and the report itself with the assessee (Dana, 1980). Both Bill Smith (1978) and Walt Klopfer (1983) have raised objections to this practice by suggesting the potential complexity of feedback and its effects upon assessees. While the mechanics, process, and limits of honest feedback are still not fully known, the rationale that consumers are entitled to full disclosure of their own assessment data and our interpretations is becoming more widely accepted.

The benefits of shared process ultimately accrue to assessors in terms of additional knowledge of instruments and assessment process, including the relative contributions of assessor eisegesis and skill. Professional growth occurs as a result of more stringent and more personal accountability to assessees. Moreover, as Timothy Leary first suggested (1970), the self-knowledge of each person cannot be omitted from our professional attempts to conceptualize assessee experience and to provide information that is relevant to decision-making.

Projective assessment. Coequal participation by assessees is only one part of a more selective, sophisticated, and intensive use of the Rorschach as a "fascinating set of stimuli" (Klopfer, 1968, p. 149). Sustained and consistent use of projective techniques has been documented by recent surveys (Piotrowski & Heller, 1984; Weiner, 1983), a spate of books on single instruments, continued exploration and refinement of usage at the Menninger Clinic, and by the most recent annual review chapter on projective techniques (Klopfer & Taulbee, 1976).

To some extent this continued usage and enthusiasm may be a byproduct of a contemporary emergence of assessment as a legitimate professional specialization (e.g., Goldstein & Hersen, 1984; McReynolds, 1981; Newmark, in press; Spielberger & Butcher, 1982; Woody, 1980), but projective techniques also constitute part of the high touch of personality assessment. Instruments of idiographic origin have a unique role in illuminating not only experience but the contextualization of the individual within a variety of life situations and treatment milieus. These instruments will continue to humanize and enrich relationships between care-providers and consumers.

Service model. Assessment services are moving away from a doctor-patient model toward more equal status encounters for the purpose of information processing and subsequent use of such information primarily by the assessee. If we genuinely respect other persons, we must assign to them both the capacity and the responsibility for self-managed lifestyles. Our professional assessment service contribution consists of attempts to understand a unique individual predicament. The communication of this understanding to assessees is the essential professional contribution to assessment procedure. The informational component of assessment may become secondary since there are now a variety of alternative information sources, including self-assessment.

Training. Over time our scientist-professional training programs have become more impersonal, technique-centered, and less sensitive to individual styles or personal problems of students. We seem to be so enamored by the high technology potential of our profession that temporarily we have lost sight of the fact that our students are still persons who require care. For several years, I have been trying to assemble an edited book (Dana, in preparation) pertaining to personal growth in graduate school and find a curious reluctance among some contributors to describe what happens in their own programs — programs that recognize and respond to needs of students. It is almost as if there is something professionally suspect about the topic of personal growth in graduate school or internship.

There are several strands to this dilemma which relate to perennial concerns over the adequacy of Boulder Model training: (a) research versus practice; (b) predisposing student orientations and values; (c) caring for others. First, we still experience a relative failure to fuse our research origins with our practical applications. I share Sarason's lament (1981) that historically, at least, psychology has been misdirected, although the present research base for practice does begin to address a variety of limited service delivery problems. As a profession we are just beginning to acknowledge Lipsey's (1974) clinical psychology graduate students who voiced their anguish over training programs in which social concern and relevance were largely missing from required research. We cannot remediate this deficiency in training by preoccupation with a technologization of clinical practice that blurs the distinction between research and practice and between training and practice without concomitant fostering of the human constituents of training, research, and practice.

Second, there is accumulating evidence that we have not been sufficiently sensitive to student values that emphasize service instead of research. George Frank (1984) has carefully examined the Boulder Model history and faults the simultaneous requirement for students to be both practitioner and scientist without provision for equal training in both roles. He documents dichotomous orientations, scientist and humanist or practitioner, that lead to scientist or professional training programs. These orientations not only provide different vocational interests, but are characterized by different needs, personality traits, cognitive abilities, childhood experiences, and cerebral dominance.

Conway (1982) surveyed young clinical psychologists who were nominated as scientists, professionals, or scientist-professionals and examined their self-reported personal competencies using categorization derived from the Jackson Personality Research Form. The scientists reported cognitive skills and intellectual curiosity, the professionals identified interpersonal skills of nurturance (empathy, acceptance, sensitivity to clients, warmth, rapport) and affiliation (friendly, good interpersonal skills, personable), while the scientist-professionals included cognitive skills as well as nurturance or affiliation.

These young clinical psychologists bear striking resemblance to my own juxtaposition of graduate student personality with Alpha (experimental) or Beta (clinical) orientations (Dana, 1982). Alpha students adhere to objective reality, a normative ideology, and social responsibility ethics. Beta students perceive reality subjectively, espouse a humanistic ideology, and abide by personal conscience ethics.

The cultural foment of the 1960s produced the Vail or practitioner training model which sought to reverse the figure/ground relationship between research and practice, an oversimplified solution but one that emphasized values, motives, and personality dimensions. These personality dimensions affect not only the kind of practice but the quality of all practice. For example, Beta persons have values that make primary/secondary prevention especially attractive problem-solving recourses since they potentially involve social structures and persons as proactive agents for their own well-being. Beta persons also honor understanding in terms of perception that uses natural empathy. Such perception is a response to contents that are ordinarily latent in interpersonal communication (i.e., regression to cultural assumptions, values and patterns of thought) (Bergin & Fisch, 1969; Stewart, 1976). Understanding may ultimately involve sensing the state of mind (being) of others that is predicated on a capacity to cherish the feelings of another person (Scheler as cited by Allport, 1968).

Such understanding may be related to humanism as Frank suggested. Gitelman (1984) has described one basis for humanism in Judaism — the *Halakha* which presents an attitude toward life that emphasizes deeds of the "good heart," kindness and charity. The levels of charity, or giving, are directly relevant to the humanizing effects of service provision by professionals. There are eight levels in which giving is grudging, cheerful, upon being asked, without being asked, wherein giver does not know recipient, wherein recipient does not know giver, wherein both giver and recipient are unaware of one another, and helping before any need is apparent.

These levels speak to our interventions in professional psychology. Tertiary prevention is professional giving upon being asked by the individual, or level 3, whereas primary prevention constitutes professional giving before the need is apparent in the individual, or level 8. The level of consciousness in a society determines the prevailing and sanctioned interventions. By the same token, the level of consciousness, or ego development, in the professional psychologist determines the choice of intervention strategies that constitute professional service delivery. If our Boulder Model programs foster Alpha students, society may have to settle for preoccupation with level 3 giving, at least for the immediate future.

Since the 1960s graduate students, especially in Boulder Model programs, have changed dramatically. To be sure our society now has different priorities — conservation has replaced consciousnous-expanding and the private sector is attempting to compensate for federal unresponsiveness to public welfare. Graduate students are now more conforming, acceptant of our doctrines and our technology, task-oriented and competent, but somehow lacking a world view, a sense of wonder/awe as to what they are about, and a helping/caring attitude. These students are more often "preppies" who are akin to medical students with their values of impersonality, status, personal achievement, and affluence.

Third, the issue of concern or caring for others — students, clients, patients — is central to training in a high technology society. There has been an unwitting separation of high tech and high touch components between scientist-professional and practitioner programs that has occurred as a result of differences in program values, training priorities, and student selection. Again, Sarason (1984) has unerringly identified lack of caring as central to the dilemmas of professional psychologists, physicians, and teachers.

While I would not minimize selection of students, or the goodness-of-fit between their values and training experiences, I would suggest that we need to build into training programs the humanizing elements which high technology threatens to disrupt. Programs have done this in the past, albeit by very different strategies. For example (Dana, 1978), the University of Alabama began with a set of training values and translated those values into a training model that was benevolent, nurturant, and predicated on belief in a matrix of knowledge and skills which could be learned by apprenticeship. This program has maintained contact with all graduates and I know of no other program that is so respected and even cherished by former students. The University of Kansas program achieved high touch by treating students as professional persons from the onset. This resulted in major control by the student over an individualized training program, responsibility for selection of candidacy exam components, and a genuine share in program governance. While there are many avenues to high touch in professional training, all are predicated on careful program planning with an intent to foster a sense of integrity and wholesomeness throughout the entire experience.

Population-specificity

Cross-cultural assessment. Many new assessment instruments are population-specific in their development and source of normative data. Nonwhite persons who are becoming recipients of assessment services with increasing frequency may be pathologized or otherwise denigrated by these etic instruments. Whenever behaviors are compared across cultures using normative criteria from the dominant (white) culture, the degree of acculturation will confound the intended measurement purpose. As a result, there are palliative attempts to provide "corrections" for some standardized tests as well as awareness that emic, or culture-specific measures may be the only culture-fair assessment devices.

However, the etic-emic controversy is merely one of a number of antinomies which frustrate simple or permanent solutions to ethnic minority issues in professional psychology practice (S. Sue, 1983). There are now reviews which delineate issues (Sundberg & Gonzales, 1981), describe culture-appropriate instruments (Brislin, Thorndike, & Lonner, 1973), and suggest the extent of invidious cross-cultural comparison in a context of measurement alternatives (Dana, 1984-b), although current training in assessment has not taken cross-cultural perspectives seriously. The clear message from cross-cultural psychology to assessors is that ignorance in training, practice, and research has ethical, legal, and moral implications.

Cross-cultural assessment also illustrates the insufficiency of an exclusively high tech approach. In doing projective assessment with reservation Sioux assessees, I soon learned that specific knowledge (e.g., tribal history and values, ethnography, acculturation of assessee) and relevant behaviors (e.g., preassessment socialization, social etiquette of process) were necessary ingredients. However, the quality of an assessment relationship which led to adequate data was directly determined by the assessee's gut reactions to my intentions and feeling tone in a context of sensitivity to a history of intercultural relations that contained repeated betrayals of trust in the interests of eventual genocide. White assessors may find as I did that their reports do not describe real persons who are recognizable by their informed peers

(Dana, Hornby, & Hoffman, in press). The tragedy herein is that a false belief in the efficacy of projective instruments for cross-cultural assessment leads to acceptance of data fragments as a representative sample for that assessee. Selection and nurturance of students who embody characteristics making for unconditional acceptance and regard that can be communicated unequivocably constitutes a high touch training imperative.

Psychology of women. A few years ago I asked the women students in a graduate personality course to present materials on personality theory applied to women. The men subsequently had to take an exam prepared by the women on this content. Since the male students paid little attention to presentations by their female peers, they did poorly on this exam and a rift was created between the sexes that took several years to heal. While I had not intended to be divisive, I unwittingly discovered that male professionals still exhibit sexism and sex-role stereotypy.

We are now aware of the potential for pathologization of women clients by male clinicians as a result of sex-role stereotypy. We also know enough to be sensitive to the wisdom of referrals to same sex therapists but have not extended this notion to same-sex assessors. Male clinicians still derogate women clients (Bowman, 1982; Steuer, 1982). There is little training to elucidate cross-sex professional gambits involving power, sexuality, and prejudice (e.g., Gallessich, Gilbert, & Holahan, 1980), in spite of accumulating evidence that these behaviors have negative training consequences (Rozsnafszky, 1979).

We have the beginnings of a credible psychology of women by women and clear delineation of sex differences in competitiveness and self-perceptions of masculinity and femininity (Babladelis, Deaux, Helmreich, & Spence, 1983). This knowledge must be countered by the reality that nourishment of intimate relationships is the single most difficult contemporary life task in this culture. As a result, students need training in how to apply this knowledge both in their own lives and in services provided to clients. While it is possible to train psychologists to be attentive to impingement of personal bias upon assessment or intervention process, such high touch professional training still occurs largely by demonstration or research (Gallessich & McDonald, 1981).

Self-assessment

External assessment involves a professional assessor who gathers data and makes interpretations or predictions. Self-assessment makes the person primarily responsible for generating information and subsequent interpretations or predictions. Professional assessors are skeptical concerning self-assessment, believing that people do not, in fact, know themselves and are prone to response bias. Nonetheless, recent literature suggests that people can be perceptive observers of their own behavior, have a larger data base than professional assessors, are aware of changes affecting behavior, and may be more attentive to situational determinants (Shrauger & Osberg, 1981).

Self-assessment is an avenue to self-knowledge and psychologists now affirm that self-knowledge is linked to behavior by self-relevance (Marcus, 1983). A high inner focus of attention augments the validity of self-assessment by increasing motivation for accurate self-report and rendering overt behavior more consistent with attitudes (Gibbons, 1983). Moreover, self-assessment contributes to this sense of personal responsibility for information about the self in a manner that an external aegis for assessment cannot readily duplicate. For example, Cioffi (1979) discovered that feedback from health hazard appraisal did not lead to changes in perception of the self, perhaps because assessment was conducted in a conventional manner.

However, these findings pertain to the general utility of self-assessment rather than to goodness-to-fit with particular assessee attitudes. Self-assessment is probably most useful for persons who experience an internal locus of control and have expectations for personal mastery. D. W. Sue (1978) has indicated that belief in personal responsibility for problems and use of personal power for change is a typical prerogative of the white middle-class. Self-efficacy may be the characteristic that determines the extent to which individuals can make constructive use of self-assessment. A Self-Efficacy Scale (Sherer et al., 1982) has linked personal mastery expectations to internal locus of control, ego strength, and interpersonal competency.

Self-assessment questionnaires are currently widely available in books and popular magazines. These item collections pertain either to single dimensions or to several dimensions which may be labeled as holistic health. Most of these instruments have not been evaluated psychometrically and are part of a do-it-yourself study of personality. People respond to these self-report items voluntarily, use a scoring key to obtain scores, and then have immediate access to the purported meaning of their own scores. While it is easy for professional psychologists to deride the popularization of these instruments, consumers often have a proprietary stance regarding the self-knowledge being generated. As a result they believe the interpretations and may base subsequent actions on instruments of unknown authenticity. Since self-assessment may be more valid than external assessment for predictions of achievement, vocation, and intervention (Shrauger & Osberg, 1981), it is evident that psychometrically acceptable instruments are desirable.

Historically, assessors made use of TAT interpretation by assessees to increase knowledge of defenses, to suggest degree of repression (Bettelheim, 1947), or to provide information on the nature of personality (Luborsky, 1953). Rorschach administration has been augmented by assessee-created and self-interpreted stories to each response (Elizur, 1976) and by the Instruction-Insight Method (Harrower, 1977) used to teach students self-interpretation in group sessions, although the earliest self-interpretation may have been an example of the facility of schizophrenic patients with content analysis (Moss, 1957). It has also been demonstrated that TAT card selection by assessees results in greater verbal responsiveness and increases in transcendence, personality revealingness, and emotional tone (Kalter, 1970; Pieper, 1972).

More recently, there have been relatively large scale applications of self-assessment to career and personal decision-making by college students (Comer, 1980; McWhirter, Nichols, & Banks, 1984) and community persons (Dana & Fitzgerald, 1976) in courses designed for this purpose. In addition, clients in a community mental health center (Prager, 1980) and patients in a partial hospitalization program (Maynard, 1982) have provided primary and relevant input into their own assessment. Such participation assists unmotivated clients to assume ownership of treatment process.

Shrauger and Osberg (1981) have succinctly described the contribution to assessment practice of the person-centering inherent in self-assessment. Self-assessment emphasizes a relationship between assessor and assessee that is open, candid, and collegial. Both parties work toward a common assessment goal in which genuine informed consent maximizes motivation. Whenever assessment precedes intervention, there will be feelings of assessee responsibility for subsequent behavior changes.

Many professional assessors have minimized the potential contributions of assessees to assessment because of reluctance to diminish their own role as expert providers of assessment services. As a result not only has the subjective world of the consumer been largely ignored but also the reality that decisions and their behavioral consequences ultimately have to be owned by assessees. Moreover, it has been easy to overlook the fact that nonprofessionals may have as much knowledge of the determinants of behavior as we do and are much less prone to be preoccupied with personality attributes as the singular explanation for behavior. The immediate task for professional assessors is to recognize that their special skills need to be used to amplify self-assessment instruments and to encourage assessees to incorporate their own enormous capacity for self-knowledge into the assessment process.

A Human Science for Professional Psychology

I have long espoused a human science approach that emerges from a prizing of human beings. This approach has three cardinal components: (a) intentionality; (b) phenomenal level descriptions; (c) shared endeavor. Lest these labels seem cryptic, I will describe each component, suggest historical origins, and illustrate with examples.

Our science must be predicated on human intentionality which includes values that celebrate life and encourage the transformations of awareness, knowledge, and problem-solving that foster quality of life for all persons. Values determine what is relevant for research scrutiny and research problems should precurse and suggest method. The phenomenal level regards description of life-world as basic. The origins of human data are experiential/subjective. This approach demands probity, completeness, and contextualization in dealing with observed human data which can be rendered more intelligible by shared interpretation. Since our professional acts — at best — are generative and enabling for our clients and ultimately for ourselves, we should be privileged to share a human transaction in research, teaching, and practice.

Participation by persons as coequals in all of our professional activities is a primary ingredient. With all of our technology generated by experts we cannot hope to understand other persons without their active, informed, continuous, and shared involvement in an open-ended relationship. Research, training, and practice are part of a continuous cycle in which the person who is the object of study is also the author of each endeavor and a vital partner without whom our technology is sterile. The critical issue is ownership of our psychological science and our clinical art. The locus of power is ultimately with the assessee, the research participant, and student for they have the content to implement any vision of a human science. To the extent that we practice a human science, we will be able to make meaningful applications of knowledge to human behavior.

Historically, as Giorgi (1970), Polkinghorne (1983), and others have noted, human science as described by Dilthey, Brentano, and Husserl provides for different approaches to natural and human phenomena. Dilthey believed that "life is what we experience in our attitudes and reflections as we live out our personal histories (Polkinghorne, 1983, p. 25)." The meaning of another person is shared by understanding mental process, situational context, and socio-cultural system. Brentano believed that the heart of humanness lies in a capacity for intentionality, a quality inherent in acts of loving, hating, judging, etc. Humanness means that we are inextricably bound to whatever we do. All experience is embodied in the present whereby we preserve, enhance, and reaffirm not only individual identities but our continuity with a human past. Husserl provided method in which selected examples — objects of consciousness — were described by free imaginative variation, using addition or deletions in order to look for necessary or invariant features, intuiting essential ingredients, and validating by others or self. Careful and systematic description not only can illumine the nature of psychological phenomena but the presence of the researcher/clinician as well (Giorgi, 1983).

Phenomenology has not been embraced by professional psychology in spite of widespread and longstanding discontent with the prevailing scientific perspective. There are now many "human science" approaches to professional psychology. For example, Arnold (1976) edited a symposium that contains eight metatheories, or "differing conceptual frameworks, where the decisions that we make will define what are to be regarded as psychological 'facts,' how they are to be determined, and what they mean" (p. viii).

While I will not reiterate the assaults on methodology that have accompanied the search for a new paradigm, both Koch (1981) and Conway (1984) have provided recent summarizations. Koch distinguished between ameaningful thinking — knowledge as a result of processing or methodology — and meaningful thinking in the sense of discovery. Koch foresees area-specific methods while lamenting the current status of our professional humanity: "the false hubris that has been our way of containing our existential anguish in a terrifying age has led us to prefer easy yet grandiose pseudoknowledge to the hard and spare fruit that is knowledge" (p. 269). Conway decries a zealous pursuit of simplicity, a misconstrued role of experimental method, and an obsolete neopositivist metatheory. Prerequisites for an adequate human science include discoveries from the "unarticulated experience base," study of exceptional clinicians, description of complex phenomena, and subjective/phenomenal experience. Advances in our science may be byproducts of the tension between traditionalist and iconoclast.

I would like to illustrate with two human science assessment examples. Rychlak (1984) argues that Newtonian science has diminished our humanity by omitting formal causes (pattern/order) and final cause (intentions) from the primary description of objects and events. He believes that because method and theory are confounded that facts and their interpretations become indistinguishable. Only the conceptual/introspective activity of the person who is the research participant (or assessee) can render interpretation intelligible and relevant to the human experience. Rychlak proposes to recapture intentionality by studying telic descriptions using the *telosponse,* or "behavior done for the sake of a premised reason (purpose, intention)" (p. 92). Telic descriptions, or final cause explanations, constitute the essence of human behavior. Rychlak (1982) has provided a research example of this process in which tests sampled the premises of young male managers.

Dana (1982) teaches personality assessment as a collaboration between student assessors, assessees, and instructors. Students write independent reports from the same data set and one or more criterion reports are written by more experienced assessors. The concepts are abstracted from all reports for comparison across student reports and between student reports and reports by more experienced assessors. The assessee evaluates the personal relevance of all concepts in all reports and this information is available to all assessors. Finally, a composite report is written based on consensual and unique concepts in all reports and with the benefit of assessee reaction/commentary. This composite report is evaluated by the assessee and subsequent feedback is provided to all assessors. The research basis for these procedures is summarized elsewhere (Dana, Bolton, & West, 1983). While this teaching device may sound formal and mechanical, it is contextualized within an experiential process of administration, interpretation, and report preparation. Fischer (1980) provides a similar perspective in which client participation enables life events to become primary assessment data while tests access style of shaping/being shaped, and reports serve explanatory (structured description), interpretive (hermeneutic), and illustrative (re-presentational) purposes. Assessment becomes not only a preface to intervention, but also can assume interventional characteristics as a result.

Professional Training

Assessment megatrends are relevant for an informed and effective professional psychology. To be a competent practitioner, students must find technical competence in the research basis for practice. Moreover, there must be an application of this technology with an awareness of the importance of a biopsychosocial orientation for adequate diagnosis and intervention. Whatever students do with technical knowledge in service delivery should be personal and

Table 2
Components for a Hypothetical Professional Psychology Training Program

Selection	Placement	Student Participation	Professional Training	Academics
Criteria: personality experience academic work	Evaluation of competence/ knowledge	Individual program: planning candidacy Training program: governance Personal growth: individual/group psychotherapy growth groups workshops	Practica: captive diagnostic center captive Community Mental Health Center affiliated hospital	Human Science: Professional Psychology Health Care Delivery System Cross-Cultural Psychology Method-Research Literacy Psychology core: Biopsychology Cognitive/Affective Personality/Social Individual Differences
Internship		**Evaluation**		
captive internship desirable		continuity of relationship with all graduates		Specialization: Clinical/Counseling School Clinical/Child Health Community Minorities Geriatrics Candidacy exam Project/paper

subjective as well as impersonal and objective. Person-centering invokes respect for the integrity of consumers that becomes apparent in wanting to help others, quality of caring, cherishing feelings and thereby sensing states of being. Students need to honor all sources of understanding, particularly their unverbalizeable and intuitive emotional resources in applying their technical knowledge. Research should be relevant to applications of knowledge to human problem-solving. Those persons who are recipients of services should represent the entire population, particularly minorities and those whose health or well-being status is at risk.

David Shakow (1976) wanted a scientist-professional — a high tech/high touch practitioner. The Boulder Model could not fulfill his dream because the implementers did not understand the necessary complementarity between science and person, or the ego developmental demands on mentor and student. Instead — at its worst — Boulder Model training masks the humanity of students by professionalism. At best — and infrequently — it inspires Conway's young scientist-professionals to fuse their technology with an investment in high touch professional transactions. Training for professional psychology in this generation is thus a reinvestment in the Boulder Model, a return to our 1947 origins, but with a distinct difference — the recognition that professional psychology is a human science research-based métier that demands caring and personal growth as touchstones for competence.

A hypothetical program

Over a period of years several of us have considered the training of professional psychologists, devoured the literature, and made fantasy pilgrimages into program terrain. From this process there are certain constituents which illustrate the human science aegis of this paper as applied to training. Table 2 presents these components chronologically: selection, placement, student ownership, locus of professional training, academic preparation, evaluation, and continuity.

First, we would require masters' degrees in areas relevant to professional psychology with at least three years of post-academic work experience. On the basis of experienced qualities of those students/interns we have known who became professional embodiments of Rozsnafszky's (1979) integrity and maturity, we would look for Beta personalities. For example, we include world view and a position on values issues, a helping/caring orientation, next-to-top intellectual credentials, commitment to a task-orientation, moral competence (trustworthiness), openness and gentleness, and a sustaining sense of awe/wonder/appreciation of life. This list invites comparison with the original Boulder Model catalog of attributes (Raimy, 1950, p. 212-213). Identification of these characteristics should be feasible from applicant self-descriptions (Smith, 1984).

Since this program would entail only two academic years with concurrent practica plus an internship and would accept students from a variety of relevant academic backgrounds, delineation of entry level professional skills and knowledge would facilitate individual training plans. This process would be accomplished during the summer prior to admission and consist of individual/group experiences with faculty, observation, and role-play, as well as examination for academic preparation.

Ownership by the student of her/his own training experience coupled with opportunities for personal/professional growth provides a special and intense motivation. Within a range of options, students would decide on content areas and format of their candidacy examinations. Growth groups would be available as well as opportunities for individual/group psychotherapy. Workshops that provided structure for dealing with issues of power and sex would be included. Such structures need to be built into programs at their inception, as does the capacity for planned change, rather than added piecemeal as a result of internal pressures. Nor is it sufficient for students to be major authors of their own training agenda without the concomitant commitment to responsibilities for good functioning of the program. As a result, mechanisms that endow students with shared responsibility for decision-making are necessary. Enumeration of these activities does not guarantee that treatment with respect and understanding will occur, but does provide opportunities for communication and shared use of power. Ultimately, it is the quality of relationships with faculty and peers and a generative use of faculty power that becomes nourishing and growth-inducing for students.

The locus of professional training, or practica, would be in three settings, a captive clinic which provided supervised experience in assessment of neuropsychological and learning disabilities, a captive Community Mental Health Center in which students receive supervised experience in all facets of service delivery, and an affiliated hospital to make available supervised experience with inpatients. All supervisors would be program faculty and practicum experience would occur concurrently with course work.

The academic component would consist of required courses to provide a human science background and a psychology core (Table 2). The human science core is designed to foster values that include a systems perspective and sensitization to opportunities for primary and secondary intervention. Specialization would enable acquisition of the research basis for practice in one of seven areas. The candidacy examination would include observation of professional behaviors in the specialty area. The project/paper would require that the problem selected antedate and determine the choice of method. Cognitive process and empirical activity would have equal merit. The internship would occur following the completion of all academic work and a captive setting for some students would be desirable. An evaluation component would make possible a continuity of relationship between the program and all graduates. As a result, information would be potentially available on training outcomes and satisfaction with program.

Assessment would be integrated within each one of the seven specialization areas in this hypothetical training program. Since assessment training can no longer be considered separately from intervention procedures, it is inefficient to provide generic training in projective techniques or self-report instruments and to assume that such training will generalize across populations or specialty areas. In addition, practica in all three settings would coordinate didactic assessment content with supervised applications to particular individuals. Moreover, each student's prior knowledge of psychological testing/psychometrics would be demonstrated by examination during the summer prior to admission. Students would be able to specialize in assessment within or across specialty areas, demonstrate assessment proficiency on the candidacy exam, and fulfill research requirements by assessment projects/papers. This section constitutes an example of the potential impact of megatrends on the design of professional psychology training programs.

The Rorschach: A Test of Perception or an Evaluation of Representation

Sidney J. Blatt

I am deeply honored to be the recipient of the Bruno Klopfer Award, especially during this 50th anniversary year of the Society for Personality Assessment. At nodal points in one's career such as this, one looks back and recalls the people and the experiences that have made it all possible. It is always difficult to decide how personal to make such recollections and remembrances and how much to share aspects of one's early life with colleagues, without running the risk of being overly sentimental and boring. Let me just say that it has not always been easy, and it has not always been simple. In my most outlandish fantasies as a young man, I would have never dared to imagine that I would have earned a PhD from the University of Chicago, spent most of my professional life at Yale, and received the Bruno Klopfer Award for distinguished contributions to personality assessment. As the saying goes, perhaps from a bygone era before the feminist movement, there is a woman behind this man's accomplishments. And I want to dedicate my receiving this award to my wife Ethel whose support and encouragement over these many years has been an essential part of what I have been able to do and what I have been able to accomplish. I want also to acknowledge the support and encouragement of my children, Susan, Judith, and David, who had the patience to tolerate a father who was never without his brief case, even on vacations.

In my development in the area of personality assessment, I was first introduced to projective techniques many years ago by a new faculty member at Penn State who had just arrived from the Midwest filled with "knowledge" about the unreliability and invalidity of the Rorschach. He fortunately decided to demonstrate the absurdity of this procedure by administering the Rorschach to the class as a group and asking each of us to consider whether our responses to such a procedure could contribute to the understanding of our personality. In the days that followed, I reflected on a number of my responses and became aware somewhat consciously, but mostly intuitively and preconsciously, that my responses expressed a greal deal about me and my personal experiences and preoccupations.

I left Penn State with a master's degree and took a position as a vocational counselor at the Jewish Vocational Service of Chicago. There I met two gifted clinical psychologists, Dr. Walter Neff and Dr. Nat Glaser, who both did a fair amount of psychological assessment. Frequent chats with them confirmed my earlier impressions that projective techniques had remarkable potential for revealing subtle and important aspects of an individual's psychological world. I applied and was admitted to the graduate program in psychology at the University of Chicago, but my enrolling required some special arrangements. I shall always be indebted to Dr. William Gellman, then Executive Director of the Jewish Vocational Service, and Ms. Charlotte Ellis, then Registrar of the Department of Psychology at the University of Chicago, for the arrangements that enabled me to return to graduate training.

The University of Chicago turned out to be an intellectual paradise. In my 3 years there as a graduate student (including an internship with Carl Rogers and his colleagues at the Counseling Center) and later as a post doctoral research fellow and a lecturer at The University College, I had the good fortune to meet and study with Professors Morris Stein, Joseph Wepman, Samuel Beck, William Henry, Carl Rogers, Hedda Bolgar, and Donald Fiske. In terms of projective techniques, learning the Rorschach from Sam Beck and the Thematic Apperception Test (TAT) from Bill Henry were astounding experiences. And Morris Stein, who had been trained at Harvard by Henry Murray in the tradition of the Office of Strategic Services (OSS) selection methodology, alerted me to the research potential inherent in these procedures. Subsequently, during a clinical postdoctoral fellowship at the University of Illinois Medical Center and at Michael Reese Hospital in Chicago, I studied and worked with Drs. Alan Rosenwald, Sheldon Korchin, Erika Fromm, Sara Polka, Mary Engel, Joseph Kepecs, and Roy Grinker. Using projective techniques in a clinical context with supervision from Rosenwald, Korchin, Polka, Fromm, and Engel enabled me to realize the vast potential inherent in these methods, especially if one took the time to study responses carefully and if one had a comprehensive theory of personality that provided a framework for integrating the remarkable diversity of observations that became available through these procedures. Polka and Engel had been trained at the Menninger Foundation where they had learned the Rapaport approach (Rapaport, Gill, & Schafer, 1945) to psychological assessment, and they shared this orientation with me. I left Chicago and Michael Reese Hospital in the summer of 1960 to join the faculty in the Department of Psychology at Yale where I met Roy Schafer and Carl Zimet. Roy invited me to attend his Friday morning clinical conference in which he and the group microscopically examined responses to the Wechsler Adult Intelligence Test, the TAT, and the Rorschach. It was a rare opportunity from which I learned a great deal. And Carl Zimet and I later initiated collaboration on a book on psychological assessment which eventually led to *The Interpretation of Psychological Tests* which was published in 1968 with Joel Allison (Allison, Blatt, & Zimet, 1968/1988). In 1961, I began psychoanalytic training at the Western New England Psychoanalytic Institute; this training proved to be invaluable to my learning to listen to and understand the flow of thought, especially the more subtle and less conscious aspects of an individual's experience.

I have also had the good fortune to have taught, and more important, to have learned from almost 30 years of students at Yale University in undergraduate, graduate, and postdoctoral seminars. Over the years, these students, most of them remarkably bright and energetic, have asked wise and penetrating questions and, at times, have had fascinating insights that enriched my understanding of personality development, psychopathology, and various methods for assessing these dimensions. A number of these former students are now among the outstanding younger people in contemporary clinical psychology and personality assessment. It would be difficult to mention adequately all or even a portion of these students but I do want to note just one—the late Dr. Cynthia Wild. Cynthia was among the first and among the most talented of my graduate students and postdoctoral fellows. She was a remarkable and gentle woman, with understanding and insight well beyond her years. In 1976, we published our book on schizophrenia (Blatt & Wild, 1976; Blatt, Wild, & Ritzler, 1975), and just a few years later, Cynthia prematurely passed away from a stroke caused by arterial deterioration deriving from infantile diabetes. From Cynthia and from so many of my students, I learned a great deal and am indebted to them.

When I first began graduate school in 1950, psychology as an academic discipline was concerned primarily with sensation and perception and the prediction and control of manifest behavior. The properties of the stimulus field and its impact on perceptual processes, as well as the careful observation of behavior and the specification of the manifest antecedent conditions of behavioral responses, were the primary focus of psychological discourse and investigation. Cognitive processes and the mind were considered unavailable for scientific study because they were subjective experiences—unobservable processes that occurred in what was called the mysterious, impenetrable "black box." Because the processes in the black box, the unobservable links between stimulus input and subsequent behavioral response, were considered beyond the realm of scientific inquiry, many psychologists focused on the analysis of behavioral responses and developed theories about the manifest antecedent conditions that influenced overt behavior. Psychology was considered a "behavioral science" and the basic model was the stimulus–response paradigm, on the order of a reflex arc, with little attention given to the more personal, individual processes that mediate between stimulus input and behavioral response. In addition, the primary motivational force was viewed as essentially hedonic—drive determined—with little relation to the interpersonal field.

Some clinical psychologists found this behavioral orientation quite compatible and developed theories that attempted to predict behavior from empirical observations of current and/or prior antecedent environmental events. Some of these psychologists also developed behavioral intervention strategies for altering maladaptive behavior, particularly around focal problems such as anxiety and phobias. A large number of clinical psychologists, however, found that stimulus–response theories had little relevance for their clinical work. Many turned instead to theories of psychological development and psychopathology that were available in the psychiatric literature. The theoretical models as well as the procedures and techniques of clinical psychologists in those early years were based either on theories of perception and stimulus–response (behavioral) paradigms or their approach to clinical phenomena was based on a psychiatric model that usually viewed psychological disorders as diseases rather than disruptions of, and/or deviations from, essentially normal development. The commitment to psychiatric models of psychopathology had its advantages, but it also had major disadvantages conceptually and clinically as well as politically in terms of the professional relationship between psychology and psychiatry. The involvement with psychiatric facilities provided psychologists with access to a wide range of patients and clinical resources, as well as to colleagues with extensive clinical experience, but it also had the potential to place psychologists in a dependent and secondary role. In addition, psychologists began to lose ties with basic psychological theory and with conceptions of normal psychological development throughout the life cycle that could serve as a baseline from which clinical deviations could be evaluated. Instead some psychologists began viewing various forms of psychopathology as disease entities, often with the assumption that these were essentially biological disorders. I believe that for the past 30 to 40 years clinical psychology has been struggling to free itself from these early behavioral and psychiatric traditions which have hampered and limited its growth and development.

In the mid-1950s expressed partly in the publication of Charles Osgood's (1953) highly acclaimed text, *Method and Theory in Experimental Psychology*, psychologists began to consider the processes that might be occurring in the black box—the possible "mediational processes" that seemed to influence the nature and quality of the link between stimulus input and behavioral response. And beginning in the early 1960s, psychology entered into what Howard Gardner (1985) called the "cognitive revolution." Psychologists became increasingly interested in cognitive processes and issues of mental representation. Although perception and cognition (or mental representation) are interrelated, there is a fundamental distinction between them. Perception involves the relatively clear-cut recognition and relatively immediate reading of primarily figurative aspects of available stimuli, whereas cognition and representation involves the construction of meaning and the establishment of operations and transformations of objects in ways that are different from how they appear in the perceptual field (Piaget, 1937/1954). Perception provides the basic information for the development of cognition, but cognition (or representation) goes beyond perception. And contemporary psychology, in many of its subareas, began to investigate how individuals establish cognitive structures—schema, plans, scripts, and templates—and how these cognitive structures guide and influence behavior.

Psychology also moved beyond the formulations of a primarily hedonic theory of motivation in which drive reduction, in either stimulus–response or drive-defense paradigms, is viewed as the primary motivational force of human behavior. More recent theoretical formulations stress the powerful motivational forces of bonding, attachment, exploration, play, and curiosity that develop relatively independently of basic biological needs and drives. And increasing attention has been given to the role of caring interpersonal relationships in psychological development and especially in the building of the cognitive structures that determine much of human behavior. Research in developmental, social, and cognitive psychology has increasingly indicated the importance of investigating cognitive schema. Cognitive structures have been studied in a number of different ways—as schema (Bartlett, 1932; Neisser, 1967, 1976; Piaget, 1945/1962), plans (Miller, Galanter, & Pribram, 1960), prototypes (Fiske & Taylor, 1984), expectancies (Feather, 1966), scenes (Tomkins, 1979), scripts (Shank & Abelson, 1977), and, more generally, as the tendency and capacity to construct meaning. We now recognize that an essential part of human functioning involves the establishment and creation of meaning—in what has been called a "constructivist" approach (e.g., Bruner, 1986; Gardner, 1985; Goodman, 1984). These contemporary approaches emphasize how individuals develop cognitive structures (schema, plans, expectations, or scripts) that organize and shape their experiences. Cognitive structures or meaning systems have both content and structure—they are appraisal systems that influence the experiencing of events and the processing of information. But these cognitive schema are more than memory structures or forms of information processing. Rather, they are relatively stable and enduring psychological structures that emerge during the life cycle and determine the full range of human experiences and guide and direct all human behavior and experience. Given this new emphasis on cognitive processes, it is important to recognize that psychology is now no longer just a science of behavior; it has become a science of the construction of meaning. The emphasis on cognitive structures and meaning systems in psychology is consistent with the contemporary emphasis in a number of other disciplines on structuralism and semiotics as basic philosophic and conceptual models. This emerging emphasis in psychology not only provides links between psychology and other disciplines; I believe it provides a new basis for integrating clinical psychology within the mainstream of psychological science.

This new emphasis on cognitive processes and the construction of meaning can be seen in research in child development, in social psychology, and, of course, in cognitive psychology. In child development, for example, Piaget (e.g., 1937/1954, 1945/1962) and Werner (1948; Werner & Kaplan, 1963) have studied the development of the representational world in considerable detail. Other more recent developmental investigators, such as Mary Ainsworth (e.g., 1969) and Mary Main (e.g., Main, Kaplan, & Cassidy, 1985) and their respective colleagues, deriving in part from the psychoanalytic formulations of John Bowlby (1973, 1988), have studied attachment behavior and its role in the development of "mental models of caring relationships" (e.g., Bowlby, 1973, 1988; Main et al., 1985). Psychological science has increasingly begun to recognize that many basic cognitive structures emerge and develop in the intimacy of caring relationships. Thus, considerable attention is now directed toward the study of normal development throughout the life cycle and the interpersonal factors that influence the development of cognitive structures that express aspects of the child's emerging sense of self and of reality and influence his or her subsequent interpersonal experiences. Research evidence clearly indicates the important for psychological development of affective bonding and secure emotional attachment between child and parent during the very early years of life. And from a different theoretical perspective, developmental psychoanalytic investigators, such as Margaret Mahler (e.g., Mahler, Pine, & Bergman, 1975), Anna Freud (1965), Selma Fraiberg (1969), John Bowlby (1973), and Daniel Stern (1985), have also studied the child's development of attachment and the capacity for separation and their role in the development of the concept of the self and of others. This emphasis on cognitive processes has also had a major impact in social psychology. Increasing attention has been given, for example, to issues of social cognition (e.g., Fiske & Linville, 1980; Hastie, 1981; Taylor & Crocker, 1981)—the cognitive and interpersonal factors that determine patterns of social behavior. Social psychological research has also increasingly begun to address issues of person perception and of self-concept. Research in social psychology is also now directed toward experiences of bereavement, loss, intimacy, and loneliness, and the role of cognitive structures in these experiences. And, of course, cognitive psychology itself has become a major subspecialty within psychological science in which the processes of mental representation have been investivated in multiple ways.

It is important to note that this new cognitive emphasis in psychology is also highly congruent with aspects of psychoanalytic theory which, since its inception, has sought to identify cognitive structures and how complex systems of meaning are established and result in adaptive and maladaptive functioning. From the very beginning, psychoanalysis has been a structuralist theory interested in semiotics and the functioning of the mind. Thus, there has been increasing recognition of a potential meeting ground between aspects of contemporary cognitive theory and aspects of psychoanalysis such as the current investigation within cognitive psychology of a dual representational system (e.g., Paivio, 1986) for lexical and nonlexical material and its relationship to Freud's formulations about the differences between word and thing representation (Buci, 1985).

It is clear that the cognitive revolution with its emphasis on representational processes and the construction of meaning has had major impact in many areas of psychological science (e.g., developmental, social, cognitive, and clinical). But what have been the implications of the cognitive revolution for psychological assessment? In an article prepared for the Fiftieth Anniversary Edition of the *Journal of Personality Assessment*, I (Blatt, 1986) began to consider some of these issues for personality assessment. I pointed out that utilization of Rorschach's (1921, 1942) remarkably creative method for assessing personality was limited by the scientific zeitgeist and theoretical models dominant in the first half of the 20th century. Rorschach's method was developed within a scientific tradition that emphasized perceptual processes and behavioral response, and so Hermann Rorschach naturally considered his method as "a test of perception" from which one could infer behavioral tendencies (e.g., extra- or intratensive proclivities). Personality dimensions were inferred from the tendency to perceive, for example, large or small segments of the stimulus and to perceive them somewhat accurately or inaccurately, or by the differential perceptual responsiveness to the various dimensions of form, color, and shading. The findings in the late 1940s and early 1950s of the "new look" in perception, (e.g., Bruner, 1948; Bruner & Goodman, 1947; Klein, 1951; Postman, Bruner, & McGinnies, 1948), which indicated that personal needs could influence perception, provided further experimental support for viewing the Rorschach as a perceptual test for assessing personality dimensions.

More recently, however, psychological science has become increasingly aware that the way individuals acquire, organize, and represent knowledge—their basic cognitive schemas—have a fundamental influence on the way they conduct their lives and establish relationships. Psychology has also begun to realize that reality is not always so clearly defined and that we need to understand how individuals construct both conventional (consensual) and idiosyncratic or unique interpretations of reality (Goodman, 1984). Thus, one of the primary tasks in contemporary personality assessment must be to understand the assumptions and the cognitive structures that influence how individuals create their conceptions of reality and construct meaning (semiotic) systems. The cognitive revolution in psychology creates exciting new possibilities for the use of the Rorschach and other projective techniques in clinical practice and research, especially if we have the imagination and creativity to develop methods for evaluating cognitive processes and the structures of mental representation from an individual's responses to relatively ambiguous stimuli.

This new theoretical emphasis in psychology, a view of psychology as a science of the construction of meaning as well as a behavioral science, has begun to be reflected in personality assessment. The Rorschach has begun to be viewed not so much as a perceptual test but rather as an experimental procedure that systematically presents an individual with ambiguity and allows us to observe and study how the individual constructs meaning from relative ambiguity. The response process to the Rorschach, as well as to the TAT, is no longer viewed just as a perceptual experience, but as a process through which an individual attempts to construct meaning in response to well specified, carefully defined, but relatively ambiguous, segments of reality. This new approach to personality assessment reflects an interest in cognition as well as perception, an interest in the construction of meaning as well as manifest behavior—an interest in understanding the relativism of individual cognitive constructions and interpretations as well as nomothetic descriptions of individuals in reference to established norms. Rorschach's inkblots have now become an experimental procedure that can be used to study the processes of cognitive construction and the relationships of cognitive structures and mental representations to a host of other dimensions, including personality organization.[1]

---

[1]This emphasis on the processes of mental representation rather than on perception provides a theoretical rationale for David Rapaport et al.'s (1945) remarkably intuitive recommendation that

Certainly the earlier perceptual approach to the Rorschach has been productive. It has been useful, for example, to differentiate an individual's tendency to respond to small details versus global or well-differentiated large details, to perceive the stimuli accurately or inaccurately, or to respond to certain perceptual determinants (e.g., form, color, or shading) and to explore the relationships of these dimensions to aspects of personality organization. But if one were to identify the single most important dimension of the Rorschach, most clinicians and clinical researchers would agree that the movement response is probably the most informative determinant. It is important to note that the movement response is not a perceptual variable—the stimulus is not moving. Rather, the movement response is a mental representation—it is the result of a construction of meaning imposed on or created out of perceptual experiences. The movement response is often so remarkably informative precisely because it is primarily a representational variable. Likewise, research (e.g., Aronow & Reznikoff, 1976; Schafer, 1954) consistently indicates that the content of Rorschach responses can express a great deal about an individual's interests and preoccupations. Content is also primarily a representational variable—it reflects the meaning systems an individual attributes to relatively ambiguous perceptual experiences.

As discussed by Piaget (1937/1954, 1945/1962), perception and representation are interrelated. Representation is based on perception, but it also goes beyond perception. And the same is true for the Rorschach. Interpretations of a Rorschach protocol as a perceptual test are still valid, but they are insufficient. The use of the Rorschach as a method of personality assessment can be greatly enhanced if we also consider responses not just as a perceptual experience but rather as indicating cognitive–representational processes that allow us to observe how individuals construct meaning in response to relatively ambiguous stimuli.

Aspects of Rorschach responses can be viewed along a continuum from perception to representation. More perceptual dimensions would include the relative response to color, shading, and form. The accuracy or consensual validity of a response, the degree of convergence of the response with the form of the stimulus, reflects more of a blend of perceptual and representational processes. The attribution of content, including movement, is more representational than perceptual. We have developed quite fully ways of analyzing the more perceptual dimensions of the Rorschach, but we now have to move beyond the ratios and percentages of various perceptual dimensions and develop ways to capture the more cognitive or representational dimensions of a protocol. We need to find ways of reflecting the dynamic processes of thought, the sequence and flow of thinking as it moves across various content areas and

---

inquiry into Rorschach responses be conducted after each card and with the card out of sight. This mode of inquiry reduces the perceptual input of the stimulus and highlights instead the cognitive processes through which the individual constructed the response.

different levels of thought organization both within and between the sequence of responses to the various stimuli. And we need to consider the relationship of these various qualities of thought process to aspects of personality organization and psychopathology.

It is important to note that an analysis of thought processes reflects a search for more latent cognitive structures that exist below the surface of perceptual experience, manifest behavior, and conscious awareness. Thus, the relationship of aspects of cognitive processes to personality organization and psychopathology necessitates the utilization of theories that deal with more than just manifest symptoms and behavioral response. A cognitive approach to the Rorschach will require more than descriptive taxonomies of psychopathology based on atheoretical categorizations of different manifest symptoms, such as in the *Diagnostic and Statistical Manual of Mental Disorders* (3rd ed., rev. [*DSM–III–R*]; American Psychiatric Association, 1987). Rather, we will need conceptions of psychopathology that are based on an understanding of psychological development throughout the life cycle and on differences in cognitive structure inherent in different types of psychological disorders (Blatt, 1988). We will need more than checklists of manifest symptoms and categories of different types of behavioral response; we will need personality theories that identify more basic structures of psychological organization.

There have been several recent attempts to approach the Rorschach as a method for studying cognitive processes. Robert Holt (1962a, 1962b, 1977) developed an extensive methodology for evaluating primary and secondary process thinking on the Rorschach, and Barry Ritzler and I (Blatt & Ritzler, 1974) developed a conceptualization of different types of thought disorder as expressions of various degrees of cognitive boundary disturbances. Several groups of investigators have begun to analyze Rorschach responses, as well as responses to other "projective" procedures, from an object relations perspective and have begun to investigate the relationship of personality organization to an individual's concept of the object—concepts of self and of others and their actual and potential interactions. A research group at the University of Michigan (Hatcher & Krohn, 1980; Krohn & Mayman, 1974; Mayman, 1967; Urist, 1977, 1980, Urist & Shill, 1982) investigated object representation from the vantage point of psychosexual theory and different types of ego states; research groups at Yale (e.g., Blatt, Brenneis, Schimek, & Glick, 1976; Blatt, Chevron, Quinlan, Schaffer, & Wein, 1988) integrated cognitive developmental theory with aspects of developmental psychoanalytic theory to study the differentiation, articulation, and integration of the concept of the object; Sheila Coonerty (1986) developed a method for evaluating Rorschach responses for themes of separation–individuation derived from the theoretical model proposed by Margaret Mahler; Steve Cooper and his colleagues (Cooper, Perry, Hoke, & Richman, 1985) evaluated Rorschach responses in terms of Winnicott's theories of transitional phenomena; and Walter Burke and his colleagues (Burke,

Friedman, & Gorlitz, 1988; Burke, Summers, Selinger, & Polonus, 1986) applied a "comprehensive" theory of the development of object relations, from symbiosis to individuation, to the analysis of Rorschach responses. Several research teams (e.g., Thompson, 1986; Westen, Buttenheim, & Silk, 1985; Westen, Lohr, Silk, Kerber, & Goodrich, 1985/1989) have taken a similar approach to the TAT and assessed individuals' concept of the object and their level of affective development.

Thus, we seem to be entering a new phase of Rorschach analysis, one that has remarkable potential for both clinical practice and research. Although prior approaches to the Rorschach based on ratios and percentages of various perceptual dimensions are still useful, it is clear that these are only the beginning of the utilization of the Rorschach as a method for assessing personality organization. Our task now is to articulate theoretical models that will enable us to assess systematically the underlying cognitive schemas and representational structures that are expressed in responses to the Rorschach. But in order to approach the Rorschach as an experimental method for assessing cognitive or representational processes, we need theoretical models of personality development and functioning that go beyond manifest behavior and identify instead more basic psychological structures. We need concepts of psychopathology that are more than descriptive lists and taxonomies of manifest symptoms; we need theories of psychopathology that specify underlying morphological cognitive structures that differentiate among various forms of psychological disturbances (cf. Blatt, 1988). We need personality theories that appreciate how different levels of psychological functioning emerge throughout the life cycle and how this understanding of normal development identifies various principles of structural organization that can account for similarities and differences across a wide range of manifest behavior. Although there is much to be done and a long way to go, it is important to recognize that a most important revolution has occurred in psychological science and that we are at the threshold of a new era in personality assessment, one that holds the potentiality for beginning to appreciate more fully the fascinating complexities of the human condition.

ACKNOWLEDGMENT

This article was presented at the Bruno Klopfer Award Address at the meetings of the American Psychological Association, New Orleans, LA, August 1989.

Reflections on Fifty Years of Personality Assessment and Future Directions for the Field

EDWIN I. MEGARGEE
and
CHARLES D. SPIELBERGER

This volume begins with Morris Krugman's 1939 Presidential Address to the Rorschach Institute and concludes with Sidney Blatt's Distinguished Contributions Award Address given in 1989 at the 50th Anniversary Meeting of the Society for Personality Assessment. Between these covers, we have reviewed 50 years of personality assessment in America as seen from the perspective of distinguished members of the Society. In this concluding chapter, we will comment on some of the trends and events that occurred during the past half-century, discuss the current status of personality assessment, and speculate on what the future might hold in store.

PERSONALITY ASSESSMENT: 1939–1965

Projective Tests

We have seen how a handful of individuals who learned the Rorschach technique in Europe from followers of Hermann Rorschach introduced the method in the United States in the 1920s and 1930s. We have also seen how Bruno Klopfer, one of these pioneers, founded the *Rorschach Research Exchange* in 1935 and then established in 1939 the Rorschach Institute, the predecessor of the SPA. Almost all of the original Rorschach workers, as they referred to themselves, shared a psychoanalytic orientation, most of them Freudian and a few Jungian. The strong commitment to this orientation can be seen most clearly in Samuel Beck, who considered a personal psychoanalysis to be an essential requirement for a Rorschach interpreter.

In the early days, assessment was an integral part of the training and practice of clinical psychology, and psychodiagnosis was considered an essential prerequisite for planning therapeutic interventions. From the writings of the founding members of the Rorschach Institute, it is clear that they would never have conceived of a world in which psychologists might question the importance of personality assessment. Sharing unbounded optimism about the viability and the future of the Rorschach technique, their primary concern was focused on how to integrate projective test data with basic psychological theory and research, especially in the areas of personality and perceptual processes.

During World War II, as we noted earlier, the U.S. government began a major program of training psychologists for military service and, subsequently, to work as clinical psychologists in the Veterans Administration where they were involved in the diagnosis and treatment of the psychiatric casualties from the war. Psychodiagnosis and personality assessment were central components of this training. An unprecedented number of psychology trainees studied and used a textbook entitled *Military Clinical Psychology* (Departments of the Army and Air Force, 1951). The centrality of personality assessment can be seen in this brief text, which contained chapters on the Rorschach, the TAT and the MMPI written, respectively, by Bruno Klopfer, Henry Murray and Starke Hathaway. Under the auspices of the VA and the G.I. Bill, many of these military psychologists, including several future Klopfer Award winners, entered graduate school and obtained their doctoral degrees in clinical psychology. Never again will a common core of assessment techniques be taught to such a large proportion of America's future clinicians.

In the 1950s, the use of projective techniques in personality assessment was a growth industry. As we have already seen, several different scoring techniques and approaches to the interpretation of the Rorschach and the TAT were developed, some relying primarily on formal aspects and others on content. To improve the psychometric qualities of the Rorschach, a number of alternative modes of administration were advocated. For example, Holtzman and his associates (Holtzman et al., 1961) developed two parallel sets of 45 blots, specially designed to elicit certain determinants; subjects were required to give a single response to each blot. A number of different types of apperceptive methods were also devised. Some applied the same basic procedures used in the TAT to new problem areas or populations. The Children's Apperception Test (Bellak, 1954), the Michigan Picture Study (Andrew et al., 1951), the Symonds Picture Story Method (1949) and the Roberts Apperception Test (McArthur & Roberts, 1982), all applied Murray's (1943) basic apperceptive approach to younger age groups, and Thompson (1949) adapted Murray's TAT cards for use with blacks.

Several psychologists devised innovations that supplemented or supplanted the traditional apperceptive procedures. For example, Shneidman's (1949) Make-A-Picture Story (MAPS) technique allowed respondents to select paper dolls representing various characters, which they placed in settings of their choice before telling stories about the scenes they had assembled. The Twitchell-Allen Three Dimensional Apperception Test (Horrocks, 1964) provided clay figures that served as apperceptive stimuli for visually impaired clients.

Other apperceptive tests required respondents to answer standard sets of questions after they had finished telling their stories. These included the Blacky Pictures (Blum, 1950) which assessed psychoanalytic constructs, the Michigan Pictures (Andrew et al., 1951), and the Roberts Apperception Test (McArthur & Roberts, 1982). The Rosenzweig Picture-Frustration Study (Rosenzweig, Fleming & Clarke, 1947) used cartoons in which one character made an obnoxious or frustrating remark to another to assess the aggressiveness of the victim's response.

In addition to the inkblot and apperceptive measures, a number of other projective methods were developed and used. These included a variety of graphic or drawing tasks (e.g., Machover, 1949), and word association and sentence completion techniques, to mention but a few (Anderson & Anderson, 1951). These methods all shared a fundamental problem that has plagued the Rorschach and the TAT; they did not conform to conventional criteria for evaluating reliability and validity, a key issue noted by Krugman in his 1939 Presidential Address. Confronting this problem has stimulated reconsideration of the traditional methods for establishing reliability and validity. Among the questions asked, for example, is it really desirable for all the items on a sentence completion test to measure the same thing? If not, is it necessary for the measure to have a high coefficient of internal consistency? On a measure of mood or affect, is temporal stability desirable?

Under certain specifiable circumstances, projective techniques and other personality tests might be exempt from some of the traditional requirements for reliability, but inter-examiner differences were less excusable. One would expect, of course, differences between adherents of schools with diverse theoretical orientations who might use different methods of administration and scoring. On the TAT, for example, the pictures differ considerably in their stimulus value, and it is not uncommon for different examiners to use different sets of cards, or for a single examiner to vary the array and the order of cards presented from one client to the next (Murstein, 1963). But differences in the responses elicited by various projective tests as a function of examiner characteristics or the setting in which the test was administered were more troubling (Lord, 1950; Masling, 1960; Megargee, Lockwood, Cato & Jones, 1966).

With regard to validity, the difficulty of finding adequate criteria for the unobservable personality traits projective techniques purported to assess led Cronbach and Meehl (1955) to propose the concept of "construct" validation. From this validation perspective, a "nomological net" of hypotheses is formulated, relating to the construct and to the operations by which it is measured. These hypotheses are then tested as one would evaluate a theoretical proposition.

It was also apparent that the validity of predictions made on the basis of projective techniques such as the Rorschach and TAT cannot be separated from the skill and acumen of the interpreter. How do researchers validate the combination of clinician and instrument, as Hammond (1954) had suggested? Were blind analyses, such as the one Rorschach himself had performed (Rorschach & Oberholzer, 1923), the answer? And if a particular test/clinician combination proved to be valid, or invalid for that matter, could this finding be generalized to other clinicians using that instrument? Or to the same clinician examining a different client? Concerns such as these led Shneidman (1959) to propose that, instead of referring to a test's validity as if it was a single unvarying entity, we delineate validity for whom, for when, and for which, as well as how that validity was established.

Yet another difficulty was that projective tests were replete with configural patterns in which the interpretation of one test sign depended on other test parameters. For example, a large proportion of Rorschach responses using the whole inkblot means one thing if these responses are of good form quality and involve a creative integration of disparate blot elements in a record with many responses, but whole responses mean something quite different in a sparse protocol with poor form and many animal responses. The fact that the physical sciences have similar difficulties, as Kutash noted in his 1954 Presidential address, does not make them any easier to resolve, but the advent of multivariate techniques and affordable large capacity computers has certainly helped. Turning to structured techniques, we will find that they share many of these problems and have others of their own.

Structured Techniques

During the 1940s and '50s members of The Rorschach Institute and its successor, the Society for Projective Techniques, viewed structured personality measures such as the MMPI with suspicion, if not downright hostility. Although Meehl attempted to bridge the gap with his 1945 paper, "The dynamics of structured personality tests," in which he cogently explained why the external criterion method of item selection did not assume or require veridical answering, many projective testers were convinced that paper and pencil questionnaires were too subject to distortion and dissimulation to be valid. Some may also have felt structured instruments required less clinical acumen to interpret than the more arcane and esoteric projective techniques.

Whatever the reason, it was not until 1965 that the Society welcomed the advocates of structured assessment techniques. This broadening of the Society's perspective was formally reflected by its changing its name to "The Society for Projective Techniques *and Personality Assessment.*" Since the earlier presentations by members of the Society were typically not, for the most part, concerned with issues peculiar to objective assessment instruments, we shall summarize a few.

In the early 1940s, Hathaway and McKinley's Minnesota Multiphasic Personality Inventory (MMPI) provided clinical psychologists with their first viable wide-band, structured personality test. Like the Rorschach, its strength came from the fact that its items and their scoring were empirically derived. Although most clinicians in those years tended to be either MMPIers *or* Rorschachers, the two instruments actually complement each other quite nicely. The MMPI is the stronger for the assessment of the neuroses and personality disorders and the Rorschach is superior for evaluating thought disorders and cognitive impairment (Megargee, 1966).

After the MMPI was created, a number of other structured personality assessment techniques were introduced, some wide-band and many narrow-band. One of the earliest was the California Psychological Inventory (CPI) developed by Harrison Gough (1960). Employing some of Hathaway and McKinley's (1967) MMPI construction techniques and items, Gough developed new items as well to assess "folk culture" traits in nonclinical populations. Researchers who devised structural personality inventories to measure constructs identified in factor analytic research included Raymond B. Cattell (Cattell & Eber, 1966; Cattell & Scheier, 1963), Hans Eysenck (1959; Eysenck & Eysenck, 1975), and J. P. Guilford (Guilford & Zimmerman, 1949; 1956).

As we noted earlier, "construct" validity was introduced to provide a way for researchers to test the proposition that a particular test pattern was related to some characteristic that was not directly observable (American Psychological Association, 1954). While acknowledging that no single criterion measure was completely adequate, it was only after a number of tests using a variety of criteria were completed that any conclusions could be drawn. In the beginning, researchers only examined "convergent" validity, that is, whether the test sign or scale correlated significantly with other measures of the same construct. Before long, however, "discriminant" validity was introduced as a further test of construct validity (Campbell, 1960; Campbell & Fiske, 1959). For this type of validity the requirement was that a test sign *not* correlate substantially with conceptually *un*related measures. For example, in order to validate a scale that supposedly assessed "leadership," using sociometric ratings obtained in college dormitories as criteria, the leadership scale should not only correlate with sociometric ratings of leadership, thus supporting the scale's "convergent" validity, but it should also fail to correlate with sociometric ratings of popularity, good looks, or other conceptually unrelated attributes if we are to infer "discriminant" validity.

In the mid-1960s, many structured personality tests were criticized for their lack of discriminant validity because of their supposed susceptibility to two "response sets," social desirability, i.e., the tendency to answer all items in a socially desirable fashion (Edwards, 1953), and acquiescence, a disposition to respond affirmatively regardless of content (Jackson & Messick, 1961). After a deluge of studies correlating measures of these response sets with virtually every test scale ever produced, the furor eventually subsided as a number of investigators demonstrated that controlling for response sets did not increase clinicians' ability to predict behavior (Block, 1965; Dicken, 1963; Rorer, 1965). Since response sets continued to concern some personality researchers, new inventories such as the Edwards (1954) Personal Preference Schedule (EPPS) and the Jackson (1967) Personality Research Form (PRF) were introduced to minimize their effects.

Unfortunately, many structured personality inventories were found to have a great deal of "method" variance, which detracted from their discriminant validity. Diverse scales on a given inventory often correlated more closely with one another, even though they were supposed to be measuring different traits, than they did with relevant criterion measures of the same trait that were obtained using different procedure.

The 1960s also witnessed a proliferation of new scales that were derived for established instruments. In 1962, Megargee and Mendelsohn, noting that over 200 MMPI scales had already been published, facetiously remarked that the number of MMPI scales might soon exceed the number of 556 MMPI items, never dreaming that within 10 years there would actually be well over 700 scales. Other tests also had new scales constructed by investigators who were not involved in the initial development of the inventory. These new scales vary widely in validity, reliability, and the methods used to construct them.

Thus far, we have focused on wide-band instruments that simultaneously assess a number of different characteristics, but many narrow-band tests have also been introduced such as the State-Trait Anxiety Inventory (STAI: Spielberger, Gorsuch & Lushene, 1970). Since narrow-band techniques focus on a limited number of traits or characteristics, they are comprised of fewer items, thereby requiring less time and effort for both the examiner and the examinee. Moreover, since all of the items often concentrate on a single dimension, such measures generally have greater internal consistency, ensuring that equivalent scores on the scale will have the same meaning.

PERSONALITY ASSESSMENT: 1965 TO THE PRESENT

Beginning in 1965, proponents of structured as well as projective approaches to personality assessment were included within the Society. As before, most members were psychologists with a dynamic theoretical orientation who were primarily interested in clinical assessment. Recently, the number of members with a cognitive behavioral perspective has increased. Individuals interested in personality assessment who worked in educational and vocational settings have been less numerous, as have those belonging to the "factor analytic" schools of personality theory and research (Spielberger & Piotrowski, 1992).

The years from 1965 through 1975 or so were difficult ones for personality assessment, as the papers by Marguerite Hertz (1970) and Irving Weiner (1983) noted. This was a time of widespread questioning of many orthodox traditions, including various American institutions and standards. In clinical psychology, personality assessment had definitely been perceived as being part of the "Establishment." For decades, clinical psychologists had been trained to administer and interpret individual intelligence and personality tests, whether they were interested in assessment or not. But differential diagnosis and treatment planning are only challenging when they actually influence what happens to clients. With psychiatrists often determining the course of treatment, many psychologists felt that their appraisals had little influence on the treatment plan. Psychotherapy and mental health administration appeared to offer much more status and prestige than assessment.

At about this same time, as was noted by Marguerite Hertz, there was increasing skepticism regarding the validity and utility of psychodiagnosis and assessment. Some maintained that situational influences rather than hypothetical personality traits were the primary determinants of behavior (Mischel, 1968). Others felt that behavior modification was a universally effective treatment of choice, regardless of diagnosis. Behavioral rather than personality assessment was advocated by many, especially since the new diagnostic nomenclature (American Psychiatric Association, 1980) had changed the emphasis from traits to symptom checklists. Traditional personality assessment seemed anachronistic and was consequently deemphasized in many training programs.

The advent of powerful psychotropic medications made it possible to discharge many patients who were treated as outpatients in the community. Whereas 77% of patient care occurred in inpatient settings in 1955, the proportion had shrunk to less than 25% by 1975. Since many community settings were poorly funded, time was often at a premium and brief screening evaluations were preferred to lengthy assessment batteries. There was also a proliferation of short-form intelligence and personality tests, few of which demonstrated satisfactory validity (Megargee, 1986).

One major topic of debate is particularly worth noting because it has continued in one form or another for four decades. Although the real issue is how best to utilize actuarial methods in clinical assessment, it was forever polarized when Paul Meehl entitled what he called his "wicked" 1954 book, *Clinical vs. Statistical Prediction.* After reviewing all the studies he could find in which the two methods were directly compared, Meehl concluded that the actuarial technique was superior.

By "actuarial," Meehl was referring to how the data are combined into a decision function. The input data could be either "statistical," such as test scores, or "clinical," such as subjective judgments. Nevertheless, many clinicians were outraged. They protested that Meehl's prediction problems were atypical and contrived, often being limited to simple dichotomies such as succeeding or failing in college. In several studies, a "sophisticated" actuarial formula derived from previous cases was pitted against a "naive" clinician, who nevertheless had accepted the challenge (Holt, 1958). We will examine these issues in more detail when we discuss computer-based test interpretation.

PERSONALITY ASSESSMENT: CURRENT STATUS

We noted in our introductory chapter that the Society for Personality Assessment weathered the vicissitudes of the 1970s and is presently vigorous and healthy. Several of the more recent papers in this volume suggested reasons why this came to be. Contrary to his reputation as the arch actuary, Paul Meehl (1979) attested to the superiority of clinicians, as compared to multivariate techniques, in delineating new syndromes. John Exner (1980) described his work on improving interexaminer reliability, and thereby the norms for the Rorschach. Irving Weiner (1983) noted that many clinicians have come to appreciate the complicated role of a consultant, which is based on assessing the problem and determining the most effective solution. Not only is there more prestige in tackling the problems others have not been able to resolve, but one also sees the most interesting and challenging cases. Finally, Sidney Blatt (1990) discussed the unique contributions that personality assessment can make to the burgeoning area of cognitive psychology.

Perhaps the two most cogent explanations for the revitalization of personality assessment are that: (1) practicing clinicians have found that assessment aids intervention, and (2) most psychology training directors have insisted that pre-doctoral clinical interns should be familiar with the basic assessment techniques. Another major reason that assessment has survived is that measurement is fundamental to research in all areas of psychology. Moreover, personality variables often interact with other variables in predicting behavior. In clinical research, for example, investigators selecting subjects for studies of anxiety, depression, or psychopathy must demonstrate that their samples indeed have that condition. It may also be necessary to establish that they do *not* have some other disorder that might confound the research.

Scales such as Beck's widely used Depression Inventory (BDI) (Beck et al., 1961) allow clinical investigators to establish actual levels of depression among their research subjects so they can be compared with the levels reported in other studies, or used to establish subgroups differing in depression, or to assess the level of depression before and after the occurrence of life events or clinical interventions. Psychiatric diagnoses are unsatisfactory for these purposes. Even if they could be made inexpensively and reliably, they only provide nominal scale (categorical) measurement, thus limiting the statistical analyses that can be performed.

Personality assessment was also strengthened by research demonstrating that situational factors were not as overpowering determinants of behavior as some social psychologists had maintained. For example, a series of studies using the CPI Dominance (Do) scale demonstrated that neither personality nor situational factors alone could predict who would assume leadership roles, but when *both* trait *and* situational factors were considered, highly accurate predictions could be made (Megargee & Carbonell, 1988). Research indicating the continuity of personality traits over time (Rabin, 1977) further strengthened the case for trait measurement.

New and Revised Assessment Techniques

During the past decade, the infrastructure for personality assessment has been greatly strengthened by major revisions and re-standardizations of several important assessment instruments, including the MMPI and the CPI. Similarly, Exner's (1974; 1978) development of his comprehensive system has given new life to the Rorschach, while in the closely related field of intelligence appraisal both the Binet and the Wechsler procedures have been updated. Among the major improvements these revisions have accomplished is providing norms that are sensitive to differences in age, gender, education, culture and other demographic factors.

A number of new instruments have also been introduced, as was noted by Weiner (1983). The Millon (1982) Clinical Multi-Axial Inventory (MCMI) addressed the constructs defined in the third edition of the *Diagnostic and Statistical Manual (DSM III).* Spielberger introduced state and trait measures to assess the experience, expression and control of anger (Spielberger, 1988; Spielberger et al., 1983; 1985). Other new scales focused on specific clinical syndromes such as suicidal ideation (Beck et al., 1979) and thought disorders (Andreasen, 1979). Although we have focused on examples from clinical psychology, other measures have been introduced which are equally useful in personality and social psychological research with nonclinical subjects.

A whole new array of techniques are now available for neuropsychological assessment, most requiring specialized post-doctoral training, as was noted by Weiner (1983) in his Klopfer Award Address. Numerous behavioral assessment measures have also been developed, many of which can be administered by nonprofessional personnel (Barlow, 1981; Hersen & Bellak, 1981). Buss and Craik (1983) introduced the "act-frequency" approach, which complements traditional methods of personality assessment, as do recently devised structured clinical interviews. Some of these procedures can be administered by computers to assess mental health status, depression, adaptation to the community, interpersonal maturity level, health related behaviors, sexual history and practices, family background, and so on.

A variety of new measures have also been introduced by psychologists for use in medical settings, such as measures of Type A Behavior and the agonistic emotions related to coronary heart disease (Chesney & Rosenman, 1985). Forensic assessment has benefited from the development of several standardized instruments for assessing legal competency (Golding & Roesch, 1987; Roesch & Golding, 1987), and Brodsky and Smitherman (1951) have compiled a handbook containing hundreds of scales that can be used in research on crime and delinquency. Many other examples could be cited.

Some experts in personality assessment feared that behavioral and computerized assessment techniques might make psychologists redundant. Instead, they have provided the diagnostician with a broader array of data and more refined referral questions. Neuropsychology provides an excellent example. A generation ago, a neurological referral for a psychological examination typically posed diagnostic questions such as, "Does psychological testing suggest there is organic involvement?" Using various memory, perceptual-motor, and even inkblot tests, the psychologist attempted to determine the presence of a lesion and, if possible, detect its location. While admittedly imperfect, psychological tests were one of the few non-invasive procedures available. Moreover, in at least one early study, Zygmunt Piotrowski's signs of organicity on the Rorschach compared favorably with the EEG and surpassed the pneumoencephalograph (Fisher, Gonda & Little, 1955).

Today there are a number of computer-assisted high technology devices available that permit non-invasive scanning of brain tissue and functioning. Instead of making psychological assessment obsolete, these technological advances have freed psychologists to address other questions they can answer much better, such as "Has this temporal lobe lesion made the patient more impulsive? What has been the impact on memory and cognition? On interpersonal relations? How is the patient coping with the disability? Will the patient be able to resume employment as an airline pilot?"

Improving the infrastructure of a test is always an expensive undertaking. The days when a test author like Harrison Gough could construct CPI scales by tallying item frequencies with his wife's help at their kitchen table are gone (Megargee, 1972). In 1954, the American Psychological Association issued technical recommendations that test authors should adhere to. Over the years, these guidelines have grown more demanding; authors and their publishers must do increasingly more extensive and expensive research in investigating reliability and validity, establishing norms and standards for various groups and, in effect, preparing the psychometric equivalent of an environmental impact statement before a test is published.

These requirements result in better but also more expensive instruments. Consequently, the prices charged consumers for test materials and scoring services have risen sharply in recent years, and some consumers have been priced out of the market. For example, a major correctional agency that used to administer a personality inventory routinely to all new admissions had to abandon such screening when the price they formerly paid tripled over a two-year period. In some clinical settings, third party payments or public subsidies may help defray increased assessment costs, but cautious clinicians who once administered an extensive battery may now think twice before scheduling additional tests.

Unfunded researchers face a similar dilemma when publishers do not make test materials or services available at reduced rates for research use. Investigators interested in only one or two scales from an expensive comprehensive inventory sometimes abstract these scales from the larger instrument. Quite apart from the legal and ethical issues, some scales simply do not work when they are administered in isolation. Other investigators substitute homemade instruments whose reliability and validity are uncertain at best. The net effect is that such economies tend to retard progress by adding research based on questionable measures to the literature.

Conceptual Advances

Personality theory, research, and assessment are all interdependent. While it is obvious that advances in each area can benefit the others, it may be less apparent that problems encountered in assessment may contribute new insights to personality theory. This has certainly been true in the editors' research. For example, Megargee's early search for personality tests that could differentiate assaultive from nonassaultive criminals eventually led him to formulate a comprehensive theoretical framework for the analysis of aggressive behavior. Within this conceptual framework, assaultive behavior can be evaluated as a function of intrinsic and extrinsic motivation, habit strength, internal inhibitions and practical constraints that interact with situational factors that can facilitate or impede aggression (Megargee, 1982; 1986; in press).

Spielberger's (1966a) studies on the effects of anxiety on complex learning and academic achievement demonstrated the need, ". . . to distinguish between anxiety as a transitory state and as a relatively stable personality trait . . ." (Spielberger, 1966b). This distinction not only clarified issues in anxiety research, but also led directly to the development of the State-Trait Anxiety Inventory (STAI) which operationalized these constructs (Spielberger et al., 1970). Since then the STAI has been substantially revised (Spielberger, 1983), and the state/trait distinction has been extended and incorporated into other instruments for assessing constructs such as anger (Spielberger et al., 1983; 1985; 1988) and curiosity (Spielberger, Peters & Frain, 1980). Many other examples of this interdependence could also be cited.

Other conceptual advances have led to a greater understanding of the factors involved in the practical utility of a personality test, as distinguished from its psychometric validity. While formal validity might be established by statistically significant correlation coefficients in large samples, small correlations though statistically reliable might not be clinically useful. On the other hand, a rare nonlinear pattern might generate a clinical hypothesis that is extremely important in the case of a particular client, but is impossible to validate statistically.

According to Paul Meehl, the 1979 SPA Klopfer Award winner, the minimum criterion for convergent validation is that a test should allow us to make accurate, semantically clear statements about a client. However, to be *optimally useful* (Meehl, 1959), the information that the test provides should be:

1. not readily available from other less expensive sources,
2. provided earlier in time, and
3. relevant for practical applications.

In testing the concurrent validity of a "criminality" test, for example, we may find that prisoners obtain significantly higher scores than correctional officers. However, we could have differentiated between the two groups faster, more accurately, and at less cost by simply checking the prison's personnel and prisoner rosters. Moreover, even if the test findings indicate that some officers or inmates are in the wrong group, there is little that can be done about it. Public policy rightly prohibits reclassifying prisoners as correctional officers and vice versa on the basis of their test scores.

There are assessment situations in which all of Meehl's criteria are met, such as in the selection of Peace Corps volunteers. Personality test data obtained early in training can suggest which trainees are not appropriate, which are psychologically suited for overseas service, and who among them needs additional training or counseling. The success of the Peace Corps over the past 30 years shows that this selection process has achieved a high level of predictive validity.

Another of Meehl's important contributions was his demonstration of the importance of considering "base rates" in clinical assessment. Specifically, Meehl and Rosen (1955) showed that if one attempts to predict a rare event, a test with even a modest false positive rate will inevitably produce an abundance of predictive errors. To maximize hit rate, clinicians should focus on selection tasks with base rates approximating 50%.

In assessing infrequent events, clinicians should seek subgroups in which the base rates more nearly approximate 50%. For example, a test designed to predict who will suffer a myocardial infarction will have a better chance of success if it is applied to a high base-rate group, such as middle-aged men who have already experienced a heart attack, than if it is administered to contestants in the Miss America Pageant. In predicting infrequent events, it is best to concentrate on situations in which a false positive has relatively benign consequences, such as being referred for further evaluation. Airports seeking to identify potential hijackers by means of metal detectors have an astronomical false positive rate for this low base-rate event, but the consequences are so minor that few passengers object.

In some circumstances, an externally imposed selection ratio can overcome a high false positive rate or enhance the utility of a test with poor validity. In NASA's original Mercury astronaut program, for example, there were over 1,000 applicants for six positions. In such circumstances, one need not worry overly about the consequences of falsely rejecting a potentially qualified applicant because the selection ratio and the cost of training ensure that almost all candidates would be rejected in any event.

Turning from screening to individualized clinical assessment, a broad array of treatment options and interventions are generally available. Moreover, our increased understanding of the complex biopsychosocial etiology of many disorders has heightened the need for accurate diagnosis. Clients can be treated in a number of different settings, ranging from a total institutional environment with various levels of security and control, through halfway house and community settings, to full outpatient status, with or without medication and aftercare. A wide variety of change agents and therapies, both group and individual, are also available. Planning the best treatment, change agent and setting for each client requires careful individualized assessment. One point on which virtually all of our distinguished authors would probably agree is that although psychological assessment and research have become increasingly nomothetic, clinical psychology should not lose sight of its idiographic roots.

Advances in Technology

In addition to new assessment devices and conceptual advances, there has been immense progress in the development of the mathematical and statistical infrastructure for the construction and evaluation of personality assessment devices. There have also been important advances in providing consumers with economical data processing hardware and software. In the area of inferential statistics, personality assessment has greatly benefited from the development of nonparametric tests that are better suited to the ordinal scale data produced by many tests. Multiple range tests and multivariate analyses of variance and covariance that can evaluate profile comparisons and the array of interrelated scores that one often finds in assessment research are important additions to our statistical armamentarium. Because there is no shortage of tests, psychologists tackling new prediction tasks may benefit from a variety of multiple regression techniques that can suggest the best weighted linear or nonlinear combination of existing measures.

Factor analytic and cluster analytic techniques are not only useful for identifying the sources of reliable variance in complex criterion measures, but can also be used in other ways. For example, the same year Meehl delivered his address on using cluster analysis to search for latent entities or syndromes, a system for classifying criminal offenders based on cluster analyses of their MMPI profiles was introduced that has since been successfully applied in a number of federal, state and local correctional institutions (Megargee et al., 1979). These and many other mathematical and statistical advances have been made more available by the widespread proliferation of relatively inexpensive computers. Today suburban shoppers tally their purchases on inexpensive, hand-held, solar-powered calculators that can outperform the mechanical behemoths costing thousands of dollars used to derive test scales in the 1950s. Much of the work on this book was done at sea using a four pound portable computer with over 1000 times more memory than the mainframes that occupied entire rooms 25 years ago.

These technological advances have had many applications in assessment. Practitioners can use computers to schedule appointments, interview and test clients, and write narrative reports. Researchers can use them to access the literature, help prepare grant proposals, select subjects, present stimuli, record and score responses, analyze data, and help prepare reports. While such labor saving devices have freed psychologists from performing many tedious tasks, the results have not been entirely beneficial. We will focus on three problem areas: research design, test construction and test interpretation. In each area the problem is, of course, not the computers themselves, but the way they have been used or misused.

Research Design. In recent years, an increasing number of research proposals and completed projects unknowingly duplicate ones that have long since been carried out and reported in the literature. Others use long-discredited scales as operational definitions of important constructs. This state of affairs appears to be an unfortunate side effect of the computerization of the literature. Since many older studies were never entered into these information systems, they might as well be inscribed in Sanskrit on the walls of a Babylonian tomb for all the influence they have today.

Test Construction. The availability of powerful computers and software has made it possible for people with relatively little knowledge about test construction and development to devise and disseminate poorly constructed measures. One recently published 38-item inventory offers 15 scales, three of which have only two items each. This makes it difficult to calculate meaningful measures of internal consistency and impossible to determine split half reliabilities!

Unfortunately journal editors are not entirely successful in preventing the literature from being polluted with unreliable and invalid scales. A common source of contamination comes from measures devised for use in one-shot studies because such measures typically do not go through the rigorous procedures prescribed for formally published instruments (American Psychological Association, 1954). Another source of inadequate measures are instruments devised by people with insufficient training in test construction, who may see a market for measures that promise to identify dishonest employees or match potential marital partners. In 1939, Morris Krugman worried about quacks misusing assessment; 50 years later we should all share his concern.

Computer-Based Test Interpretation. A major source of concern in regard to the validity of the utilization of computers in assessment is with respect to computer-based test interpretation (CBTI) (Butcher, 1987; Matarazzo, 1986; Rubenzer, 1991; Spielberger & Piotrowski, 1991a). Current discussions of CBTI are reminiscent of the debates about validating clinicians' interpretations that appeared long ago in the *Rorschach Re-*

search Exchange. Similarly, the controversy over the reliability and validity of interpretive programs recapitulates the arguments regarding statistical vs. clinical prediction (Holt, 1958; Holtzman, 1960; Lindzey, 1965; Meehl, 1954; 1957; 1965). The primary difference, however, is that whereas actuarial interpretation was hypothetical in the 1950s and 1960s, CBTI is now a present reality. As Spielberger and Piotrowski (1992) recently noted, over 500 articles on CBTI have appeared in the literature, and several books and special issues of journals have been devoted to the topic. Space permits us to list only a few of the many issues that are relevant to this controversy:

1. There is general agreement that computers are superior to humans in the tedious work of scoring and profiling tests with limited response options, such as true/false or multiple choice paper-and-pencil tests. Projective techniques in which the examinees are free to create their responses are much less amenable to computer scoring. With regard to paper-and-pencil tests, automated scoring equipment such as optical scanners and high speed computers are many times faster and more reliable than human psychometrists, but this does not necessarily mean they are more accurate. Scoring programs are written by humans, and humans make errors. If a high speed computer is programmed incorrectly, it will simply make errors more consistently and more quickly than a human scorer.[1]

2. Given the same input, actuarial procedures will always produce the same output, unless, of course, someone has tinkered with the program. Clinicians are more variable.

3. Information that can not be incorporated into an actuarial formula can not influence a CBTI interpretation. However, such information, such as the circumstances under which the test was administered, may be extremely important. Megargee has reported an MMPI profile [Welsh code = *975′61384*-2/0: F-KL/] obtained on a young man the day after he was convicted of slaughtering a mother and her young daughter and sentenced to the electric chair. Clinicians who know this interpret the profile quite differently than those who are unaware of the situation. No computer program we are aware of can utilize such information.

4. Since clinicians are more creative than computers, they are better able to detect new syndromes or deal with atypical cases. No actuary could ever have diagnosed Seal Eskimo psychosis in a native Floridian, as one clinician of our acquaintance did. But although it saved that young woman's life, by definition such rare cases account for little variance when the actuaries' overall performance is compared with that of the clinicians. Of course, whenever a clinician succeeds in validating a new diagnostic sign, there is an actuary lurking in the wings ready to incorporate it into a CBTI.

5. There is no quality control over the decision functions utilized by either the actuary or the clinician. Either may be based on sound empirical data, unvalidated folklore, or wild-eyed hunches. Clinicians may not always be able to specify which test parameters led to a particular interpretation; actuaries should be able to do so, but often will not for proprietary reasons. The interpretations and recommendations of both are, of course, subject to validation. In comparing clinicians with programmers who prepare CBTI programs, it is important to remember that clinical psychologists can practice only they have demonstrated their competence by: (1) obtaining a doc-

[1]Mistakes do happen. Megargee discovered errors in two vendors' programs for assigning MMPI profiles into types according to his classification system. One company substituted totally different, less complex solutions for the actual classification rules. Another programmed the rules correctly, but inadvertently reversed the sequence of two important steps when they later translated the system into a different programming language.

toral degree, including a one year predoctoral internship; (2) engaging in a year or more of closely supervised postdoctoral clinical work; and (3) passing a licensing examination. Programmers are not subject to any such review.

6. Clinicians typically have more direct contact with clients than CBTI purveyors, and, as licensed professionals, they are held to strict codes of ethical conduct and important legal safeguards. Therefore, many clinicians feel they are better able to give appropriate feedback and aftercare than CBTI vendors, while preserving the confidentiality of their clients. It is this factor, as well as test validity, that leads many to agree with the conclusion of Fowler and Butcher (1986, p. 95), "There must be a clinician between the client and the computer."

7. Most CBTI interpretations are based on a single data source, typically a test such as the MMPI. Research has shown that case history information is superior to test data and that clinicians with access to multiple sources of information do better than those making inferences on the basis of a single test (Kostlan, 1954; Little & Shneidman, 1959). Most commercial vendors stipulate that CBTI should never be used as the sole basis for diagnostic or treatment decisions (Spielberger & Piotrowski, 1991b).

8. The results of a recent survey of the members of the Society for Personality Assessment indicated that 85% felt that CBTI narratives were a cause for concern, and that 62% did not feel that the psychometric issues they raised had been adequately addressed (Spielberger & Piotrowski, 1991a). The authors concluded that most respondents felt that the data included in computer-generated narratives, ". . . must be validated against sound clinical judgment" (Spielberger & Piotrowski, 1991a, p. 62).

Rubenzer (1991) has recently challenged the adequacy of clinical judgment as a criterion, citing comparisons of clinical and statistical assessment that favored the latter approach. It should be noted that in these studies, dating back to Meehl (1954), the clinician and the actuary play on a level field, with each having access to the same limited data sources. In real life, of course, clinicians can utilize many sources of data and avail themselves of professional consultation when needed. With professional reputations and livelihoods at stake, not to mention the consequences to clients, debate over the relative superiority of clinical versus computerized assessment can become very heated. We will discuss the appropriate role of CBTI when we examine the future of assessment.

Personnel and Training

Intellectual and personality assessment were once the cornerstones of clinical psychology, and rigorous training in the administration and interpretation of psychological tests once occupied a major part of the curriculum in graduate training programs. In the late 1950s, one stalwart psychologist who had worked with Terman maintained that until an examiner had administered at least 250 Stanford Binets, the results were not worth scoring. (Learning to score or interpret the Binet properly would take considerably longer.) This daunting criterion was considered excessive even in those days, but there is little doubt that training in assessment is currently much less extensive than it was previously. One training program, for example, "teaches" the Rorschach, TAT, MMPI and CPI in a single semester (Megargee, 1986).

The fact that many graduate students in clinical and other areas of applied psychology now arrive at their internships having had relatively little preparation in assessment is probably a major reason why many professional training centers now favor a two year clinical internship (Belar et al., 1987). We will discuss training issues at greater length when we examine future trends.

QUO VADEMUS? REFLECTIONS ON THE FUTURE

There are those who maintain that history always repeats itself. This maybe true in the humanities, politics, or social mores, but it does not apply to science and technology. Barring some cataclysm, a discovery once made, a device once invented, cannot be undone. Using Krugman's (1939) metaphor, the "demons" that Hermann Rorschach turned loose can never be returned to the ink well. Thus, the one thing we can predict with absolute certainty is that the next half-century of personality assessment in America will not replicate the first 50 years.

Factors Influencing the Future Course of Assessment

Several sets of factors that we discussed in our review of the current status of personality assessment seem likely to influence the future course of the field. The first is the continuing expansion of clinical psychology. Since the Rorschach Institute was founded there has been an exponential increase in the number of clinical psychologists, professional training programs, and personality assessment techniques, as well as in the volume of clinical information being generated and disseminated. Clinical psychologists now have many more career paths and opportunities open to them than ever before. Inevitably, the women and men who graduate from professional training programs in the years to come will have a greater range of interests, goals, skills, theoretical orientations and factual knowledge than previous generations.

It also seems likely that many clinical psychologists will not be as well trained or as interested in personality assessment as their predecessors. Moreover, among those psychologists who share an interest in personality assessment, there appear to be fewer who are intrinsically interested in personality assessment as a field of study in its own right. Instead, more appear to be concerned with assessment as a means to achieving specific measurement goals. A researcher may develop a scale in order to operationalize an important construct. An applied psychologist may devise an instrument to help solve a specific selection problem.

A second set of factors that seem destined to influence the future consists of the technological developments we have noted. There are now available a wide range of tests that profess to assess virtually every conceivable personality construct, as well as some one might not think of such as "success in baseball" and "pharisaic virtue." Many of these tests can be administered, scored and interpreted by people with minimal training or education using commercial software packages. Item analyses, regression analyses, factor analyses, almost every complex procedure except psychoanalyses, can be performed with little time, effort or expertise. While the results may not be valid, they can be made to appear slick and professional to the unwary or unsophisticated consumer.

A third factor is society's need for assessment services. While clinical psychologists in mental health settings may not be doing as much formal assessment as they once did, overall consumer demand for assessment services appears to be as strong as ever. Indeed, in law, medicine, and business the utilization of personality tests for screening and classification has probably increased. As more people compete for available resources in educational, medical, commercial, and even in correctional institutions, there is an even greater need for screening procedures.

A fourth factor of contemporary life is that testing has become a political issue. Tests are currently being used to assign students to educational tracks, assess educational achievement, screen applicants for employment, determine legal competency, classify prisoners and predict their recidivism, evaluate claims for disability compensation, select patients for medical procedures, and assist in deciding who is eligible for certain health benefits or rehabilitation programs. They may even play a role in deciding which capital offenders should be sentenced to death, and which of those so sentenced is competent for execution (Litwack & Schlesinger, 1987; Golding & Roesch, 1987). Obviously, there is a compelling public interest in ensuring that tests meet the highest standards of reliability and validity.

As a consequence of the widespread use of psychological tests, many groups have become concerned about their validity, fairness and costs. Minority groups are sensitive to bias on the basis of age, race, gender, and ethnicity. The common concern is to ensure that tests which can influence such important decisions are fair and valid. Consumers question whether the costs are justified by the validity. Because they feel testing is too important to be left to the testers, individuals are increasingly turning to the courts for protection.

Given these trends and circumstances, what are the implications for personality assessment? We will discuss issues relating to test development and validation, computer-based test interpretation, problems in prediction, and the training and qualifications of professionals engaged in personality assessment.

Implications for Test Development and Validation

Publishing a major wide-band personality test has become a prodigious undertaking. The costs and requirements have increased enormously since the days when Hermann Rorschach descended from the Herislau Cantonal Asylum with the inkblots he had been experimenting with in his spare time. Given the important uses to which tests are being applied, included among them applications that Rorschach, Murray and Hathaway never imagined, society can be expected to hold future test developers to strict standards of accountability.

In view of the expense and time involved in properly producing a new test, it seems likely that we will see more utilization of already developed instruments, especially if publishers make tests available to unfunded researchers at minimal cost. This development is desirable since more progress can be made if those working within an area can agree to use a common set of measures. Most new measures are likely to be narrow-band instruments addressing focal questions in well defined subject groups. Most will be relatively brief, nomothetic questionnaires that are suitable for automated or computerized administration and scoring. Many of these new scales will probably be designed for use in nonclinical populations, and to assess constructs that are more relevant to behavioral medicine and to educational and vocational assessment than to psychopathology.

Although free response instruments such as inkblot tests, story telling techniques, and graphic or drawing tasks occupy a unique and valuable place in our assessment repertoire, the difficulties associated with reliably administering, scoring and interpreting such devices, not to mention the time and effort required, will induce most researchers and practitioners to use structured instruments whenever possible, especially if large numbers of subjects are being assessed.

Ben-Porath and Butcher (1991, p. 147) suggest that "adaptive" testing, in which a computer program varies the items administered to each client as a function of the client's previous responses, are, ". . . likely to be one of the more significant trends in the future of personality assessment." They correctly note that this will require the development of appropriate software, but it will also depend on the availability of the necessary hardware. While adaptive testing may be useful in settings in which individual clients come to well equipped assessment centers, the computers needed make it unlikely that this approach can be used for testing large groups or for outreach assessments that have to be conducted in settings such as schools, jails and hospital wards.

Supply, Demand, and CBTI

Increased demand for personality assessment techniques and services runs counter to projected decreases in the number of psychologists actively involved in personality assessment. How will such a shortfall be met?

Some testing will no doubt continue to be done by individuals trained as clinical psychologists, who keep a favored instrument, a sentence completion test perhaps, or maybe a TAT or even a Rorschach, tucked away in a desk drawer.

Not every structured test will be administered by a psychologist. Many measures are developed by investigators who have no special expertise in test construction or validation for use in personality, social, motivational and other areas of psychological research. Outside psychology, physical education, movement sciences, family life, criminology and education are among the disciplines making use of personality assessment devices.

Overall, computer-based interpretive testing is probably the major substitute for direct clinical assessment. Most of the controversy over CBTI is focused on whether it is superior or inferior to individual personality assessment, but other salient issues are cost-effectiveness and availability. If there is no clinician to stand between the client and the computer, as Fowler and Butcher (1986) recommended, should the mental health worker who is unschooled in testing forego using a computerized assessment service?

Because computer-based test interpretation is here to stay, the question is how best to deal with it. A universal recommendation is for additional validational research for CBTI programs (Butcher, 1987). Many researchers seem daunted by the prospect of determining the validity of each interpretive statement, especially when the relationships between test signs and specific statements are not published. However, much information could be contributed by more macroscopic studies similar to those used to test the validity of clinical interpretations in the 1950s. Interested investigators might find the designs and approaches used by Datel and Gengerelli (1955), Davenport (1952), Holsopple & Phelan (1954), Holtzman and Sells (1954), Kostlan (1954), and Little and Shneidman (1954, 1955, 1959) to be stimulating and useful.

It would also be helpful if authoritative training programs and courses designed to educate CBTI users were developed. In particular, clear statements should warn the user when referral for a more comprehensive evaluation is needed. Finally, Spielberger and Piotrowski's (1991a) call for the formulation of ethical guidelines governing the appropriate use of CBTI should be heeded.

Screening and the Vanishing Variance Component

In his later years, Starke Hathaway often remarked that what puzzled him most about the MMPI was the lack of further progress. He had fully expected that new developments in testing would soon make the MMPI obsolete. As we have seen, many new tests and scales, both projective and structured, have been formulated and considerable technological progress has been made. But none of these developments has produced increases in the number and size of validity coefficients.

In order to maximize their impact, psychologists interested in personality assessment should be guided by the conceptual advances that have been noted, concentrating on situations in which the nature of the assessment problem provides the greatest chance for a test to demonstrate incremental validity and utility. Effectiveness of assessment can be enhanced by focusing on meaningful problems where the results have applied implications, subpopulations with high base rates, and situations with favorable selection ratios.

We must also realize that there is a limit to the degree to which behavior can be predicted on the basis of personality assessments alone because behavior is a function of the interaction of personal and situational factors. On the personal side of the ledger, there is only a finite amount of reliable variance to be assessed. The more existing instruments measure this pool of reliable variance, the less there is left to be accounted for by newer techniques. One can build instruments that are shorter, ones that have improved statistical characteristics or boast more representative standardization samples, but it is unrealistic to expect these refinements to produce massive increases in validity coefficients.

In a book celebrating personality assessment, the next statement probably seems heretical. However, given all the work that has gone into assessing personality traits and states in the last 50 years, psychologists interested in improving practical prediction might do better to concentrate on developing instruments to assess the relatively untapped situational variance. Aside from the scales produced by Rudolf Moos (1984, 1986), there has been precious little investment in developing measures for the assessment of the environmental variables that interact with personal factors to determine behavior.

Personnel and Training

Despite increasing demand for high quality personality assessment in a variety of fields and the need for rigorous research investigating the validity of tests and test interpretations, both clinical and computerized, education and training in psychological assessment appears to be declining. In the past, a major portion of graduate training in clinical psychology was devoted to assessment. It was expected that all clinical psychologists would attain at least journeyman status by the time they received the doctoral degree, but this no longer appears to be the case.

It is our impression that many graduate programs have reduced the emphasis on assessment in order to acquaint students with the vastly increased knowledge base of psychological science without significantly increasing the time required to obtain the doctoral degree. While most internship training centers still place a high priority on traditional assessment, there are limits in what they can accomplish if trainees have had relatively little prior assessment training. And some internships have all but abandoned personality assessment; one internship training director recently boasted that for the past 15 years no one at his center had even seen a Rorschach, much less administered one (Megargee, 1990).

Given the number and the diversity of training programs in clinical psychology, both university based and free standing, it is probably unrealistic to expect them all to agree on the proper role of assessment in the clinical curriculum. But it would behoove each program to formulate explicit training goals and objectives with respect to assessment. Should every graduate student in clinical, counseling and school psychology be required to demonstrate proficiency in the administration, scoring and interpretation of intelligence and personality tests? Or should they merely be expected to attain sufficient familiarity to become intelligent consumers of assessments, with expertise being reserved for those who choose to take advanced specialty training? Either of these options is preferable to a slow drift toward mediocrity which allows minimally trained students to believe they are competent diagnosticians.

In his 1939 Presidential Address to the Rorschach Institute, Morris

Krugman argued that a Rorschach diagnosis only as good as the person who makes it. He believed that a major responsibility of the organization was to ". . . prevent the Rorschach from being misused by incompetents or charlatans." In particular, he warned about poorly trained individuals who, ". . . cannot use it properly, but they can misuse it, they can make unwarranted diagnoses and they can mislead people and do damage" (Krugman, 1939, p. 100). Although Krugman was focusing on the Rorschach, his remarks apply generally to personality assessment, whether it is for research or practice, by clinician or computer. As the Society for Personality Assessment begins its second half-century, it could do far worse than to accept Krugman's challenge to ensure that, in the years to come, psychological assessment is kept, ". . . on the high professional level it deserves."

REFERENCES

American Psychiatric Association, Task Force on nomenclature and statistics (1980). *Diagnostic and statistical manual of mental disorders* (3rd ed.). Washington, DC: Author.

American Psychological Association (1954). Technical recommendations for psychological tests and diagnostic techniques. *Psychological Bulletin, 51,* 1-38.

Anderson, H. H., & Anderson, G. L. (1951). *Introduction to projective techniques.* Englewood Cliffs, NJ: Prentice Hall.

Andreasen, N. C. (1979). Thought language and communication disorders II: diagnostic significance. *Archives of General Psychiatry, 36,* 1325-1330.

Andrew, G., Walton, R. E., Hartwell, S. W., & Hutt, M. L. (1951). The Michigan Picture Test: The stimulus value of the cards. *Journal of Consulting Psychology, 15,* 51-54.

Barlow, D. H. (Ed.) (1981). *Behavioral assessment of adult disorders.* New York: Guilford Press.

Beck, A. et al. (1961). An inventory for measuring depression. *Archives of General Psychiatry, 4,* 561-571.

Beck, A. et al. (1979). Assessment of suicidal ideation. *Journal of Consulting and Clinical Psychology, 47,* 343-352.

Beck, S. J. (1939, October). Thoughts on an impending anniversary. *American Journal of Orthopsychiatry,* 806-807.

Beck, S. J. (1972). How the Rorschach came to America. *Journal of Personality Assessment, 36,* 105-108.

Belar et al. (Eds.) (1987). *Proceedings of the National Conference on Internship Training in Psychology.* Washington, DC: Association of Psychology Internship Centers.

Bellak, L. (1954). *The Thematic Apperception Test and the Children's Apperception Test in clinical use.* New York: Grune and Stratton.

Ben-Porath, Y. S., & Butcher, J. N. (1991). The historical development of personality assessment. In C. E. Walker (Ed.), *Clinical psychology: Historical and research foundations* (pp. 121-156). New York: Plenum.

Blatt, S. J. (1990). The Rorschach: A test of perception or an evaluation of representation. *Journal of Personality Assessment, 55,* 394-416.

Block, J. (1965). *The challenge of response sets.* New York: Appleton Century.

Blum, G. S. (1950). *The Blacky Pictures: A manual of instructions.* New York: Psychological Corp.

Brodsky, S. L., & Smitherman, H. O. (1951). *Handbook of scales for research in crime and delinquency.* New York: Plenum.

Buss, D. M., & Craik, K. H. (1983). The act-frequency approach to personality. *Psychological Review, 96,* 105-126.

Butcher, J. N. (Ed.) (1987). *Computerized psychological assessment.* New York: Basic Books.

Campbell, D. T. (1960). Recommendations for APA test standards regarding construct, trait, or discriminant validity. *American Psychologist, 15,* 546-553.

Campbell, D. T., & Fiske, D. W. (1959). Convergent and discriminant validation by the multitrait-multimethod matrix. *Psychological Bulletin, 56,* 81-105. [Reprinted in Megargee (1966).]

Cattell, R. B., & Eber, H. J. (1966). *The 16 Personality Factor Questionnaire* (3rd ed.). Champaign, IL: IPAT.

Cattell, R. B., & Scheier, I. H. (1963). *The IPAT Anxiety Scale Questionnaire.* Champaign, IL: IPAT.

Chesney, M. A., & Rosenman, R. H. (Eds.) (1985). *The dynamics of aggression and their application to cardiovascular disorders.* New York: Hemisphere.

Cronbach, L. J., & Meehl, P. E. (1955). Construct validity in psychological tests. *Psychological Bulletin, 52,* 281-302. [Reprinted in Megargee (1966).]

Datel, W. E., & Gengerelli, J. A. (1955). The reliability of Rorschach interpretations. *Journal of Projective Techniques, 19,* 372-381.

[Reprinted in Megargee (1966).]
Davenport, B. F. (1952). The semantic validity of TAT interpretations. *Journal of Consulting Psychology, 16,* 171–175. [Reprinted in Megargee (1966).]
Departments of the Army and Air Force. (1951). *Military clinical psychology.* TM 8-242/AFM 160-45. Washington, DC: U.S. Government Printing Office.
Dicken, C. W. (1963). Good impression, social desirability and acquiescence as suppressor variables. *Educational and Psychological Measurement, 23,* 699–720. [Reprinted in Megargee (1966).]
Edwards, A. L. (1953). *The social desirability variable in personality assessment.* New York: Holt.
Edwards, A. L. (1954). *The Edwards Personal Preference Schedule Manual.* New York: Psychological Corp.
Exner, J. E. (1974). *The Rorschach: A comprehensive system* (Vol. 1). New York: Wiley.
Exner, J. E. (1978). *The Rorschach: A comprehensive system* (Vol. 2). New York: Wiley.
Exner, J. E. (1980). But it's only an inkblot. *Journal of Personality Assessment, 44,* 563–576.
Eysenck, H. J. (1959). *The Maudsley Personality Inventory.* London: University of London Press.
Eysenck, H. J., & Eysenck, S. B. G. (1975). *Manual for the Eysenck Personality Questionnaire.* San Diego: Educational and Industrial Testing Service.
Fisher, J., Gonda, T. A., & Little, K. B. (1955). The Rorschach and central nervous system pathology: A cross validation study. *American Journal of Psychiatry, 3,* 487–492.
Fowler, R. E., & Butcher, J. N. (1986). Critique of Matarazzo's views on computerized testing: All sigmas and no meaning. *American Psychologist, 41,* 94–96.
Golding, S. L., & Roesch, R. (1987). The assessment of criminal responsibility: A historical approach to a current controversy. In I. B. Weiner & A. K. Hess (Eds.), *Handbook of forensic psychology* (pp. 395–436). New York: Wiley.
Gough, H. G. (1960). *Manual for the California Psychological Inventory.* Palo Alto, CA: Consulting Psychologists Press.
Guilford, J. P., & Zimmerman, W. S. (1949). *The Guilford-Zimmerman Temperament Survey Manual.* Beverly Hills: Sheridan Supply Co.
Guilford, J. P., & Zimmerman, W. S. (1956). Fourteen dimensions of temperament. *Psychological Monographs, 70* (Whole No. 417).
Hammond, K. R. (1954). Representative vs. systematic design in clinical psychology. *Psychological Bulletin, 51,* 208–211. [Reprinted in Megargee (1966).]
Hathaway, S. R., & McKinley, J. C. (1967). *Minnesota Multiphasic Personality Inventory. Manual for administration and scoring.* New York: Psychological Corp.
Hersen, M., & Bellak, A. S. (Eds.) (1981). *Behavioral assessment: A practical handbook.* New York: Pergamon.
Hertz, M. (1970). Projective techniques in crisis. *Journal of Projective Techniques and Personality Assessment, 34,* 449–467.
Holsopple, J. Q., & Phelan, J. G. (1954). The skills of clinicians in analysis of projective tests. *Journal of Clinical Psychology, 10,* 307–320. [Reprinted in Megargee (1966).]
Holt, R. R. (1958). Clinical *and* statistical prediction: A reformulation and some new data. *Journal of Abnormal and Social Psychology, 56,* 1–12. [Reprinted in Megargee (1966).]
Holtzman, W. H. (1960). Can the computer supplant the clinician? *Journal of Clinical Psychology, 16,* 119–122. [Reprinted in Megargee (1966).]
Holtzman, W. H. (1988). Beyond the Rorschach. *Journal of Personality Assessment, 52,* 578–609.
Holtzman, W. H., & Sells, S. B. (1954). Prediction of flying success by clinical analysis of test protocols. *Journal of Abnormal and Social Psychology, 49,* 485–490. [Reprinted in Megargee (1966).]
Holtzman, W. H., Thorpe, J. S., Swartz, J. D., & Herron, E. W. (1961). *Inkblot perception and personality.* Austin, TX: University of Texas.
Horrocks, J. E. (1964). *Assessment of behavior: The methodology and content of psychological measurements.* Columbus, OH: Charles E. Merrill.
Jackson, D. N. (1967). *Personality Research Form.* Goshen, NY: Research Psychologists Press.
Jackson, D. N., & Messick, S. J. (1961). Acquiescence and desirability as response determinants of the MMPI. *Educational and Psychological Measurement, 21,* 771–792.
Kostlan, A. (1954). A method for the empirical study of psychodiagnosis. *Journal of Consulting Psychology, 18,* 83–88. [Reprinted in Megargee (1966).]
Krugman, M. (1939). Out of the inkwell: The Rorschach method. *Rorschach Research Exchange, 4,* 91–100.
Kutash, S. B. (1955). The impact of projective techniques on basic psychological science. *Journal of Projective Techniques, 19,* 453–469.
Lindzey, G. (1965). Seer vs. sign. *Journal of Experimental Research in Personality, 1,*

17-26. [Reprinted in Megargee (1966).]

Little, K. B., & Shneidman, E. S. (1954). The validity of MMPI interpretations. *Journal of Consulting Psychology, 18,* 425–428. [Reprinted in Megargee (1966).]

Little, K. B., & Shneidman, E. S. (1959). Congruencies among interpretations of psychological test data and anamnestic data. *Psychological Monographs, 73* (6, Whole No. 476). [Reprinted in Megargee (1966).]

Litwack, T. R., & Schlesinger, L. B. (1987). Assessing and predicting violence: Research, law, and applications. In I. B. Weiner & A. K. Hess (Eds.), *Handbook of forensic psychology* (pp. 205–257). New York: Wiley.

Lord, E. (1950). Experimentally induced variations in Rorschach performance. *Psychological Monographs, 64* (10, Whole No. 316).

Machover, K. (1949). *Personality projection in the drawing of the human figure: A method of personality investigation.* Springfield, IL: Charles C. Thomas.

Masling, J. (1960). The influence of situational and personal variables in projective testing. *Psychological Bulletin, 57,* 6–85.

Matarazzo, J. D. (1986). Computerized psychological test interpretation: Unvalidated plus all mean and no sigma. *American Psychologist, 41,* 14–24.

McArthur, D. S., & Roberts, G. E. (1982). *Roberts Apperception Test.* Los Angeles: Western Psychological Services.

Meehl, P. E. (1945). The dynamics of structured personality tests. *Journal of Clinical Psychology, 1,* 296–303.

Meehl, P. E. (1954). *Clinical vs. statistical prediction: A theoretical analysis and review of the evidence.* Minneapolis: University of Minnesota Press.

Meehl, P. E. (1957). When shall we use our heads instead of the formula? *Journal of Counseling Psychology, 4,* 268–273. [Reprinted in Megargee (1966).]

Meehl, P. E. (1959). Some ruminations on the validation of clinical procedures. *Canadian Journal of Psychology, 13,* 10–128. [Reprinted in Megargee (1966).]

Meehl, P. E. (1965). Seer vs. sign: The first good example. *Journal of Experimental Research in Personality, 1,* 27–32. [Reprinted in Megargee (1966).]

Meehl, P. E. (1979). A funny thing happened to us on the way to the latent entities. *Journal of Personality Assessment, 42,* 564–577.

Meehl, P. E., & Rosen, A. (1955). Antecedent probability and the efficacy of psychometric signs, patterns or cutting scores. *Psychological Bulletin, 52,* 194–216. [Reprinted in Megargee (1966).]

Megargee, E. I. (Ed.) (1966). *Research in clinical assessment.* New York: Harper & Row.

Megargee, E. I. (1972). *California Psychological Inventory handbook.* Palo Alto, CA: Consulting Psychologists Press.

Megargee, E. I. (1982). Psychological correlates and determinants of criminal violence. In M. Wolfgang & N. Weiner (Eds.), *Criminal violence* (pp. 81–170). Beverly Hills, CA: Sage.

Megargee, E. I. (1986, June). *Buffalo Bill and the boy on the pony: The assessment tradition and its ramifications in clinical psychology.* Invited address delivered at the Edward Chace Tolman Centennial Celebration, Berkeley, CA.

Megargee, E. I. (1990). *A guide to obtaining a psychology internship.* Muncie, IN: Accelerated Development.

Megargee, E. I. (in press). Aggression and violence. In H. Adams and P. Sutker (Eds.), *Comprehensive handbook of psychopathology* (Rev. Ed.). New York: Plenum.

Megargee, E. I., & Bohn, Jr., M., with Meyer, Jr., J., & Sink, F. (1979). *Classifying criminal offenders: A new system based on the MMPI.* Beverly Hills, CA: Sage Publications.

Megargee, E. I., & Carbonell, J. L. (1988). Evaluating leadership with the CPI. In C. D. Spielberger & J. N. Butcher (Eds.), *Advances in personality assessment* (Vol. 7, pp. 203–219). New York: Lawrence Erlbaum.

Megargee, E. I., Lockwood, V., Cato, J., & Jones, J. K. (1966). Effects of differences in examiner, tone of administration, and sex of subject on scores on the Holtzman Inkblot Technique. *Proceedings of the 74th Annual Convention of the American Psychological Association, 2,* 234–236.

Megargee, E. I., & Mendelsohn, G. A. (1962). A cross-validation of 12 MMPI measures of hostility and control. *Journal of Abnormal and Social Psychology, 65,* 431–438.

Millon, T. (1982). *Millon Clinical Multiaxial Inventory manual* (2nd ed.). Minneapolis: National Computer Systems.

Mischel, W. (1968). *Personality and assessment.* New York: Wiley.

Moos, R. H. (1984). Context and coping: Toward a unifying conceptual framework. *American Journal of Community Psychology, 12,* 5–25.

Moos, R. H. (1986). *Coping with life crises: An integrated approach.* New York: Plenum.

Murray, H. A. (1943). *Thematic Apperception Test Manual.* Cambridge, MA: Harvard University Press.

Murstein, B. I. (1963). *Theory and research in projective techniques (Emphasizing the TAT).* New York: Wiley.

Piaget, J. (1954). The construction of reality an the child. [Translated from the French by M. Cock.] New York: Basic Books. [Original

published in 1937.]
Rabin, A. I. (1977). Enduring sentiments: The continuity of personality over time. *Journal of Personality Assessment, 41,* 564–572.
Rickers-Ovsiankina, M. (1943). Some theoretical considerations regarding the Rorschach method. *Rorschach Research Exchange, 7,* 41–53.
Robins et al. (1981). National Institute of Mental Health Diagnostic Interview Schedule. *Archives of General Psychiatry, 38,* 381–389.
Roesch, R., & Golding, S. L. (1987). Defining and assessing competency to stand trial. In I. B. Weiner & A. K. Hess (Eds.), *Handbook of forensic psychology* (pp. 378–394). New York: Wiley.
Rorer, L. G. (1965). The great response-style myth. *Psychological Bulletin, 63,* 129–156.
Rorschach, H., & Oberholzer, E. (1923). Zur Auswertung des Formdeutversuchs fuer die Psychoanalyse. *Zsch. f. d. ges. Neur. u. Pschiatr., 82,* 240–273. [Translated as: The application of the interpretation of form to psychoanalysis. *Journal of Nervous and Mental Disease,* 1924, *60,* 225–248; 359–379.]
Rosenzweig, S., Fleming, E. E., & Clark, H. J. (1947). Scoring manual for the Rosenzweig Picture-Frustration Study. *Journal of Psychology, 24,* 165–208.
Rubenzer, S. (1991). Computerized testing and clinical judgment: A cause for concern. *The Clinical Psychologist, 44,* 63–66.
Shneidman, E. S. (1949). *The Make-A-Picture Story (MAPS) Test.* New York: Psychological Corp.
Shneidman, E. S. (1959). Suggestions for the delineation of validational studies. *Journal of Projective Techniques, 23,* 259–262. [Reprinted in Megargee (1966).]
Spielberger, C. D. (1966a). The effects of anxiety on complex learning and academic achievement. In C. D. Spielberger (Ed.), *Anxiety and behavior* (pp. 361–398). New York: Academic Press.
Spielberger, C. D. (1966b). Theory and research on anxiety. In C. D. Spielberger (Ed.), *Anxiety and behavior* (pp. 3–20). New York: Academic Press.
Spielberger, C. D. (1983). *Manual for the State-Trait Anxiety Inventory.* Palo Alto: Consulting Psychologists Press.
Spielberger, C. D. (1988). *State-Trait Anger Expression Inventory (STAXI) Professional Manual* (Research ed.). Odessa, FL: Psychological Assessment Resources, Inc. (PAR).
Spielberger, C. D., Jacobs, G., Russell, S., & Crane, R. S. (1983). Assessment of Anger: The State-Trait Anger Scale (STAS). In J. N. Butcher & C. D. Spielberger (Eds.), *Advances in personality assessment* (Vol. 2). Hillsdale, NJ: Lawrence Erlbaum Associates, Inc.
Spielberger, C. D., Krasner, S. S., & Solomon, E. P. (1988). The experience, expression, and control of anger. In M. P. Janisse (Ed.), *Health psychology: Individual differences and stress.* New York: Springer-Verlag Publishers.
Spielberger, C. D., Johnson, E. H., Russell, S. F., Crane, R. J., Jacobs, G. A., & Worden, T. J. (1985). The experience and expression of anger: Construction and validation of an anger expression scale. In M. A. Chesney & R. H. Rosenman (Eds.), *Anger and hostility in cardiovascular and behavioral disorders* (pp. 5–30). New York: Hemisphere.
Spielberger, C. D., Peters, R. A., & Frain, F. (1980). Curiosity and anxiety. In H. G. Voss & H. Keller (Eds.), *Curiosity research: Basic concepts and results.* Weinheim, Germany: Beltz.
Spielberger, C. D., & Piotrowski, C. (1991a). Clinician's attitudes toward computer-based testing. *The Clinical Psychologist, 43,* 60–63.
Spielberger, C. D., & Piotrowski, C. (1991b). Clinician or technician? A reply to Rubenzer. *The Clinical Psychologist, 44,* 67–68.
Spielberger, C. D., & Piotrowski, C. (1992). Profile of the membership of the Society for Personality Assessment: Comparison between 1987 and 1990. *Journal of Personality Assessment, 58,* 423–429.
Symonds, P. M. (1949). *Adolescent fantasy: An investigation of the picture-story method of personality study.* New York: Columbia University.
Thompson, C. E. (1949). The Thompson modification of the Thematic Apperception Test. *Rorschach Research Exchange, 13,* 469–478.
Weiner, I. B. (1983). The future of psychodiagnosis revisited. *Journal of Personality Assessment, 47,* 451–459.
Werner, H. (1948). *Comparative psychology of mental development.* New York: International Universities Press.

Combined Reference List for the Key Contributions

Reference Notes

In 1973, in the Second Edition of its *Publication Manual,* the American Psychological Association instructed authors to cite unpublished references such as technical reports, papers read at meetings, manuscripts under review and personal communications as "Reference Notes." These notes were listed in a separate section before the Reference List. Three articles reprinted in the present volume adopted this practice which was discontinued in 1983 when the Third Edition of the *Publication Manual* was issued.

Since Reference Notes used consecutive numbers for citations in the text, modifying them for incorporation into our comprehensive Reference List would have required expensive changes in the body of each article. Instead we have chosen to list them separately as was done in the original publications.

Meehl, P. E. (1979). A funny thing happened to us on the way to the latent entities. *Journal of Personality Assessment, 42,* 564–577.

1. Blashfield, R. K. *Failure of cluster analysis in psychiatric research.* Paper presented at the meeting of the American Psychological Association, Toronto, Canada, August 30, 1978.
2. Golden, R. R. & Meehl, P. E. *Taxometric analysis of causal entities: Detection of the schizoid taxon.* New York: Academic Press, to appear.
3. Golden, R. R. & Meehl, P. E. *Detection of biological sex: An empirical test of six cluster methods.* Manuscript submitted for publication, 1979.
4. Meehl, P. E., Lykken, D. T., Burdick, M. R., & Schoener, G. R. *Identifying latent clinical taxa, III: An empirical trial of the normal single-indicator method, using MMPI Scale 5 to identify the sexes* (Tech. Rep. PR-69-1). Minneapolis, University of Minnesota Psychiatry Research Laboratory, 1969.
5. Meehl, P. E. *Detecting latent clinical taxa by fallible quantitative indicators lacking an accepted criterion* (Tech. Rep. PR-65-2). Minneapolis, University of Minnesota Psychiatry Research Laboratory, 1965.
6. Meehl, P. E. *Detecting latent clinical taxa, II: A simplified procedure, some additional hit-max cut locators, a single-indicator method, and miscellaneous theorems* (Tech. Rep. PR-684). Minneapolis, University of Minnesota Psychiatry Research Laboratory, 1968.

Exner, J. E. (1980). But it's only an inkblot. *Journal of Personality Assessment, 44,* 563–576.

1. Thomas, E. & Exner, J. *Temporal consistency among six- and nine-year-olds over a 24 to 30 month interval.* Workshop Study 346 (unpublished). Rorschach Workshops, 1980.
2. Brent, P. & Exner, J. *Temporal consistency among eight-year-olds retested after seven days.* Workshop Study 361 (unpublished). Rorschach Workshops, 1980.
3. Alinsky, D. & Exner, J. *Temporal consistency among seven- and fifteen-year-olds retested after nine months.* Workshop Study 352 (unpublished). Rorschach Workshops, 1980.
4. Thomas, E. & Exner, J. *The effects of instructions to give different responses during retest on the consistency of scores for eight-year-olds.* Workshop Study 372 (unpublished). Rorschach Workshops, 1980.

Weiner, I. B. (1983). The future of psychodiagnosis revisited. *Journal of Personality Assessment, 47,* 451–459.

1. Lubin, B., Matarazzo, J. D. & Larsen, R. M. *Patterns of psychological test usage in the United States: 1935–1982.* Paper presented at the meeting of the American Psychological Association, Anaheim, August, 1983.
2. Leventhal, D. B., personal communication. April, 1983.

References

Abel, T. M. (1945). Responses of Negro and white morons to the Thematic Apperception Test. *American Journal Mental Deficiency, 49,* 463-468.

Adelson, J. (1969). Personality. *Annual Review of Psychology, 20,* 217-252.

Ainsworth, M. D. S. (1969). Object relations, dependency and attachment: A theoretical view of the mother-infant relationship. *Child Development, 40,* 969-1025.

Allison, J., Blatt, S. J., & Zimet, C. N. (1988). *The interpretation of psychological tests* (Original work published in 1968). New York: Hemisphere.

Allport, G. W. (1968). The historical background of modern social psychology. In G. Lindzey & E. Aronson (Eds.), *The handbook of social psychology* (Vol. 1., pp. 3-56). Cambridge, MA: Addison-Wesley.

American Psychiatric Association. (1987). *Diagnostic and statistical manual of mental disorders* (3rd ed., rev.). Washington, DC: Author.

Ames, L. B. (1960). Age changes in the Rorschach responses of a group of elderly individuals. *Journal of Genetic Psychology, 97,* 257-285.

Ames, L. B. (1966). Changes in Rorschach response throughout the human life span. *Genetic Psychology Monographs, 74,* 89-125.

Ames, L. B., & August, J. (1966). Rorschach responses of Negro and white 5 to 10 year olds. *Journal of Genetic Psychology, 109,* 297-309.

Ames, L. B., & Ilg, F. L. (1967). Search for children showing academic promise in a presdominantly Negro school. *Journal of Genetic Psychology, 110,* 217-231.

Angyal, A. (1942). Speed and pattern of perception in schizophrenic and normal persons. *Char. & Pers., 11.*

Appelbaum, S. A. (1976). Objections to diagnosis and diagnostic psychological testing diagnosed. *Bulletin of the Menninger Clinic, 40,* 559-564.

Arnhoff, F. N., & Jenkins, J. W. (1969). Subdoctoral education in psychology: A study of issues and attitudes. *American Psychologist, 24,* 430-443.

Arnold, W. J. (Ed.). (1976). *Nebraska symposium on motivation.* 1975. Lincoln, NE: University of Nebraska Press.

Aronow, E., & Reznikoff, M. (1976). *Rorschach content interpretation.* New York: Grune & Stratton.

Atkinson, J. W. (Ed.). (1958). *Motives in fantasy, action, and society.* Princeton, NJ: D. Van Nostrand Co.

Atkinson, J. W. (1981). Studying personality in the context of an advanced motivational psychology. *American Psychologist, 31,* 117-128.

Babladelis, G., Deaux, K., Helmreich, R. L., & Spence, J. T. (1983). Sex-related attitudes and personal characteristics in the United States. *International Journal of Psychology, 18,* 111-123.

Bach, G. R. (1952). Who are the discoverers of psychological knowledge? *American Psychologist, 7,* 131-132.

Bartlett, F. C. (1932). *Remembering.* Cambridge, England: Cambridge University Press.

Baruch, R. (1967). The achievement motive in women: Implications for career development. *Journal of Personality and Social Psychology, 5,* 260-267.

Baudelaire, C. (1921). *Oeuvrews compl.* Goutier.

Baughman, E. E. (1959). An experimental analysis of the relationship between stimulus structure and behavior on the Rorschach. *Journal of Projective Techniques, 23,* 134-183.

Bauman, G., & Roman, M. (1968). Interaction product analysis in group and family diagnosis. *Journal of Projective Techniques & Personality Assessment, 32,* 331-337.

Beck, S. J. (1932). The Rorschach test as applied to a feeble-minded group. *Arch. of Psychology, 136.* (Columbia University)

Beck, S. J. (1933). Configurational tendencies in Rorschach responses. *Am J. Psychol., 45.*

Beck, S. J. (1937). Introduction to the Rorschach method. *The American Orthopsychiatric Assn.*

Beck, S. J. (1942). Error, symbol and method in the Rorschach test. *Journal Abnormal Social Psychology, 37,* 83-103.

Beck, S. J. (1944). *Rorschach's test.* Vol. 1. New York: Grune & Stratton. (A variety of personality pictures)

Beck, S. J. (1954). *The six schizophrenias.* Research monogr. No. 6. New York: American Orthopsychiatric Association.

Beck, S. J. (1965). *Psychological processes in the schizophrenic adaptation.* New York: Grune & Stratton.

Beck, S. J. (1967). Schizophrenia: Interadaptation of person, family and culture. In J. Romana (Ed.), *The origins of schizophrenia* (pp. 249-267). New York: Excerpta Medica Foundation. (Proceedings of the First Rochester International Conference of Schizophrenia)

Beck, S. J., Beck, A. G., Levitt, E. E., & Molish, H. B. (1961). *Rorschach's test: Basic processes.* Vol. 1, 3rd ed. New York: Grune & Stratton.

Beck, S. J., & Molish, H. B. (1967). *Rorschach's test: A variety of personality pictures.* Vol. 2. New York: Grune & Stratton.

Beck, S. J., & Nunnally, J. C. (1953). Two researches in schizophrenia. *American Journal of Orthopsychiatry, 23,* 223–235.

Beitman, B. D., Williamson, R., Featherstone, N., & Katon, W. (1982). Resistance to physician use of the biopsychosocial model. *General Hospital Psychiatry, 4,* 81–83.

Beizmann, C. (1961). *Le Rorschach chez l'enfant de 3 a 10 ans.* Neuchatel, Switzerland: Delachaux et Niestle.

Beizmann, C. (1966). *Livret de cotation des formes dans le Rorschach.* Paris, France: Centre de Psychologie Appliquee.

Bell, A., Trosman, H., & Ross, W. D. (1952). The use of projective techniques in the investigation of emotional aspects of general medical disorders. *Journal of Projective Techniques, 16,* 428–443.

Bell, J. E. (1953). Projective techniques and the development of personality. *Journal of Projective techniques, 17,* 391–400.

Benfari, R. C., & Calogeras, R. C. (1968). Levels of cognition and conscience typologies. *Journal of Projective Techniques & Personality Assessment, 32,* 466–474.

Berg, M. (1984). Expanding the parameters of psychological testing. *Bulletin of the Menninger Clinic, 48*(1), 10–24.

Bergin, T. G., & Fisch, M. H. (1969). *The new science of Giambattista Vico.* Ithaca: Cornell University Press.

Bersoff, D. N. (1973). Silk purses into sow's ears: The decline of psychological testing and a suggestion for its redemption. *American Psychologist, 28,* 892–899.

Bettelheim, B. (1947). Self-interpretation of fantasy: The Thematic Apperception Test as an education and therapeutic device. *American Journal of Orthopsychiatry, 17,* 80–100.

Binswanger-Bemerkungen zu, H. (1923). Rorschach's psychodiagnostik. *Intern. Zsch. Psychoanal., 9.*

Blashfield, R. K. (1976). Mixture model tests of cluster analysis: Accuracy of four agglomerative hierarchical methods. *Psychological Bulletin, 83,* 377–388.

Blashfield, R. K., & Aldenderfer, M. S. (1978). The literature on cluster analysis. *Multivariate Behavioral Research, 13,* 291–295.

Blashfield, R. K., & Draguns, J. G. (1976). Toward a taxonomy of psychopathology: The purpose of psychiatric classification. *British Journal of Psychiatry, 129,* 574–583.

Blatt, S. J. (1958). An experimental study of the problem-solving process. A. *American Psychologist, 13,* 373. (Abstract)

Blatt, S. J. (1959). Recall and recognition vocabulary: Implications for intellectual deterioration. *Archives of General Psychiatry, 1,* 473–476.

Blatt, S. J. (1975). The validity of projective techniques and their research and clinical contribution. *Journal of Personality Assessment, 39,* 327–343.

Blatt, S. J. (1986). Where have we been and where are we going?: Reflections on fifty years of personality assessment. *Journal of Personality Assessment, 50,* 343–346.

Blatt, S. J. (1988, August). *A cognitive morphology for psychopathology* (Paper presented at the First International Conference of Disorders of Personality, Copenhagen, Denmark). Copenhagen, Denmark.

Blatt, S. J., Brenneis, C. B., Schimek, J. G., & Glick, M. (1976). Normal development and psychopathological impairment of the concept of the object on the Rorschach. *Journal of Abnormal Psychology, 86,* 364–373.

Blatt, S. J., Chevron, E. S., Quinlan, D. M., Schaffer, C. E., & Weiss, S. (1988). *The assessment of qualitative and structural dimensions of object representations* (rev. ed.). New Haven: Hale University.

Blatt, S. J., & Ritzler, B. A. (1974). Thought disorder and boundary disturbances in psychosis. *Journal of Consulting and Clinical Psychology, 42,* 370–381.

Blatt, S. J., & Stein, M. I. (1957). Some personality, value and cognitive characteristics of the creative person. *American Psychologist, 12,* 406. (Abstract)

Blatt, S. J., & Stein, M. I. (1959). Efficiency in problem solving. *The Journal of Psychology, 48,* 193–213.

Blatt, S. J., & Wild, C. M. (1976). *Schizophrenia: A developmental analysis.* New York: Academic.

Blatt, S. J., Wild, C. M., & Ritzler, B. A. (1975). Disturbances of object representation in schizophrenia. *Psychoanalysis and Contemporary Science, 4,* 235–288.

Block, W. E. (1962). Psychometric aspects of the Rorschach technique. *Journal of Projective Techniques, 26,* 162–172.

Bloom, B. L. (Ed.). (1969). Training the psychologist for a role in community change. *Newsletter, Division of Community Psychology, 3.* (No. 3 Special Issue)

Bodin, A. M. (1968). Conjoint family assessment: An evolving field. In P. McReynold (Ed.), *Advances in psychological assessment.* Vol. 1. Palo Alto, CA: Science & Behavior Books.

Boll, T. J. (1981). The Halstead-Reitan neuropsychology battery. In S. Filskov & T. J. Boll (Eds.), *Handbook of clinical neuropsychology.* New York: Wiley.

Boll, T. J. (1983). Neuropsychological assessment. In I. B. Weiner (Ed.), *Clinical methods in psychology* (2nd ed.). New York: Wiley.

Bowlby, J. (1973). *Attachment and loss, Volume 2: Separation, anxiety, and anger.* New York: Basic Books.

Bowlby, J. (1988). Developmental psychology comes of age. *American Journal of Psychiatry, 145,* 1-10.

Bowman, P. R. (1982). An analog study with beginning therapists suggesting bias against "activity" in women. *Psychotherapy: Training, Research and Practice, 19,* 318-324.

Boyer, L. B., Boyer, R. M., Hayao, K., & Klopfer, B. (1965). Effects of acculturation on the personality traits of the old people of the Mescalero and Chiricahua Apaches. *International Journal of Social Psychiatry, 11,* 264-271.

Boyer, L. B., Boyer, R. M., Hayao, K., & Klopfer, B. (1967). Apache "learners" and "nonlearners". *Journal of Projective Techniques & Personality Assessment, 31,* 22-29.

Boyer, L. B., Boyer, R. M., Klopfer, B., & Scheiner, Z. B. (1968). Apache "learners" and "nonlearners": II. Quantitative Rorschach signs of influential adults. *Journal of Projective Techniques and Personality Assessment, 32,* 146-159.

Bradway, K. P., Lion, E. G., & Corrigan, H. G. (1946). The use of the Rorschach in the psychiatric study of promiscuous girls. *Rorschach Res. Exch., 10,* 105-110.

Brian, C., & Goodenough, F. (1929). The relative potency of color and form perception at various ages. *J. Exp. Psychol., 12.*

Brislin, R. W., Thorndike, R. M., & Lonner, W. J. (1973). *Crosscultural research methods.* New York: Wiley.

Brosin, H., & Fromm, E. (1942). Some principles of Gestalt psychology in the Rorschach experiment. *Rorschach Res. Exch., 6.*

Brown, F. (1965). The Bender Gestalt and acting out. In L. E. Abt & S. L. Weissman (Eds.), *Acting out: Theoretical and clinical aspects.* New York: Grune & Stratton.

Brown, W. R., & McGuire, J. M. (1976). Current psychological assessment practices. *Professional Psychology, 7,* 476-484.

Bruner, J. (1948). Symbolic value as an organizing factor in perception. *Journal of Social Psychology, 27,* 203-208.

Bruner, J. (1986). *Actual minds, possible worlds.* Cambridge, MA: Harvard University Press.

Bruner, J. S., & Goodman, C. C. (1947). Value and need as organizing factors in perception. *Journal of Abnormal and Social Psychology, 42,* 33-42.

Brunswik, E. (1947). *Systematic and representative design of psychological experiments.* Berkeley, CA: University of California Press.

Buci, W. (1985). Dual coding: Cognitive model for psychoanalytic research. *Journal of the American Psychoanalytic Association, 33,* 571-607.

Burchard, E. M. L. (1952). The use of projective techniques in the analysis of creativity. *Journal of Projective Techniques, 16,* 412-427.

Burke, W. F., Friedman, G., & Gorlitz, P. (1988). The psychoanalytic Rorschach profile: An integration of drive, ego and object relations perspectives. *Psychoanalytic Psychology, 5,* 193-212.

Burke, W. F., Summers, F., Selinger, D., & Polonus, T. (1986). The comprehensive object relations profile: A preliminary report. *Psychoanalytic Psychology, 3,* 173-185.

Butcher, J. N. (1978). Computerized scoring and interpreting services. In O. K. Buros (Ed.), *The eighth mental measurements yearbook* (pp. 942-945). Highland Park, NJ: Gryphon Press.

Butcher, J. N. (Ed.). (1979). *New developments in the use of the MMPI.* Minneapolis, MN: University of Minnesota Press.

Butler, J. M., & Fiske, D. W. (1955). Theory and techniques of assessment. *Annual Review of Psychology, 6,* 327-356.

Cattell, R. B., Cattell, A. K. S., & Rhymer, R. M. (1947). P-technique demonstrated in determining psychophysiological source traits in a normal individual. *Psychometrika, 12,* 267-288.

Caudill, W., & DeVos, G. (1967). Achievement, culture and personality: The case of the Japanese Americans. In J. I. Roberts (Ed.), *School children in the urban slum.* New York: The Free Press.

Ciminero, A. R., Calhoun, K. S., & Adams, H. E. (Eds.). (1977). *Handbook of behavioral assessment.* New York: Wiley.

Clair, T. N., Osterman, R. L., Kiraly, J., Klausmeier, R. D., & Griff, M. M. (1971). Practicum and internship experiences in school psychology: Recent trends in graduate training. *American Psychologist, 26,* 566-574.

Cleveland, S. E. (1976). Reflections on the rise and fall of psychodiagnosis. *Professional Psychology, 7,* 309-318.

Coleman, J. C. (1968). Rorschach content as a means of studying child development. *Journal of Projective Techniques and Personality Assessment, 32,* 435-442.

Comer, P. (1982). An undergraduate, preprofessional course-in-oneself. In R. H. Dana (Ed.), *Personal growth in professional training programs* (in preparation).

Conant, J. B. (1951). *Science and common sense.* New Haven: Yale University Press.

Conway, J. B. (1982, June). *Some characteristics of exemplary young clinical psychologists: The scientists, the professionals, and the scientific-professional.* Paper presented at the meeting of the Canadian Psychological Association, Montreal.

Conway, J. B. (1984). A place for discontent and tensions in psychology. *Canadian Psychology, 25,* 96–104.

Connerty, S. (1986). An exploration of separation-individuation themes in the borderline personality disorder. *Journal of Personality Assessment, 50,* 501–512.

Cooper, G. D., Adams, H. B., & Cohen, L. D. (1965). Personality changes after sensory deprivation. *Journal of Nervous & Mental Disorders, 40,* 103–118.

Cooper, S. H., Perry, J. C., Hoke, L., & Richman, N. (1985). Transitional relatedness and borderline personality disorder. *Psychoanalytic Psychology, 2,* 115–128.

Cowen, E. L., Gardner, E. A., & Zax, M. (Eds.). (1967). *Emergent approaches to mental health problems.* New York: Appleton-Century-Crofts.

Coyne, J. (1942). *An experiment on the interpretative value of color in the Rorschach test.* Unpublished manuscript in the library of Wheaton College.

Craddick, R. A. (1975). Sharing oneself in the assessment procedure. *Professional Psychology, 6,* 279–282.

Cronbach, L. J. (1948). A validation design for qualitative studies of personality. *Journal Consult. Psychol., 12,* 365–374.

Cronbach, L. J. (1949). Statistical methods applied to Rorschach scores. *Psychol. Bulletin, 46,* 393–429.

Cronbach, L. J. (1975). Beyond the two disciplines of scientific psychology. *American Psychologist, 30,* 116–127.

Cronbach, L. J., & Meehl, P. E. (1956). Construct validity in psychological tests. In Feigl & Scriven (Eds.), *Minnesota studies in the philosophy of science* (Vol. 1, pp. 174–204). Minneapolis: University of Minnesota Press.

Cumming, E., Dean, L. R., Newell, D. S., & McCaffrey, I. (1959). *Disengagement: A tentative theory of aging.* Paper read in meeting of Division 20, American Psychological Association. Cincinatti, OH.

Cushing, R. (1896). Outlines of Zuni creation myths. *13th Report Bur. Am. Ethnology.*

Cutter, F. (1968). Role complements and changes in consensus Rorschachs. *Journal of Projective Techniques & Personality Assessment, 32,* 338–347.

Cutter, F., Jorgensen, M., & Farberow, N. L. (1968). Replicability of Rorschach signs with known degrees of suicidal intent. *Journal of Projective Techniques & Personality Assessment, 32,* 428–434.

Dana, R. H. (1978). Comparisons of competence training in two successful clinical programs. *Psychological Reports, 42,* 919–926.

Dana, R. H. (1980). Receptivity to clinical interpretation. In R. H. Woody (Ed.), *Encyclopedia of clinical assessment* (Vol. 2, pp. 1042–1049). San Francisco: Jossey-Bass.

Dana, R. H. (1982). *A human science model for personality assessment with projective techniques.* Springfield, IL: Thomas.

Dana, R. H. (1984). Personality assessment: Practice and teaching for the next decade. *Journal of Personality Assessment, 48,* 46–57.

Dana, R. H. (In press-a). The Thematic Apperception Test with adolescents. In A. I. Rabin (Ed.), *Projective techniques for children and adolescents.* New York: Springer.

Dana, R. H. (In press-b). Assessment for health psychology. *Clinical Psychology Review.*

Dana, R. H., Bolton, B., & West, V. (1983). *Validation of eisegesis concepts in assessment reports using the 16 PF: A training method with examples.* Third International 16 PF Conference Proceedings. Champaign, IL: IPAT.

Dana, R. H., Dana, J., & Comer, P. (1972). Role-playing effects on Rorschach scoring and interpretation. *Journal of Personality Assessment, 36,* 435.

Dana, R. H., & Fitzgerald, J. (1976). Educational self-assessment: A course-in-oneself. *College Student Journal, 10,* 317–323.

Dana, R. H., Hornby, R., & Hoffmann, T. (Eds.). (In press). Personality assessment of Rosebud Sioux: A comparison of Rorschach, Millon Clinical Multiaxial Inventory and 16 PF reports. *White Cloud Journal.*

Daston, P. G., & Sakheim, G. A. (1960). Prediction of successful suicide from the Rorschach test, using a sign approach. *Journal of Projective Techniques, 24,* 355–361.

Dawes, R. M. (1979). The robust beauty of improper linear models in decision making. *American Psychologist, 34,* 571–582.

Dawes, R. M., & Corrigan, B. (1974). Linear models in decision making. *Psychological Bulletin, 81,* 95–106.

Dawes, R. M., & Meehl, P. E. (1966). Mixed group validation: A method for determining the validity of diagnostic signs without using criterion groups. *Psychological Bulletin, 66,* 63–67.

Depue, R. A., & Monroe, S. M. (1978). The unipolar-bipolar distinction in the depressive disorders. *Psychological Bulletin, 85,*1001–1029.

Descoeudres, A. C. (1914). Forme ou Nombre. *Arch. de Psychol.*

DeVos, G. A. (1965a). Achievement orientation, social self-identity and Japanese economic growth. *Asian Survey, 5,* 575-589 (a).

DeVos, G. A. (1965b). Transcultural diagnoses of mental health by means of psychological tests. In A. V. S. deReuck & R. Porter (Eds.), *Ciba Foundation symposium on transcultural psychiatry.* London, England: J. and A. Churchill, Ltd.

DeVos, G. A. (1966). *A comparison of the personality differences in two generations of Japanese Americans by means of the Rorschach test.* Hawaii: University of Hawaii Social Science Research Institute. (Reprint no. 14)

DeVos, G. A. (1968). Achievement and innovation in culture and personality. In E. Norback, D. Price-William, & W. M. McCord (Eds.), *The study of personality: An interdisciplinary appraisal* (pp. 348-370). New York: Holt, Reinhart & Winston. (Rice University Symposium)

DeVos, G. A., & Hippler, A. E. (1969). Cultural psychology: Comparative studies of human behavior. In G. Lindzey & E. Aronson (Eds.), *The handbook of social psychology* (Revised). Reading, MA: Addison-Wesley Publishing Co.

Dewey, J. (1938). *Logic: The theory of inquiry.* New York: Holt.

Dubois, C. (1944). *The people of Alor.* Minneapolis: University of Minnesota Press. (Summary of the use of the Rorschach by E. Oberholzer)

Dudek, S. Z. (1968). Regression and creativity. *Journal of Nervous & Mental Disease, 147,* 535-546.

Dudek, S. Z. (1969). Interaction testing as a measure of therapeutic change in groups. *Journal of Projective Techniques & Personality Assessment, 33,* 127-137.

Dunnette, M. D. (1966). Fads, fashions, and folderol in psychology. *American Psychologist, 21,* 343-352.

Eisdorfer, C. (1963). Rorschach performance and intellectual functioning in the aged. *Journal of Gerontology, 18,* 358-363.

Elizur, B. (1976). Content analysis of the Rorschach in two phases: Imaginary story and self-interpretation. *Perceptual and Motor Skills, 43,* 43-46.

Eljasch, M. (1928). Neue Absraktionsversuche bei vorschulpfichtigen Kindern. *Zsch. Psychol., 105.*

Endicott, N. A., & Endicott, J. (1963). "Improvement" in untreated psychiatric patients. *Archives of General Psychiatry, 9,* 575-585.

Endler, N. S., & Magnusson, D. (1976). Toward an interactional psychology of personality. *Psychological Bulletin, 83,* 956-974.

Engel, G. L. (1980). The clinical application of the biopsychosocial model. *Psychiatry, 137,* 535-544.

Engel, P. (1935). Ueber die teilinhaltliche Beachtung von Farbe und Form. *Zsch. paed. Psychol., 36.*

Erikson, E. H. (Ed.). (1959). Identity and the life cycle. *Psychological Issues, 1*(No. 1).

Exner, J. (1969). *The Rorschach systems.* New York: Grune & Stratton.

Exner, J. E. (1974). *The Rorschach: A comprehensive system.* Vol. 1. New York: Wiley.

Exner, J. E. (1978). *The Rorschach: A comprehensive system.* Vol. 2. New York: Wiley. (Current research and advanced interpretation)

Exner, J. E. (1983). Rorschach assessment. In I. B. Weiner (Ed.), *Clinical methods in psychology* (2nd ed.). New York: Wiley.

Exner, J. E., Armbrusher, G. L., & Viglione, D. (1978). The temporal stability of some Rorschach features. *Journal of Personality Assessment, 42,* 474-482.

Exner, J. E., & Weiner, I. B. (1982). *The Rorschach: A comprehensive system.* Vol. 3. New York: Wiley. (Assessment of children and adolescents)

Feather, N. T. (1966). Effects of prior success and failure on expectations of success and subsequent performance. *Journal of Personality and Social Psychology, 3,* 287-298.

Feigl, H. (1951). Principles and problems of theory construction in psychology. In *Current Trends in Psychological Theory,* pp. 179-213. (University Press)

Feirstein, A. (1967). Personality correlates of tolerance for unrealistic experiences. *Journal of Consulting Psychology, 31,* 387-395.

Fenichel, O. (1945). *The psychoanalytic theory of the neuroses.* New York: Norton.

Fischer, C. T. (1970). The testee as co-evaluator. *Journal of Counseling Psychology, 17,* 70-76.

Fischer, C. T. (1973). Contextural approach to assessment. *Community Mental Health Journal, 9,* 38-45.

Fischer, C. T. (1980). Phenomenology and psychological assessment: Representational description. *Journal of Phenomenological Psychology, 11,* 79-105.

Fisher, R. (1947). *The design of experiments.* 4th ed. New York: Hofner.

Fisher, S. (1967). Projective methodologies. *Annual Review of Psychology, 18,* 165-191.

Fiske, S. E., & Linville, F. W. (1980). What does the schema concept buy us? *Personality and Social Psychology Bulletin, 6,* 543-557.

Fiske, S. T., & Taylor, S. E. (1984). *Social cognition.* Reading, MA: Addison-Wesley.

Fosberg, I. A. (1938). Rorschach reactions under various instructions. *Rorschach Research Exchange, 3,* 12-30.

Fraiberg, S. (1969). Libidinal object constancy and mental representation. *Psychoanalytic Study of the Child, 24,* 9–47.

Francis-Williams, J. (1969). *The diagnostic use of Rorschach with children.* Elmsford, NY: Pergamon Publishing Co.

Frank, G. H. (1967). A review of research with measures of ego strength derived from the MMPI and the Rorschach. *Journal of General Psychology, 77,* 183–206.

Frank, G. H. (1984). The Boulder model: History, rationale, and critique. *Professional Psychology: Research and Practice, 15*(3), 417–435.

Frank, L. K. (1939). Projective methods for the study of personality. *Journal of Psychology, 8,* 389–413.

Frenkel-Brunswik, E. (1949). Intolerance of ambiguity as an emotional and perceptual variable. *Journal Perseonal., 18,* 108–143.

Frenkel-Brunswik, E., & Sanford, R. N. (1945). Personality factors in anti-semitism. *Journal Psychology, 13,* 425–459.

Freud, A. (1965). *Normality and pathology in childhood.* New York: International Universities Press.

Freud, S. (1927). *The ego and the id.* Joan Riviere translation. London, England: Leonard and Virginia Woolf & Institute of Psychoanalysis.

Fromme, A. (1941). On the use of certain qualitative methods of attitude research. *Journal Soc. Psychol., 13,* 425–459.

Fulkerson, S. (1965). Some implications of the new cognitive theory for projective tests. *Journal of Consulting Psychology, 29,* 191–197.

Gallessich, J. M., Gilbert, L., & Holahan, C. (1980). A training model to facilitate professional effectiveness in power-salient and sex-salient situations. *Professional Psychology, 11,* 15–23.

Gallessich, J. M., & MacDonald, J. (1981). Facilitating professional development through group analogic methods. *Professional Psychology, 12,* 209–215.

Gardner, H. (1985). *The mind's new science: A history of the cognitive revolution.* New York: Basic Books.

Garfield, S. L. (1980). *Psychotherapy: An eclectic approach.* New York: Wiley.

Garfield, S. L. (1982). Eclecticism and integration in psychotherapy. *Behavior Therapy, 13,* 610–623.

Garfield, S. L., & Kurtz, R. M. (1973). Attitudes toward training in diagnostic testing: A survey of directors of internship training. *Journal of Consulting and Clinical Psychology, 40,* 350–355.

Garfield, S. L., & Kurtz, R. M. (1977). A study of eclectic views. *Journal of Consulting and Clinical Psychology, 45,* 78–83.

Gaylin, N. L. (1966). Psychotherapy and psychological health: A Rorschach function and structure analysis. *Journal of Consulting Psychology, 30,* 494–500.

Gibbons, F. X. (1983). Self-attention and self-report: The "veridicality" hypothesis. *Journal of Personality, 51,* 517–542.

Gibby, R. G. (1952). Examiner influence on the Rorschach inquiry. *Journal Consult. Psychol., 16,* 449–455.

Giorgi, A. (1970). *Psychology as a human science.* New York: Harper & Row.

Giorgi, A. (1983). Concerning the possibility of phenomenological psychological research. *Journal of Phenomenological Psychology, 14,* 129–169.

Gitelman, M. (1984, April). *Jewish humanism.* Presented at the Ben B. Kimpel Lecture Series, Perspectives on Humanism. Fayetteville, AR.

Gleser, G. C. (1963). Projective methodologies. *Annual Review of Psychology, 14,* 391–422.

Goethe von, W. (1867). Zur Farbenlehre, Cott, sche Buchhandlung. *Stuttgart, 33 & 34.*

Goldberg, L. R. (1965). Diagnosticians vs. diagnostic signs: The diagnosis of psychosis vs. neurosis from the MMPI. *Psychological Monographs, 79.* (9, Whole No. 602)

Golden, C. J. (1981). A standardized version of Luria's neuropsychological tests: A quantitative and qualitative approach to neuropsychological evaluation. In S. Filskov & T. J. Boll (Eds.), *Handbook of clinical neuropsychology.* New York: Wiley.

Golden, R. R., & Meehl, P. E. (1969). Detection of the schizoid taxon with MMPI indicators. *Journal of Abnormal Psychology, 88,* 217–233.

Goldenberg, I. I. (1969). The clinician and the community: Contemporary responsibilities and historical imperatives. *Transactions of the New York Academy of Sciences, 31,* 611–617.

Goldfried, M. R. (1966). The assessment of anxiety by means of the Rorschach. *Journal of Projective Techniques & Personality Assessment, 30,* 364–380.

Goldfried, M. R. (Ed.). (1982). *Converging themes in psychotherapy: Trends in psychodynamic, humanistic and behavioral assessment.* New York: Pergamon.

Goldfried, M. R. (1982). On the history of therapeutic integration. *Behavior Therapy, 13,* 572–593 (b).

Goldfried, M. R. (1983). Behavioral assessment. In I. B. Weiner (Ed.), *Clinical methods in psychology* (2nd ed.). New York: Wiley.

Goldfried, M. R., & Kent, R. N. (1972). Traditional vs. behavioral personality assessment: A comparison of methodological and theoretical assumptions. *Psychological Bulletin, 77,* 409–420.

Goldstein, K. (1939). *The organism.* New York: Am. Book Co.

Goldstein, K. (1942). Some experimental observations concerning the influence of colors on the function of the organism. *Occupational Therapy and Rehabilitation, 21.*

Goodenough, F. (1929). The emotional behavior of young children during mental tests. *Journal Delinquency, 13,* 204–219.

Goodman, N. (1984). *Of mind and other matters.* Cambridge, MA: Harvard University Press.

Gough, H. G. (1962). Clinical vs. statistical prediction in psychology. In L. Postman (Ed.), *Psychology in the making: Histories of selected research problems.* New York: Knopf.

Grant, D. L., Katkovsky, W., & Bray, D. W. (1967). Contributions of projective techniques to assessment of management potential. *Journal of Applied Psychology, 51,* 226–232.

Grebstein, L. C. (1967). Defensive behavior in an interpersonal situation. *Journal of Consulting Psychology, 31,* 529–535.

Grinker, R. R. (1932). A comparison of psychological "repression" and neurological "inhibition." *Journal of Mental and Nervous Disorders, 89,* 765–781.

Grotjahn, M. (1955). Analytic psychotherapy with the elderly. *Psychoanalytic Review, 42,* 419–427.

Guerney, B. G. (1969). *Psychotherapeutic agents: New roles for nonprofessionals, parents, and teachers.* New York: Holt, Rinehart & Winston.

Gutmann, D. L., Henry, W. E., & Neugarten, B. (1959). Personality development in middle-aged man. *American Psychologist, 14,* 351. (Abstract)

Gynther, M. D., & Gynther, R. A. (1983). Personality inventories. In I. B. Weiner (Ed.), *Clinical methods in psychology* (2nd ed.). New York: Wiley.

Haan, N. (1964). An investigation of the relationship of Rorschach scores, patterns, and behavior to coping and defense mechanisms. *Journal of Projective Techniques & Personality Assessment, 28,* 429–442.

Haley, E. M., Draguns, J. G., & Phillips, L. (1967). Studies of Rorschach content: A review of research literature. Part II: Nontraditional uses of content indicators. *Journal of Projective Techniques & Personality Assessment, 31,* 3–38.

Hall, D. M., & Abramson, Y. (1968). Frequency of the Rorschach human-movement response in Negro and white emotionally disturbed children. *Journal of Consulting and Clinical Psychology, 32,* 158–163.

Hallowell, A. I. (1942). Acculturation processes and personality changes as indicated by the Rorschach technique. *Rorschach Res. Exch., 6,* 42–50.

Hammer, E. F. (1965). Acting out and its prediction by projective drawing assessment. In L. C. Abt & S. L. Weissman (Eds.), *Acting out* (pp. 288–319). New York: Grune & Stratton.

Hammond, K. R. (1951). Relativity and representativeness. *Phil. Sci., 18,* 208–211.

Hammond, K. R. (1954). Representative vs. systematic design in clinical psychology. *Psychol. Bull, 51,* 150–159.

Harrower, M. (1977). The Rorschach and self-understanding: The Instruction-Insight Method. *Journal of Personality Assessment, 41,* 451–460.

Hartigan, J. A. (1975). *Clustering algorithms.* New York: Wiley.

Hartley, E. L. (1946). *Problems in prejudice.* New York: King's Crown Press.

Hastie, R. (1981). Schematic principles in human memory. In E. T. Higgins, P. Herman, & M. P. Zanna (Eds.), *Social cognition: The Ontario symposium* (pp. 39–88). Hillsdale, NJ: Lawrence Erlbaum Associates, Inc.

Hatcher, R. L., & Krohn, A. (1980). Level of object representation and capacity for intensive psychotherapy in neurotics and borderlines. In J. S. Kwawer, H. D., Lerner, P. M. Lerner, & A. Sugarman (Eds.), *Borderline phenomena and the Rorschach Test* (pp. 299–320). New York: International Universities Press.

Hathaway, S. R. (1959). Increasing clinical efficiency. In B. M. Bass & I. A. Berg (Eds.), *Objective approaches to personality assessment.* Princeton, NJ: D. Van Nostrand.

Hayworth, M. R. (1968). Symposium: The Children's Apperception Test: Its use in developmental assessment of normal children. *Journal of Projective Techniques & Personality Assessment, 32,* 402–427.

Hemmendinger, L. (1960). Developmental theory and the Rorschach method. In M. A. Rickers-Ovsiankina (Ed.), *Rorschach psychology.* New York: John Wiley and Sons.

Henry, W. E. (1947). The Thematic Apperception Technique in the study of culture-personality relations. *Genet. Psychol. Monogr., 35,* 3-135.

Henry, W. E. (1956). *The analysis of fantasy.* New York: Wiley.

Hersch, C. (1962). The cognitive functioning of

the creative person: A developmental analysis. *Journal of Projective Techniques, 26,* 193–200.

Hersen, M., & Bellack, A. S. (Eds.). (1976). *Behavioral assessment: A practical handbook.* New York: Pergamon.

Hertz, M. R. (1935). The Rorschach ink-blot test: Historical summary. *Psychol. Bulletin, 32,* 33–36.

Hertz, M. R. (1942a). Personality patterns in adolescence as portrayed by the Rorschach ink-blot method. *Journal General Psychol. I, 27,* 119–188.

Hertz, M. R. (1942b). Rorschach: Twenty years after. *Psychol. Bull., 39,* 529–572.

Hertz, M. R. (1943a). Personality patterns in adolescence as portrayed by the Rorschach ink-blot method. *Journal Gen. Psychol. II, 28,* 3–61.

Hertz, M. R. (1943b). Personality patterns in adolescence as portrayed by the Rorschach ink-blot method. *Journal Gen. Psychol. III, 28,* 225–276.

Hertz, M. R. (1943c). Personality patterns in adolescence as portrayed by the Rorschach ink-blot method. *Journal Gen. Psychol. IV, 29,* 3–45.

Hertz, M. R. (1963). Objectifying the subjective. *Rorschachiana VIII,* pp. 25–54.

Hertz, M. R. (1965). Detection of suicidal risks with the Rorschach. In L. Abt & S. Weissman (Eds.), *Acting out* (pp. 257–270). New York: Grune & Stratton.

Hertz, M. R. (1968). Hertz interpretation. Ellen: A girl, ten years of age. In J. Exner (Ed.), *The Rorschach systems* (pp. 321–374). New York: Grune & Stratton.

Hertz, M. R. (1970). *Frequency tables for scoring Rorschach responses.* 5th ed., revised. Cleveland, OH: press of Case Western Reserve University.

Hertz, M. R., & Baker, E. (1943). Personality patterns in adolescence as portrayed by the Rorschach ink-blot method: II. The color factors. *J. Gen. Psychol., 28.*

Hertzman, M., & Seitz, C. P. (1942). Rorschach reactions at high attitudes. *Journal of Psychology, 14,* 245–257.

Hertzman, M., Seitz, C. P., & Orlansky, J. (1944). Personality organization and anoxia tolerance. *Psychosom. Med., 4,* 317–331.

Heston, L. L. (1966). Psychiatric disorders in foster home reared children of schizophrenic mothers. *British Journal of Psychiatry, 112,* 819–825.

Heston, L. L. (1970). The genetics of schizophrenia and schizoid disease. *Science, 167,* 249–256.

Hirt, M. L., & Kaplan, M. L. (1967). Psychological testing: II. Current practice. *Comprehensive Psychiatry, 8,* 310–320.

Holt, R. R. (1950). An approach to the validation of the Szondi test through a systematic study of unreliability. *Journal Proj. Tech., 14,* 435–444.

Holt, R. R. (1958). Clinical and statistical prediction: A reformulation and some new data. *Journal of Abnormal and Social Psychology, 56,* 1–12. (Reprinted in E. I. Megargee (Ed.) *Research in clinical assessment.* New York: Harper & Row, 1966, 657–671.)

Holt, R. R. (1961). Clinical judgment as a disciplined inquiry. *Journal of Nervous and Mental Disease, 133,* 369–382.

Holt, R. R. (1962). *Manual for the scoring of primary process manifestation in Rorschach responses* (8th ed.). New York: Research Center for Mental Health, New York University.

Holt, R. R. (1966). Measuring libidinal and aggressive motives and their controls by means of the Rorschach test. In D. Levine (Ed.), *Nebraska symposium on motivation,* vol. 13 (pp. 1–47). Lincoln: University of Nebraska Press.

Holt, R. R. (1967). Diagnostic testing: Present status and future prospects. *Journal of Nervous and Mental Disease, 144,* 444–465.

Holt, R. R. (1970). Yet another look at clinical and statistical prediction: Or, is clinical psychology worthwhile? *American Psychologist, 25,* 327–349.

Holt, R. R. (1977). A method for assessing primary process manifestations and their control in Rorschach responses. In M. Rickers-Ovsiankina (Ed.), *Rorschach psychology* (pp. 375–420). Huntington, NY: Krieger.

Holt, R. R., & Luborsky, L. (1958). *Personality patterns of psychiatrists: A study in selection techniques.* 2 vols. New York: Basic Books.

Holtzman, W. H., Thorpe, J. S., Swartz, J. D., & Herron, E. W. (1961). *Inkblot perception and personality.* Austin, TX: University of Texas.

Holzberg, J. D. (1968). Psychological theory and projective techniques. In A. I. Rabin (Ed.), *Projective techniques in personality assessment.* New York: Springer.

Honigman, J. J. (1969). Psychological anthropology. *The Annals of the American Academy of Political and Social Science, 383,*145–158.

Horn, D. (1943). *An experimental study of the diagnostic process in the clinical investigation of personality.* Ph.D. Thesis, Department of Psychology, Harvard University. New York.

Horn, D. (1950). Intra-individual variability in the study of personality. *Journal Clin. Psychol., 6,* 43–47.

Hulstart, B. (1979). *The effects of a "second change" instructional set on the Rorschach records of emotionally disturbed and culturally deprived children.* Unpublished doctoral dissertation. Long Island: Long Island University.

Hunt, J. M. (1952). Psychological services in the tactics of psychological science. *Am. Psychol., 7,* 608–622.

Ichimura, J. (1966). Ten year follow-up on the early prediction of juvenile delinquency by means of the Rorschach test. *Japanese Psychological Research, 8,* 151–160.

Ilg, F. L., Ames, L. B., & Apell, R. J. (1965). School readiness as evaluated by Gesell developmental, visual, and projective tests. *Genetic Psychology Monographs, 71,* 61–91.

Ittelson, W. H., & Cantril, H. (1954). *Perception: A transactional approach.* Garden City, NY: Doubleday Papers in Psychology.

Ivnik, R. J. (1977). Uncertain status of psychological tests in clinical psychology. *Professional Psychology, 8,* 206–213.

Jackson, H. (1932). *Selected writings.* London, England: Hodder.

Jaensch, E. (1937). Gefuehl und empfindung. *15-Kongress d. Ges. f. Psychol.*

Jolles, I. A. (1947). The diagnostic implications of Rorschach's test in case studies of mental defectives. *Gen. Psychol. Mon., 36,* 93–197.

Jung, C. (1926). *Psychological types.* New York: Harcourt, Brace and Co.

Kalter, N. (1970). Self-selection of TAT cards: A technique for assessing test-resistant children. *Journal of Projective Techniques and Personality Assessment, 34,* 324–327.

Kantor, R. E., & Herron, W. G. (1966). *Reactive and process schizophrenia.* Palo Alto, CA: Science & Behavior Books.

Kaplan, M. L. (1967). Ego impairment and ego adaptation in schizophrenia. *Journal of Projective Techniques & Personality Assessment, 31,* 7–17.

Kaplan, M. L., Hirt, M. L., & Kurtz, R. M. (1967). Psychological testing: I. History and current trends. *Comprehensive Psychiatry, 8,* 299–309.

Katz, D. (1913). *Studien zur Kinderpsychologie.* Leipzig.

Kaufman, A. S., & Kaufman, N. L. (1983). *Kaufman assessment battery for children.* Circle Pines, MN: American Guidance Services.

Kelly, E. L., & Fiske, D. W. (1951). *The prediction of performance in clinical psychology.* Ann Arbor: University of Michigan Press.

Kendall, P. C., & Hollon, S. D. (Eds.). (1981). *Assessment strategies for cognitive-behavioral interventions.* New York: Academic.

Kinslinger, H. J. (1966). Application of projective techniques in personnel psychology since 1940. *Psychological Bulletin, 66,* 134–150.

Klein, G. S. (1951). The personal world through perception. In R. R. Blake & G. V. Ramsey (Eds.), *Perception: An approach to personality.* New York: Ronald Press Co.

Kleinman, A. (1983). The cultural meanings and social uses of illness: A role for medical anthropology and clinically oriented social science in the development of primary care theory and research. *Journal of Family Practice, 16,* 539–545.

Kline, M. H., Dittman, A. T., Parloff, M. B., & Gill, M. M. (1969). Behavior therapy: Observations and reflections. *Journal of Consulting and Clinical Psychology, 33,* 259–266.

Klopfer, B. (Ed.). (1936–1940). *Rorschach research exchange.* New York: Klopfer.

Klopfer, B., Ainsworth, M., Klopfer, W., & Holt, R. (1954). *Developments in the Rorschach technique.* Vol. 1. Yonkers-on-Hudson, New York: World Book.

Klopfer, B., & Kelley, D. (1942). *The Rorschach technique.* Yonkers-on-Hudson, New York: World Book.

Klopfer, W. G. (1945). The efficacy of group therapy as indicated by the group Rorschach record. *Rorschach Res. Exch., 9,* 207–209.

Klopfer, W. G. (1968a). Current status of the Rorschach test. In P. McReynolds (Ed.), *Advances in psychological assessment* (Vol. 1, pp. 131–149). Palo Alto, CA: Science and Behavior Books.

Klopfer, W. G. (1968b). Integration of projective techniques in the clinical case study. In A. I. Rabin (Ed.), *Projective techniques in personality assessment.* New York: Springer Publishing Co.

Klopfer, W. G. (1983). Writing psychological reports. In C. E. Walker (Ed.), *Clinical psychology: Theory, research, and practice* (Vol. 1, pp. 502–527). Homewood, IL: Dow Jones-Irwin.

Klopfer, W. G., & Borstelmann, L. J. (1950). The associative valences of the Szondi pictures. *Journal of Personality, 19,* 23–29.

Klopfer, W. G., & Taulbee, E. S. (1976). Projective tests. *Annual Review of Psychology, 27,* 543–567.

Knott, P. D. (1969). On the manpower problem and graduate training in clinical psychology. *American Psychologist, 24,* 675–679.

Koch, S. (1981). The nature and limits of psychological knowledge. *American Psychologist, 36,* 257–269.

Koffka, K., & Harrower, M. (1931). Color and organization, I. *Psychol. Forsch., 15.*

Korchin, S. J., & Schuldberg, D. (1981). The future of clinical assessment. *American Psychologist, 36,* 1147–1158.

Korman, A. K. (1968). The prediction of managerial performance. A review. *Personnel Psy-*

chology, 21, 295-322.

Kroh, O., & Scholl, R. (1926). Ueber die teilinhaltliche Beachtung von Form und Farbe beim Haushuhn. *Zsch. Psychol., 100.*

Krohn, A., & Mayman, M. (1974). Object representations in dreams and projective tests. *Bulletin of the Menninger Clinic, 38,* 445-466.

Kuelpe, O. *Versuche ueber Abstraktion, 1.* Kongress Exp. Psychol.

Kutash, S. B. (1943). Performance of psychopathic defective criminals on the Thematic Apperception Test. *Journal Crim. Psychopath., 5,* 319-340.

Kutash, S. B. (1954). The East Orange research program in perceptual changes in psychopathology. *Information Bulletin.* (VA Psychiatry and Neurology Service)

Kutash, S. B., & Gehl, R. H. (1954). *The graphomotor projection techniques: Clinical use and standardization.* Springfield, IL: Charles C. Thomas Co.

Lacks, P. (in press). *Clinical use of the revised Bender Gestalt test.* New York: Wiley.

Lacks, P. B. (1984). *Bender Gestalt screening for brain dysfunctions.* New York: Wiley-Interscience.

Landau, R. J., & Goldfried, M. R. (1981). The assessment of schemata: A unifying framework for cognitive, behavioral and traditional assessment. In P. C. Kendall & S. D. Hollon (Eds.), *Assessment strategies for cognitive-behavioral interventions.* New York: Academic.

Landsberger, H. A. (1956). Final report on a research project in mediation. *Labor Law Journal, 7,* 501-507.

Lanyon, R. I. (1984). Personality assessment. *Annual of Review of Psychology, 35,* 667-701.

Lazarus, L. W., & Weinberg, J. (1982). Psychosocial intervention with the aged. *Psychiatric Clinics of North America, 5,* 215-227.

Leary, T. F. (1957). *The interpersonal diagnosis of personality.* New York: Ronald Press.

Leary, T. F. (1970). The diagnosis of behavior and the diagnosis of experience. In A. Mahrer (Ed.), *New approaches to personality classification* (pp. 211-236). New York: Columbia University Press.

Leigh, H., & Reiser, M. F. (1980). *The patient: Biological, psychological and social dimensions of medical practice.* New York: Plenum Press.

Levine, K., & Grassi, J. (1942). The relation between blot and concept in graphic Rorschach responses. *Rorschach Res. Exch., 6.*

Levine, M., & Spivack, G. (1964). *The Rorschach index of repressive style.* Springfield, IL: Charles C. Thomas.

Levitt, E. E. (1973). Internship versus campus: 1964 and 1971. *Professional Psychology, 4,* 129-132.

Levy, J., & Epstein, N. B. (1964). An application of the Rorschach test in family investigation. *Family Process, 3,* 344-376.

Levy, M. R. (1970). Issues in the personality assessment of lower class patients. *Journal of Projective Techniques & Personality Assessment, 34,* 6-9.

Levy, M. R., & Fox, H. H. (1975). Psychological testing is alive and well. *Professional Psychology, 6,* 420-424.

Levy, M. R., & Kahn, M. W. (1969). Interpreter bias on the Rorschach test as a function of patients' socioeconomic status. *Proceedings of the 77th Annual Convention of the American Psychological Association, 4,* 525-526.

Lewandowski, D. G., & Saccuzzo, D. P. (1976). The decline of psychological testing. *Professional Psychology, 7,* 177-184.

Lewin, K. (1936). *Principles of topological psychology.* New York: McGraw Hill Book Co.

Lewin, K. (1951). *Field theory in social science.* New York: Harper.

Lezak, M. D. (1976). *Neuropsychological assessment.* New York: Oxford University Press.

Liebmann (Ed.). (1927). Ueber das Verhalten farbiger Forman bei Helligkeitsgleichheit von Figur un Grund. *Psychol. Forsch., 9.*

Lindzey, G. (1961). *Projective techniques and cross-cultural research.* New York: Appleton-Century-Crofts.

Lindzey, G. (1965). Seer versus sign. *Journal of Experimental Research in Personality, 1,* 17-26.

Lindzey, G., Bradford, J., Tejessy, C., & Davis, A. (Eds.). (1959). The Thematic Apperception Test: An interpretive lexicon. *Journal of Clinical Psychology Monograph Supplement, 12.*

Lipsey, M. (1974). Research and relevance: A survey of graduate students and faculty in psychology. *American Psychologist, 29,* 541-555.

Lohrenz, L. J., & Gardner, R. W. (1967). The Mayman form-level scoring method: Scorer reliability and correlates of form level. *Journal of Projective Techniques & Personality Assessment, 31,* 39-43.

Loveland, N. T., Wynne, L. C., & Singer, M. T. (1963). The family Rorschach: A new method for studying family interaction. *Family Process, 2,* 187-215.

Lubin, B., Wallis, R. R., & Paine, C. (1971). Patterns of psychological test usage in the United States: 1935-1969. *Professional Psychology, 2,* 70-74.

Luborsky, L. (1953). Self-interpretation of the TAT as a clinical technique. *J. Proj. Tech., 17,* 217-223.

Lutz, A. T. B. (1929). Auffassungsumfang und persoenlichkeitstypus. *Zsch. Psychol., 14.*
Lykken, D. T. (1956). A method of actuarial pattern analysis. *Psychological Bulletin, 53,* 102-107.
Lykken, D. T., & Rose, R. (1963). Psychological prediction from actuarial tables. *Journal of Clinical Psychology, 19,* 139-151.
Mahler, M. S., Pine, F., & Bergman, A. (1975). *The psychological birth of the human infant.* New York: Basic Books.
Main, M., Kaplan, N., & Cassidy, J. (1985). Security in infancy, childhood and adulthood: A move to the level of representation. In I. Bretherton & E. Waters (Eds.), *Growing points in attachment theory and research* (pp. 66-104). Chicago, IL: University of Chicago Press.
Maloney, M. P., & ward, M. P. (1976). *Psychological assessment: A conceptual approach.* New York: Guilford University Press.
Marburg, G. S. (1983). Mental health and Native Americans: Responding to the challenge of the biopsychosocial model. *White Cloud Journal, 3,* 43-51.
Marcus, H. (1983). Self-knowledge: An expanded view. *Journal of Personality, 51,* 544-565.
Masling, J. (1960). The influence of situational and interpersonal variables in projective testing. *Psychological Bulletin, 57,* 65-85.
Maslow, A. H. (1962). *Toward a psychology of being.* Princeton, NJ: Van Nostrand.
May, W. T., & Dana, R. H. (1984, March). *Megatrends in health psychology.* Paper presented at the meeting of the Southeastern Psychological Association. New Orleans, LA.
Mayman, M. (1967). Object-representations and object-relations in Rorschach responses. *Journal of Projective Techniques and Personality Assessment, 32,* 303-316.
Maynard, L. B. (1982). The integration of patient self-assessment in partial hospitalization programming. *International Journal of Partial Hospitalization, 1*(3), 213-220.
McDougall, W. (1929). A chemical theory of temperament applied to introversion and extraversion. *J. Abn. Soc. Psychol., 24.*
McNeil, E. B. (1962). Aggression in fantasy and behavior. *Journal of Consulting Psychology, 26,* 232-240.
McReynolds, P. (Ed.). (1968). *Advances in psychological assessment.* Vol. 1. Palo Alto, CA: Science & Behavior Books.
McReynolds, P. (Ed.). (1981). *Advances in psychological assessment.* Vol. 5. San Francisco: Jossey-Bass.
McWhirter, J. J., Nichols, E., & Banks, N. M. (1984). Career awareness and self-exploration (CASE) groups: A self-assessment model for career decisionmaking. *Personnel and Guidance Journal, 62,* 580-582.
Mead, M. (1968). *The mountain Arapesh: I. The record of Unabelin with Rorschach analyses.* Garden City, NY: Natural History Press.
Meehl, P. E. (1945a). The dynamics of structured personality tests. *Journal of Clinical Psychology, 1,* 296-303.
Meehl, P. E. (1954b). *Clinical versus statistical prediction: A theoretical analysis and a review of the evidence.* Minneapolis, MN: University of Minnesota Press.
Meehl, P. E. (1965). Seer over sign: The first good example. *Journal of Experimental Research in Personality, 1,* 27-32.
Meehl, P. E. (1970a). Some methodological reflections on the difficulties of psychoanalytic research. In M. Radner & S. Winokur (Eds.), *Minnesota studies in the philosophy of sciences* (Vol. 4, pp. 403-416). Minneapolis: University of Minnesota Press. (Reprinted in *Psychological Issues,* 1973, *8,* 104-115.)
Meehl, P. E. (1970b). Theory-testing in psychology and physics: A methodological paradox. In D. E. Morrison & R. E. Henkel (Eds.), *The significance test controversy.* Chicago: Aldine. (Originally published in *Philosophy of Science,* 1967, *34,* 103-115.)
Meehl, P. E. (1973a). MAXCOV-HITMAX: A taxometric search method for loose genetic syndromes. In P. E. Meehl (Ed.), *Psychodiagnosis: Selected papers.* Minneapolis: University of Minnesota Press.
Meehl, P. E. (1973b). Some ruminations on the validation of clinical procedures. In P. E. Meehl (Ed.), *Psychodiagnosis: Selected papers.* Minneapolis: University of Minnesota Press. (Originally published in *Canadian Journal of Psychology,* 1959, *13,* 102-128.)
Meehl, P. E. (1973c). Specific genetic etiology, psychodynamics and therapeutic nihilism. In P. E. Meehl (Ed.), *Psychodiagnosis: Selected papers.* Minneapolis: University of Minnesota Press.
Meehl, P. E. (1973d). Why I don't go to case conferences. In P. E. Meehl (Ed.), *Psychodiagnosis: Selected papers.* Minneapolis: University of Minnesota Press.
Meehl, P. E. (1977). Specific etiology and other forms of strong influence: Some quantitative meanings. *Journal of Medicine and Philosophy, 2,* 33-53.
Meehl, P. E. (1978). Theoretical risks and tabular asterisks: Sir Karl, Sir Ronald and the slow progress of soft psychology. *Journal of Consulting and Clinical Psychology, 46,* 806-834.
Meehl, P. E., Lykken, D. T., Schofield, W., & Tellegen, A. (1971). Recaptured-item technique (RIT): A method for reducing somewhat the subjective element in factor-naming.

Journal of Experimental Research in Personality, 5, 171-190.

Megargee, E. I. (1966a). A comparison of the scores of white and Negro male juvenile delinquents on three projective tests. *Journal of Projective Techniques & Personality Assessment, 30,* 530-535.

Megargee, E. I. (1966b). Undercontrolled and over-controlled personality types in extreme anti-social aggression. *Psychological Monographs, 80.* (No. 3, Whole No. 611)

Megargee, E. I., & Cook, P. E. (1967). The relation of TAT and inkblot aggressive content scales with each other and with criteria of overt aggressiveness in juvenile delinquents. *Journal of Projective Techniques & Personality Assessment, 31,* 48-60.

Mensh, I. N. (1950). Statistical techniques in present-day psychodiagnostics. *Psychol. Bull., 47,* 475-492.

Metzger, W. (1930). Optische Untersuchungen am Ganzfeld II. Zur Phaenomenologie des Homogene Ganzfelds. *Psychol. Forsch., 13.*

Meyer, M., & Caruth, E. (1965). Rorschach indices of ego process. *Journal of Projective Techniques & Personality Assessment, 29,* 200-219.

Miller, G. A., Galanter, E., & Pribram, K. (1960). *Plans and the structure of behavior.* New York: Holt, Rinehart and Winston.

Miller, J. G. (1950). Contemporary trends in psychodiagnosis. In *Recent advances in diagnostic psychological testing.* Springfield, IL: Charles C. Thomas Co.

Millon, T. (1982). *Millon Clinical Multiaxial Inventory manual.* 2nd ed. Minneapolis, MN: National Computer Systems.

Mischel, W. (1968). *Personality and assessment.* New York: Wiley.

Moss, C. S. (1957). A note on the use of the schizophrenic in Rorschach content analysis. *Journal of Projective Techniques, 21,* 384-390.

Mucchielli, R. (1968). *La dynamique du Rorschach.* Paris: Presses Universitaires de France.

Mueller, W. J., & Abeles, N. (1964). The components of empathy and their relationship to projection of human movement responses. *Journal of Projective Techniques & Personality Assessment, 28,* 322-330.

Muench, G. A. (1950). The application of diagnostic psychological methods to counseling and psychotherapy. In *Recent advances in diagnostic psychological testing* (pp. 53-72). Springfield, IL: Charles C. Thomas Co.

Munroe, R. L. (1945). Considerations on the place of the Rorschach in the field of general psychology. *Rorschach Res. Exch., 9,* 30-40.

Munroe, R. L. (1948). The use of projective methods in group testing. *Journal Consult. Psychol., 12,* 8-15.

Murphy, E. A. (1964). One cause? many causes? the argument from a bimodal distribution. *Journal of Chronic Diseases, 17,* 301-324.

Murphy, G. (1945). The freeing of intelligence. *Psychol. Bulletin, 42,* 1-19.

Murphy, G. (1954). *Personality through perception.* Introduction to Witkin, Lewis, Hertzman et al. New York: Harper & Brothers.

Murray, H. A. (1947). Problems in clinical research, Round Table. *American Journal Orthopsychiat., 17,* 196-230.

Murray, H. A., et al. (1938). *Explorations in personality.* New York: Oxford University Press.

Murstein, B. I. (1963). *Theory and research in projective techniques (emphasizing the TAT).* New York: Wiley.

Murstein, B. I. (Ed.). (1965). *Handbook of projective techniques.* New York: Basic Books.

Naisbitt, J. (1982). *Megatrends.* New York: Warner.

Neiger, S., Slemon, A. G., & Quirk, D. A. (1965). Rorschach scales of regression in psychosis. *Genetic Psychology Monographs, 71,* 93-136.

Neisser, U. (1967). *Cognitive psychology.* New York: Appleton-Century-Crofts.

Neisser, U. (1976). *Cognition and reality: Principles and implications of cognitive psychology.* San Francisco, CA: Freeman.

Neuringer, C. (1965). The Rorschach test as a research device for the identification, prediction, and understanding of suicidal ideation and behavior. *Journal of Projective Techniques & Personality Assessment, 29,* 71-82.

Neuringer, C. (1967). Art and science in projective techniques. *Journal of Consulting Psychology, 31,* 85-88.

Newmark, C. S. (Ed.). (1985). *Major psychological assessment instruments.* Newton, MA: Allyn & Bacon.

Norcross, J. D., & Prochaska, J. O. (1982). A national survey of clinical psychologists: Affiliations and orientations. *Clinical Psychologist, 35,* 1-6.

Oberleder, M. (1967). Adapting current psychological techniques for use in testing the aging. *Georontologist, 7,* 188-191.

Oeser, O. (1932). Some experiments on the abstraction of form and color, Part I and Part II. *Br. J. Psychol., 22.*

Offer, D., & Offer, J. (1968). Profiles of normal adolescent girls. *Archives of General Psychiatry, 19,* 513-522.

Osgood, C. (1953). *Method and theory in experimental psychology.* New York: Oxford University Press.

Osgood, C. E., Suci, G. J., & Tannenbaum, I. H. (1957). *The measurement of meaning.* Urbana: The University of Illinois Press.

Paivio, A. (1986). *Mental representations: A dual coding approach.* New York: Oxford University Press.

Palmer, J. O. (1983). *The psychological assessment of children.* 2nd ed. New York: Wiley.

Pankratz, L. D., & Taplin, J. R. (1982). Issues in psychological assessment. In J. R. McNamara & A. G. Barclay (Eds.), *Critical issues, developments, and trends in professional psychology.* New York: Praeger.

Parker, K. A. (1983). A meta-analysis of the reliability and validity of the Rorschach. *Journal of Personality Assessment, 47,* 227–231.

Pati, G. (1966). Personality pathology of delinquents. *Psychological Studies, 11,* 35–41.

Perry, L. S., & Dana, R. H. (Eds.). (In press). Macroconceptual analysis of psychological literature. *Professional Psychology: Research and Practice.*

Peterson, D. R. (1954a). The diagnosis of subclinical schizophrenia. *Journal of Consulting Psychology, 18,* 198–200.

Peterson, D. R. (1954b). Predicting hospitalization of psychiatric outpatients. *Journal of Abnormal and Social Psychology, 49,* 260–265.

Peterson, D. R. (1968). *The clinical study of social behavior.* New York: Appleton-Century-Crofts.

Petzel, T. P., & Berndt, D. J. (1980). APA internship selection criteria: Relative importance of academic and clinical preparation. *Professional Psychology, 11,* 792–796.

Phillips, H. P. (1965). *Thai peasant personality.* Berkeley and Los Angeles, CA: University of California Press.

Piaget, J. (1954). *The construction of reality in the child.* M. Cook, trans. New York: Basic Books. (Original work published 1937)

Piaget, J. (1962). *Play, dreams, and imitation in childhood.* C. Cattegno & F. M. Hodgson, trans. New York: Norton. (Original work published 1945)

Pieper, B. E. (1972). *Stimulus transcendence, personality revelation and emotional tone as functions of card selection of the Thematic Apperception Test.* Unpublished master's thesis, Marquette University. Milwaukee, WI.

Piotrowski, C., & Keller, J. W. (1978). Psychological test usage in southeastern outpatient mental health facilities in 1975. *Professional Psychology, 9,* 63–67.

Piotrowski, C., & Keller, J. W. (1984). Psychodiagnostic testing in APA-approved clinical psychology programs. *Professional Psychology: Research and Practice, 15*(3), 450–456.

Piotrowski, Z. A. (1937-38). Recent Rorschach literature. *Rorschach Res. Exch., 2,* 172–175.

Piotrowski, Z. A. (1941). The Rorschach method as a prognostic aid in the insulin shock treatment of schizophrenics. *Psychiatr. Quart., 15,* 807–822.

Piotrowski, Z. A. (1964). Digital-computer interpretation of inkblot data. *The Psychiatric Quarterly, 38,* 1–26.

Piotrowski, Z. A. (1965). Predicting acting out by means of the Thematic Apperception Test. In L. A. Abt & S. L. Weissman (Eds.), *Acting out* (pp. 271–287). New York: Grune & Stratton.

Piotrowski, Z. A., & Rock, M. R. (1963). *The perceptanalytic executive scale.* New York: Grune & Stratton.

Polanyi, M. (1964). *Personal knowledge: Toward a postcritical philosophy.* rev. ed. New York: Harper & Torch Books.

Polkinghorne, D. (1983). *Methodology for the human sciences.* Albany, NY: State University of New York Press.

Popper, K. R. (1962). *Conjectures and refutations.* New York: Basic Books.

Popper, K. R. (1976). A note on verisimilitude. *British Journal for the Philosophy of Science, 27,* 147–195.

Poppinga, O. (1931). Die teilinhaltliche Beachtung von Form und Farbe bei Erwachsenen in ihrer Beziehung zur strukturpsychologischen Typenlehre. *Zsch. Psychol., 121.*

Poser, E. G. (1951). Personality factors in patients with duodenal ulcer: A Rorschach study. *Journal of Proj. Tech., 15,* 131–143.

Postman, L., Bruner, J. S., & McGinnies, E. (1948). Personal values as selective factors in perception. *Journal of Abnormal and Social Psychology, 43,* 142–154.

Prabu, G. G. (1967). The Rorschach technique with normal adult Indians. *Indian Psychological Review, 3,* 97–106.

Praeger, E. H. (1980). A client-developed measure of self-assessment in mental health. *Dissertation Abstracts International, 41,* 1778A.

Preston, C. E. (1964). Psychological testing with northwest coast Alaskan Eskimos. *Genetic Psychological Monographs, 69,* 323–419.

Propper, M. M. (1970). Direct and projective assessment of alienation among affluent adolescent males. *Journal of Projective Techniques & Personality Assessment, 34,* 41–44.

Proschansky, H. M. (1950). Projective techniques in action research: Disguised diagnosis and measurement. In Abt & Bellak (Eds.), *Projective psychology* (pp. 462–485). New York: Alfred A. Knopf.

Purcell, K. (1965). The Thematic Apperception Test and antisocial behavior. In B. I. Murstein (Ed.), *Handbook of projective tech-*

niques. New York: Basic Books.

Rabin, A. I. (1968a). Adapting and devising projective methods for special purposes. In A. I. Rabin (Ed.), *Projective techniques in personality assessment*. New York: Springer.

Rabin, A. I. (1968b). *Projective techniques in personality assessment*. New York: Springer.

Ramey, V. (Ed.). (1950). *Training for clinical psychology*. New York: Prentice-Hall.

Rapaport, D., Gill, M. M., & Schafer, R. (1945). *Diagnostic psychological testing*. Vol. 1. Chicago: Year Book Medical.

Rapaport, D., Gill, M. M., & Schafer, R. (1946). *Diagnostic psychological testing*. Vol. 2. Chicago: Yearbook Publishers.

Rawls, J. R., & Slack, G. K. (1968). Artists versus nonartists: Rorschach determinants and artistic creativity. *Journal of Projective Techniques & Personality Assessment, 32,* 233–237.

Reiser, M. F. (1980). Implications of the biopsychosocial model for research in psychiatry. *Psychosomatic Medicine, 42*(Suppl. 1), 141–151.

Reissman, F., & Miller, S. M. (1958). Social class and projective tests. *Journal of Projective Techniques, 22,* 432–439.

Rickers-Ovsiankina, M. A. (1943). Some theoretical considerations regarding the Rorschach method. *Rorschach Res. Exch., 7,* 41–53.

Rickers-Ovsiankina, M. A (1977). *Rorschach psychology*. 2nd ed. Huntington, NY: Krieger.

Ritzler, B. A., & Del Gaudio, A. C. (1976). A survey of Rorschach teaching in APA-approved clinical graduate programs. *Journal of Personality Assessment, 40,* 451–453.

Rodolfa, E. R., & Hungerford, L. (1982). Self-help groups: A referral source for professional therapists. *Professional Psychology, 13,* 345–353.

Roe, A. (1949). Analysis of group Rorschachs of biologists. *Rorschach Res. Exch., 13,* 25–43.

Roe, A. (1950). Analysis of group Rorschachs of physical scientists. *Journal Proj. Tech.,* 385–398.

Roe, A. (1952). Analysis of group Rorschachs of psychologists and anthropologists. *Journal Proj. Tech., 16,* 212–224.

Rogers, C. R. (1961). *On becoming a person*. Boston: Houghton-Mifflin.

Rogolsky, M. (1968). Artistic creativity and adaptive regression in third grade children. *Journal of Projective Techniques & Personality Assessment, 32,* 53–62.

Rorer, L. G., & Widiger, T. A. (1983). Personality structure and assessment. *Annual Review of Psychology, 34,* 431–463.

Rorschach, H. (1921a). *Psychodiagnostik. Methodik und Ergebnisse eines Warhenhmungsdiagnostischen experiments*. Bern: Bircher.

Rorschach, H. (1921b). *Psychodiagnostik: Methodik und ergebnisse eines warnesmungsdiagnostischen experiment. Deutenlassen von sufalls formen*. Published in 1942 in English: *Psychodiagnostics* [P. Lemkau & B. Kronenbourg, trans.]. Bern: Huber and New York: Grune & Stratton.

Rorschach, H. (1923). Zur Auswertung des Formdeutversuchs fuer die Psychoanalyse. posthumously published by Oberholzer. *Zsch. ges. Neurol. Psychiat., 82.*

Rorschach, H. (1932). *Psychodiagnostik: Methodik und Ergebnisse eines wahrnehmungs-diagnostischen experiments*. 2nd ed. Bern and Berlin: Huber 1932. (Translated P. Lemkau and B. Kronenberg, New York: Grune & Stratton, 1942)

Rorschach, H., & Oberholzer, E. (1923). Zur Auswertung des Formdeutversuche fur die Psychoanalyse. *Zsch, f.d. ges. Neur. u. Psychiatr., 82,* 240–273. (Translated as: The application of the interpretation of form to psychoanalysis. *J. Nerv. and Ment. Dis.,* 1924, *60,* 225–248; 359–379)

Rosen, J. L., & Neugarten, B. L. (1960). Ego functions in the middle and later years: A thematic apperception study of normal adults. *Journal of Gerontology, 15,* 62–67.

Rosenthal, R. (1966). *Experimenter effects in behavioral research*. New York: Appleton-Century-Crofts.

Rosenthal, R. (1967). Covert communication in the psychological experiment. *Psychological Bulletin, 67,* 356–367.

Rosenwald, G. R. (1963). Psychodiagnostics and its discontents. *Psychiatry, 26,* 222–240.

Rosenzweig, S. (1950). A method of validation by successive clinical predictions. *Journal Abnormal Soc. Psychol., 45,* 507–509.

Ross, D. C. (1968). Computer processing of inkblot test data. *Journal of School Psychology, 6,* 200–205.

Ross, W. D. (1945). The Rorschach performance with neurocirculatory asthenia. *Psychosom. Med., 7,* 80–84.

Ross, W. D., & McNaughton, S. L. (1945). Objective personality studies in migraine by means of the Rorschach method. *Psychosom. Med., 7,* 73–79.

Rozsnafszky, J. (1979). Beyond schools of psychotherapy: Integrity and maturity in therapy supervision. *Psychotherapy: Theory, Research, and Practice, 16,* 190–198.

Reusch, J., & Fensinger, J. (1941). The relation of the Rorschach color response to the use of color in drawings. *Psychosomatic Medicine, 3.*

Russ, S. W. (1978). Teaching psychological assessment: Training issues and teaching approaches. *Journal of Personality Assessment, 42,* 452–456.

Rychlak, J. F. (1982). *Personality and life-style of young male managers.* New York: Academic Press.

Rychlak, J. F. (1984). Newtonianism and the professional responsibility of psychologists: Who speaks for humanity? *Professional Psychology: Research and Practice, 15,* 82–95.

Sakheim, G. A. (1955). Suicidal responses on the Rorschach test: A validation study. *Journal of Nervous & Mental Disease, 123,* 332–344.

Sanford, F. H., & Rosenstock, I. M. (1952). Proj. techniques on the doorstep. *Journal Abnormal Soc. Psychol., 47,* 3–16.

Sarason, S. B. (1943). The use of the Thematic Apperception Test with mentally deficient children, I: A study of high grade girls, II: A study of high grade boys. *American Journal of Mental Deficiency, 47; 48,* 414–421; 169–173.

Sarason, S. B. (1949). *Psychological problems in mental deficiency.* New York: Harper & Brothers.

Sarason, S. B. (1981). *Psychology misdirected.* New York: Free Press.

Sarason, S. B. (1984, April). *Caring in America: A critique of the clinical endeavor.* Paper presented at the Memphis State University Colloquium.

Sawyer, J. (1966). Measurement and prediction, clinical and statistical. *Psychological Bulletin, 66,* 178–200.

Schachtel, E. G. (1966). *Experiential foundations of Rorschach's test.* New York: Basic Books.

Schafer, R. (1948). *The clinical application of psychological tests.* New York: International Universities Press.

Schafer, R. (1949). Psychological tests in clinical research. *Journal Consult. Psychol., 13,* 328–334.

Schafer, R. (1954). *Psychoanalytic interpretation in Rorschach testing.* New York: Grune & Stratton.

Schank, R., & Abelson, R. P. (1977). *Scripts, plans, goals and understanding.* Hillsdale, NJ: Lawrence Erlbaum Associates, Inc.

Schaw, L. C., & Henry, W. E. (1956). A method for the comparison of groups: A study in thematic apperception. *Genet. Psych. Monogr., 54,* 207–253.

Schimek, J. G. (1968). Cognitive style and defenses: A longitudinal study of intellectualization and field independence. *Journal of Abnormal Psychology, 73,* 575–580.

Schmidt, B. (1936). Reflektorische reaktiionen auf Form und Farbe. *Zsch. Psychol., 37.*

Scholl, R. (1927). Untersuchungen ueber teilinhaltliche Beachtun von Farbe und Form bei Erwachsenen und Kinder. *Zsch. Psychol., 101.*

Schwartz, G. E. (1982). Testing and biopsychological model: The ultimate challenge facing behavioral medicine? *Journal of Consulting and Clinical Psychology, 50,* 1040–1053.

Sell, J. M., & Torres-Henry, R. (1979). Testing practices in university and college counseling centers in the United States. *Professional Psychology, 10,* 774–779.

Selosse, J., Mazerol, M. T., & Jacquey, M. (1967). Reflexions a propos d'une recherche sur la reeducation des adolescents delinquants. *Bulletin de Psychologie, 20,* 897–904.

Shakow, D. (1976). What is clinical psychology? *American Psychologist, 31,* 553–560.

Shemberg, K. M., & Keeley, S. M. (1974). Training practices and satisfaction with preinternship preparation. *Professional Psychology, 5,* 98–105.

Shemberg, K. M., & Leventhal, D. B. (1981). Attitudes of internship directors toward preinternship training and clinical training models. *Professional Psychology, 12,* 639–646.

Sherer, M., Maddux, J. E., Mercandente, B., Prentice-Dunn, S., Jacobs, B., & Rogers, R. W. (1982). The self-efficacy scale: construction and validation. *Psychological Reports, 51,* 663–671.

Shore, M. F., Massimo, J. L., & Mack, R. (1964). The relationship between levels of guilt in thematic stories and unsocialized behavior. *Journal of Projective Techniques & Personal Assessment, 28,* 346–349.

Shrauger, J. S., & Osberg, T. M. (1981). The relative accuracy of self-predictions and judgments by others in psychological assessment. *Psychological Bulletin, 90,* 322–351.

Shuffield, G., & Dana, R. H. (1984, March). *Wellness assessment: A rationale, a measure, and physical/psychological components.* Paper presented at the meeting of the Society for Personality Assessment. Tampa, FL.

Siegel, M. G. (1948). The diagnostic and prognostic validity of the Rorschach test in a child guidance clinic. *American Journal Orthopsychiat., 18,* 119–193.

Singer, J. L. (1968). Research applications of projective methods. In A. I. Rabin (Ed.), *Projective techniques in personality assessment.* New York: Springer.

Singer, M. T. (1968). The consensus Rorschach and family transaction. *Journal of Projective Techniques & Personality Assessment,* pp. 348–351.

Singer, M. T., & Wynne, L. C. (1965a). Thought disorder and family relations of schizophrenics: III. Methodology using projective techniques. *Archives of General Psychiatry, 12,* 187–200.

Singer, M. T., & Wynne, L. C. (1965b). Thought disorder and family relations of schizophrenics: IV. Results and implications. *Archives of General Psychiatry, 12,* 201–212.

Singer, M. T., & Wynne, L. C. (1966). Principles for scoring communication defects and deviances in parents of schizophrenics: Rorschach and TAT scoring manuals. *Psychiatry, 29,* 260–288.

Skolnick, A. (1966). Motivational imagery and behavior over twenty years. *Journal of Consulting Psychology, 30,* 463–478.

Sloan, W. (1948). Prediction of extramural adjustment of mental defectives by use of the Rorschach test. *Journal Consult. Psychol., 12,* 303–309.

Smith, R. G., & Soper, W. B. (1978). A survey of master's-level staffing patterns and clinical roles. *Professional Psychology, 9,* 9–15.

Smith, R. J. (1967). Explorations in nonconformity. *Journal of Social Psychology, 71,* 133–150.

Smith, W. H. (1978). Ethical, social and professional issues in patients' access to psychological test reports. *Bulletin of the Menninger Clinic, 42*(2), 150–155.

Smith, W. H. (1984, March). *The use of self-descriptive statements in student selection.* Paper presented at the Society for Personality Assessment. Tampa, FL.

Smith, W. H., & Allen, J. G. (1984). Identity conflicts and the decline of psychological testing. *Professional Psychology: Research and Practice, 15,* 49–55.

Sneath, P. H. A., & Sokal, R. R. (1973). *Numerical taxonomy.* San Francisco, CA: W. H. Freeman.

Sokal, R. R. (1974). Classification: Purposes, principles, progress, prospects. *Science, 185,* 1115–1123.

Spielberger, C., & Butcher, J. N. (Eds.). (1982). *Advances in personality assessment.* Vol. 1. Hillsdale, NJ: Lawrence Erlbaum Associates, Inc.

Stephenson, W. (1949). The Q. technique study of personality. *Trans. N. Y. Acad. Sci., 11,* 215–219.

Stephenson, W. (1953). *The study of behavior.* Chicago: University of Chicago Press.

Stern, D. N. (1985). *The psychological world of the infant.* New York: Basic Books.

Steuer, J. L. (1982). Psychotherapy with older women: Ageism and sexism in traditional practice. *Psychotherapy: Training, Research and Practice, 19,* 429–436.

Stevens, J., Yock, T., & Perlman, B. (1979). Comparing master's clinical training with professional responsibilities in community mental health centers. *Professional Psychology, 10,* 20–27.

Stewart, E. C. (1976). Cultural sensitivities in counseling. In P. Pederson, W. J. Lonner, & D. J. Draguns (Eds.), *Counseling across cultures* (pp. 98–122). Honolulu, HI: University of Hawaii Press.

Suczek, R. F., & Klopfer, W. G. (1952). Interpretation of the Bender-Gestalt: Associative value of the figures. *Journal of Orthopsychiatry, 12,* 33–37.

Sue, D. W. (1978). Eliminating cultural oppression in counseling: Toward a general theory. *Journal of Counseling Psychology, 25,* 419–428.

Sue, S. (1983). Ethnic minority issues in psychology: A reexamination. *American Psychologist, 38,* 583–592.

Sugarman, A. (1978). Is psychodiagnostic assessment humanistic? *Journal of Personality Assessment, 42,* 11–21.

Sundberg, N. D. (1961). The practice of psychological testing in clinical services in the United States. *American Psychologist, 16,* 79–83.

Sundberg, N. D., & Gonzales, L. R. (1981). Cross-cultural and cross-ethnic assessment: Overview and issues. In P. McReynolds (Ed.), *Advances in psychological assessment* (Vol. 5, pp. 460–541). San Francisco, CA: Jossey-Bass.

Takahashi, S., & Zax, M. (1966). The stimulus value of Rorschach inkblots: A comparison of Japanese and American students. *Japanese Psychological Research, 8,* 38–45.

Tatibana, S. N. S. (1936). *Psychology of Color.* Tokyo, Japan: Toen Syobs.

Taylor, A. (1965). Maternal deprivation: Its effects on conceptual development. *Bulletin of the Institute of Child Study, 27,* 4–11.

Taylor, S. E., & Crocker, J. (1981). Schematic bases of social information processing. In E. T. Higgins, C. P. Herman, & M. P. Zanna (Eds.), *Social cognition: The Ontario symposium on personality and social psychology* (pp. 89–134). Hillsdale, NJ: Lawrence Erlbaum Associates, Inc.

Thomas, C. B., Ross, D. C., & Freed, E. S. (1964). *An index of Rorschach responses: Studies on the psychological characteristics of medical students. I.* Baltimore, MD: The Johns Hopkins Press.

Thomas, C. B., Ross, D. C., & Freed, E. S. (1965). *An index of responses to the group Rorschach Test. II.* Baltimore, MD: The Johns Hopkins Press.

Thompson, A. E. (1986). An object-relational theory to affect maturity: Applications to the

Thematic Apperception Test. In M. Kissen (Ed.), *Assessing object relations phenomena* (pp. 207-224). Madison, CT: International Universities Press.

Tinbergen, N. (1951). *The study of instinct.* Oxford, England: Oxford University Press.

Tobie, H. (1927). Die Entwicklung der teilinhaltlichen Beachtun von Farbe und Form im vorschulpflichtigen kindesalter. *Zsch. angew. Psychol., 38.* (Beiheft)

Tolor, A., & Brannigan, G. G. (1980). *Research and clinical applications of the Bender-Gestalt test.* Springfield, IL: Thomas.

Tomkins, S. S. (1979). Script theory: Differential magnification of affects. In H. E. Howe & R. A. Dientsbier (Eds.), *Nebraska symposium on motivation* (Vol. 26, pp. 201-236). Lincoln, NE: University of Nebraska Press.

Townsend, J. K. (1967). The relation between Rorschach signs of aggression and behavioral aggression in emotionally disturbed boys. *Journal of Projective Techniques & Personality Assessment, 31,* 13-21.

Urist, J. (1977). The Rorschach test and the assessment of object relations. *Journal of Personality Assessment, 41,* 3-9.

Urist, J. (1980). Object relations. In R. H. Woody (Ed.), *Encyclopedia of clinical assessment* (Vol. 1, pp. 821-833). San Francisco: Jossey Bass.

Urist, J., & Shill, M. (1982). Validity of the Rorschach mutuality of autonomy scale: A replication using excerpted responses. *Journal of Personality Assessment, 46,* 450-454.

Vernon, P. E. (1933). The Rorschach ink-blot test. *Brit. J. Med Psychol., 13,* 89-118; 179-200; 271-291.

Vernon, P. E. (1935). Recent work on the Rorschach test. *J. Ment. Sci., 81,* 894-920.

Vernon, P. E. (1936-1937). Rorschach bibliography No. III. *Rorschach Res. Exch., 1,* 89-93.

Volkelt, H. (1926). Fortschritte der Kinderpsychologie, 9. *Kongress exp. Psychol.*

von Allesch, G. (Ed.). (1925). Die aesthetische Erscheinungsweise der Farben. *Psychol. Forsch, 6.*

von Bertalanffy, L. (1949). *Problems of life.* New York: Wiley.

Wachtel, P. L. (1973). Psychodynamics, behavior therapy, and the implacable experimenter: An inquiry into the consistency of personality. *American Psychologist, 35,* 399-408.

Wachtel, P. L. (1977). *Psychoanalysis and behavior therapy: Toward an integration.* New York: Basic Books.

Wachtel, P. L. (1982). What can dynamic therapists contribute to behavior therapy? *Behavior Therapy, 13,* 594-609.

Wade, T. C., & Baker, T. B. (1977). Opinions and use of psychological tests: A survey of clinical psychologists. *American Psychologist, 32,* 874-882.

Wade, T. C., Baker, T. B., Morton, T. B., & Baker, L. J. (1978). The status of psychological testing in clinical psychology: Relationships between test use and professional activities and orientations. *Journal of Personality Assessment, 42,* 3-10.

Wainer, H. (1976). Estimating coefficients in linear models: It don't make no nevermind. *Psychological Bulletin, 83,* 312-317.

Wallach, J. (1978). *Affective-symbolic connotations of the Rorschach inkblots. Fact or fantasy.* Unpublished doctoral dissertation. Long Island: Long Island University.

Watson, R. I. (1959). Historical review of objective testing: The search for objectivity. In M. Bass & I. A. Berg (Eds.), *Objective approaches to personality assessment.* Princeton, NJ: Van Nostrand.

Weaver, W. (1948). Science and complexity. *American Scientist, 36,* 536-544.

Wechsler, D. (1974). *Manual for the Wechsler intelligence scale for children.* Rev. WISC-R. New York: Psychological Corporation.

Wechsler, D. (1981). *Manual for the Wechsler adult intelligence scale.* Rev. WAIS-R. New York: Psychological Corporation.

Weinberg, R. M. (1968). Personality characteristics of African children: A projective analysis. *Journal of Genetic Psychology,* pp. 65-77.

Weiner, I. B. (1966). *Psychodiagnosis in schizophrenia.* New York: John Wiley.

Weiner, I. B. (1972). Does psychodiagnosis have a future? *Journal of Personality Assessment, 36,* 534-546.

Weiner, I. B. (1977). Approaches to Rorschach validation. In M. A. Rickers-Ovsiankina (Ed.), *Rorschach psychology* (2nd ed.). Huntington, NY: Krieger.

Weiner, I. B. (1983a). The future of psychodiagnosis revisited. *Journal of Personality Assessment, 47,* 451-459.

Weiner, I. B. (1983b). Theoretical foundations of clinical psychology. In M. Hersen, A. E. Kazdin, & A. S. Bellack (Eds.), *American handbook of clinical psychology.* New York: Pergamon.

Weissman, S. L. (1964). Some indicators of acting out behavior from the Thematic Apperception Test. *Journal of Projective Techniques & Personality Assessment, 29,* 366-375.

Wells, F. L. (1935). Rorschach and the free association test. *J. Gen. Psychol., 13.*

Wender, P. H. (1967). On necessary and sufficient conditions in psychiatric explanation.

Archives of General Psychiatry, 16, 41–47.
Werner, H. (1940). Comparative psychology of mental development. New York: Harper Brothers.
Werner, H. (1945). Perceptual behavior of brain-injured, mentally defective children: An experimental study by means of the Rorschach technique. *Gen. Psychol. Mon., 31,* 51–110.
Werner, H. (1948). *Comparative psychology of mental development.* New York: International Universities Press.
Werner, H., & Kaplan, B. (1963). *Symbol formation.* New York: Wiley.
Wertheimer, M. (1925). Ueber Gestaltheorie. *Symposion.*
Westen, D. (1989). *Object relations and social cognition TAT scoring manual* (In collaboration with Lohr, N., Kerber, K., & Goodrich, S.) [Unpublished manual]. University of Michigan. (Original research performed 1985)
Westen, D., Buttenheim, M., & Silk, K. R. (1985, August). *Measuring object relations using TAT stories and early memories.* Paper presented at the annual meeting of the American Psychological Association.
Whipple, G. M. (1910). *Manual of mental and physical tests.* Baltimore: Warwick & Hork. (Chapter XI, Tests of Imagination and Invention, Test 45, Ink-Blots, pp. 430–435)
Williams, G. F. (1968). Frequency of the Rorschach human movement response in Negro and white emotionally disturbed children. *Journal of Consulting and Clinical Psychology, 32,* 158–163.
Witkin, H. A., Dyk, R. B., Faterson, H. F., Goodenough, D. R., & Karp, S. A. (1962). *Psychological differentiation.* New York: John Wiley & Sons.
Witkin, H. A., Lewis, H. B., Hertzman, M., & et al. (1954). *Personality through perception: An experimental and clinical study.* New York: Harper & Brothers.
Wohlwill, J. F. (1970). The emerging discipline of environmental psychology. *American Psychologist, 25,* 303–312.
Woody, R. H. (Ed.). (1980). *Encyclopedia of clinical assessment.* Vols. 1 & 2. San Francisco, CA: Jossey-Bass.
Wyatt, F. (1947). The scoring and analysis of the Thematic Apperception Test. *Journal of Psychology, 24,* 319–330.
Wyatt, F. (1967). How objective is objectivity? *Journal of Projective Techniques & Personality Assessment, 31,* 3–19.
Wynne, L. C. (1968). Consensus Rorschachs and related procedures for studying interpersonal patterns. *Journal of Projective Techniques & Personality Assessment, 32,* 352–356.
Zubin, J. (1950). Introduction: Symposium on statistics for the clinician. *Journal Clin. Psychol., 6,* 1–6.
Zubin, J. (1966). Clinical vs. actuarial prediction: A pseudo-problem. In A. Anastasi (Ed.), *Testing problems in perspective: 25th anniversary volume of topical readings from the invitational Conference on Testing Problems* (pp. 625–637). Washington, DC: American Council on Education.
Zubin, J. (1967). Classification of the behavior disorders. *Annual Review of Psychology,* 373–406.
Zubin, J., Eron, L. D., & Schumer, F. (1965). *An experimental approach to projective techniques.* New York: Wiley.
Zubin, J., & Young, K. M. (1948). *Manual of projective and cognate techniques.* Madison, WI: College Typing Co.

For Product Safety Concerns and Information please contact our EU representative GPSR@taylorandfrancis.com
Taylor & Francis Verlag GmbH, Kaufingerstraße 24, 80331 München, Germany

www.ingramcontent.com/pod-product-compliance
Ingram Content Group UK Ltd.
Pitfield, Milton Keynes, MK11 3LW, UK
UKHW022202190926
475702UK00003B/169
* 9 7 8 0 8 0 5 8 0 9 2 8 2 *